DISCOVERING THE
AMERICAN PAST

DISCOVERING THE AMERICAN PAST

A LOOK AT THE EVIDENCE

THIRD EDITION

∞ VOLUME II: SINCE 1865 ∞

William Bruce Wheeler
University of Tennessee

Susan D. Becker
University of Tennessee

HOUGHTON MIFFLIN COMPANY   Boston   Toronto

Geneva, Illinois   Palo Alto   Princeton, New Jersey

Sponsoring Editor: Sean Wakely
Senior Development Editor: Frances Gay
Editorial Assistant: Traci Beane
Managing Editor: Kathy Brown
Editorial Assistant: Stefanie Jacobs
Production/Design Coordinator: Jennifer Waddell
Senior Manufacturing Coordinator: Marie Barnes
Marketing Manager: Becky Dudley

Acknowledgments

Source 4 (p. 173): Excerpts from *Middletown: A Study in American Culture* by Robert S. Lynd and Helen Merrell Lynd. Copyright 1929 by Harcourt Brace & Company and renewed 1957 by Robert S. Lynd and Helen Merrell Lynd. Reprinted by permission of the publisher.

CHAPTER ONE

Sources 1–12: From Morton Keller, *The Art and Politics of Thomas Nast* (New York: Oxford University Press, 1968), plates 108; 55 and 56; 22; 17; 27; 32; 47; 50; 38; 196; 197; 155; 209, respectively. Courtesy of the publisher.

Source 13: From J. Chal Vinson, *Thomas Nast, Political Cartoonist* (Athens: University of Georgia Press, 1967). Courtesy of the publisher.

CHAPTER TWO

Source 3: From Edwin S. Redkey, ed., *Respect Black: The Writings and Speeches of Henry McNeal Turner* (New York: Armo Press, 1971) pp. 167–171. Reprinted by permission.

Acknowledgments are continued on pp. 347–348 which constitute an extension of the copyright page.

Cover: Postcard of *Skyline, Cincinnati, Ohio*, 1933. Lake County (Illinois) Museum, Curt Teich Postcard Archives.

Printed in the U.S.A.
Library of Congress Catalog Card Number: 93-78664
ISBN: 0-395-66866-2

3 4 5 6 7 8 9-DH-97 96 95

CONTENTS

∽ CHAPTER THREE ∾

How They Lived:
Middle-Class Life, 1870–1917   58

∽ CHAPTER FOUR ∾

Justifying American Imperialism:
The Louisiana Purchase
Exposition, 1904   102

∽ CHAPTER FIVE ∾

Homogenizing a Pluralistic Culture:
Propaganda During
World War I   129

∽ **CHAPTER SIX** ∾

The "New" Woman of the 1920s: Image and Reality   160

∽ **CHAPTER SEVEN** ∾

Documenting the Depression: The FSA Photographers and Rural Poverty   183

∽ CHAPTER EIGHT ∾

The Burdens of Power:
The Decision to
Drop the Atomic Bomb, 1945

∽ CHAPTER NINE ∾

The Second Red Scare:
HUAC vs. Hollywood, 1947

∽ CHAPTER TEN ∾

A Generation in War and Turmoil:
The Agony of Vietnam

ʑ **CHAPTER ELEVEN** ʐ

The Reinvention of America: Who "Owns" Our History? 318

PREFACE

This book is based on the premise that students have a strong desire to learn about United States history and will put forth considerable effort to do so, provided the nation's history is presented in a challenging and stimulating way. Students tell us they enjoy "doing history" rather than simply being told about it and welcome the opportunity to become "active learners" rather than passive notetakers.

The third edition of *Discovering the American Past: A Look at the Evidence* follows, both in spirit and in format, the effective approach established by its predecessors. The unique structure of this book clusters primary sources around a set of historical questions that students are asked to "solve." Unlike a source reader, this book prompts students to actually *analyze* a wide variety of authentic primary source material, to make inferences, and to draw conclusions in much the same way that historians do.

As in previous editions, we expose students to the broad scope of the American experience by providing a mixture of types of historical problems and a balance among political, social, diplomatic, economic, intellectual, and cultural history. This wide variety of historical topics and events engages students' interest and rounds out their view of American history.

FORMAT OF THE BOOK

Historians are fully aware that everything that is preserved from the past can be used as evidence to solve historical problems. In that spirit, we have included as many different *types* of historical evidence as we could. Almost every chapter gives students the opportunity to work with a different type of evidence: works of art, first-person accounts, trial transcripts, statistics, maps, letters, charts, biographical sketches, court decisions, music lyrics, prescriptive literature, newspaper accounts, congressional debates, speeches, diaries, proclamations and laws, political cartoons, photographs, architectural plans, advertisements, posters, film reviews, fiction, memoirs, oral interviews, and interpretations by past historians. In this book, then, we have created a kind of historical sampler that we believe will help students learn the methods and skills historians use, as well as help them learn historical content.

Each type of historical evidence is combined with an introduction to the appropriate methodology in an effort to teach students a wide variety of research skills. As much as possible, we have tried to let the evidence speak for itself and have avoided leading students to one particular interpretation or another. This approach is effective in many different classroom situations, including seminars, small classes, discussion sections, and large lecture classes. Indeed, we have found that the first and second editions of *Discovering the American Past* have proven themselves equally stimulating and effective in very large classes as well as very small ones. An Instructor's Resource Manual that accompanies the book offers numerous suggestions on how *Discovering the American Past* can be used effectively in large classroom situations.

Each chapter is divided into six parts: The Problem, Background, The Method, The Evidence, Questions to Consider, and Epilogue. Each of the parts relates to or builds upon the others, creating a uniquely integrated chapter structure that helps guide the reader through the analytical process. "The Problem" section begins with a brief discussion of the central issues of the chapter and then states the questions students will explore. A "Background" section follows, designed to help students understand the historical context of the problem. The section called "The Method" gives students suggestions for studying and analyzing the evidence. "The Evidence" section is the heart of the chapter, providing a variety of primary source material on the particular historical event or issue described in the chapter's "Problem" section. The section called "Questions to Consider" focuses students' attention on specific evidence and on linkages among different evidence material. The "Epilogue" section gives the aftermath or the historical outcome of the evidence—what happened to the people involved, who won the election, the results of a debate, and so on.

CHANGES IN THE THIRD EDITION

In response to student and faculty reactions, we have made significant alterations in the content of this edition. Six new chapters have been written, three for Volume I and three for Volume II. As with all other chapters, the six new chapters have been tested extensively in the classroom.

Volume I begins with a completely revised chapter on Europeans' first encounters with Native Americans. The first chapter now includes Native American as well as European accounts of the same event: the encounter between the Aztecs and Hernando Cortés and his troops. Chapter 6 is entirely new, an examination of Chief Justice Taney's decision in the *Charles River Bridge* v. *Warren Bridge* Supreme Court case (1837). The chapter focuses on the issue of the proper role of government in the private economic sector, a continuing controversy in America's past and present. Chapter 9 is also new. This chapter examines the difficult problem of the responsibilities of Americans during wartime, in this case the Mexican War. Henry David Thoreau's "Civil Disobedience" is juxtaposed against President James Knox Polk's Second Annual Message and Stephen A. Douglas's speech on that subject in the House of Representatives.

New chapters in Volume II include Chapter 6, which uses popular fiction and memoirs to examine the "new" woman of the 1920s. Fictional portrayals of women are presented side-by-side with selected women's own memories of the "roaring" decade. Chapter 7, a new treatment of the Great Depression of the 1930s, uses photographic evidence from the archives of the Farm Security Administration to discuss the problems of work, unemployment, and poverty during that difficult era. Finally, Chapter 11, on cultural diversity and American history, is entirely new. In this chapter, students will read five distinctly different accounts of the same event written by six historians (George Bancroft, Charles and Mary Beard. John A. Garraty, Howard Zinn, and their own textbook) to see how historical treatments have changed during the past century.

In addition to these six new chapters, all the chapters from the second editon have been rethought, discussed, revised, and tested in classrooms.

∽ INSTRUCTOR'S RESOURCE MANUAL ∾

An Instructor's Resource Manual suggests ways that might be useful in guiding students through the evidence, provides answers to questions students often ask, and explains a variety of ways in which the students' learning may be evaluated. Many of those ideas have come from instructors who have used the first and second editions. For this edition, we have added a new section explaining how this book can be used with large classes, based on the authors' own experience with the text.

∽ ACKNOWLEDGMENTS ∾

We would like to thank the many students and instructors who have helped us in our effort. In addition to our colleagues across the United States, we would like to thank especially our colleagues at the University of Tennessee, who offered suggestions, read chapter drafts, and tested the new problems in their own classes. John R. Finger, Michael J. McDonald, Charles W. Johnson, and Jonathan G. Utley were especially helpful. Mary Ann Bright and Lisa Medlin were helpful in preparing the manuscript. Finally, colleagues at other institutions who reviewed chapter drafts made significant contributions to this edition, and we would like to thank them for their generosity, both in time and in helpful ideas and suggestions. These reviewers were:

Sherri Broder
  Boston College
Kenneth Bruce
  DeAnza College
Margaret Caffrey
  Memphis State University

Catherine Caraher
  University of Detroit—Mercy
Wilton Fowler
  University of Washington
Theresa McGinley
  North Harris College
Burton Peretti
  University of California—Berkeley
Ingrid Scobie
  Texas Women's University
Stan Underdal
  Sam Jose State University
Sue Zschoche
  Kansas State University

As with our first and second editions, we dedicate this effort to our colleagues who seek to offer a challenging and stimulating academic experience to their students and to those students themselves, who make all our efforts so worthwhile.

CHAPTER 1

RECONSTRUCTING RECONSTRUCTION: THE POLITICAL CARTOONIST AND THE NATIONAL MOOD

❧ THE PROBLEM ❧

The Civil War took a tremendous toll on North and South alike. In the defeated South, more than one-fourth of all men who had borne arms for the Confederacy died, and an additional 15 percent were permanently disabled. Indeed, in 1865 Mississippi spent one-fifth of the state's total revenue on artificial arms and legs for Confederate veterans. Combined with the damage to agriculture, industry, and railroads, the human cost of the Civil War to the South was nearly catastrophic. For its part, the North had suffered frightful human losses as well, although proportionately less than those of the South.

And yet the Civil War, although appalling in its human, physical, and psychological costs, did settle some important issues that had plagued the nation for decades before that bloody conflict. First, the triumph of Union arms had established the United States as "one nation indivisible," from which no state could secede.[1] No less important, the "peculiar institution" of slavery was eradicated, and African Americans at last were free. In truth, although the Civil War had been costly, the issues it settled were momentous.

1. In response to President Benjamin Harrison's 1892 appeal for schoolchildren to mark the four hundredth anniversary of Columbus's discovery with patriotic exercises, Bostonian Francis Bellamy composed the pledge of allegiance to the American flag, from which the phrase "one nation indivisible" comes. In 1942, Congress made it the official pledge to the flag, and in 1954 Congress added the words "under God" in the middle of Bellamy's phrase.

CHAPTER 1

RECONSTRUCTING
RECONSTRUCTION:
THE POLITICAL
CARTOONIST
AND THE
NATIONAL MOOD

The victory of the United States, however, raised at least as many questions as it settled. There was the question of what should happen to the defeated South. Should the states of the former Confederacy be permitted to take their natural place in the Union as quickly and smoothly as possible, with minimum concessions to their northern conquerors? Or should the North insist on a thorough reconstruction of the South, with new economic and social institutions to replace the old? Tied to this issue was the thorny constitutional question of whether the South actually had left the Union at all in 1861. If so, then the southern states in 1865 were territories, to be governed and administered by Congress. If not, then the Civil War had been an internal insurrection and the president, as commander in chief, would administer the South's re-entry into the Union.

Perhaps the most difficult question the Union's victory raised was the status of the former slaves. To be sure, they were no longer in bondage. But should they possess all the rights that whites had? Should they be assisted in becoming landowners; if not, how would they earn a living? Should they be allowed to vote and run for elective office? Indeed, no more complex and difficult issue confronted the country than the "place" of the newly freed slaves in the nation.

In all these questions, public opinion in the victorious North was a critical factor in shaping or altering the policies designed to reconstruct the South. Earlier democratic reforms made it unlikely that either the president or Congress could defy public opinion successfully. Yet public opinion can shift with remarkable speed, and political figures forever must be sensitive to its sometimes fickle winds.

Among the many influences on public opinion in the second half of the nineteenth century were writers and artists who worked for newspapers and magazines. In this chapter, you will be examining and analyzing the work of one man who attempted to shape public opinion in the North: editorial cartoonist Thomas Nast (1840–1902). Nast was not the only person who attempted to influence public opinion in the North, but at the peak of his career, he and his cartoons were well-known and widely appreciated. What were Nast's views on the controversial issues of the Reconstruction era, and how did he try to influence public opinion?

∽ BACKGROUND ∾

By early 1865, it was evident to most northerners and southerners that the Civil War was nearly over. While Grant was hammering at Lee's depleted forces in Virginia, Union general William Tecumseh Sherman broke the back of the Confederacy with his devastating march through Georgia and then northward into the Carolinas. Atlanta fell to Sherman's troops in September 1864, Savannah in December, and Charleston and Columbia, South Carolina, in February 1865. Two-thirds of Columbia lay in ashes. Meanwhile, General Philip Sheridan had driven the Confederates out of the Shenandoah Valley of Virginia, thus blocking any escape attempts by Lee and further cutting southern supply routes. The Union naval blockade of the South was taking its fearful toll, as parts of the dying Confederacy were facing real privation. Hence, although northern armies had suffered terrible losses, by 1865 they stood poised on the brink of victory.

In the South, all but the extreme die-hards recognized that defeat was inevitable. The Confederacy was suffering in more ways than militarily. The Confederate economy had almost completely collapsed, and Confederate paper money was nearly worthless. Slaves were abandoning their masters and mistresses in great numbers, running away to Union armies or roaming through the South in search of better opportunities. In many areas, civilian morale had almost totally deteriorated, and one Georgian wrote, "The people are soul-sick and heartily tired of the hateful, hopeless strife. . . . We have had enough of want and woe, of cruelty and carnage, enough of cripples and corpses."[2] As the Confederate government made secret plans to evacuate Richmond, most southerners knew that the end was very near.

Yet even with victory almost in hand, many northerners had given little thought to what should happen after the war. Would southerners accept the changes that defeat would almost inevitably force on them (especially the end of slavery)? What demands should the victors make on the vanquished? Should the North assist the South in rebuilding after the devastation of war? If so, should the North dictate how that rebuilding, or reconstruction, should take place? What efforts should the North make to ensure that the former slaves were receiving the rights of free men and women? During the war, few northerners had seriously considered these questions. Now that victory was within their grasp, they could not avoid them.

One person who had been wrestling with these questions was Abraham Lincoln. In December 1863, the president announced his own plan for reconstructing the South, a plan in keeping with his later hope, as expressed in his second inaugural address, for "malice toward none; with charity for all; . . . Let us . . . bind up the nation's wounds."[3] In Lincoln's plan, a southern state could resume its normal activities in the Union as soon as 10 percent of the voters of 1860 had taken an oath of loyalty to the United States. High-ranking Confederate leaders would be excluded, and some blacks might gain the right to vote. No men-

2. The letter probably was written by Georgian Herschel V. Walker. See Allan Nevins, *The Organized War to Victory, 1864–1865,* Vol. IV of *The War for the Union* (New York: Charles Scribner's Sons, 1971), p. 221.

3. The full text of Lincoln's second inaugural address, delivered on March 4, 1865, can be found in Roy P. Basler, ed., *The Collected Works of Abraham Lincoln,* Vol. VIII (New Brunswick, N.J.: Rutgers University Press, 1953), pp. 332–333.

CHAPTER 1

RECONSTRUCTING
RECONSTRUCTION:
THE POLITICAL
CARTOONIST
AND THE
NATIONAL MOOD

tion was made of protecting the civil rights of former slaves; it was presumed that this matter would be left to the slaves' former masters and mistresses.

To many northerners, later known as Radical Republicans, Lincoln's plan was much too lenient. In the opinion of these people, a number of whom had been abolitionists, the South, when conquered, should not be allowed to return to its former ways. Not only should slavery be eradicated, they claimed, but freed blacks should be assisted in their efforts to attain economic, social, and political equity. Most of the Radical Republicans favored education for African Americans, and some advocated carving the South's plantations into small parcels to be given to the freedmen. To implement these reforms, Radical Republicans wanted detachments of the United States Army to remain in the South and favored the appointment of provisional governors to oversee the transitional governments in the southern states. Lincoln approved plans for the Army to stay and supported the idea of provisional governors. But he opposed the more far-reaching reform notions of the Radical Republicans, and as president he was able to block them.

In addition to having diametrically opposed views of Reconstruction, Lincoln and the Radical Republicans differed over the constitutional question of which branch of the federal government would be responsible for the reconstruction of the South. The Constitution made no mention of secession, reunion, or reconstruction. But Radical Republicans, citing passages in the Constitution giving Congress the power to guarantee each state a republican government, insisted that the reconstruction of the South should be carried out by Congress.[4] For his part, however, Lincoln maintained that as chief enforcer of the law and as commander in chief, the president was the appropriate person to be in charge of Reconstruction. Clearly, a stalemate was in the making, with Radical Republicans calling for a more reform-minded Reconstruction policy and Lincoln continuing to block them.

President Lincoln's death on April 15, 1865 (one week after Lee's surrender at Appomattox Court House),[5] brought Vice President Andrew Johnson to the nation's highest office. At first, Radical Republicans had reason to hope that the new president would follow policies more to their liking. A Tennessean, Johnson had risen to political prominence from humble circumstances, had become a spokesperson for the common white men and women of the South, and had opposed the planter aristocracy. Upon becoming president, he excluded from amnesty all former Confederate political and military leaders as well as all southerners who owned taxable property worth more than $20,000 (an obvious slap at his old planter-aristocrat foes). Moreover, Johnson issued a proclamation setting up provisional mil-

4. See Article IV, Section 4, of the Constitution. Later Radical Republicans also justified their position using the Thirteenth Amendment, adopted in 1865, which gave Congress the power to enforce the amendment ending slavery in the South.
5. The last Confederate army to give up, commanded by General Joseph Johnston, surrendered to Sherman at Durham Station, North Carolina, on April 18, 1865.

itary governments in the conquered South and told his cabinet he favored black suffrage, although as a states' rightist he insisted that states adopt the measure voluntarily. At the outset, then, Johnson appeared to be all the Radical Republicans wanted, preferable to the more moderate Lincoln.

Yet it did not take Radical Republicans long to realize that President Johnson was not one of them. Although he spoke harshly, he pardoned hundreds of former Confederates, who quickly captured control of southern state governments and congressional delegations. Many northerners were shocked to see former Confederate generals and officials, and even former Confederate vice president Alexander Stephens, returned to Washington. The new southern state legislatures passed a series of laws, known collectively as black codes, that so severely restricted the rights of former slaves that they were all but slaves again. Moreover, Johnson privately told southerners that he opposed the Fourteenth Amendment to the Constitution, which was intended to confer full civil rights on the newly freed slaves. He also used his veto power to block Radical Republican Reconstruction measures in Congress and seemed to do little to combat the general defiance of the former Confederacy (exhibited in many forms, including insults thrown at Union occupation soldiers, the desecration of the United States flag, and the formation of organized resistance groups such as the Ku Klux Klan).

To an increasing number of northerners, the unrepentant spirit of the South and Johnson's acquiescence to it were nothing short of appalling.

Had the Civil War been fought for nothing? Had more than 364,000 federal soldiers died in vain? White southerners were openly defiant, African Americans were being subjugated by white southerners and virtually ignored by President Johnson, and former Confederates were returning to positions of power and prominence. Radical Republicans had sufficient power in Congress to pass harsher measures, but Johnson kept vetoing them, and the Radicals lacked the votes to override his vetoes.[6] Indeed, the impasse that had existed before Lincoln's death continued.

In such an atmosphere, the congressional elections of 1866 were bitterly fought campaigns, especially in the northern states. President Johnson traveled throughout the North, defending his moderate plan of Reconstruction and viciously attacking his political enemies. However, the Radical Republicans were even more effective. Stirring up the hostilities of wartime, they "waved the bloody shirt" and excited northern voters by charging that the South had never accepted its defeat and that the 364,000 Union dead and 275,000 wounded would be for nothing if the South was permitted to continue its arrogant and stubborn behavior. Increasingly, Johnson was greeted by hostile audiences as the North underwent a major shift in public opinion.

The Radical Republicans won a stunning victory in the congressional elections of 1866 and thus broke the stalemate between Congress and the

6. Congress was able to override Johnson's vetoes of the Civil Rights Act and a revised Freedmen's Bureau bill.

CHAPTER 1

RECONSTRUCTING
RECONSTRUCTION:
THE POLITICAL
CARTOONIST
AND THE
NATIONAL MOOD

president. Armed with enough votes to override Johnson's vetoes almost at will, the new Congress proceeded rapidly to implement the Radical Republican vision of Reconstruction. The South was divided into five military districts to be ruled by martial law. Southern states had to ratify the Fourteenth Amendment and institute black suffrage before being allowed to take their formal places in the Union. The Freedmen's Bureau, founded earlier, was given additional federal support to set up schools for African Americans, negotiate labor contracts, and, with the military, help monitor elections. Only the proposal to give land to blacks was not adopted, being seen as too extreme even by some Radical Republicans. Congressional Reconstruction had begun.

President Johnson, however, had not been left completely powerless. Determined to undercut the Radical Republicans' Reconstruction policies, he issued orders increasing the powers of civil governments in the South and removed military officers who were enforcing Congress's will, replacing them with commanders less determined to protect black voting rights and more willing to turn the other way when disqualified white southerners voted. Opposed most vigorously by his own secretary of war, Edwin Stanton, Johnson tried to discharge Stanton. To an increasing number of Radicals, it became clear that the president would have to be removed from office.

In 1868, the House of Representatives voted to impeach Andrew Johnson. Charged with violating the Tenure of Office Act and the Command of the Army Act (both of which had been passed over Johnson's vetoes), the president was tried in the Senate, where two-thirds of the senators would have to vote against Johnson for him to be removed.[7] The vast majority of senators disagreed with the president's Reconstruction policies, but they feared that impeachment had become a political tool that, if successful, threatened to destroy the balance of power between the branches of the federal government. The vote on removal fell one short of the necessary two-thirds, and Johnson was spared the indignity of removal. Nevertheless, the Republican nomination of General Ulysses Grant and his subsequent landslide victory (running as a military hero, Grant carried twenty-six out of thirty-four states) gave Radical Republicans a malleable president, one who, although not a Radical himself, could ensure the continuation of their version of Reconstruction.[8]

The Democratic party, however, was not dead, even though the Republican party dominated national politics in the immediate aftermath of the Civil War. In addition to white farmers and planters in the South and border states, the Democratic party contained many northerners who favored conservative ("sound money") policies, voters who opposed Radical Reconstruction, and first- and second-generation Irish immigrants who had settled in urban

7. See Article I, Sections 2 and 3, of the Constitution.
8. In 1868, southern states, where the Democratic party had been strong, either were not in the Union or were under the control of Radical Reconstruction governments. Grant's victory, therefore, was not as sweeping as it may first appear.

areas and had established powerful political machines such as Tammany Hall in New York City.

By 1872, a renewed Democratic party believed it had a chance to oust Grant and the Republicans. The Grant administration had been rocked by a series of scandals, some involving men quite close to the president. Although honest himself, Grant had lost a good deal of popularity by defending the culprits and naively aiding in a cover-up of the corruption. These actions, along with some of his other policies, triggered a revolt within the Republican party, in which a group calling themselves Liberal Republicans bolted the party ranks and nominated well-known editor and reformer Horace Greeley to oppose Grant for the presidency.[9] Hoping for a coalition to defeat Grant, the Democrats also nominated the controversial Greeley.

Greeley's platform was designed to attract as many different groups of voters as possible to the Liberal Republican-Democratic fold. He favored civil service reform, the return to a "hard money" fiscal policy, and the reservation of western lands for settlers rather than for large land companies. He vowed an end to corruption in government. But the most dramatic part of Greeley's message was his call for an end to the bitterness of the Civil War, a thinly veiled promise to bring an end to Radical Reconstruction in the South. "Let us," he said, "clasp hands over the bloody chasm."

For their part, Radical Republicans attacked Greeley as the tool of die-hard southerners and labeled him as the candidate of white southern bigots and northern Irish immigrants manipulated by political machines. By contrast, Grant was labeled as a great war hero and a friend of blacks and whites alike. The incumbent Grant won easily, capturing 55 percent of the popular vote. Greeley died soon after the exhausting campaign.

Gradually, however, the zeal of Radical Republicanism began to fade. An increasing number of northerners grew tired of the issue. Their commitment to full civil rights for African Americans had never been strong, and they had voted for Radical Republicans more out of anger at southern intransigence than out of any lofty notions of black equality. Thus northerners did not protest when, one by one, southern Democrats returned to power in the states of the former Confederacy.[10] As an indication of how little their own attitudes had changed, white southerners labeled these native Democrats "Redeemers."

Although much that was fruitful and beneficial was accomplished in the South during the Reconstruction period (most notably black suffrage and public education), some of this was to be temporary, and many opportunities for progress were lost. By the

9. See Volume I, Chapter 10, for a discussion of Greeley's position on the emancipation of slaves in 1862.

10. Southerners regained control of the state governments in Tennessee and Virginia in 1869, North Carolina in 1870, Georgia in 1871, Arkansas and Alabama in 1874, and Mississippi in early 1876. By the presidential election of 1876, only South Carolina, Louisiana, and Florida were still controlled by Reconstruction governments.

CHAPTER 1

RECONSTRUCTING
RECONSTRUCTION:
THE POLITICAL
CARTOONIST
AND THE
NATIONAL MOOD

presidential election of 1876, both candidates (Rutherford B. Hayes and Samuel Tilden) promised an end to Reconstruction, and the Radical Republican experiment, for all intents and purposes, was over.

It is clear that northern public opinion from 1865 to 1876 was not static but was almost constantly shifting. This public opinion was influenced by a number of factors, among them speeches, newspapers, and word of mouth. Especially influential were editorial cartoons, which captured the issues visually, often simplifying them so that virtually everyone could understand them. Perhaps the master of this style was Thomas Nast, a political cartoonist whose career, principally with *Harper's Weekly,* spanned the tumultuous years of the Civil War and Reconstruction. Throughout his career, Nast produced more than three thousand cartoons, illustrations for books, and paintings. He is credited with originating the modern depiction of Santa Claus, the Republican elephant, and the Democratic donkey. Congratulating themselves for having hired Nast, the editors of *Harper's Weekly* once exclaimed that each of Nast's drawings was at once "a poem and a speech."

Apparently, Thomas Nast developed his talents early in life. Born in the German Palatinate (one of the German states) in 1840, Nast was the son of a musician in the Ninth Regiment Bavarian Band. The family moved to New York City in 1846, at which time young Thomas was enrolled in school. It seems that art was his only interest. One teacher admonished him, "Go fin-

ish your picture. You will never learn to read or figure." After unsuccessfully trying to interest their son in music, his parents eventually encouraged the development of his artistic talent. By the age of fifteen, Thomas Nast was drawing illustrations for *Frank Leslie's Illustrated Newspaper.* He joined *Harper's Weekly* in 1862 (at the age of twenty-two), where he developed the cartoon style that was to win him a national reputation, as well as enemies. He received praise from Abraham Lincoln, Ulysses Grant, and Samuel Clemens (also known as Mark Twain, who in 1872 asked Nast to do the illustrations for one of his books so that "then I will have good pictures"). In contrast, one of Nast's favorite targets, political boss William Marcy Tweed of New York's Tammany Hall, once shouted, "Let's stop these damn pictures. I don't care so much what the papers say about me—my constituents can't read; but damn it, they can see pictures!"

It is obvious from his work that Nast was a man of strong feelings and emotions. In his eyes, those people whom he admired possessed no flaws. Conversely, those whom he opposed were, to him, capable of every conceivable villainy. As a result, his characterizations often were terribly unfair, gross distortions of reality and more than occasionally libelous. In his view, however, his central purpose was not to entertain but to move his audience, to make them scream out in outrage or anger, to prod them to action. The selection of Nast's cartoons in this chapter is typical of the body of his work for *Harper's Weekly:* artistically inventive and polished, blatantly slanted, and brimming with indignation and emotion.

Your tasks in this chapter are (1) to identify the principal issues and events of the Reconstruction era, (2) to analyze Nast's cartoons to determine what he thought about each issue or event, and (3) to trace any changes in Nast's beliefs between 1865 (Source 1) and the end of Reconstruction in 1876 (Source 13).

∞ THE METHOD ∞

Although Thomas Nast developed the political cartoon into a true art form, cartoons and caricatures had a long tradition in both Europe and America before Nast. English artists helped bring forth the cartoon style that eventually made *Punch* (founded in 1841) one of the liveliest illustrated periodicals on both sides of the Atlantic. In America, Benjamin Franklin is traditionally credited with publishing the first newspaper cartoon in 1754—the multidivided snake (each part of the snake representing one colony) with the ominous warning "Join or Die." By the time Andrew Jackson sought the presidency, the political cartoon had become a regular and popular feature of American political life. Crude by modern standards, these cartoons influenced some people far more than did the printed word.

As we noted, the political cartoon, like the newspaper editorial, is intended to do more than objectively report events. It is meant to express an opinion, a point of view, approval or disapproval. Political cartoonists want to move people, to make them laugh, to anger them, or to move them to action. In short, political cartoons do not depict exactly what is happening; rather, they portray popular reaction to what is happening and try to persuade people to react in a particular way.

How do you analyze political cartoons? First, using your text and the Problem and Background sections of this chapter, make a list of the most important issues and events (including elections) of the period between 1865 and 1876. As you examine the cartoons in this chapter, try to determine what event or issue is being portrayed. Often a cartoon's caption, dialogue, or date will help you discover its focus.

Next, look closely at each cartoon for clues that will help you understand the message that Nast was trying to convey. People who saw these cartoons more than one hundred years ago did not have to study them so carefully, of course. The individuals and events shown in each cartoon were immediately familiar to them, and the message was obvious. But you are historians, using these cartoons as evidence to help you understand how people were reacting to important events many years ago.

CHAPTER 1

RECONSTRUCTING
RECONSTRUCTION:
THE POLITICAL
CARTOONIST
AND THE
NATIONAL MOOD

As you can see, Nast was a talented artist. Like many political cartoonists, he often explored the differences between what he believed was the ideal (justice, fairness) and the reality (his view of what was actually happening). To "read" Nast's cartoons, you should identify the issue or event on which the cartoon is based. Then look at the *imagery* Nast used: the situation, the setting, the clothes people are wearing, and the objects in the picture. It is especially important to note how people are portrayed: Do they look handsome and noble, or do they look like animals? Are they happy or sad? Intelligent or stupid?

Political cartoonists often use *symbolism* to make their point, sometimes in the form of an *allegory*. In an allegory, familiar figures are shown in a situation or setting that everyone knows—for example, a setting from the Bible, a fairy tale, or another well-known source. For instance, a cartoon showing a tiny president of the United States holding a slingshot, dressed in sandals and rags, and fighting a giant, muscular man labeled "Congress" would remind viewers of the story of David and Goliath. In that story, the small man won. The message of the cartoon is that the president will win in his struggle with Congress.

Other, less complicated symbolism is often used in political cartoons. In Nast's time, as today, the American flag was an important symbol of the ideals of our democratic country, and an olive branch or dove represented the desire for peace. Some symbols have changed, however. Today, the tall, skinny figure we call Uncle Sam represents the United States. In Nast's time, Columbia, a tall woman wearing a long classical dress, represented the United States. Also in Nast's time, an hourglass, rather than a clock, symbolized that time was running out. And military uniforms, regardless of the fact that the Civil War had ended in 1865, were used to indicate whether a person had supported the Union (and, by implication, was a Republican) or the Confederacy (by implication, a Democrat).

As you can see, a political cartoon must be analyzed in detail to get the full meaning the cartoonist was trying to convey. From that analysis, one can discover the message of the cartoon, along with the cartoonist's views on the subject and the ways in which the cartoonist was trying to influence public opinion. Now you are ready to begin your analysis of the Reconstruction era through the cartoons of Thomas Nast.

Sources 1 through 12 from Morton Keller, *The Art and Politics of Thomas Nast* (New York: Oxford University Press, 1968), plates 55 and 56, 22, 17, 27, 32, 47, 50, 38, 196, 197, 155, 209. Courtesy of the publisher.

1.

FRANCHISE.

And Not This Man?"

August 5, 1865

PARDON.

Columbia.—"Shall I Trust These Men,

CHAPTER 1

RECONSTRUCTING
RECONSTRUCTION:
THE POLITICAL
CARTOONIST
AND THE
NATIONAL MOOD

2.

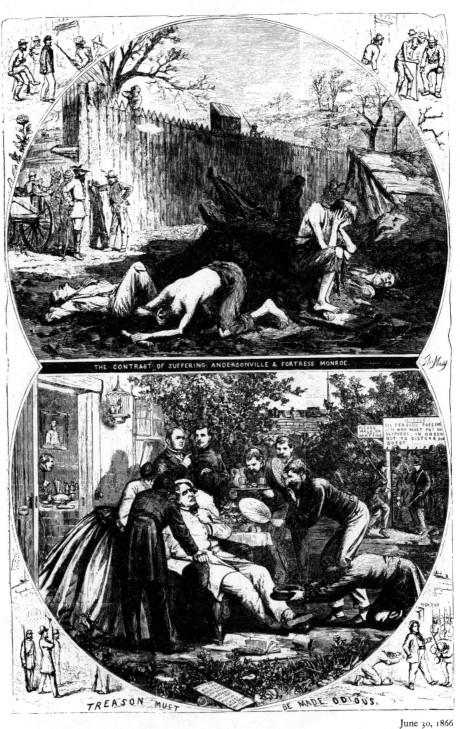

THE CONTRAST OF SUFFERING. ANDERSONVILLE & FORTRESS MONROE.

TREASON MUST BE MADE ODIOUS.

June 30, 1866

March 30, 1867.

Amphitheatrum Johnsonianum—Massacre of the Innocents
At New Orleans, July 30, 1866.

CHAPTER 1

RECONSTRUCTING
RECONSTRUCTION:
THE POLITICAL
CARTOONIST
AND THE
NATIONAL MOOD

4.

September 5, 1868

"This Is a White Man's Government."

"We regard the Reconstruction Acts (so called) of Congress as usurpations, and unconstitutional, revolutionary, and void."—*Democratic Platform.*

The Modern Samson.

October 3, 1868

CHAPTER 1

RECONSTRUCTING
RECONSTRUCTION:
THE POLITICAL
CARTOONIST
AND THE
NATIONAL MOOD

6.

August 3, 1872

Baltimore 1861–1872.

"Let Us Clasp Hands over the Bloody Chasm."

September 7, 1872

The Whited Sepulchre.

Covering the monument of infamy with his white hat and coat.

CHAPTER 1

RECONSTRUCTING
RECONSTRUCTION:
THE POLITICAL
CARTOONIST
AND THE
NATIONAL MOOD

8.

April 13, 1872

The Republic Is Not Ungrateful.

"It is not what is *charged* but what is *proved* that damages the party defendant. Any one may be accused of the most heinous offenses; the Saviour of mankind was not only arraigned but convicted; but what of it? Facts alone are decisive."—*New York Tribune*, March 13, 1872.

9.

March 14, 1874

Colored Rule in a Reconstructed (?) State.

(THE MEMBERS CALL EACH OTHER THIEVES, LIARS, RASCALS, AND COWARDS.)

COLUMBIA. "You are aping the lowest whites. If you disgrace your race in this way you had better take back seats."

CHAPTER 1

RECONSTRUCTING
RECONSTRUCTION:
THE POLITICAL
CARTOONIST
AND THE
NATIONAL MOOD

10.

September 26, 1874

The Commandments in South Carolina.

"We've pretty well smashed that; but I suppose, Massa Moses, you can get another one."

December 9, 1876

The Ignorant Vote—Honors Are Easy.

CHAPTER 1

RECONSTRUCTING
RECONSTRUCTION:
THE POLITICAL
CARTOONIST
AND THE
NATIONAL MOOD

12.

October 24, 1874

A Burden He Has To Shoulder.
And they say, "He wants a third term."

Source 13 from J. Chal Vinson, *Thomas Nast, Political Cartoonist* (Athens: University of Georgia Press, 1967), plate 103.

13.

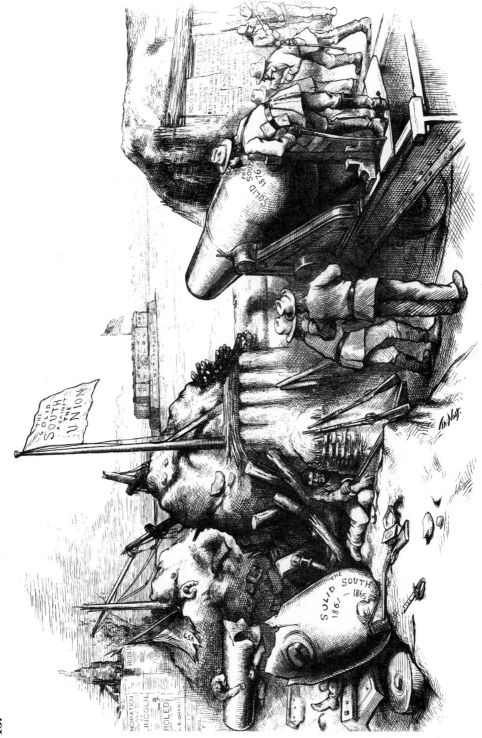

CHAPTER 1

RECONSTRUCTING
RECONSTRUCTION:
THE POLITICAL
CARTOONIST
AND THE
NATIONAL MOOD

❧ QUESTIONS TO CONSIDER ❧

Begin by reviewing your list of the important issues and events of the Reconstruction era. Then systematically examine the cartoons, answering the following questions for each one:

1. What issue or event is represented by this cartoon?
2. Who are the principal figures, and how are they portrayed?
3. What *imagery* is used?
4. Is this cartoon an *allegory?* if so, what is the basis of the allegory?
5. What *symbols* are used?
6. How was Nast trying to influence public opinion through this cartoon?

You may find that making a chart is the easiest way to do this.

Sources 1 through 3 represent Nast's views of Reconstruction under President Andrew Johnson. Sources 4 and 5 deal with an issue crucial to Radical Republicans. Sources 6 and 7 focus on the presidential election of 1872, and Sources 8 through 12 evaluate Radical Reconstruction in its later years. The cartoons are roughly in chronological order, and you should watch for any changes in Nast's portrayal of the major issues between the end of the Civil War in 1865 and the end of Radical Reconstruction after the election of 1876.

Who is the woman in Source 1? What emotions do her two different poses suggest? Who are the people asking for pardon in the first frame? Look carefully at the black man in the second frame. Who does he represent? Can you formulate one sentence that summarizes the message of both parts of Source 1?

Source 2 is more complex: two drawings within two other drawings. If you do not already know what purpose Andersonville and Fortress Monroe served, consult a text on this time period, an encyclopedia, or a good Civil War history book. Then look at the upper left and upper right outside drawings. Contrast the appearance of the man entering with the man leaving. Now examine the lower left and lower right outside drawings the same way. What was Nast trying to tell? The larger inside drawings explain the contrast. What were the conditions like at Andersonville? At Fortress Monroe? What did the cartoonist think were the physical and psychological results?

On July 30, 1866, several blacks attending a Radical Republican convention in New Orleans were shot and killed by white policemen. Who is the emperor in Source 3, and how is he portrayed? What kind of setting is used in this cartoon? Who is the person in the lower left intending to represent? What did Nast think caused this event? What was his own reaction to it?

Each of the three people standing in Source 4 represents part of the Democratic party coalition, and each has something to contribute to the party. Can you identify the groups that the man on the right and the man in the center represent? What do they offer the party? Notice the facial features of the man on the left as well as his dress, particularly the hatband from Five Points (a notorious slum section of New York City). Who is this man supposed to represent, and what does he give the party? Notice what the black man lying on the ground has dropped. What does he represent? What is he reaching for? What is happening in the background of the cartoon?

What issue does Source 5 explore? What story are people supposed to remember when they see this cartoon? Who is the woman, and what has she done? Who are her supporters at the left? What other things do they advocate? Who is the figure in the upper right-hand corner? What has he promised African Americans? What has he done?

Sources 6 and 7 were published just before the presidential election of 1872. Who is the plump little man with the white beard and glasses who appears in both cartoons? What part of this man's campaign did Nast find especially objectionable? Why? What is wrong with what the character is trying to do? Who is portrayed in Source 8? Why is the woman protecting him from attack?

Sources 9 through 12 reflect Nast's thinking in the later years of Reconstruction. Sources 9 and 10 portray his opinion of Reconstruction in South Carolina, presided over by Radical Republican governor Franklin J. Moses (caricatured in Source 10). How are African Americans pictured (compare to Sources 1, 4, and 5)? To whom are African Americans compared in Source 11? What does this say about Nast's opinion of Reconstruction? Source 12 portrays President Ulysses Grant (compare to Sources 3 and 8). How is he pictured?

The last cartoon (Source 13) shows Nast's opinion of the South in 1876, near the end of Reconstruction. What scene was Nast re-creating? What is the significance of this scene? How is the black man depicted? What was Nast trying to show? How would you compare or contrast this cartoon with Sources 9 through 12? How did Nast's views change? In the final analysis, what did he think had been accomplished by more than a decade of Reconstruction?

Now return to the central questions asked earlier. What significant events took place during Reconstruction? How did Nast try to influence public opinion on the important issues of the era? How did Nast's own views change between 1865 and 1876? Why did Reconstruction finally end?

∽ EPILOGUE ∾

Undoubtedly, Nast's work had an important impact on northern opinion of Reconstruction, the Democratic party, Horace Greeley, the Irish Americans, and other issues. Yet gradually, northern ardor began to decline as other issues and concerns eased Reconstruction out of the limelight and as it ap-

CHAPTER 1

RECONSTRUCTING
RECONSTRUCTION:
THE POLITICAL
CARTOONIST
AND THE
NATIONAL MOOD

peared that the crusade to reconstruct the South would be an endless one. Radical Republicans, who insisted on equality for the freed slaves, received less and less attention, and southern Democrats, who regained control of southern state governments, were essentially allowed a free hand as long as they did not obviously violate the Constitution and federal law. By 1877, the South was once again in the hands of white Democrats.

As long as African Americans did not insist on their rights, white southern leaders allowed them to retain, in principle, all that the Civil War and Reconstruction had won. In other words, as long as black voters did not challenge the "Redeemers," they were allowed to retain their political rights. Economically, many African Americans gradually slipped into the status of tenant farmer, sharecropper, or even peon. The political structure, local courts, and law-enforcement agencies tended to support this arrangement. For his part, African American leader Booker T. Washington was praised by white southerners for urging that blacks seek education and economic opportunities but not "rock the boat" politically in the white-controlled South. Finally, in the late 1880s, when white southerners realized that the Reconstruction spirit had waned in the North, southern state legislatures began instituting rigid segregation of schools, public transportation and accommodations, parks, restaurants and theaters, elevators, drinking fountains, and so on. Not until the 1950s did those chains begin to be broken.

As the reform spirit waned in the later years of Reconstruction, Nast's popularity suffered. The public appeared to tire of his anger, his self-righteousness, his relentless crusades. The new publisher of *Harper's Weekly* sought to make the magazine less political, and in that atmosphere there was no place for Nast. He resigned in 1886.

Nast continued to free-lance for a number of magazines and tried unsuccessfully to start his own periodical, *Nast's Weekly*. Financially struggling, he appealed to friends, who influenced President Theodore Roosevelt to appoint Nast to a minor consular post in Ecuador. He died there of yellow fever in 1902.

Thomas Nast was a pioneer of a tradition and a political art form. His successors, people such as Herbert Block (Herblock), Bill Mauldin, Oliphant, and even Garry Trudeau ("Doonesbury"), have continued to prick the American conscience, fret and irritate newspaper readers, and assert through their art the proposition that no evildoer can escape the scrutiny and ultimate justice of the popular will. Sometimes these successors are effective, sometimes not.

CHAPTER 2

THE ROAD TO TRUE FREEDOM: AFRICAN AMERICAN ALTERNATIVES IN THE NEW SOUTH

◌⊙ THE PROBLEM ⊙◌

By 1895, when the venerable Frederick Douglass died, African Americans in the South had been free for thirty years. Yet in many ways, their situation had barely improved from that of servitude, and in some ways, it had actually deteriorated. Economically, very few had been able to acquire land of their own, and the vast majority continued to work for white landowners under various forms of labor arrangements and sometimes under outright peonage.[1] Political and civil rights supposedly had been guaranteed under the Fourteenth and Fifteenth amendments to the Constitution (ratified in 1868 and 1870, respectively), but those rights often were violated, federal courts offered little protection, and, beginning in the early 1890s, southern states began a successful campaign to disfranchise black voters and to institute legal segregation through legislation that collectively became known as Jim Crow laws.[2] In some ways more threatening, violence against African Americans

---

1. Whatever names were given to these labor arrangements (tenancy, sharecropping, and so on), in most of the arrangements a white landowner or merchant furnished farm workers with foodstuffs and fertilizer on credit, taking a percentage of the crops grown in return. For a fascinating description of how the system worked, see Theodore Rosengarten, *All God's Dangers: The Life of Nate Shaw* (New York: Alfred A. Knopf, 1974).

2. The term "Jim Crow," generally used to refer to issues relating to African Americans, originated in the late 1820s with white minstrel singer Thomas "Daddy" Rice, who performed the song "Jump Jim Crow" in blackface makeup. By the 1840s, the term was used to refer to racially segregated facilities in the North.

CHAPTER 2

THE ROAD TO
TRUE FREEDOM:
AFRICAN
AMERICAN
ALTERNATIVES
IN THE NEW
SOUTH

was increasing and in most cases going unpunished. Between 1889 and 1900, 1,357 lynchings of African Americans were recorded in the United States, the vast majority in the states of the former Confederacy. In 1898, in New Bern, North Carolina, one white orator proposed "choking the Cape Fear River with the bodies of Negroes." In truth, by the 1890s it had become evident for all who cared to see that Lincoln's emancipation of southern slaves had been considerably less than complete.

A number of spokespersons offered significantly different strategies for improving the situation of African Americans in the South. We have chosen four such spokespersons, all of them extremely well-known to blacks in the New South. Ida B. Wells (1862–1931) was a journalist, lecturer, and crusader who was well-known in both the United States and Europe. Booker T. Washington (1856–1915) was a celebrated educator, author, and political figure who many believed should inherit the mantle of Frederick Douglass as the principal spokesperson for

African Americans. Henry McNeal Turner (1834–1915) was a bishop of the African Methodist Episcopal Church and a controversial speaker and writer. W. E. B. Du Bois (pronounced DuBoys', 1868–1963) was an academician and editor and one of the founders of the National Association for the Advancement of Colored People (NAACP). Each of these spokespersons offered a contrasting alternative for African Americans.

In this chapter, you will be analyzing the situation that African Americans in the South faced in the years after Reconstruction and identifying the principal alternatives open to them. What different strategies did Wells, Washington, Turner, and Du Bois offer African Americans? Were there other options they did not mention? Finally, based on your examination of the evidence and on the use of your historical imagination, which alternative do you think was the best one for African Americans at the turn of the twentieth century? How would you go about proving your hypothesis?

∽ BACKGROUND ∾

The gradual end of Reconstruction by the federal government left the South in the hands of political and economic leaders who chose to call themselves "Redeemers." Many of these men came from the same landowner and planter-lawyer groups that had led the South prior to the Civil War, thus giving the post–Reconstruction South a high de-

gree of continuity with earlier eras. Also important, however, was a comparatively new group of southerners, men who called for a "New South" that would be highlighted by increased industrialization, urbanization, and diversified agriculture.

In many ways, the New South movement was an undisguised attempt to imitate the industrialization that was sweeping through the North just prior to, during, and after the Civil War. Indeed, the North's industrial prowess had been one reason for its ultimate military victory. As Reconstruction gradually came to an end in the southern states, many southern bankers, business leaders, and editors became convinced that the South should not return to its previous, narrow economic base of plantations and one-crop agriculture but instead should follow the North's lead toward modernization through industry. Prior to the Civil War, many of these people had been calling for economic diversification, but they had been overwhelmed by the plantation aristocracy that controlled southern state politics and had used that control to further its own interests. By the end of Reconstruction, however, the planter elite had lost a good deal of its power, thus creating a power vacuum into which advocates of a New South could move.

Nearly every city, town, and hamlet of the former Confederacy had its New South boosters. Getting together in industrial societies or chambers of commerce, the boosters called for the erection of mills and factories. Why, they asked, should southerners export their valuable raw materials elsewhere, only to see them return from northern and European factories as costly finished products? Why couldn't southerners set up their own manufacturing establishments and become prosperous within a self-contained economy? And if the southerners were short of capital, why not encourage rich northern investors to put up money in re-

turn for promises of great profits? In fact, the South had all the ingredients required of an industrial system: raw materials, a rebuilt transportation system, labor, potential consumers, and the possibility of obtaining capital. As they fed each other's dreams, the New South advocates pictured a resurgent South, a prosperous South, a triumphant South, a South of steam and power rather than plantations and magnolias.

Undoubtedly, the leading spokesman of the New South movement was Henry Grady, editor of the *Atlanta Constitution* and one of the most influential figures in the southern states. Born in Athens, Georgia, in 1850, Grady was orphaned in his early teens when his father was killed in the Civil War. Graduating from his hometown college, the University of Georgia, Grady began a long and not particularly profitable career as a journalist. In 1879, aided by northern industrialist Cyrus Field, he purchased a quarter interest in the *Atlanta Constitution* and became that newspaper's editor. From that position, he became the chief advocate of the New South movement.

Whether speaking to southern or northern audiences, Grady had no peer. Addressing a group of potential investors in New South industries in New York in 1886, he delighted his audience by saying that he was glad the Confederacy had lost the Civil War, for that defeat had broken the power of the plantation aristocracy and provided the opportunity for the South to move into the modern industrial age. Northerners, Grady continued, were welcome: "We have sown

CHAPTER 2

THE ROAD TO
TRUE FREEDOM:
AFRICAN
AMERICAN
ALTERNATIVES
IN THE NEW
SOUTH

towns and cities in the place of theories, and put business above politics . . . and have . . . wiped out the place where Mason and Dixon's line used to be."[3]

To those southerners who envisioned a New South, the central goal was a harmonious, interdependent society in which each person and thing had a clearly defined place. Most New South boosters stressed industry and the growth of cities because the South had few factories and mills and almost no cities of substantial size. But agriculture also would have its place, although it would not be the same as the cash-crop agriculture of the pre–Civil War years. Instead, New South spokesmen advocated a diversified agriculture that would still produce cash crops for export but would also make the South more self-sufficient by producing food crops and raw materials for the anticipated factories. Small towns would be used for collection and distribution, a rebuilt railroad network would transport goods, and northern capital would finance the entire process. Hence each part of the economy and, indeed, each person would have a clearly defined place and role in the New South, a place and role that would ensure everyone a piece of the New South's prosperity.

But even as Grady and his counterparts were fashioning their dreams of a New South and selling those dreams to both northerners and southerners, a less beneficial, less prosperous side of the New South was taking shape.

In spite of the New South advocates' successes in establishing factories and mills (for example, Knoxville, Tennessee, witnessed the founding of more than ninety such enterprises in the 1880s alone), the post–Reconstruction South remained primarily agricultural. Furthermore, most of the farms were worked by sharecroppers or tenant farmers who eked out a bare subsistence while the profits went to the landowners or to the banks. This situation was especially prevalent in the lower South, where by 1890 a great proportion of farms were worked by tenants: South Carolina (61.1 percent), Georgia (59.9 percent), Alabama (57.7 percent), Mississippi (62.4 percent), and Louisiana (58.0 percent). Even as factory smokestacks were rising on portions of the southern horizon, a high percentage of southerners remained in agriculture and in poverty.

Undeniably, African Americans suffered the most. More than four million African American men, women, and children had been freed by the Civil War. During Reconstruction, some advances were made, especially in the areas of public education and voter registration. Yet even these gains were either impermanent or incomplete. By 1880 in Georgia, only 33.7 percent of the black school-age population was enrolled in schools, and by 1890 (twenty-five years after emancipation) almost half of all black people ages ten to fourteen in the Deep South were still illiterate.[4] As for voting rights,

3. Grady's speech is in Richard N. Current and John A. Garraty, eds., *Words That Made American History*, Vol. II (Boston: Little, Brown and Company, 1962), pp. 23–31.

4. Roger L. Ransom and Richard Sutch, *One Kind of Freedom: The Economic Consequences of Emancipation* (Cambridge: Cambridge University Press, 1977), pp. 28, 30.

the vast majority of African Americans chose not to exercise them, fearing intimidation and violence.

Many blacks and whites at the time recognized that African Americans would never be able to improve their situation economically, socially, or politically without owning land. Yet even many Radical Republicans were reluctant to give land to the former slaves. Such a move would mean seizing land from the white planters, a proposal that clashed with the notion of the sanctity of private property. As a result, most African Americans were forced to take menial, low-paying jobs in southern cities or work as farmers on land they did not own. By 1880, only 1.6 percent of the landowners in Georgia were black, and most of them owned the most marginal and least productive land.

As poor urban laborers or tenant farmers, African Americans were dependent on their employers, landowners, or bankers and prey to rigid vagrancy laws, the convict lease system, peonage, and outright racial discrimination. Moreover, the end of Reconstruction in the southern states was followed by a reimposition of rigid racial segregation, at first through a return to traditional practices and later (in the 1890s) by state laws governing nearly every aspect of southern life. For example, voting by African Americans was discouraged, initially by intimidation and then by more formal means such as poll taxes and literacy tests. African Americans who protested or strayed from their "place" were dealt with harshly. Between 1880 and 1918, more than twenty-four hundred African Americans were lynched by southern white mobs, each action being a grim reminder to African Americans of what could happen to those who challenged the status quo. For their part, the few southern whites who spoke against such outrages were themselves subjects of intimidation and even violence. Indeed, although most African American men and women undoubtedly would have disagreed, African Americans' relative position in some ways had deteriorated since the end of the Civil War.

Many New South advocates openly worried about how potential northern investors and politicians would react to this state of affairs. Although the dream of the New South rested on the concept of a harmonious, interdependent society in which each component (industry, agriculture, and so forth) and each person (white and black) had a clearly defined place, it appeared that African Americans were being kept in their "place" largely by intimidation and force. Who would want to invest in a region in which the status quo of mutual deference and "place" often was maintained by force? To calm northern fears, Grady and his cohorts assured northerners that African Americans' position was improving and that southern society was one of mutual respect between the races. "We have found," Grady stated, "that in the summing up the free Negro counts more than he did as a slave." Most northerners believed Grady because they wanted to, because they had no taste for another bitter Reconstruction, and in many cases because they shared white southerners' prejudice against African Americans. Grady was able to reassure them because they wanted to be reassured.

CHAPTER 2

THE ROAD TO
TRUE FREEDOM:
AFRICAN
AMERICAN
ALTERNATIVES
IN THE NEW
SOUTH

Thus for southern African Americans, the New South movement had done little to better their collective lot. Indeed, in some ways their position had deteriorated. Tied economically either to land they did not own or to the lowest-paying jobs in towns and cities, subjects of an increasingly rigid code of racial segregation and loss of political rights, and victims of an upswing in racially directed violence, African Americans in the New South had every reason to question the oratory of Henry Grady and other New South boosters. Jobs in the New South's mills and factories generally were reserved for whites, so the opportunities that European immigrants in the North had to work their way gradually up the economic ladder were closed to southern blacks.

How did African Americans respond to this deteriorating situation? In the 1890s, numerous African American farmers joined the Colored Alliance, part of the Farmers' Alliance Movement that swept the South and Midwest in the 1880s and 1890s. This movement attempted to reverse the farmers' eroding position through the establishment of farmers' cooperatives (to sell their crops together for higher prices and to purchase manufactured goods wholesale) and by entering politics to elect candidates sympathetic to farmers (who would draft legislation favorable to farmers). Many feared, however, that this increased militancy of farmers—white and black—would produce a political backlash that would leave them even worse off. Such a backlash occurred in the South in the 1890s with the defeat of the Populist revolt.

Wells, Washington, Turner, and Du Bois offered southern African Americans four other alternatives to meet the economic, social, and political problems they faced. And, as African American men and women soon discovered, there were other options as well.

Your task in this chapter is to analyze the evidence to answer the following central questions:

1. What were the different alternatives offered by Wells, Washington, Turner, and Du Bois?
2. Were there options those four spokespersons did not mention?
3. Which alternative do you think was the best one for African Americans in the South at the turn of the twentieth century?
4. How would you support your conclusion?

⌾ THE METHOD ⌾

In this chapter, the evidence is arranged chronologically. The piece by Ida B. Wells is from a pamphlet published simultaneously in the United States and England in 1892. It is likely that parts of the pamphlet were delivered as a speech by Wells earlier that year. The selections by Washington and Turner and the two selections by Du Bois are transcriptions or printed versions of speeches delivered in September 1895, December 1895, and 1903 and 1906, respectively. Finally, there is one set of statistics (Source 6) that suggests an additional alternative open to African Americans.

Ida Bell Wells was born a slave in Holly Springs, Mississippi, in 1862. After emancipation, her father and mother, as a carpenter and a cook, respectively, earned enough money to send her to a freedmen's school. In 1876, her parents died in a yellow fever epidemic. Only fourteen years old, Wells lied about her age and got a job teaching in a rural school for blacks, eventually moving to Memphis, Tennessee, to teach in the city's schools for African Americans. In 1884, she was forcibly removed from a railroad passenger car for refusing to move to the car reserved for "colored" passengers; she sued the railroad company.[5] About this time, Wells began writing articles for many black-owned newspapers, mostly on the subject of unequal educational opportunities for whites and blacks in Memphis. As a result, the Memphis school board discharged her, and she became a full-time journalist and lecturer. By 1892, she had become co-owner of the *Memphis Free Speech* newspaper. In that year, three of her friends were lynched in Memphis, an event that propelled her into the antilynching movement. In 1895, she married black lawyer-editor Ferdinand Lee Barnett and from that time went by the name Ida Wells-

Barnett, a somewhat radical practice in 1895.

Like Wells, Booker T. Washington was born a slave, in Franklin County, Virginia. Largely self-taught before entering Hampton Institute, a school for African Americans, at age seventeen, he worked his way through school, mostly as a janitor. At age twenty-five, he was chosen to organize a normal school for blacks at Tuskegee, Alabama. Washington spent thirty-four years as the guiding force at Tuskegee Institute, shaping the school into his vision of what African Americans must do to better their lot. Tuskegee became nationally known as a school where blacks could learn skilled trades (carpentry, masonry, home economics, and the like) and acquire the skills to teach other African Americans. In great demand as a speaker to white and black audiences alike, Washington received an honorary degree from Harvard College in 1891. Four years later, he was chosen as the principal speaker at the opening of the Negro section of the Atlanta Exposition.

Henry McNeal Turner was born a free black near Abbeville, South Carolina. Mostly self-taught, he joined the Methodist Episcopal Church, South, in 1848 and was licensed to preach in 1853. In 1858, he abandoned that denomination to become a minister in the African Methodist Episcopal Church, and by 1862 he was the pastor of the large Israel Church in Washington, D.C. In 1863, he became a chaplain in the Union army, assigned to the 1st U.S. Colored Regiment. After the war, he became an official of the Freedmen's Bureau in Georgia and afterward held a succession of political

5. The Tennessee Supreme Court ruled in favor of the Chesapeake and Ohio Railroad and against Wells in 1887.

CHAPTER 2

THE ROAD TO
TRUE FREEDOM:
AFRICAN
AMERICAN
ALTERNATIVES
IN THE NEW
SOUTH

appointments. One of the founders of the Republican party in Georgia, Turner was made bishop of the African Methodist Episcopal Church in Georgia in 1880. By the time Turner made the speech reproduced in part here as Source 3, he had visited Africa three times and had spoken extensively on his travels and other subjects. Turner delivered the speech at a conference on Africa and the American Negro held at the Gammon Theological Seminary in Atlanta.

William Edward Burghardt Du Bois was born in Great Barrington, Massachusetts, one of approximately fifty blacks in a town of five thousand people. He was educated with the white children in the town's public school and in 1885 was enrolled at Fisk University, a college for African Americans in Nashville, Tennessee. It was there, according to his autobiography, that he first encountered overt racial prejudice. Graduated from Fisk in 1888, he entered Harvard as a junior. He received his bachelor's degree in 1890 and his Ph.D. in 1895. His book *The Philadelphia Negro* was published in 1899. In this book, Du Bois asserted that the problems African Americans faced were the results of their history (slavery and racism) and environment, not of some imagined genetic inferiority. He was the principal founder of the Niagara Movement (named after the site of its first meeting) in 1905. The movement called for protests against all forms of segregation and racial injustice.

This is not the first time that you have had to analyze speeches. Our society is almost literally bombarded by speeches delivered by politicians, business figures, educators, and others, most of whom are trying to convince us to adopt a set of ideas or actions. As we listen to such speeches, we invariably weigh the options presented to us, often using other available evidence (in this case, the Background section of this chapter) to help us make our decisions. One purpose of this exercise is to help you think more critically and use evidence more thoroughly when assessing different options.

It is logical to begin by analyzing each of the speeches in turn. As you read each selection, make a rough chart like the one on page 35 to help you remember the main points. Then examine Source 6 for another option open to southern African Americans. Remember that when we analyze statistics, we need to ask three principal questions:

1. What is being measured?
2. How did that variable change over time?
3. How can that change be explained?

Once you have carefully defined the alternatives presented by Wells, Washington, Turner, Du Bois, and Source 6, return to the Background section of this chapter. As you reread that section, use your historical imagination to determine which was the best alternative.

African American Alternatives			Your Reaction (Fill in later)
Speaker	Suggested Alternatives	How Does Speaker Develop Her/His Arguments?	
Wells			
Washington			
Turner			
Du Bois			

∽ THE EVIDENCE ∽

Source 1 from Ida B. Wells, *United States Atrocities* (London: Lux Newspaper and Publishing Co., 1892), pp. 13–18. In the United States, the pamphlet was titled *Southern Horrors*.

1. Wells's *United States Atrocities,* 1892.

Mr. Henry W. Grady, in his well-remembered speeches in New England and New York, pictured the Afro-American as incapable of self-government. Through him and other leading men the cry of the South to the country has been "Hands off! Leave us to solve our problem." To the Afro-American the South says, "The white man must and will rule." There is little difference between the Ante-bellum South and the New South. Her white citizens are wedded to any method however revolting, any measure however extreme, for the subjugation of the young manhood of the dark race. They have cheated him out of his ballot, deprived him of civil rights or redress in the Civil Courts thereof, robbed him of the fruits of his labour, and are still murdering, burning and lynching him.

The result is a growing disregard of human life. Lynch Law has spread its insidious influence till men in New York State, Pennsylvania and on the free Western plains feel they can take the law in their own hands with impunity, especially where an Afro-American is concerned. The South is brutalised to a degree not realised by its own inhabitants, and the very foundation of government, law, and order are imperilled.

CHAPTER 2

THE ROAD TO
TRUE FREEDOM:
AFRICAN
AMERICAN
ALTERNATIVES
IN THE NEW
SOUTH

Public sentiment has had a slight "reaction," though not sufficient to stop the crusade of lawlessness and lynching. The spirit of Christianity of the great M. E. Church was sufficiently aroused by the frequent and revolting crimes against a powerless people, to pass strong condemnatory resolutions at its General Conference in Omaha last May. The spirit of justice of the grand old party[6] asserted itself sufficiently to secure a denunciation of the wrongs, and a feeble declaration of the belief in human rights in the Republican platform at Minneapolis, June 7th. A few of the great "dailies" and "weeklies" have swung into line declaring that Lynch Law must go. The President of the United States issued a proclamation that it be not tolerated in the territories over which he has jurisdiction. . . .

These efforts brought forth apologies and a short halt, but the lynching mania has raged again through the past twelve months with unabated fury. The strong arm of the law must be brought to bear upon lynchers in severe punishment, but this cannot and will not be done unless a healthy public sentiment demands and sustains such action. The men and women in the South who disapprove of lynching and remain silent on the perpetration of such outrages are *particeps criminis*—accomplices, accessories before and after the fact, equally guilty with the actual law-breakers, who would not persist if they did not know that neither the law nor militia would be deployed against them.

In the creation of this healthier public sentiment, the Afro-American can do for himself what no one else can do for him. The world looks on with wonder that we have conceded so much, and remain law-abiding under such great outrage and provocation.

To Northern capital and Afro-American labour the South owes its rehabilitation. If labour is withdrawn capital will not remain. The Afro-American is thus the backbone of the South. A thorough knowledge and judicious exercise of this power in lynching localities could many times effect a bloodless revolution. The white man's dollar is his god, and to stop this will be to stop outrages in many localities.

The Afro-Americans of Memphis denounced the lynching of three of their best citizens, and urged and waited for the authorities to act in the matter, and bring the lynchers to justice. No attempt was made to do so, and the black men left the city by thousands, bringing about great stagnation in every branch of business. Those who remained so injured the business of the street car company by staying off the cars, that the superintendent, manager, and treasurer called personally on the editors of the *Free Speech,*

6. The Republican party.

and asked them to urge our people to give them their patronage again. Other business men became alarmed over the situation, and the *Free Speech* was suppressed that the coloured people might be more easily controlled. A meeting of white citizens in June, three months after the lynching, passed resolutions for the first time condemning it. *But they did not punish the lynchers.* Every one of them was known by name because they had been selected to do the dirty work by some of the very citizens who passed these resolutions! Memphis is fast losing her black population, who proclaim as they go that there is no protection for the life and property of any Afro-American citizen in Memphis who will not be a slave.

The Afro-American citizens of Kentucky, whose intellectual and financial improvement has been phenomenal, have never had a separate car law until now. Delegations and petitions poured into the Legislature against it, yet the Bill passed, and the Jim Crow Car of Kentucky is a legalised institution. Will the great mass of Negroes continue to patronise the railroad? A special from Covington, Kentucky, says:—

"Covington, June 13th.—The railroads of the State are beginning to feel very markedly the effects of the separate coach Bill recently passed by the Legislature. No class of people in the State have so many and so largely attended excursions as the blacks. All these have been abandoned, and regular travel is reduced to a minimum." A competent authority says the loss to the various roads will reach 1,000,000 dols. this year.

A call to a State Conference in Lexington, Kentucky, last June, had delegates from every county in the State. Those delegates, the ministers, teachers, heads of secret and other orders, and the heads of families should pass the word around for every member of the race in Kentucky to stay off railroads unless obliged to ride. If they did so, and their advice was followed persistently, the Convention would not need to petition the Legislature to repeal the law or raise money to file a suit. The railroad corporations would be so affected they would, in self defence, "lobby" to have the separate car law repealed. On the other hand, as long as the railroads can get Afro-American excursions they will always have plenty of money to fight all the suits brought against them. They will be aided in so doing by the same partisan public sentiment which passed the law. White men passed the law, and white judges and juries would pass upon the suits against the law, and render judgment in line with their prejudices, and in deference to the greater financial power.

The appeal to the white man's pocket has ever been more effectual than all the appeals ever made to his conscience. Nothing, absolutely nothing, is to be gained by a further sacrifice of manhood and self-respect. By the

CHAPTER 2

THE ROAD TO
TRUE FREEDOM:
AFRICAN
AMERICAN
ALTERNATIVES
IN THE NEW
SOUTH

right exercise of his power as the industrial factor of the South, the Afro-American can demand and secure his rights, the punishment of lynchers, and a fair trial for members of his race accused of outrage.

Of the many inhuman outrages of this present year, the only case where the proposed lynching did *not* occur, was where the men armed themselves in Jacksonville, Florida, and Paducah, Kentucky, and prevented it. The only times an Afro-American who was assaulted got away has been when he had a gun, and used it in self-defence. The lesson this teaches, and which every Afro-American should ponder well, is that a Winchester rifle should have a place of honour in every black home, and it should be used for that protection which the law refuses to give. When the white man, who is always the aggressor, knows he runs a great risk of biting the dust every time his Afro-American victim does, he will have greater respect for Afro-American life. The more the Afro-American yields and cringes and begs, the more he has to do so, the more he is insulted, outraged, and lynched.

. . .

The assertion has been substantiated that the Press[7] contains unreliable and doctored reports of lynchings, and one of the most necessary things for the race to do is to get these facts before the public. The people must know before they can act, and there is no educator to compare with the Press.

The Afro-American papers are the only ones which will print the truth, and they lack means to employ agents and detectives to get at the facts. The race must rally a mighty host to the support of their journals, and thus enable them to do much in the way of investigation. . . .

Nothing is more definitely settled than that he must act for himself. I have shown how he may employ the "boycott," emigration, and the Press; and I feel that by a combination of all these agencies Lynch Law—the last relic of barbarism and slavery—can be effectually stamped out. "The gods help those who help themselves."

7. Wells was referring here to newspapers owned by whites.

Source 2 from Louis R. Harlan, ed., *The Booker T. Washington Papers* (Urbana: University of Illinois Press, 1974), Vol. III, pp. 583–587.

2. The Standard Printed Version of Booker T. Washington's Atlanta Exposition Address.

[Atlanta, Ga., Sept. 18, 1895]

Mr. President and Gentlemen of the Board of Directors and Citizens:

One-third of the population of the South is of the Negro race. No enterprise seeking the material, civil, or moral welfare of this section can disregard this element of our population and reach the highest success. I but convey to you, Mr. President and Directors, the sentiment of the masses of my race when I say that in no way have the value and manhood of the American Negro been more fittingly and generously recognized than by the managers of this magnificent Exposition at every stage of its progress. It is a recognition that will do more to cement the friendship of the two races than any occurrence since the dawn of our freedom.

Not only this, but the opportunity here afforded will awaken among us a new era of industrial progress. Ignorant and inexperienced, it is not strange that in the first years of our new life we began at the top instead of at the bottom; that a seat in Congress or the state legislature was more sought than real estate or industrial skill; that the political convention or stump speaking had more attractions than starting a dairy farm or truck garden.

A ship lost at sea for many days suddenly sighted a friendly vessel. From the mast of the unfortunate vessel was seen a signal, "Water, water; we die of thirst!" The answer from the friendly vessel at once came back, "Cast down your bucket where you are." A second time the signal, "Water, water; send us water!" ran up from the distressed vessel, and was answered, "Cast down your bucket where you are." And a third and fourth signal for water was answered, "Cast down your bucket where you are." The captain of the distressed vessel, at last heeding the injunction, cast down his bucket, and it came up full of fresh, sparkling water from the mouth of the Amazon River. To those of my race who depend on bettering their condition in a foreign land or who underestimate the importance of cultivating friendly relations with the Southern white man, who is their next-door neighbour, I would say: "Cast down your bucket where you are"—cast it down in making friends in every manly way of the people of all races by whom we are surrounded.

CHAPTER 2

THE ROAD TO
TRUE FREEDOM:
AFRICAN
AMERICAN
ALTERNATIVES
IN THE NEW
SOUTH

Cast it down in agriculture, mechanics, in commerce, in domestic service, and in the professions. And in this connection it is well to bear in mind that whatever other sins the South may be called to bear, when it comes to business, pure and simple, it is in the South that the Negro is given a man's chance in the commercial world, and in nothing is this Exposition more eloquent than in emphasizing this chance. Our greatest danger is that in the great leap from slavery to freedom we may overlook the fact that the masses of us are to live by the productions of our hands, and fail to keep in mind that we shall prosper in proportion as we learn to dignify and glorify common labour, and put brains and skill into the common occupations of life; shall prosper in proportion as we learn to draw the line between the superficial and the substantial, the ornamental gewgaws of life and the useful. No race can prosper till it learns that there is as much dignity in tilling a field as in writing a poem. It is at the bottom of life we must begin, and not at the top. Nor should we permit our grievances to overshadow our opportunities.

To those of the white race who look to the incoming of those of foreign birth and strange tongue and habits for the prosperity of the South, were I permitted I would repeat what I say to my own race, "Cast down your bucket where you are." Cast it down among the eight millions of Negroes whose habits you know, whose fidelity and love you have tested in days when to have proved treacherous meant the ruin of your firesides. Cast down your bucket among these people who have, without strikes and labour wars, tilled your fields, cleared your forests, builded your railroads and cities, and brought forth treasures from the bowels of the earth, and helped make possible this magnificent representation of the progress of the South. Casting down your bucket among my people, helping and encouraging them as you are doing on these grounds, and to education of head, hand, and heart, you will find that they will buy your surplus land, make blossom the waste places in your fields, and run your factories. While doing this, you can be sure in the future, as in the past, that you and your families will be surrounded by the most patient, faithful, law-abiding, and unresentful people that the world has seen. As we have proved our loyalty to you in the past, in nursing your children, watching by the sick-bed of your mothers and fathers, and often following them with tear-dimmed eyes to their graves, so in the future, in our humble way, we shall stand by you with a devotion that no foreigner can approach, ready to lay down our lives, if need be, in defense of yours, interlacing our industrial, commercial, civil, and religious life with yours in a way that shall make the interests of both races one. In all things that are purely social we can be as separate as the fingers, yet one as the hand in all things essential to mutual progress.

There is no defense or security for any of us except in the highest intelligence and development of all. If anywhere there are efforts tending to curtail the fullest growth of the Negro, let these efforts be turned into stimulating, encouraging, and making him the most useful and intelligent citizen. Effort or means so invested will pay a thousand per cent interest. These efforts will be twice blessed—"blessing him that gives and him that takes."

There is no escape through law of man or God from the inevitable:—

"The laws of changeless justice bind
  Oppressor with oppressed;
And close as sin and suffering joined
  We march to fate abreast."

Nearly sixteen millions of hands will aid you in pulling the load upward, or they will pull against you the load downward. We shall constitute one-third and more of the ignorance and crime of the South, or one-third [of] its intelligence and progress; we shall contribute one-third to the business and industrial prosperity of the South, or we shall prove a veritable body of death, stagnating, depressing, retarding every effort to advance the body politic.

Gentlemen of the Exposition, as we present to you our humble effort at an exhibition of our progress, you must not expect overmuch. Starting thirty years ago with ownership here and there in a few quilts and pumpkins and chickens (gathered from miscellaneous sources), remember the path that has led from these to the inventions and production of agricultural implements, buggies, steam-engines, newspapers, books, statuary, carving, paintings, the management of drug stores and banks, has not been trodden without contact with thorns and thistles. While we take pride in what we exhibit as a result of our independent efforts, we do not for a moment forget that our part in this exhibition would fall far short of your expectations but for the constant help that has come to our educational life, not only from the Southern states, but especially from Northern philanthropists, who have made their gifts a constant stream of blessing and encouragement.

The wisest among my race understand that the agitation of questions of social equality is the extremest folly, and that progress in the enjoyment

CHAPTER 2

THE ROAD TO
TRUE FREEDOM:
AFRICAN
AMERICAN
ALTERNATIVES
IN THE NEW
SOUTH

of all the privileges that will come to us must be the result of severe and constant struggle rather than of artificial forcing. No race that has anything to contribute to the markets of the world is long in any degree ostracized. It is important and right that all privileges of the law be ours, but it is vastly more important that we be prepared for the exercise of these privileges. The opportunity to earn a dollar in a factory just now is worth infinitely more than the opportunity to spend a dollar in an opera-house.

In conclusion, may I repeat that nothing in thirty years has given us more hope and encouragement, and drawn us so near to you of the white race, as this opportunity offered by the Exposition; and here bending, as it were, over the altar that represents the results of the struggles of your race and mine, both starting practically empty-handed three decades ago, I pledge that in your effort to work out the great and intricate problem which God has laid at the doors of the South, you shall have at all times the patient, sympathetic help of my race; only let this be constantly in mind, that, while from representations in these buildings of the product of field, of forest, of mine, of factory, letters, and art, much good will come, yet far above and beyond material benefits will be that higher good, that, let us pray God, will come, in a blotting out of sectional differences and racial animosities and suspicions in a determination to administer absolute justice, in a willing obedience among all classes to the mandates of law. This, coupled with our material prosperity, will bring into our beloved South a new heaven and a new earth.

Source 3 from Edwin S. Redkey, ed., *Respect Black: The Writings and Speeches of Henry McNeal Turner* (New York: Arno Press, 1971), pp. 167–171.

3. Turner's "The American Negro and His Fatherland," 1895.

It would be a waste of time to expend much labor, the few moments I have to devote to this subject, upon the present status of the Negroid race in the United States. It is too well-known already. However, I believe that the Negro was brought to this country in the providence of God to a heaven-permitted if not a divine-sanctioned manual laboring school, that he might have direct contact with the mightiest race that ever trod the face of the globe.

The heathen Africans, to my certain knowledge, I care not what others may say, eagerly yearn for that civilization which they believe will elevate them and make them potential for good. The African was not sent and brought to this country by chance, or by the avarice of the white man, single and alone. The white slave-purchaser went to the shores of that continent and bought our ancestors from their African masters. The bulk who were brought to this country were the children of parents who had been in slavery a thousand years. Yet hereditary slavery is not universal among the African slaveholders. So that the argument often advanced, that the white man went to Africa and stole us, is not true. They bought us out of a slavery that still exists over a large portion of that continent. For there are millions and millions of slaves in Africa today. Thus the superior African sent us, and the white man brought us, and we remained in slavery as long as it was necessary to learn that a God, who is a spirit, made the world and controls it, and that that Supreme Being could be sought and found by the exercise of faith in His only begotten Son. Slavery then went down, and the colored man was thrown upon his own responsibility, and here he is today, in the providence of God, cultivating self-reliance and imbibing a knowledge of civil law in contradistinction to the dictum of one man, which was the law of the black man until slavery was overthrown. I believe that the Negroid race has been free long enough now to begin to think for himself and plan for better conditions [than] he can lay claim to in this country or ever will. *There is no manhood future in the United States for the Negro*. He may eke out an existence for generations to come, but he can never be a *man*—full, symmetrical and undwarfed. Upon this point I know thousands who make pretensions to scholarship, white and colored, will differ and may charge me with folly, while I in turn pity their ignorance of history and political and civil sociology. We beg here to itemize and give a cursory glance at a few facts calculated to convince any man who is not biased or lamentably ignorant. Let us note a few of them.

1. There is a great chasm between the white and black, not only in this country, but in the West India Islands, South America, and as much as has been said to the contrary, I have seen inklings of it in Ireland, in England, in France, in Germany, and even away down in southern Spain in sight of Morocco in Africa. We will not, however, deal with foreign nations, but let us note a few facts connected with the United States.

I repeat that a great chasm exists between the two race varieties in this country. The white people, neither North or South, will have social contact as a mass between themselves and any portion of the Negroid race. Although they may be as white in appearance as themselves, yet a drop of African blood imparts a taint, and the talk about two races remaining in the same country with mutual interest and responsibility in its institutions and progress, with no social contact, is the jargon of folly, and no man who has read the history of nations and the development of countries, and the agencies which have culminated in the homogeneity of racial variations,

CHAPTER 2

THE ROAD TO
TRUE FREEDOM:
AFRICAN
AMERICAN
ALTERNATIVES
IN THE NEW
SOUTH

will proclaim such a doctrine. Senator Morgan,[8] of Alabama, tells the truth when he says that the Negro has nothing to expect without social equality with the whites, and that the whites will never grant it.

This question must be examined and opinions reached in the light of history and sociological philosophy, and not by a mere think-so on the part of men devoid of learning. When I use the term learning, I do not refer to men who have graduated from some college and have a smattering knowledge of Greek, Latin, mathematics and a few school books, and have done nothing since but read the trashy articles of newspapers. That is not scholarship. Scholarship consists in wading through dusty volumes for forty and fifty years. That class of men would not dare to predict symmetrical manhood for the Negroid race in this or any other country, without social equality. The colored man who will stand up and in one breath say that the Negroid race does not want social equality and in the next predict a great future in the face of all the proscription of which the colored man is the victim, is either an ignoramus, or is an advocate of the perpetual servility and degradation of his race variety.[9] I know, as Senator Morgan says, and as every white man in the land will say, that the whites will not grant social equality to the Negroid race, nor am I certain that God wants them to do it. And as such, I believe that two or three millions of us should return to the land of our ancestors, and establish our own nation, civilization, laws, customs, style of manufacture, and not only give the world, like other race varieties, the benefit of our individuality, but build up social conditions peculiarly our own, and cease to be grumblers, chronic complainers and a menace to the white man's country, or the country he claims and is bound to dominate.

The civil status of the Negro is simply what the white man grants of his own free will and accord. The black man can demand nothing. He is deposed from the jury and tried, convicted and sentenced by men who do not claim to be his peers. On the railroads, where the colored race is found in the largest numbers, he is the victim of proscription, and he must ride in the Jim Crow car or walk. The Supreme Court of the United States decided, October 15th, 1883, that the colored man had no civil rights under the general government,[10] and the several States, from then until now, have been enacting laws which limit, curtail and deprive him of his civil rights,

8. John Tyler Morgan (1824–1907), U.S. senator from 1877 to 1907. Morgan was an ardent expansionist and white supremacist. See Joseph A. Fry, *John Tyler Morgan and the Search for Southern Autonomy* (Knoxville: University of Tennessee Press, 1992).
9. The reference is to Booker T. Washington.
10. In October 15, 1883, the Supreme Court handed down one decision that applied to five separate cases that had been argued before the Court, all of them having to do with racial

immunities and privileges, until he is now being disfranchised, and where it will end no one can divine.

They told me in the Geographical Institute in Paris, France, that according to their calculation there are not less than 400,000,000 of Africans and their descendants on the globe, so that we are not lacking in numbers to form a nationality of our own.

2. The environments of the Negroid race variety in this country tend to the inferiority of them, even if the argument can be established that we are equals with the white man in the aggregate, notwithstanding the same opportunities may be enjoyed in the schools. Let us not[e] a few facts.

The discriminating laws, all will concede, are degrading to those against which they operate, and the degrader will be degraded also. "For all acts are reactionary, and will return in curses upon those who curse," said Stephen A. Douglass [sic], the great competitor of President Lincoln. Neither does it require a philosopher to inform you that degradation begets degradation. Any people oppressed, proscribed, belied, slandered, burned, flayed and lynched will not only become cowardly and servile, but will transmit that same servility to their posterity, and continue to do so *ad infinitum,* and as such will never make a bold and courageous people. The condition of the Negro in the United States is so repugnant to the instincts of respected manhood that thousands, yea hundreds of thousands, of miscegenated will pass for white, and snub the people with whom they are identified at every opportunity, thus destroying themselves, or at least *unracing* themselves. They do not want to be black because of its ignoble condition, and they cannot be white, thus they become monstrosities. Thousands of young men who are even educated by white teachers never have any respect for people of their own color and spend their days as devotees of white gods. Hundreds, if not thousands, of the terms employed by the white race in the English language are also degrading to the black man. Everything that is satanic, corrupt, base and infamous is denominated *black,* and all that constitutes virtue, purity, innocence, religion, and that which is divine and heavenly, is represented as *white.* Our Sabbath-school children, by the time they reach proper consciousness, are taught to sing to the laudation of white and to the contempt of black. Can any one with an ounce of common sense expect that these children, when they reach

---

segregation by private businesses (inns, hotels, theaters, and a railroad). Writing for the majority, Justice Joseph P. Bradley ruled that the thirteenth, fourteenth, and fifteenth amendments did not give the federal government the power to outlaw discriminatory practices by private organizations, but only by states. See 109 U.S. 3, 3 S.Ct., 18, 27, L.Ed. 835 (1883).

CHAPTER 2

THE ROAD TO
TRUE FREEDOM:
AFRICAN
AMERICAN
ALTERNATIVES
IN THE NEW
SOUTH

maturity, will ever have any respect for their black or colored faces, or the faces of their associates? But, without multiplying words, the terms used in our religious experience, and the hymns we sing in many instances, are degrading, and will be as long as the black man is surrounded by the idea that *white* represents God and black represents the devil. The Negro should, therefore, build up a nation of his own, and create a language in keeping with his color, as the whites have done. Nor will he ever respect himself until he does it.

3. In this country the colored man, with a few honorable exceptions, folds his arms and waits for the white man to propose, project, erect, invent, discover, combine, plan and execute everything connected with civilization, including machinery, finance, and indeed everything. This, in the nature of things, dwarfs the colored man and allows his great faculties to slumber from the cradle to the grave. Yet he possesses mechanical and inventive genius, I believe, equal to any race on earth. Much has been said about the natural inability of the colored race to engage in the professions of skilled labor. Yet before the war, right here in this Southland he erected and completed all of the fine edifices in which the lords of the land luxuriated. It is idle talk to speak of a colored man not being a success in skilled labor or the fine arts. What the black man needs is a country and surroundings in harmony with his color and with respect for his manhood. Upon this point I would delight to dwell longer if I had time. Thousands of white people in this country are ever and anon advising the colored people to keep out of politics, but they do not advise themselves. If the Negro is a man in keeping with other men, why should he be less concerned about politics than any one else? Strange, too, that a number of would-be colored leaders are ignorant and debased enough to proclaim the same foolish jargon. For the Negro to stay out of politics is to level himself with a horse or a cow, which is no politician, and the Negro who does it proclaims his inability to take part in political affairs. If the Negro is to be a man, full and complete, he must take part in everything that belongs to manhood. If he omits a single duty, responsibility or privilege, to that extent he is limited and incomplete.

Time, however, forbids my continuing the discussion of this subject, roughly and hastily as these thoughts have been thrown together. Not being able to present a dozen or two more phases, which I would cheerfully and gladly do if opportunity permitted, I conclude by saying the argument that it would be impossible to transport the colored people of the United States back to Africa is an advertisement of folly. Two hundred millions of dollars would rid this country of the last member of the Negroid race, if such a thing was desirable, and two hundred and fifty millions would give every man, woman and child excellent fare, and the general government could furnish that amount and never miss it, and that would only be the pitiful sum of a million dollars a year for the time we labored for nothing, and for which somebody or some power is responsible. The emigrant agents at New York, Boston, Philadelphia, St. John, N.B., and Halifax, N.S., with whom I have talked, establish beyond contradiction, that over a million, and from that to twelve hundred thousand persons, come to this country every year, and yet there is no public stir about it. But in the case of African emigration, two or three millions only of self-reliant men and women would be necessary to establish the conditions we are advocating in Africa. . . .

Source 4 from Nathan Huggins, comp., *W. E. B. Du Bois Writings* (New York: Library of America, 1986), pp. 842, 846–848, 860–861.

4. Du Bois's "The Talented Tenth" (1903).

The Negro race, like all races, is going to be saved by its exceptional men. The problem of education, then, among Negroes must first of all deal with the Talented Tenth; it is the problem of developing the Best of this race that they may guide the Mass away from the contamination and death of the Worst, in their own and other races. Now the training of men is a difficult and intricate task. Its technique is a matter for educational experts, but its objects is for the vision of seers. If we make money the object of man-training, we shall develop money-makers but not necessarily men; if we make technical skill the object of education, we may possess artisans but not, in nature, men. Men we shall have only as we make manhood the object of the work of the schools—intelligence, broad sympathy, knowledge of the world that was and is, and of the relation to men to it—this is the curriculum of that Higher Education which must underlie true life. On this foundation we may build bread-winning skill of hand and quickness of brain, with never a fear lest the child and man mistake the means of living for the object of life.

If this be true—and who can deny it—three tasks lie before me; first to show from the past that the Talented Tenth as they have risen among American Negroes have been worthy of leadership; secondly, to show how these men may be educated and developed; and thirdly, to show their relation to the Negro problem.

You misjudge us because you do not know us. From the very first it has been the educated and intelligent of the Negro people that have led and elevated the mass, and the sole obstacles that nullified and retarded their

CHAPTER 2

THE ROAD TO
TRUE FREEDOM:
AFRICAN
AMERICAN
ALTERNATIVES
IN THE NEW
SOUTH

efforts were slavery and race prejudice; for what is slavery but the legalized survival of the unfit and the nullification of the work of natural internal leadership? . . .

It is the fashion of today to sneer at them and to say that with freedom Negro leadership should have begun at the plow and not in the Senate—a foolish and mischievous lie; two hundred and fifty years that black serf toiled at the plow and yet that toiling was in vain till the Senate passed the war amendments; and two hundred and fifty years more the half-free serf of today may toil at his plow, but unless he have political rights and righteously guarded civic status, he will still remain the poverty-stricken and ignorant plaything of rascals, that he now is. This all sane men know even if they dare not say it.

And so we come to the present—a day of cowardice and vacillation, of strident wide-voiced wrong and faint-hearted compromise; of double-faced dallying with the Truth and Right. Who are today guiding the work of the Negro people? The "exceptions" of course. And yet so sure as this Talented Tenth is pointed out, the blind worshippers of the Average cry out in alarm: "These are exceptions, look here at death, disease and crime—these are the happy rule." Of course they are the rule, because a silly nation made them the rule: Because for three long centuries this people lynched Negroes who dared to be brave, raped black women who dared to be virtuous, crushed dark-hued youth who dared to be ambitious, and encouraged and made to flourish servility and lewdness and apathy. But not even this was able to crush all manhood and chastity and aspiration from black folk. A saving remnant continually survives and persists, continually aspires, continually shows itself in thrift and ability and character. Exceptional it is to be sure, but this is its chiefest promise; it shows the capability of Negro blood, the promise of black men. Do Americans ever stop to reflect that there are in this land a million men of Negro blood, well-educated, owners of homes, against the honor of whose womanhood no breath was ever raised, whose men occupy positions of trust and usefulness, and who, judged by any standard, have reached the full measure of the best type of modern European culture? Is it fair, is it decent, is it Christian to ignore these facts of the Negro problem, to belittle such aspiration, to nullify such leadership and seek to crush these people back into the mass out of which by toil and travail, they and their fathers have raised themselves?

Can the masses of the Negro people be in any possible way more quickly raised than by the effort and example of this aristocracy of talent and character? Was there ever a nation on God's fair earth civilized from the bottom upward? Never; it is, ever was and ever will be from the top downward that culture filters. The Talented Tenth rises and pulls all that are worth the saving up to their vantage ground. This is the history of human progress; and the two historic mistakes which have hindered that progress were the thinking first that no more could ever rise save the few already risen; or second, that it would better the unrisen to pull the risen down.

How then shall the leaders of a struggling people be trained and the hands of the risen few strengthened? There can be but one answer: The best and most capable of their youth must be schooled in the colleges and universities of the land. We will not quarrel as to just what the university of the Negro should teach or how it should teach it—I willingly admit that each soul and each race-soul needs its own peculiar curriculum. But this is true: A university is a human invention for the transmission of knowledge and culture from generation to generation, through the training of quick minds and pure hearts, and for this work no other human invention will suffice, not even trade and industrial schools.

All men cannot go to college but some men must; every isolated group or nation must have its yeast, must have for the talented few centers of training where men are not so mystified and befuddled by the hard and necessary toil of earning a living, as to have no aims higher than their bellies, and no God greater than Gold. This is true training, and thus in the beginning were the favored sons of the freedmen trained.

Thus, again, in the manning of trade schools and manual training schools we are thrown back upon the higher training as its source and chief support. There was a time when any aged and wornout carpenter could teach in a trade school. But not so to-day. Indeed the demand for college-bred men by a school like Tuskegee, ought to make Mr. Booker T. Washington the firmest friend of higher training. Here he has as helpers the son of a Negro senator, trained in Greek and the humanities, and graduated at Harvard; the son of a Negro congressman and lawyer, trained in Latin and mathematics, and graduated at Oberlin; he has as his wife, a woman who read Virgil and Homer in the same class room with me; he has as college chaplain, a classical graduate of Atlanta University; as teacher of science, a graduate of Fisk; as teacher of history, a graduate of Smith,—indeed some thirty of his chief teachers are college graduates, and instead of studying French grammars in the midst of weeds, or buying pianos for dirty cabins, they are at Mr. Washington's right hand helping him in a noble work. And yet one of the effects of Mr. Washington's propaganda has been to throw doubt upon the expediency of such training for Negroes, as these persons have had.

Men of America, the problem is plain before you. Here is a race transplanted through the criminal foolishness of your fathers. Whether you like it or not the millions are here, and here they will remain. If you do not lift

CHAPTER 2

THE ROAD TO
TRUE FREEDOM:
AFRICAN
AMERICAN
ALTERNATIVES
IN THE NEW
SOUTH

them up, they will pull you down. Education and work are the levers to uplift a people. Work alone will not do it unless inspired by the right ideals and guided by intelligence. Education must not simply teach work—it must teach Life. The Talented Tenth of the Negro race must be made leaders of thought and missionaries of culture among their people. No others can do this work and Negro colleges must train men for it. The Negro race, like all other races, is going to be saved by its exceptional men. . . .

Source 5 from Herbert Atheker, ed., *Pamphlets and Leaflets by W. E. B. Du Bois* (White Plains, N.Y.: Kraus-Thomson Organization Ltd., 1986), pp. 63–65.

5. Du Bois's Niagara Address (1906).

The men of the Niagara Movement coming from the toil of the year's hard work and pausing a moment from the earning of their daily bread turn toward the nation and again ask in the name of ten million the privilege of a hearing. In the past year the work of the Negro hater has flourished in the land. Step by step the defenders of the rights of American citizens have retreated. The work of stealing the black man's ballot has progressed and the fifty and more representatives of stolen votes still sit in the nation's capital. Discrimination in travel and public accommodation has so spread that some of our weaker brethren are actually afraid to thunder against color discrimination as such and are simply whispering for ordinary decencies.

Against this the Niagara Movement eternally protests. We will not be satisfied to take one jot or tittle less than our full manhood rights. We nastiness the new American creed says: Fear to let black men even try to claim for ourselves every single right that belongs to a freeborn American, political, civil and social; and until we get these rights we will never cease to protest and assail the ears of America. The battle we wage is not for ourselves alone but for all true Americans. It is a fight for ideals, lest this, our common fatherland, false to its founding, become in truth the land of the thief and the home of the Slave—a by-word and a hissing among the nations for its sounding pretensions and pitiful accomplishments.

Never before in the modern age has a great and civilized folk threatened to adopt so cowardly a creed in the treatment of its fellow-citizens born and bred on its soil. Stripped of verbiage and subterfuge and in its naked rise lest they become the equals of the white. And this is the land that professes to follow Jesus Christ. The blasphemy of such a course is only matched by its cowardice.

In detail our demands are clear and unequivocal. First, we would vote; with the right to vote goes everything: Freedom, manhood, the honor of your wives, the chastity of your daughters, the right to work, and the chance to rise, and let no man listen to those who deny this.

We want full manhood suffrage, and we want it now, henceforth and forever.

Second. We want discrimination in public accommodation to cease. Separation in railway and street cars, based simply on race and color, is un-American, undemocratic, and silly. We protest against all such discrimination.

Third. We claim the right of freemen to walk, talk, and be with them that wish to be with us. No man has a right to choose another man's friends, and to attempt to do so is an impudent interference with the most fundamental human privilege.

Fourth. We want the laws enforced against rich as well as poor; against Capitalist as well as Laborer; against white as well as black. We are not more lawless than the white race, we are more often arrested, convicted and mobbed. We want justice even for criminals and outlaws. We want the Constitution of the country enforced. We want Congress to take charge of Congressional elections. We want the Fourteenth Amendment carried out to the letter and every State disfranchised in Congress which attempts to disfranchise its rightful voters. We want the Fifteenth amendment enforced and no State allowed to base its franchise simply on color.

The failure of the Republican Party in Congress at the session just closed to redeem its pledge of 1904 with reference to suffrage conditions [in] the South seems a plain, deliberate, and premeditated breach of promise, and stamps that party as guilty of obtaining votes under false pretense.

Fifth. We want our children educated. The school system in the country districts of the South is a disgrace and in few towns and cities are the Negro schools what they ought to be. We want the national government to step in and wipe out illiteracy in the South. Either the Untied States will destroy ignorance or ignorance will destroy the United States.

And when we call for education we mean real education. We believe in work. We ourselves are workers, but work is not necessarily education. Education is the development of power and ideal. We want our children trained as intelligent human beings should be, and we will fight for all time against any proposal to educate black boys and girls simply as servants and underlings, or simply for the use of other people. They have a right to know, to think, to aspire.

CHAPTER 2

THE ROAD TO
TRUE FREEDOM:
AFRICAN
AMERICAN
ALTERNATIVES
IN THE NEW
SOUTH

These are some of the chief things which we want. How shall we get them? By voting where we may vote, by persistent, unceasing agitation, by hammering at the truth, by sacrifice and work.

We do not believe in violence, neither in the despised violence of the raid nor the lauded violence of the soldier, nor the barbarous violence of the mob, but we do believe in John Brown, in that incarnate spirit of justice, that hatred of a lie, that willingness to sacrifice money, reputation, and life itself on the altar of right. And here on the scene of John Brown's martyrdom we reconsecrate ourselves, our honor, our property to the final emancipation of the race which John Brown died to make free.

Our enemies, triumphant for the present, are fighting the stars in their courses. Justice and humanity must prevail. We live to tell these dark brothers of ours—scattered in counsel, wavering and weak—that no bribe of money or notoriety, no promise of wealth or fame, is worth the surrender of a people's manhood or the loss of a man's self-respect. We refuse to surrender the leadership of this race to cowards and trucklers. We are men; we will be treated as men. On this rock we have planted our banners. We will never give up, though the trump of doom find us still fighting.

And we shall win. The past promised it, the present foretells it. Thank God for John Brown! Thank God for Garrison and Douglass! Sumner and Phillips, Nat Turner and Robert Gould Shaw,[11] and all the hallowed dead who died for freedom! Thank God for all those today, few though their voices be, who have not forgotten the divine brotherhood of all men, white and black, rich and poor, fortunate and unfortunate.

We appeal to the young men and women of this nation, to those whose nostrils are not yet befouled by greed and snobbery and racial narrowness: Stand up for the right, prove yourselves worthy of your heritage and whether born north or south dare to treat men as men. Cannot the nation that has absorbed ten million foreigners into its political life without catastrophe absorb ten million Negro Americans into that same political life at less cost than their unjust and illegal exclusion will involve?

Courage, brothers! The battle for humanity is not lost or losing. All across the skies sit signs of promise. The Slav is rising in his might, the yellow millions are tasting liberty, the black Africans are writhing toward the light, and everywhere the laborer, with ballot in his hand, is voting open the gates of Opportunity and Peace. The morning breaks over blood-stained hills. We must not falter, we may not shrink. Above are the everlasting stars.

11. Robert Gould Shaw was a Massachusetts white man who during the Civil War commanded African American troops. While leading those soldiers into battle, Shaw was killed on July 18, 1863. He was portrayed in the film *Glory*.

Source 6 from Bureau of the Census, *Historical Statistics of the United States,
Colonial Times to 1970* (Washington, D.C.: Government Printing Office, 1975),
Vol. I, p. 95.

6. Estimated Net Intercensal Migration* of Negro Population by Region, 1870–1920 (in Thousands).

	1910–1920	1900–1910	1890–1900	1880–1890	1870–1880
New England[1]	12.0	8.0	14.2	6.6	4.5
Middle Atlantic[2]	170.1	87.2	90.7	39.1	19.2
East North Central[3]	200.4	45.6	39.4	16.4	20.8
West North Central[4]	43.7	10.2	23.5	7.9	15.7
South Atlantic[5]	−158.0	−111.9	−181.6	−72.5	−47.9
East South Central[6]	−246.3	−109.6	−43.3	−60.1	−56.2
West South Central[7]	−46.2	51.0	56.9	62.9	45.1

*A net intercensal migration represents the amount of migration that took place
between United States censuses, which are taken every ten years. The net figure
is computed by comparing in-migration with out-migration to a particular state.
A minus figure means that out-migration from a state was greater than in-
migration.

1. The following states are included in New England: Maine, New Hampshire,
Vermont, Massachusetts, Rhode Island, and Connecticut.

2. The following states are included in Middle Atlantic: New York, New Jersey,
and Pennsylvania.

3. The following states are included in East North Central: Ohio, Indiana,
Illinois, Michigan, and Wisconsin.

4. The following states are included in West North Central: Minnesota, Iowa,
Missouri, North Dakota, South Dakota, Nebraska, and Kansas.

5. The following states are included in South Atlantic: Delaware, Maryland,
District of Columbia, Virginia, West Virginia, North Carolina, South Carolina,
Georgia, and Florida.

6. The following states are included in East South Central: Kentucky, Tennessee,
Alabama, and Mississippi.

7. The following states are included in West South Central: Arkansas, Louisiana,
Oklahoma, and Texas.

☙ QUESTIONS TO CONSIDER ☙

The Background section of this chapter strongly suggests that the prospects for African Americans in the post–Reconstruction South were bleak. Although blacks certainly preferred sharecropping or tenancy to

CHAPTER 2

THE ROAD TO
TRUE FREEDOM:
AFRICAN
AMERICAN
ALTERNATIVES
IN THE NEW
SOUTH

working in gangs as in the days of slavery, neither sharecropping nor tenancy offered African Americans much chance to own their own land. Furthermore, the industrial opportunities available to European immigrants, which allowed many of them gradually to climb the economic ladder, for the most part were closed to southern blacks, in part because the South was never able to match the North in the creation of industrial jobs and in part because what jobs the New South industrialization did create often were closed to blacks. As we have seen, educational opportunities for African Americans in the South were severely limited—so much so that by 1890, more than 75 percent of the adult black population in the Deep South still was illiterate (as opposed to 17.1 percent of the adult white population). In addition, rigid segregation laws and racial violence had increased dramatically. Indeed, the prospects for southern blacks were far from promising.

Begin by analyzing Ida B. Wells's response (Source 1) to the deteriorating condition of African Americans in the South. In her view, how did blacks in Memphis and Kentucky provide a model for others? What was that model? In addition to that model, Wells tells us how blacks in Jacksonville, Florida, and Paducah, Kentucky, were able to prevent lynchings in those towns. What alternative did those blacks present? Was Wells advocating it? Finally, what role did Wells see the African American press playing in preventing lynchings?

The alternative offered by Booker T. Washington (Source 2) differs markedly from those offered by Wells. In

his view, what *process* should African Americans follow to enjoy their full rights? How did he support his argument? What did Washington conceive the role of southern whites in African Americans' progress to be? Before you dismiss Washington's alternative, remember that his *goals* were roughly similar to those of Wells. Also use some inference to imagine how Washington's audiences would have reacted to his speech. How would southern whites have greeted his speech? Southern blacks? What about northern whites? Northern blacks? To whom was Washington speaking?

Now move on to Henry McNeal Turner's alternative (Source 3). At first Bishop Turner seems to be insulting blacks. What was he really trying to say? Why did he think that God ordained blacks to be brought to America in chains? In Turner's view, once blacks were freed, what was their best alternative? Why? Turner's view of whites is at serious odds with that of Washington. How do the two views differ on this point? How did Turner use his view of whites to support his alternative for blacks?

Taken together, the two speeches by Du Bois (Sources 4 and 5) present a consistent view, even though their subject matter and emphasis are different. What was the "talented tenth"? In Du Bois's view, what crucial role must that group play? How is that view at odds with Washington's view? In his Niagara Address of 1906, Du Bois states what the goals of the "talented tenth" should be. What are those objectives? How does his *process* differ from that of Washington? Furthermore, how does Du Bois's view differ from Washington's with respect to timing? Tactics? Tone? Remember, however, that the long-term goals of both men were similar.

Perhaps you have been struck by the fact that both Turner and Du Bois pinned their hopes for progress on African American *men*. Turner refers frequently to "manhood" and Du Bois to "exceptional men." Why do you think this was so? Why do you think the concept of African American manhood was important to these two thinkers?

Finally, examine Source 6. What additional alternative was open to African Americans? How did that alternative change over time? Can you use the other material in this chapter to suggest why such a change was taking place? What does this tell you about southern African Americans' reactions to the alternatives articulated by Wells, Washington, Turner, and Du Bois?

It is now time to assess the various options open to southern African Americans in the late nineteenth and twentieth centuries. To determine which option was best, you will have to answer the following questions:

1. How do I define "best"? More realistic? More morally defensible? Best in the long range? Best in the short range?
2. What would have happened if southern African Americans had adopted Wells's alternatives? Where might the process outlined by Wells have led? Were there any risks for African Americans? If so, what were they?
3. What would have happened if southern African Americans had adopted Washington's alternative? How long would it have taken them to realize Washington's goals? Were there any risks involved? If so, what were they?
4. What would have happened if southern African Americans had adopted Turner's alternative? Were there any risks involved? How realistic was Turner's option?
5. What would have happened if southern African Americans had adopted Du Bois's alternative? How long would Du Bois's process have taken? Were there any risks involved?
6. Was white assistance necessary according to Wells? To Washington? To Turner? To Du Bois? How did each spokesperson perceive the roles of the federal government and the federal courts? How did the government and courts stand on this issue at the time? [*Clue:* What was the Supreme Court decision in *Plessy* v. *Ferguson* (1896)?]

No one living in the latter part of the twentieth century can assess with absolute objectivity which of the options available to African Americans in the South almost a century before was the best one. Nor is it possible to put ourselves completely in the shoes of these men and women. Yet a thorough examination of the positive points and liabilities of each option can give us a closer approximation of which alternatives was the most attractive. As you do this, do not neglect the statistical evidence or the material provided in the Background section of this chapter or in other material you read.

CHAPTER 2

THE ROAD TO
TRUE FREEDOM:
AFRICAN
AMERICAN
ALTERNATIVES
IN THE NEW
SOUTH

∽ EPILOGUE ∽

For the advocates of a New South, the realization of their dream seemed to be just over the horizon, always just beyond their grasp. Many of the factories did make a good deal of money. But profits often flowed out of the South to northern investors. And factory owners often maintained profits by paying workers pitifully low wages, which led to the rise of a poor white urban class that lived in slums and faced enormous problems of malnutrition, poor health, family instability, and crime. To most of those who had left their meager farms to find opportunities in the burgeoning southern cities, life there appeared even worse than it had been in the rural areas. Many whites returned to their rural homesteads disappointed and dispirited by urban life.

For an increasing number of southern African Americans, the solution seemed to be to abandon the South entirely. Beginning around the time of World War I (1917–1918), a growing number of African Americans migrated to the industrial cities of the Northeast, Midwest, and West Coast. But there, too, they met racial hostility and racially inspired riots.

At least in the North, African Americans could vote and thereby influence public policy. By the late 1940s, it had become clear that northern urban African American voters, by their very number, could force American politicians to deal with racial discrimination. By the 1950s, it was evident that the South would have to change its racial policies, if not willingly then by force. It took federal courts, federal

marshals, and occasionally federal troops, but the crust of discrimination in the South began to be broken in the 1960s. Attitudes changed slowly, but the white southern politician draped in the Confederate flag and calling for resistance to change became a figure of the past. Although much work still needed to be done, changes in the South had been profound, laying the groundwork for more changes ahead. Indeed, by the 1960s the industrialization and prosperity (largely through in-migration) of the Sunbelt seemed to show that Grady's dream of a New South might become a reality.

And yet, for all the hopeful indications (black voting and office holding in the South, for instance), in many ways the picture was a somber one. By the 1970s, several concerned observers, both black and white, feared that the poorest 30 percent of all black families, instead of climbing slowly up the economic ladder, were in the process of forming a permanent underclass, complete with a social pathology that included broken families, crime, drugs, violence, and grinding poverty. Equally disturbing in the 1980s was a new wave of racial intolerance among whites, a phenomenon that even invaded many American colleges and universities. In short, although much progress had been made since the turn of the century, in many ways, as in the New South, the dream of equality and tolerance remained just over the horizon.

By this time, of course, Wells, Washington, Turner, and Du Bois were dead. Wells continued to write militant articles for the African American press, became deeply involved in the woman suffrage movement, and carried on a successful crusade to prevent the racial segregation of the Chicago city schools. She died in Chicago in 1931. For his part, Washington clung stubbornly to his notion of self-help, even though he realized privately that whites could use him as an apologist for the status quo and a supporter of racial segregation. He died in Tuskegee, Alabama, in 1915.

Turner's dream of thousands of blacks moving to Africa never materialized. In response, he grew more strident and was especially critical of African Americans who opposed his ideas. In 1898, Turner raised a storm of protest when his essay "God Is a Negro" was published. The essay began, "We have as much right . . . to believe that God is a Negro, as you buckra, or white, people have to believe that God is a fine looking, symmetrical and ornamented white man." He died while on a speaking trip to Canada in 1915. As for Du Bois, he also grew more embittered over the years, turning toward Marxism and Pan-Africanism when he believed "the system" had failed him and his people. He died in Africa in 1963.

In their time, Wells, Washington, Turner, and Du Bois were important and respected figures. Although often publicly at odds, privately they shared the same dream of African Americans living with pride and dignity in a world that recognized them as complete men and women. In an era in which few people championed the causes of African American people, these four spokespersons stood as courageous figures.

CHAPTER 3

HOW THEY LIVED: MIDDLE-CLASS LIFE, 1870–1917

∞ THE PROBLEM ∞

In the 1870s, Heinrich Schliemann, a middle-aged German archaeologist, astonished the world with his claim that he had discovered the site of ancient Troy. As all educated people of the time knew, Troy was the golden city of heroes that the blind poet Homer (seventh century B.C.) made famous in his *Iliad* and *Odyssey*. Although archaeologists continued to argue bitterly about whether it was really Troy or some other ancient city that Schliemann was excavating, the general public was fascinated with the vases, gold and silver cups, necklaces, and earrings that were unearthed.

Not only the relics and "treasure" interested Americans, however. As the magazine *Nation* pointed out in 1875, these discoveries offered an opportunity to know about Troy as it had actually existed and to understand something about the daily lives of the inhabitants. Nineteenth-century Americans were intensely curious about the art, religion, burial customs, dress, and even the foods of the ancient Greeks. "Real Trojans," noted a magazine editor in 1881, "were very fond of oysters." (He based his conclusion on the large amounts of oyster shells uncovered at the archaeological digs.)

Material culture study is the use of artifacts to understand people's lives. In this exercise, you will be looking at some artifacts of the late nineteenth and early twentieth centuries—advertisements and house plans—to try to reconstruct the lives of middle-class white Americans during a period when the country was changing rapidly. What were Americans' hopes and fears during this era? What were their values?

∽ BACKGROUND ∽

The age from approximately 1870 to 1900 was characterized by enormous and profound changes in American life. Unquestionably, the most important changes were the nation's rapid industrialization and urbanization. Aided and accelerated by the rapid growth of railroads, emerging industries could extend their tentacles throughout the nation, collecting raw materials and fuel for the factories and distributing finished products to the growing American population. By 1900, that industrial process had come to be dominated by a few energetic and shrewd men, captains of industry to their friends and robber barons to their enemies. Almost every conceivable industry, from steel and oil to sugar refining and meat packing, was controlled by one or two gigantic corporations that essentially had the power to set prices on the raw materials bought and the finished products sold. In turn, the successes of those corporations created a new class of fabulously rich industrialists, and names like Swift, Armour, Westinghouse, Pillsbury, Pullman, Rockefeller, Carnegie, and Duke literally became almost household words as much for the notoriety of the industrialists as for the industries and products they created.

As America became more industrialized, it also became more urban. In the past, the sizes of cities had been limited by the availability of nearby food, fuel, and employment opportunities. But the network of railroads and the rise of large factories had removed those limitations, and Amer-

ican cities grew phenomenally. Between 1860 and 1910, urban population increased sevenfold, and by 1920 more than half of all Americans lived in cities.[1] These urban complexes not only dominated the regions in which they were located but eventually set much of the tone for the entire nation as well.

Both processes—industrialization and urbanization—profoundly altered nearly every facet of American life. Family size began to decrease; the woman who might have had five or six children in 1860 was replaced by the "new" woman of 1900 who had only three or four children. The fruits of industrialization, distributed by new marketing techniques, could be enjoyed by a large portion of the American population. Electric lights, telephones, and eventually appliances virtually revolutionized the lives of the middle and upper classes, as did Ford's later mass production of the Model T automobile.

The nature of the work also was changed because factories required a higher degree of regimentation than did farm work or the "putting-out" system. Many industries found it more profitable to employ women and children than adult males, thus altering the home lives of many of the nation's working-class citizens. Moreover, the lure of employment brought millions

---

1. The census defined *city* as a place with a population over twenty-five hundred people. Thus, many of the cities referred to in this exercise are what we would call towns, or even small towns.

of immigrants to the United States, most of whom huddled together in cities, found low-paying jobs, and dreamed of the future. And as the cities grew grimy with factory soot and became increasingly populated by laborers, immigrants, and what one observer referred to as the "dangerous classes," upper- and middle-class Americans began to abandon the urban cores and retreat to fashionable suburbs on the peripheries, to return to the cities either in their automobiles or on streetcars only for work or recreation. In fact, the conforts of middle-class life were made possible, in part, by the exploitation of industrial workers.

Industrialization and urbanization not only changed how most Americans lived but how they *thought* as well. Faith in progress and technology was almost boundless, and there was widespread acceptance of the uneven distribution of wealth among Americans. Prior to the turn of the century, many upper- and middle-class Americans believed that life was a struggle in which the fittest survived. This concept, which applied Charles Darwin's discoveries about biological evolution to society, was called Social Darwinism. The poor, especially the immigrant poor, were seen as biologically and morally inferior. It followed, then, that efforts to help the less fortunate through charity or government intervention were somehow tampering with both God's will and Darwinian evolution. In such a climate of opinion, the wealthy leaders of gigantic corporations became national heroes, superior in prestige to both preachers and presidents.

The response of the working classes varied; although many workers rejected the concepts of Social Darwinism and Victorian morality, others aspired to middle-class status. In spite of long hours, low pay, and hazardous conditions, the men and women of the working classes engaged in a series of important labor protests and strikes during this period. A rich working-class culture developed in the saloons, vaudeville theaters, dance halls, and streets of medium-size and larger cities. Many workers sought alternatives in some form of socialism; many others, however, strove to achieve the standard of living of the rapidly expanding middle class. Across the country, young boys read the rags-to-riches tales of Horatio Alger, and girls learned to be "proper ladies" so that they would not embarrass their future husbands as they rose in society together.

Social critics and reformers of the time were appalled by the excesses of the "fabulously rich" and the misery of the "wretchedly poor." And yet a persistent belief in the opportunity to better oneself (or one's children's position) led many people to embrace an optimistic attitude and to focus on the acquisition of material possessions. New consumer goods were pouring from factories, and the housing industry was booming. Middle-class families emulated the housing and furnishing styles of the wealthy, and skilled blue-collar workers and their families aspired to own modest suburban homes on the streetcar line.

After 1900, widespread concern about the relationship of wages to the cost of maintaining a comfortable standard of living led to numerous studies of working-class families in various parts of the country. Could workers realistically hope to own homes and achieve decent standards of living as a result of their labor? In 1909, economist Robert Coit Chapin estimated that a family of five needed an annual income of about $900 to live in a decent home or apartment in New York City. A follow-up study of Philadelphia in 1917 estimated that same standard of living at approximately $1,600. Yet the average annual pay of adult male wage workers during these years ranged from only $600 to $1,700. Several other factors affected family income, however. Average wages are misleading, since skilled workers earned significantly more than unskilled or semiskilled workers. Even within the same industry and occupation, midwestern workers earned more than northeastern workers, and southern workers earned the lowest wages of all. Adult women workers, 80 percent of whom lived with families as wives or unmarried daughters, added their wages (approximately $300 to $600 a year) to the family income, as did working children. Many families, especially those of recent immigrants, also took in boarders and lodgers who paid rent.

Finally, the cost of land and building materials was much more expensive in large cities than in smaller cities and towns. In his investigation of New York, Chapin found that 28 percent of working-class families in nine upstate cities owned their own homes, compared with only 1 percent in New York City. Another study in 1915 also sharply illustrated regional differences in home ownership. Twenty percent of Paterson, New Jersey, silk workers were homeowners, but only 10 percent of Birmingham, Alabama, steelworkers owned homes. Nineteen percent of Milwaukee's working-class families owned their own homes, compared to 4.4 percent of Boston's working-class families. Nor were all these homes in the central city. Working-class suburbs expanded along streetcar lines or were developed near industries on the fringes of a city, such as the suburb of Oakwood just outside Knoxville, Tennessee.[2] In this community near textile mills and a major railroad repair shop, house lots measuring 50 by 140 feet sold for less than one hundred dollars; most homes were built for under one thousand dollars. Nearly half of the one thousand families who moved to Oakwood between 1902 and 1917 came from the older industrial sections of Knoxville.

Completely reliable income and cost statistics for early twentieth-century America do not exist, but it seems reasonable to estimate that at least one-fourth of working-class families owned or were paying for homes and that many more aspired to homeownership. But fully half of all working-class families, usually concentrated in large cities, lived in or near poverty and could not hope to own their own homes. Those with middle-class white-collar occupations were more fortunate. Lawyers, doctors, businessmen, ministers, bank tellers, newspaper editors, and even schoolteachers could—

2. Knoxville's population in 1900 was 32,637; the city had experienced a 237 percent growth in population from 1880 to 1900.

through careful budgeting and saving—realistically expect to buy or build a house.

Although technological advances and new distribution methods put many modern conveniences and new products within the reach of all but the poorest Americans, the economic growth of the period was neither constant nor steady. The repercussions from two major depressions—one in 1873 and one in 1894—made "getting ahead" difficult if not impossible for many lower-middle-class and blue-collar families. Furthermore, at times everything seemed to be changing so rapidly that many people felt insecure. Yet within middle-class families, this sense of insecurity and even fear often coexisted with optimism and a faith in progress.

One way to understand the lives of middle-class Americans during the post–Civil War era is to look at the *things* with which they surrounded themselves—their clothes, the goods and services they bought, and even their houses. Why did such fashions and designs appeal to Americans of the late nineteenth and early twentieth centuries? What kind of an impression were these people trying to make on other people? How did they really feel about themselves? Sometimes historians, like archaeologists, use artifacts such as clothes, furniture, houses, and so forth to reconstruct the lives of Americans in earlier times. Indeed, each year many thousands of tourists visit historic homes such as Jefferson's Monticello, retrace the fighting at Gettysburg, or stroll through entire restored communities such as Colonial Williamsburg. But

historians of the post–Civil War period also may use advertisements (instead of the products or services themselves) and house plans (instead of the actual houses) to understand how middle-class Americans lived and what their values and concerns were.

Every day, Americans are surrounded, even bombarded, by advertising that tries to convince them to buy some product, use some service, or compare brand X with brand Y. Television, radio, billboards, magazines, and newspapers spread the message to potential consumers of a variety of necessary—and unnecessary—products. Underlying this barrage of advertisements is an appeal to a wide range of emotions—ambition, elitism, guilt, and anxiety. A whole new "science" has arisen, called market research, that analyzes consumers' reactions and predicts future buying patterns.

Yet advertising is a relatively new phenomenon, one that began to develop after the Civil War and did not assume its modern form until the 1920s. P. T. Barnum, the promoter and impresario of mid-nineteenth-century entertainment, pointed the way with publicity gimmicks for his museum and circuses and, later, for the relatively unknown Swedish singer Jenny Lind. (Barnum created such a demand for Lind's concert tickets that they sold for as much as two hundred dollars each.) But at the time of the Civil War, most merchants still announced special sales of their goods in simple newspaper notices, and brand names were virtually unknown.

Businesses, both large and small, expanded enormously after the Civil

War. Taking advantage of the country's greatly improved transportation and communication systems, daring business leaders established innovative ways to distribute products, such as the mail-order firm and the department store. Sears Roebuck & Co. was founded in 1893, and its "wish book," or catalogue, rapidly became popular reading for millions of people, especially those who lived in rural areas. Almost one thousand pages long, these catalogues offered a dazzling variety of consumer goods and were filled with testimonial letters from satisfied customers. Lewis Thomas from Jefferson County, Alabama, wrote in 1897,

> I received my saddle and I must say that I am so pleased and satisfied with my saddle, words cannot express my thanks for the benefit that I received from the pleasure and satisfaction given me. I know that I have a saddle that will by ordinary care last a lifetime, and all my neighbors are pleased as well, and I am satisfied so well that you shall have more of my orders in the near future.

And from Granite, Colorado, Mrs. Laura Garrison wrote, "Received my suit all right, was much pleased with it, will recommend your house to my friends. . . ."

For those who lived in cities, the department store was yet another way to distribute consumer goods. The massive, impressively decorated buildings erected by department store owners were often described as consumer "cathedrals" or "palaces." In fact, no less a personage than President William Howard Taft dedicated the new Wanamaker's department store in Philadelphia in 1911. "We are here," Taft told the crowd, "to celebrate the completion of one of the most important instrumentalities in modern life for the promotion of comfort among the people."

Many of the products being manufactured in factories in the late nineteenth and early twentieth centuries represented items previously made at home. Tinned meats and biscuits, "store-bought" bread, ready-made clothing, and soap all represent the impact of technology on the functions of the homemaker. Other products were new versions of things already being used. For example, the bathtub was designed solely for washing one's body, as opposed to the large bucket or tub in which one collected rainwater, washed clothes, and, every so often, bathed. Still other products and gadgets (such as the phonograph and the automobile) were completely new, the result of a fertile period of inventiveness (1860 to 1890) that saw more than ten times more patents issued than were issued during the entire period up to 1860 (only 36,000 patents were issued prior to the Civil War, but 440,000 were granted during the next thirty years).

There was no question that American industry could produce new products and distribute them nationwide. But there *was* a problem: how could American industry overcome the traditional American ethic of thrift and create a demand for products that might not have even existed a few years earlier? It was this problem that the new field of advertising set out to solve.

America in 1865 was a country of widespread, if uneven, literacy and a vast variety of newspapers and magazines, all competing for readership. Businesses quickly learned that mass production demanded a national, even an international, market, and money spent on national advertising in newspapers and magazines rose from $27 million in 1860 to more than $95 million in 1900. By 1929, the amount spent on advertising had climbed to more than $1 billion. Brand names and catchy slogans vied with one another to capture the consumer's interest. Consumers could choose from among many biscuit manufacturers, as the president of National Biscuit Company reported to his stockholders in 1901: "We do not pretend to sell our standard goods cheaper than other manufacturers of biscuits sell their goods. They always undersell us. Why do they not take away our business?" His answer was fourfold: efficiency, quality goods, innovative packaging, and advertising. "The trademarks we adopted," he concluded, "their value we created."

Advertising not only helped differentiate one brand of a product from another, but it also helped break down regional differences as well as differences between rural and urban lifestyles. Women living on farms in Kansas could order the latest "New York–style frocks" from a mail-order catalogue, and people in small towns in the Midwest or rural areas in the South could find the newest furniture styles, appliances, and automobiles enticingly displayed in mass-circulation magazines. In this era, more and more people abandoned the old ways of doing things and embraced the new ways of life that resulted from the ap-

plication of modern technology, mass production, and efficient distribution of products. Thus, some historians have argued that advertising accelerated the transition of American society from one that emphasized production to one that stressed consumption.

The collective mentality, ideas, mood, and values of the rapidly changing society were reflected in nearly everything the society created, including its architecture. During the period from approximately 1865 to 1900, American architects designed public buildings, factories, banks, apartment houses, offices, and residential structures, aided by technological advances that allowed them to do things that had been impossible in the past. For instance, as American cities grew in size and population density, the value of real estate soared. Therefore, it made sense to design higher and higher buildings, taking advantage of every square foot of available land. The perfection of central heating systems; the inventions of the radiator, the elevator, and the flush toilet; and the use of steel framing allowed architects such as William Le Baron Jenney, Louis Sullivan, and others of the Chicago school of architecture to erect the modern skyscraper, a combined triumph of architecture, engineering, ingenuity, and construction.

At the same time, the new industrial elite were hiring these same architects to build their new homes—homes that often resembled huge Italian villas, French chateaux, and even Renaissance palaces. Only the wealthy, however, could afford homes individually designed by professional architects. Most people relied on contractors, builders, and carpenters who adapted drawings from books or magazines to suit their clients' needs and tastes. Such "pattern books," published by men like Henry Holly, the Palliser brothers, Robert Shoppell, and the Radford Architectural Company, were extremely popular. It is estimated that in the mid-1870s, at least one hundred homes a year were being built from plans published in one women's magazine, *Godey's Lady's Book*, and thousands of others were built from pamphlets provided by lumber and plumbing fixture companies and architectural pattern books. Eventually, a person could order a complete home through the mail; all parts of the prefabricated house were shipped by railroad for assembly by local workers on the owner's site. George Barber of Knoxville, Tennessee, the Aladdin Company of Bay City, Michigan, and even Sears Roebuck & Co. were all prospering in mail-order homes around the turn of the century.

From the historian's viewpoint, both advertising and architecture created a wealth of evidence that can be used to reconstruct our collective past. By looking at and reading advertisements, we can trace Americans' changing habits, interests, and tastes. And by analyzing the kinds of emotional appeals used in the advertisements, we can begin to understand the aspirations and goals as well as the fears and anxieties of the people who lived in the rapidly changing society of the late nineteenth and early twentieth centuries.

Unfortunately, most people, including professional historians, are not used to looking for values and ideas in architecture. Yet every day we pass by houses and other buildings that could tell us a good deal about how people lived in a particular time period, as well as something about the values of the time. In this chapter, you will be examining closely both advertisements and house plans to reconstruct partially how middle-class Americans of the late nineteenth and early twentieth centuries lived.

ᑐ THE METHOD ᑐ

No historian would suggest that the advertisements of preceding decades (or today's advertisements, for that matter) speak for themselves—that they tell you how people actually lived. Like almost all historical evidence, advertisements must be carefully analyzed for their messages. Advertisements are intended to make people want to buy various products and services. They can be positive or negative. Positive advertisements show the benefits—direct or indirect, explicit or implicit—that would come from owning a product. Such advertisements depict an ideal. Negative or "scare" advertisements demonstrate the disastrous consequences of not owning the product. Some of the most effective advertisements combine both negative and positive approaches ("I was a lonely 360-pound woman before I discovered Dr. Quack's Appetite Suppressors—now I weigh 120 pounds and am engaged to be married!"). Advertisements also attempt to evoke an emotional response from potential consumers that will encourage the purchase of a particular product or service.

Very early advertisements tended to be primarily descriptive, simply picturing the product. Later advertisements often told a story with pictures and words. In looking at the advertisements in this chapter, first determine whether the approach used is positive, negative, or a combination of both factors. What were the expected consequences of using (or not using) the product? How did the advertisement try to sell the product or service? What emotional response(s) were expected?

The preceding evaluation is not too difficult, but in this exercise you must go even further with your analysis. You are trying to determine what each advertisement can tell you about earlier generations of Americans and the times in which they lived. Look at (and read) each advertisement carefully. Does it reveal anything about the values of the time period in which the advertisements appeared? About the roles of men and women? About attitudes concerning necessities and luxuries? About people's aspirations or fears?

House plans also must be analyzed if they are to tell us something about how people used to live. At one time or another, you have probably looked at a certain building and thought,

"That is truly an ugly, awful-looking building! Whatever possessed the lunatic who built it?" Yet when that building was designed and built, most likely it was seen as a truly beautiful structure and may have been widely praised by its occupants as well as by those who merely passed by. Why is this so? Why did an earlier generation believe the building was beautiful?

All of us are aware that standards for what is good art, good music, good literature, and good architecture change over time. What may be pleasing to the people of one era might be considered repugnant or even obscene by those of another time. But is this solely the result of changing fads, such as the sudden rises and declines in the popularity of movie and television stars, rock 'n' roll groups, or fashionable places to vacation?

The answer is partly yes, but only partly. Tastes do change, and fads such as the Hula-Hoop and the yo-yo come and inevitably go. However, we must still ask why a particular person or thing becomes popular or in vogue at a certain time. Do these changing tastes in art, music, literature, and architecture *mean* something? Can they tell us something about the people who embraced these various styles? More to the point, can they tell us something about the *values* of those who embraced them? Obviously, they can.

In examining these middle-class homes, you should first look for common exterior and interior features. Then look at the interior rooms and their functions, comparing them with rooms in American homes today. You also must try to imagine what impression these houses conveyed to people in the late nineteenth and early twentieth centuries. Finally, you will be thinking about all the evidence—the advertisements and the house plans—as a whole. What is the relationship between the material culture (in this case, the advertisements and the house plans) and the values and concerns of Americans in the late nineteenth and early twentieth centuries?

◯◯ THE EVIDENCE ◯◯

Sources 1 through 3 from Sears Roebuck & Co. catalogues, 1897 and 1902.

1. Children's Reefer Jackets (1897) and Children's Toys (1902).

REEFER JACKETS FOR CHILDREN FROM 1 TO 5 YEARS OLD.

Reefer Jackets for little toddlers, from one to four years, nobby, stylish little coats at little bits of prices. As usual S. R. & Co. will save you money on these goods.

Do not forget to mention age and color desired when ordering.

DRESSED SAILOR DOLLS.

Sailor Girl Dolls.

No. 29R735 Sailor Girl Doll, bisque head, flowing hair, solid eyes, dressed to represent a girl in sailor costume. A very pretty doll. Length, 13 inches.
Price, each................50c

Sailor Boy Dolls.

No. 29R739 Sailor Boy Doll, dressed to represent a boy in sailor costume, companion doll to sailor girl. Length, 13 inches.
Price, each.....................50c

The Penny Saver.

No. 29R147 A perfect register-ing bank; no key, no combination. Each time a cent is dropped into the bank the bell rings and the register indicates. Opens automatically at each 50 cents. The total always in sight. They are attractive and in-teresting to children. The mechanism is made of steel, and will not break or get out of order. It is highly interesting to children, and for this reason will encourage them to save. Shipping weight, 5 pounds. Price, each........85c

2. Boys' Wash Suits and Girls' Wash Dresses (1902).

BOYS' WASH SUITS.

The extraordinary value we offer in Boys' Wash Suits can only be fully appreciated by those who order from this department. A trial order will surely convince you that we are able to furnish new, fresh, up to date, stylish and well made wash suits at much lower prices than similar value can be had from any other house.

NOTE.—Boys' wash suits can be had only in the sizes as mentioned after each description. Always state age of boy and if large or small of age.

Boy's Wash Crash Suit, 35 Cents.

Navy Blue and White Percale Wash Suit, 40 Cents.

38R2128
98c

38R2130
$1.39

38R2131
$1.48

GIRLS' WASH DRESSES.

ACES FROM 4 TO 14 YEARS.

WHEN ORDERING please state Age, Height, Weight and Number of Inches around Bust.

SCALE OF SIZES, SHOWING PROPORTION OF BUST AND LENGTH TO THE AGE OF CHILD

Age	4	6	8	10	12	14
Bust	24	27	28	29	80	81
Skirt length	18	20	22	24	26	28

No. 38R2126 GIRLS' DRESS. Some made of Madras and some made of ginghams in fancy stripes and plaids, round yokes, "V" shape yokes, some trimmed with braid, ruffles and embroidery. We show no illustration of this number on account of the differ-

3. Hip Pad and Bustle, 1902.

Parisienne Hip Pad and Bustle.

No. 18R4880 The Parisienne Hip Pad and Bustle, made of best tempered, black enameled, woven wire with hip pads of padded cloth. Perfect in shape, and light in weight. Very durable.
Price, each...**40c**

If by mail, postage extra, each, **10 cents.**

Source 4 from 1893 and 1897 advertisements.

4. Corset (1893) and Cosmetics (1897).

TOILET ARTICLE
COMBINATION.

10 Useful Articles at the Usual Price of Three·

EVERY LADY IN THE LAND Knows what a Luxury it is to have these Little Toilet Articles Around Handy.

$3.00 Worth of Useful Articles for the Toilet for 95c.

No. 26338 THIS COMBINATION CONSISTS OF:

95 c. for the entire outfit

1 bottle (8 oz.) Witch Hazel.
1 cake buttermilk soap.
1 bottle Petroleum Jelly (for burns, scalds, etc.)
1 box Swan Down Face Powder.
1 box Tooth Powder·
1 box Cold Cream (for freckles, sunburn, etc.)
1 box Toilet Powder.
1 Fancy Jug Shampoo (makes thirty shampoos.)
1 bottle Triple Extract Perfume (any odor,)
1 Face Chamois Skin.

The Entire Outfit for .... **95c.**

5. Beauty Advice Book.

A SCRAP-BOOK
FOR
"HOMELY WOMEN" ONLY.

We dedicate this collection of toilet secrets, not to the pretty women (they have advantages enough, without being told how to double their beauty), but to the plainer sisterhood, to those who look in the glass and are not satisfied with what they see. To such we bring abundant help.

CONTENTS. Part 1--Part 2.

Practical devices for ugly ears, mouths, fingertips, crooked teeth. To reduce flesh, etc. How to bleach and refine a poor skin. Freckles, Pimples, Moles, etc. Mask of Diana of Poictiers. Out of 100 Cosmetics, which to choose. How to make and apply them for daylight, evening, and the stage (one saves two thirds, and has a better article by making instead of buying Cosmetics). What goes to constitute a belle. Madame Vestris's methods for private Theatricals. How to sit for a photograph successfully, and other toilet hints.

Send $1.00, 2 two-cent stamps, and an envelope addressed to yourself.
BROWN, SHERBROOK, & CO.,
27 Hollis Street, Boston, Mass.

Source 6 from a 1912 advertisement.

6. Massage Cream for the Skin.

"Mother, here she is"

OF all moments the most try-ing—when the son brings *her* to his mother, of all critics the most exacting. Mother-love causes her to look with penetrating glance, almost *trying* to find flaws. No quality of beauty so serves to win an older woman as a skin smooth, fresh and healthy *in a natural way*, as easily provided by

POMPEIAN MASSAGE CREAM

Where artificial beautifiers—cosmetics and rouges—would only antagonize; and an uncared-for, pallid, wrinkled skin prove a negative influence—the Pompeian complexion immediately wins the mother, as it does in every other instance in social or business life.

You can have a beautiful complexion—

that greatest aid to woman's power and influence. A short use of Pompeian will surprise you and your friends. It will improve even the best complexion, and retain beauty and youthful appearance against Time's ravages.

"Don't *envy* a good complexion; use Pompeian and *have* one."

Pompeian is not a "cold" or "grease" cream, nor a rouge or cosmetic, and positively can not grow hair on the face. Pompeian simply affords a natural means toward a complete cleanliness of the facial pores. And in pores that are "Pompeian clean" lies skin health.

TRIAL JAR

sent for 6c (stamps or coin). Find out for yourself, now, why Pompeian is used and prized in a million homes where the value of a clear, fresh, youthful skin is appreciated. Clip coupon now.

All dealers 50c, 75c, $1

Cut along this line, fill in and mail today

The Pompeian Mfg. Co. 36 Prospect St., Cleveland, Ohio

Gentlemen :— Enclosed find 6c (stamps or coin) for a trial jar of Pompeian Massage Cream.

Name...

Address ....

City...State..................

7. **Croup Remedy (1895), Garment Pins (1888), and Boys' Magazine (1912).**

A LADY WRITES:—"I have to thank you for the service of your valuable SALVA-CEA, for I can testify with truth it saved the life of my dear baby.   It had bronchitis and whooping-cough severely after measles. . . . I sent for some, and rubbed it thoroughly on baby's chest, back, and soles of its feet, and in ten minutes the dear little lamb could take nourishment, and is now doing well."
[1895]

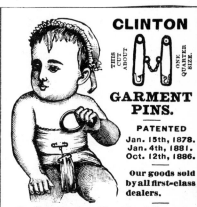

CLINTON

THIS CUT ABOUT   ONE QUARTER SIZE.

GARMENT PINS.

PATENTED
Jan. 15th, 1878.
Jan. 4th, 1881.
Oct. 12th, 1886.

Our goods sold by all first-class dealers.

Six Pairs Garment Pins 20 cents by mail.
Used as a Skirt Supporter and Dress Looper they have no equal.
CLINTON NICKEL SAFETY PINS
are the strongest and best made. Ask for them. If your dealer does not keep them send 25 cents and we will mail you 3 dozen, assorted sizes.
Solid Silver Safety Pins, 1 pair in satin-lined box by mail $1.25. **Clinton Safety Pin Co., Providence, R.I.**
[1888]

Keep your boy out of danger!

Safeguard him at every turn—particularly *his* reading. *Know* what he reads. Keep his mind clean and free from yellow-backs — from the dangerous, suggestive literature.

THE

AMERICAN BOY

Read by 500,000 boys

is red-blooded and thoroughly up to date. Fine, healthy, stirring stories and many clever, instructive departments hold the boy's continued interest. It keeps his mind free from treacherous reading.

Don't let $1.00 for a year's subscription stand between your boy and his future. Realize what pure, manly reading *means to him!* You cannot refuse to act tonight—*NOW!*

On all News-stands, 10c
The Sprague Publishing Company
160 American Bldg., Detroit, Mich.

[1912]

Sources 8 and 9 from Sears Roebuck & Co. catalogues, 1897 and 1902.

8. Ladies' and Men's Hats (1897).

LATEST DESIGNS IN STYLISH TRIMMED HATS.

AT 99 CENTS, $2.35, $3.25 AND UPWARDS.

WE SUBMIT ON THESE FOUR PAGES, the very newest effects in fashionable trimmed hats made especially for us from original designs, the same styles as will be shown by fashionable city milliners in large cities; styles that it will be impossible for you to secure in the stores in smaller towns, such goods as can be had only from the big millinery emporiums in metropolitan cities and there at two to three times our prices. These illustrations are made by artists direct from the hats, but it is impossible in a plain black and white drawing to give you a fair idea of the full beauty of these new hat creations. We ask you to read the descriptions carefully, note the illustrations and send us your order with the understanding that if the hat, when received, is not all and more than we claim for it, perfectly satisfactory, you are at liberty to return it to us at our expense and we will immediately return your money.

Wonderful Value.

99c

No. 39R101 Is a black dress shape fancy straw, slightly raised on the left. Very tastefully trimmed in the front with six large muslin roses and shaded foliage. Trimmed high to the right is a large rosette consisting of silk finished pink mull in half wheel effect, same extending all around the crown and falling over the back and caught on bandeau with loops of the same material. A very stylish young or middle aged ladies' hat. Shape can be ordered only in black or white, trimmings in any color desired, but looks very handsome as described. Price, each........ ....99c

$1.95

No. 39R107 This is a hand made fancy straw braid dress hat, drooping slightly to front and back. The wire frame is covered with an imported hand made straw braid, trimmed fully to the left with artistically designed rosettes draped in plume effect. The entire crown is covered with an imported tinted foliage and buds. The facing is neat drawn work of narrow folds of pink silk finished mull, and the bandeau is covered with nicely made loops of the same material. An exceedingly becoming and effectively designed hat. Can be ordered in all colors, Price, each............... ....$1.95

...HAT DEPARTMENT...

DO NOT BE SATISFIED WITH ANY STYLE HAT when you can have at no additional expense a hat that will be becoming and at the same time stylish and in good form. Different sections of the country have their styles, due mainly to their difference in occupation and environment. If you live on a ranch and want the proper hat for such a life, we have it. If you wish the fashionable derby or stiff hat, we can supply this.
OUR LINE OF SOFT AND FEDORA SHAPES CANNOT BE EXCELLED.

VALUE. We can sell you a hat at almost any price, but by our manufacturer to the wearer plan we are able to sell to you at almost the same price your home merchant pays for the same quality. We want your order, because we can save you 25 to 40 per cent, and at the same time fill your order with NEW, CLEAN, UP TO DATE GOODS.

MEN'S DERBY OR STIFF HATS, $1.50.
No. 33R2010 Young Men's Stiff Hat, in fashionable shape. Is a very neat block, not extreme, but stylish. Crown, 4¾ inches; brim, 1¾ inches. Fine silk band and binding. Colors, black or brown. Sizes, 6¾ to 7½.
Price, each.... $1.50
If by mail, postage extra, 34 cents.
A Fashionable Block in Men's Stiff Hats for $2.00.

Men's Large or Full Shape Stiff Hats.
No. 33R2040 A style particularly suited to large men. A shapely, staple hat, as shown in illustration. Crown, 5¼ inches; brim, 2¼ inches. Fine silk band and binding. Sizes, 6¾ to 7⅜. Color, black only.
Each.....$1.50
If by mail, postage extra, 34 cents.

Our Men's $2.25 Quality Full Shape Hat.
No. 33R2046 Men's Full Shape Hat, same style and dimensions as the above, in the high grade nonbreakable stock, with very fine silk band and binding; imported leather sweatband. Color, black only. Sizes, 6¾ to 7¾. Price, each.............$2.25
If by mail, postage extra, 34 cents.

MEN'S UNDERWEAR.

ASTONISHING TEMPTATIONS FOR ALL MANKIND.

QUALITIES THAT WILL SURPRISE YOU,

PRICES THAT WILL CONVINCE YOU.

MAKE A CHANGE, Off with the Old, on with the New. Prudence suggests it, your health demands it. Our prices protect you from over profit paying. We handle more Underwear and Hosiery than any one concern in the World. We save you nearly 50 per cent. on your purchases and give you better values than you could possible obtain anywhere else either wholesale or retail. Every garment we quote is guaranteed to be exactly as represented or money refunded. **EVERY PRICE WE QUOTE IS A REVELATION.**

OUR TERMS ARE LIBERAL. All goods sent C. O. D., subject to examination, on receipt of $1.00, balance and express charges payable at express office. **Three per cent. Discount** allowed if cash in full accompanies your order. Nearly All Our Customers Send Cash in Full.

Ventilated Health Underwear.

Summer Weight Balbriggan.

No. 2830 Men's Ventilated Natural Gray Mixed Summer Undershirts. The most comfortable as well as the most healthful balbriggan underwear ever made; fine gauge and soft finish; fancy collarette neck, pearl buttons and ribbed cuffs; ventilated all over with small drop stitch openings. Highly recommended by the best physicians as conducive to good health. Sizes 34 to 42 only. Price each..**$0.58**

MEN'S FANCY UNDERWEAR.

Men's Striped Balbriggan Underwear, 41 Cents.

No. 16R5078 Men's Fine Fancy Balbriggan Undershirts, knit from fine Egyptian cotton, made in a very narrow ⅛-inch alternating white and blue stripe. A very pretty garment that never fails to give satisfaction. Fast color. Trimmed with collarette neck and pearl buttons. **Perfect fitting ribbed cuffs.** Never retails for less than 50 to 65 cents. Stitched throughout with never-rip seams. Sizes, 34 to 44 breast measure.

Price, each.......................**41c**

Source 10 from an 1893 advertisement.

10. Shaving Soaps.

WILLIAMS' SHAVING SOAPS have enjoyed an unblemished reputation for excellence—for over HALF A HUNDRED YEARS—and are to-day the *only* shaving soaps—of absolute purity, with well-established claims for healing and antiseptic properties.

"CHEAP" and impure Shaving Soaps—are composed largely of refuse animal fats—abound in scrofulous and other disease germs—and if used—are almost sure to impregnate the pores of the skin—resulting in torturing cutaneous eruptions and other forms of blood-poisoning.

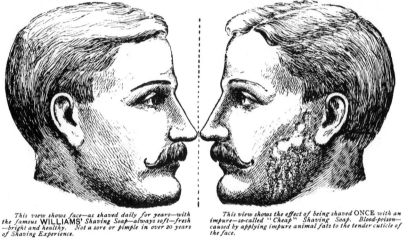

This view shows face—as shaved daily for years—with the famous WILLIAMS' Shaving Soap—always soft—fresh—bright and healthy. Not a sore or pimple in over 20 years of Shaving Experience.

This view shows the effect of being shaved ONCE with an impure—so-called "Cheap" Shaving Soap. Blood-poison—caused by applying impure animal fats to the tender cuticle of the face.

MR. CHAS. A. FOSTER,

34 SAVIN STREET,

BOSTON, MASS., writes:

"Never again will I allow a Barber to shave me unless I am *sure* he is using the only safe and reliable shaving soap made—namely WILLIAMS'. The other day—being in a hurry—I went into a shop near the Boston and Maine depot—to get a shave.

"I noticed a rank odor when the lather was put on my face, and asked the Barber if he used WILLIAMS' Shaving Soap. He said, 'No—I do not—because it costs a little more than other kinds.'

"A few days after this experience—my face was all broken out—terribly sore and smarting like fire.

"I consulted my Physician who told me it was a bad case of 'BARBER'S ITCH'—caused by the use of the Cheap Shaving Soap—containing diseased animal fats.

"I have suffered the worst kind of torture for two weeks—but I have learned a lesson."

Ask your Barber if *he* uses WILLIAMS'. Take no chances. Blood-poisoning—in some form or other is the almost sure result of using a cheaply made and impure Shaving Soap. While shaving—the pores of the Skin are open—and quickly drink in—any of the disease germs which may be contained in the diseased animal fats—so largely used in all "cheap"—inferior Toilet and Shaving Soaps.

Ask for WILLIAMS'—and *insist* that you have it—and enjoy a feeling of SECURITY—as well as of comfort—while shaving or being shaved.

In providing for the safety and comfort of visitors—it has been officially ordered that

WILLIAMS' SHAVING SOAPS

shall be used EXCLUSIVELY—in all of the Barber Shops located on the Grounds of the World's Columbian Exposition. Thus AT THE VERY START—it receives the highest possible Honor.

WILLIAMS' "JERSEY CREAM" TOILET SOAP.

Something new with us. The result of 50 years of costly and laborious experiment. Send for circular.

A most exquisite—healing and beautifying toilet soap. Containing the rich yellow cream of *our own herd* of imported Jersey Cattle. A full size cake mailed to any address for 25c. in stamps.

Do not fail to try it. Ask your Druggist—or send to us.—Address,

The J. B. Williams Co., Glastonbury, Conn., U. S. A.

"WILLIAMS' SOAPS have for a foundation—over half a hundred years of unblemished reputation."

Source 11 from a 1908 advertisement.

11. **Safety Razor.**

"Shave Yourself"

"The man who shaves himself before breakfast in the morning has a pleasure which is never known by those whose faces are not familiar with the razor or for whom it is wielded by another.

"The operation creates a sense of cleanliness, opens one's eyes to things as they are, dissipates the cobwebs in the brain which accumulate during the night, and assists in establishing amicable relations with the world for the beginning of the day."

Well lathered, you can shave yourself with the "GILLETTE" in three to five minutes any and every morning in the year at a fraction of a cent per day. The blade of my Razor, the "GILLETTE," is the only new idea in Razor Blades for over 400 years. This double-edged, thin-as-a-wafer blade is held by the Gillette frame in a perfectly rigid manner (which avoids all possibility of vibration), thus ensuring a comfortable, safe and uniform shave — which conditions are not obtainable with any other make of razor.

With the "GILLETTE" a slight turn of the handle adjusts the blade (which is always in position) for a light or close shave with a soft or hard beard.

The "GILLETTE" holder triple silver plated will last you a lifetime, and when the blades become dull, throw away and buy —

10 Brand New Double-Edged "GILLETTE" Blades for 50c.

No blades re-sharpened or exchanged. The price of the "GILLETTE" set is $5.00 everywhere.

Sold by the leading Jewelry, Drug, Cutlery and Hardware Dealers.

Ask for the "GILLETTE" and booklet. Refuse all substitutes and write me to-day for special 30-day free trial order.

King C Gillette

Care of Gillette Sales Co.

279 Times Building, New York City.

Gillette Safety Razor
NO STROPPING. NO HONING.

[77]

Source 12 from a 1912 advertisement.

12. Watch Chains.

ROBERT HILLIARD
The Famous Actor, now Appearing in New York
in " The Argyle Case," Wears a Waldemar

These are the watch chains now worn by men who set the styles

When a man buys a watch chain he chooses a *pattern* to suit his individual taste—but he wants a *style* which will always be in good taste.

A watch chain is the only piece of jewelry worn universally by men.   It is the most prominent piece a man can wear.   Every man with any regard for his personal appearance wants his watch chain right.

SIMMONS CHAINS
TRADE MARK

are always "correct" in style.   That is one reason why first-class jewelers have handled them for forty years.   A man in the smaller cities and towns can be just as sure as a New Yorker that he is getting the "proper thing" if he buys a *Simmons Chain*.

Waldemar and Dickens are the most popular styles this year.   Lapels, vests and fobs are also in good taste.   For women there are chatelaines, neck, eyeglass and guard chains and bracelets.

The beauty of design and finish and the satisfactory service of the *Simmons Chains*, have made them a standard among well-dressed men and women.

The surface of a *Simmons Chain* is not a wash or plate.   It is a rolled tube of 12 or 14 karat *solid gold*, of sufficient thickness to withstand the wear of years.

If your jeweler hasn't *Simmons Chains* write us for Style Book—make your selection and we'll see that you are supplied.

DOUGLAS FAIRBANKS
The Popular Actor who Made a Great
New York Success in "Officer 666,"
Wearing a Dickens

R. F. Simmons Co.   (Established 1873)   177 N. Main St., Attleboro, Mass.
Look for SIMMONS stamped on each piece—your protection and guarantee for wear.

Source 13 from 1899 and 1916 advertisements.

13. Smith & Wesson (1899) and Colt (1916) Revolvers.

Source 14 from an 1891 advertisement.

14. One-Volume Book.

NONE ARE TOO BUSY TO READ

IN ONE VOLUME.

"The Best Fifty Books of the Greatest Authors."

CONDENSED FOR BUSY PEOPLE.

BENJAMIN R. DAVENPORT, EDITOR.

NO EXCUSE FOR IGNORANCE.

THIS WORK of 771 pages covers the whole range of Literature from Homer's Iliad, B. C. 1200 to Gen. Lew. Wallace's Ben Hur, A. D. 1880, including a Brief Biographical Sketch and FINE FULL-PAGE PORTRAIT OF EACH AUTHOR. Every one of the Fifty Books being so thoroughly reviewed and epitomized, as to enable the READERS OF THIS VOLUME TO DISCUSS THEM FULLY, making use of Familiar Quotations properly, and knowing the connection in which they were originally used by their Great Authors.

THIS BOOK is made from material furnished by Homer, Shakespeare, Milton, Bunyan, Dickens, Stowe, Gen. Lew. Wallace. and the other great authors of thirty centuries.

BY IT A LITERARY EDUCATION MAY BE ACQUIRED WITHIN ONE WEEK, ALL FROM ONE VOLUME.

A BOOK FOR BUSY AMERICANS.
TIME SAVED. MONEY SAVED.
KNOWLEDGE IN A NUTSHELL.

NEW YORK WORLD, March 15th.—"The book is one destined to have a great sale, because it supplies, IN THE FULLEST SENSE, A LONG FELT LITERARY WANT."

Born 1504.   William Shakespeare.   Died 1616.

Opinions expressed by practical, busy and successful self-made men, as to the great value and merit of Mr. Davenport's condensations:

Mr. PHILIP D. ARMOUR writes: "I am pleased to own 'Fifty Best Books.' It certainly should enable the busy American, at small expenditure of time, to gain a fairly comprehensive knowledge of the style and scope of the authors you have selected."

GEN. RUSSELL A. ALGER writes: "I have received the beautiful volume. It is surely a very desirable work."

GOV. JOSEPH E. BROWN, of Georgia, writes: "You have shown great power of condensation. This is eminently a practical age; men engaged in the struggle for bread have no time to enter much into details in literature. What the age wants is to get hold of the substance of a book. This work entitles you to be understood as a benefactor."

Born 1783.   Washington Irving.   Died 1859.

BOSTON DAILY GLOBE, April 2, 1891.—"Men of the present generation have not time to wade through from 2,000 to 3,000 pages of any of literature's standard volumes, and as a result they do not undertake it at all, and are often placed in an embarrassing position."

BUFFALO EXPRESS, March 1st.—"The Best Fifty Books of the Greatest Authors. Condensed for Busy People," edited by Benjamin R. Davenport, deserves high praise. It not only gives busy people an introduction to literature, but takes them to its very sanctum sanctorum and bids them be at home. The editor has selected his best fifty books with the advice of the most eminent literary men in England and America. These masterpieces, from Homer's 'Iliad' to Lew. Wallace's 'Ben Hur,' he has condensed into one volume of 771 pages, working in all of the famous passages and supplying a narrative in good, straightforward, unpretentious English. The story of each book is accompanied with a brief biographical sketch and a portrait of each author. No matter how familiar one is with any of these fifty books, be it for instance, 'Don Quixote,' 'Rasselas,' 'Les Miserables,' 'Paradise Lost,' or any other, he will be forced to admit, after reading the dozen pages devoted to each one in this condensation, that there is little, if anything, to add, either with regard to plot, characters, scenes, situations, quotations, or anything else that is ever discussed by people. The result of days or weeks of reading will be the possession of hardly one single bit of information or one tangible idea concerning the book in hand that is not to be acquired by reading the dozen pages in this condensation within a half hour."

Born 1812.   Charles Dickens.   Died 1870.

SOLD BY SUBSCRIPTION ONLY.   AGENTS WANTED EVERYWHERE.

CANVASSERS who desire to represent a book which sells rapidly and without argument should send for CIRCULARS. Books forwarded, postage paid, to any address upon receipt of price.

Fine English Muslin, Sprinkled Edges, $3 75.   Full Sheep, Library Style, Marbled Edges, $4.75.
Seal Russia, Gilt Edges, $6.75.

19th CENTURY BOOK CONCERN, 40 Exchange St., Buffalo, N. Y.

[1891]

Source 15 from a 1906 advertisement.

15. Correspondence School.

What are You Worth

From The NECK UP ?

It is estimated that the average man is worth $2.00 a day from the neck *down*—what is he worth from the neck *up?*

That depends entirely upon training. If you are trained so that you can plan and direct work you are worth ten times as much as the man who can work only under orders.

The **International Correspondence Schools** go to the man who is struggling along on small pay and say to him, "We will train you for promotion right where you are, or we will qualify you to take up a more congenial line of work at a much higher salary."

What the I. C. S. says it can do, it *will* do. It has already done it for others and will do it for *you,* if you only show the inclination.

Thousands of ambitious men, realizing this fact, have marked the I. C. S. coupon, and multiplied their wages many times. During March, 403 students voluntarily reported an increase in salary and position as the direct result of **I. C. S.** training.

In this day of demand for leaders, a young man ought to be ashamed to be satisfied with small wages when he has the I. C. S. ready to qualify him for a higher salary.

Mark the coupon at once and mail it. You need not leave your present work, or your own home, while the I. C. S. prepares you to advance.

Back your *trained hand* with a *trained head!* It pays big. This coupon is for you. *Will you use it?*

International Correspondence Schools,
Box 815, SCRANTON, PA.
Please explain without further obligation on my part, how I can qualify for a larger salary in the position before which I have marked X

Bookkeeper	Mechanical Draftsman
Stenographer	Telephone Engineer
Advertisement Writer	Elec. Lighting Supt.
Show Card Writer	Mechan. Engineer
Window Trimmer	Surveyor
Commercial Law	Stationary Engineer
Illustrator	Civil Engineer
Civil Service	Building Contractor
Chemist	Architec'l Draftsman
Textile Mill Supt.	Architect
Electrician	Structural Engineer
Elec. Engineer	Bridge Engineer
	Mining Engineer

Name_____

Street and No._____

City_____ State_____

Source 16 from a 1906 advertisement.

16. Typewriter.

A Course in Practical Salesmanship
Tuition FREE~All Expenses Paid

IN these times of keen business rivalry, the services of the Trained Salesman command a high premium.

The Oliver Sales Organization is the finest body of Trained Salesmen in the world. It is composed of picked men, and is under the guidance of Sales Experts.

In less than ten years it has placed the Oliver Typewriter where it belongs—in a position of absolute leadership.

Its aggregate earnings are enormous and the individual average is high.

The scope of its activities is as wide as civilization and the greatest prizes of the commercial world are open to its membership.

The organization is drilled like an army. It affords a liberal education in actual salesmanship, and increases individual earning power many per cent, by systematic development of natural talents.

Its ranks are recruited from every walk of life. Men who had missed their calling and made dismal failures in the over-crowded professions have been developed in the Oliver School of Practical Salesmanship into phenomenal successes.

The Oliver Typewriter puts the salesman in touch with the men worth knowing—the human dynamos who furnish the brain power of the commercial world.

Because every Business Executive is interested in the very things the Oliver stands for—economy of time and money—increase in efficiency of Correspondence and Accounting Departments.

The OLIVER Typewriter

The Standard Visible Writer

is simple in principle, compactly built, durable in construction, and its touch is beautifully elastic and most responsive.

In versatility, legibility, perfect alignment, visibility, etc., it is all that could be desired in a writing machine.

It's a constant source of inspiration to the salesman, as every day develops new evidence of its wide range of usefulness.

Just as the winning personality of a human being attracts and holds friends, so does the Oliver, by its responsiveness to all demands, gain and hold an ever-widening circle of enthusiastic admirers.

If you wish to learn actual salesmanship and become a member of the Oliver Organization, send in your application **immediately,** as the ranks are rapidly being filled.

You can take up this work in spare time, or give us your entire time, just as you prefer.

Whether you earn $300 a year, or **twelve times $300** a year, depends entirely upon **yourself.**

We offer to properly qualified applicants the opportunity to earn handsome salaries and to gain a knowledge of salesmanship that will prove of inestimable value.

Can you afford to vegetate in a poorly-paid position, when the way is open to a successful business career?

Address at once,

THE OLIVER TYPEWRITER CO., 161 Wabash Ave., Chicago

WE WANT LOCAL AGENTS IN THE UNITED STATES AND CANADA.
PRINCIPAL FOREIGN OFFICE—75 QUEEN VICTORIA ST., LONDON.

Source 17 from a 1908 advertisement.

17. Life Insurance.

Don't Depend on Your Relatives When You Get Old

If you let things go kind o' slip-shod *now*, you may later have to get out of the 'bus and set your carpet-bag on the stoop of some house where your arrival will hardly be attended by an ovation.

If you secure a membership in the Century Club this sad possibility will be nipped in the bud. It is very, very comfortable to be able to sit under a vine and fig-tree of your own.

The Club has metropolitan headquarters and a national membership of self-respecting women and men who are building little fortunes on the monthly plan. Those who have joined thus far are a happy lot—it would do your heart good to read their letters.

We would just as soon send our particulars to you as to anybody else, and there is no reason in the world why you shouldn't know all about everything. You'll be glad if you do and sorry if you don't.

Be kind to those relatives—*and to yourself.*

Address, stating without fail your occupation and the exact date of your birth,

Century Life-Insurance Club
Section O

5, 7 and 9 East 42d Street, New York

RICHARD WIGHTMAN, Secretary

Source 18 from 1881 and 1885 advertisements.

18. Bicycles (1881) and Tricycles (1885).

COLUMBIA BICYCLES

The Art of wheelmanship is a gentlemanly and fascinating one, once acquired never forgotten, which no young man should neglect to acquire.

The Bicycle is practical everywhere that a buggy is, and enables you to dispense with the horse and the care and cost of keeping him. It is destined to be the prevailing light, quick, ready conveyance in country towns.

The Youth take to bicycles like ducks to water. They ride it quickly, easily, safely and gracefully. They can get more pleasure out of it than out of a horse, a boat, and a tennis or cricket outfit all together.

Parents should favor bicycle riding by their boys, because it gives them so much enjoyment, makes them lithe and strong, keeps them from evil associations, and increases their knowledge and their self-reliance. There is no out-door game or amusement so safe and wholesome.

The above paragraphs are but fragmentary suggestions; ask those who have ridden: read "The American Bicycler" (50 cts.), the "Bicycling World" (7 cts. a copy), our illustrated catalogue (3-ct. stamp).

The Columbia bicycles are of elegant design, best construction, fine finish, and are warranted. They may be had with best ball-bearings, finest nickel plate, and other specialties of construction and finish, according to choice.

The Mustang is a less expensive, plain and serviceable style of bicycle made by us for boys and youths.

Physicians, clergymen, lawyers, business men of every class, are riding our Columbias in nearly every State and Territory to-day, with profit in pocket, with benefit in health, and with delightful recreation. The L.A.W. Meet at Boston brought 800 men together on bicycles; but the **boys,** who outnumber them on bicycles, and who have their own clubs and associations in so many places, were at school and at home. Why don't every boy have a bicycle?

Send 3-cent stamp for our 24-page illustrated catalogue and price-list, with full information.

THE POPE M'F'G CO.,
598 Washington Street,
BOSTON MASS.

COLUMBIA BICYCLES.

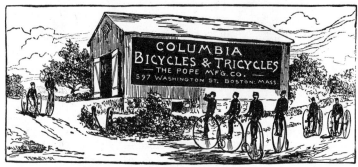

FOR HEALTH—BUSINESS—PLEASURE.

"Having examined somewhat carefully the 'wheels' of England and France, I do not believe that a better roadster is made in the world than the 'Expert Columbia.'"—ALONZO WILLIAMS, Professor of Mathematics, Brown University, Providence, R. I.

"A contractor and builder in Pennsylvania writes: 'I am using my 'wheel' night and day to make business calls, and conveying hardware and other things. . . . I would not exchange my bicycle for the best horse in the country.'"—*The Wheelman.*

"From the practical results which I determined by subjecting the different qualities of steel from which it is constructed to the recognized standard of Government

tests, I am free to assert that you may justly claim that the 'Columbia' *has not its equal in quality of material and finish;* all of which is shown in the tabulated results in your possession."—F. J. DRAKE, U. S. Inspector of Material.

"A LADY'S TESTIMONY.—A recent recruit from the fair sex, in bearing evidence as to the utility of the tricycle, writes: 'My sister and myself have just returned from a tour, having ridden from Leeds to Woodbridge (Suffolk), and home again by Halstead and Walden (Essex), or a total of 470 miles whilst we have been away; and, as we have had such a successful time of it in every respect, we intend having another tour next year.'"—*The C. T. C. Gazette.*

EVERY BOY AND MAN SHOULD HAVE A

COLUMBIA BICYCLE.

"I want to lift my voice in favor of the 'wheel' as a thing of beauty, as an instrument of pleasure, and as one of the most practical of modern inventions, looking towards practical ends."—REV. GEO. F. PENTECOST.

"But the bicycle and tricycle are not only enjoyable modes of locomotion, they are also without a peer in their hygienic capacity."—DR. S. M. WOODBURN.

EVERY LADY SHOULD RIDE A

COLUMBIA TRICYCLE.

"I am of the opinion that no exercise for women has ever been discovered that is to them so really useful. Young and middle-aged ladies can learn to ride the tricycle with the greatest facility, and they become excellently skilful. The tricycle is, in fact, now with me a not uncommon prescription, and is far more useful than many a dry, formal, medicinal one which I had to write on paper."—B. W. RICHARDSON, M. D., F. R. S.

Illustrated Catalogue Sent Free.

THE POPE M'F'G CO., Principal Office, 597 Washington St., Boston, Mass.

[1885] BRANCH HOUSES: 12 Warren St., New York; 179 Michigan Ave., Chicago.

Source 19 from 1896 and 1914 advertisements.

19. Gramophone (1896) and Victrola (1914).

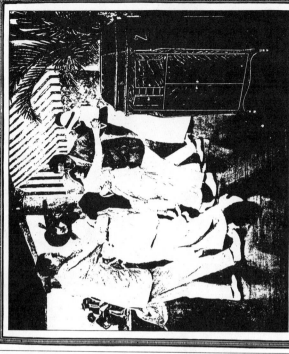

The Victrola illustrated here is the $200 style

Dancing to the music of the Victrola is the favorite pastime

With a Victrola and Victor Dance Records it is easy to learn all the new dances.

The maxixe, hesitation, tango, one-step—you can enjoy all the modern dances in your own home with the Victrola.

"How to Dance the One Step, Hesitation, and Tango" is a new Victor booklet just issued—illustrated with photos of Mr. and Mrs. Vernon Castle (who use the Victor exclusively and superintend the making of Victor Dance Records) and 288 motion-picture photographs. Ask any Victor dealer for a copy, or write us. There are Victors and Victrolas in great variety of styles from $10 to $200, and any Victor dealer will gladly play any music you wish to hear.

Victor Talking Machine Co., Camden, N. J., U.S.A.
Berliner Gramophone Co., Montreal, Canadian Distributors

Always use Victor Machines with Victor Records and Victor Needles—*the combination*. There is no other way to get the unequaled Victor tone.

[1914]

The Berliner Gramophone.

HOME is the place for your boys and girls to have a good time; amuse them and give them what they call fun and they will not want to go out evenings. A talking machine is one of the wonders of the world; Mr. Berliner, of telephone fame, has by his recent invention brought this marvellous machine to a point where it may be purchased by every household. It is simple in construction, anybody can use it and it does not get out of order. It sings solos, duets and quartette music; it reproduces exactly the cornet, clarionet, the ba jo and in fact every instrument, including an orchestra or brass band. The talking and singing records are upon indestructible disks which are easily handled and do not wear out. We have an endless variety of these disks, including practically every song you are acquainted with.

The accompanying illustration shows exactly how the machine looks and how it is operated and the pleasure it is giving the people who are hearing it. **$10.00** purchases this marvel of the ages, including two records. Extra records 60 cents each, $6.00 per dozen.

DESCRIPTION OF OUTFIT. The outfit includes the talking machine, Style No. 7½, which has a such revolving table covered with felt, nickel-plated edge, a large fly-wheel nickel-plated, balanced so as to turn evenly. Attached to the machine which holds the fly-wheel is an arm for the sound box with reproducing diaphragm; attached to this diaphragm are the rubber tubes, which are provided with a double connection so that two people may hear at the same time. (Extra tubes, 75 cents each person.) Nicely packed in box and is sent express prepaid to any express office in the United States upon receipt of price.

Send Money by Postal Note, Express Money Order or New York Draft.

Special Offer. With each Machine ordered before Nov. 20th, we will include an Amplifying Horn.

For Sale by all Music Dealers.

Send for Catalogue.   Free of Course.

NATIONAL GRAMOPHONE COMPANY, 874 to 880 Broadway, New York City.

Source 20 from 1907 and 1912 advertisements.

20. Ford Automobile (1907) and Electric Car for Women (1912).

FORD RUNABOUT
"Built for Two"

Two's company and a crowd frequently spoils a motoring trip.

When you have a large car you feel like filling up the seats—seems stingy for two to usurp so much luxury; so your tonneau is always full. Everybody's happy but—

Did you ever feel as if you'd just like to go alone—you and she—and have a day all your own? Go where you please, return when you please, drive as fancy dictates, without having to consult the wishes or the whims of others?

Ford Runabouts are ideal for such trips. Just hold two comfortably; ride like a light buggy, control easily and you can jog along mile after mile and enjoy the scenery.

Of course you can scorch if you want to—40 miles an hour easily—but you won't want to. You'll get used to the soft purr of the motor and the gentle motion of the car over the rolling country roads and—well, it's the most luxurious sensation one can imagine.

"**We've enjoyed motoring** more since we've had the Ford Runabout than we ever did before," says one lady whose purse can afford anything she desires. "Got the big car yet, but 'two's company,' and most times that's the way we go."

**$600,
F.O.B. Detroit**

Model N. 4 Cyl. 15 H.P.

FORD MOTOR COMPANY,
25 Piquette Ave., - Detroit, Mich.

BRANCH RETAIL STORES—New York, Philadelphia, Boston, Chicago, Buffalo, Cleveland, Detroit and Kansas City. Standard Motor Co., San Francisco, Oakland and Los Angeles, distributors for California. Canadian trade supplied by Ford Motor Company of Canada, Walkerville, Ont.

The Automobile for Women

Electrically Started and Lighted

Controls Itself Pumps Its Own Tires

THE advent of the Inter-State, with its marvelously simple mechanism, its electrical self-starter and its self-controller has brought a revolution in motoring. Now the powerful and magnificent Inter-State starts and obeys the will of the woman driver as readily, as easily and as simply as an electric coupe. Without moving from the driver's seat or shifting gears she starts the engine by a turn of the switch — regulates the mixture by a simple movement of the lever on the steering column, and the magnificent Inter-State is under way and under perfect and absolute control, with no more trouble than turning on an electric light. The Inter-State electric self-starter is **part of the system** and **built into it**, and the motor dynamo turns the engine itself until it picks up under its own power.

No labor to start the Inter-State

Electric Lights as in Your Own Home

ONE of the greatest features of the Inter-State is its electric light system—not a single light or two—but an entire and reliable system, front —side—rear, all correlated and so arranged that by a turn of the switch, without leaving the driver's seat, any or all of the lights may be turned on in all their brilliancy. No more gas tanks, no more oil filling, no more lamp trimming or adjusting. The system is simply perfect. The front headlights are provided with a dimming feature so that driving in city streets may be done with a medium diffused light.

Any or all lights on by turning switch

Write Today for Art Catalog

This describes fully the six 40 and 50 H. P. completely equipped Models which cost from $2,400 to $3,400. Gives complete details of all the equipment and features, and also shows the Inter-State Models 30-A and 32-B, 40 H. P., costing $1,750 and $1,700 respectively.

THAT greatest nuisance of motoring—tire pumping—is *totally eliminated* with the Inter-State equipment. Any woman can attach the valve to the tire, turn on the pump and in a few minutes have tires just as solid and as perfectly filled as if done by the greatest tire expert in the world.

The Inter-State *does* the work. You *direct* it. There is nothing to it at all and you are forearmed for any emergency with the complete and thorough equipment of the Inter-State.

Inter-State Tire Pumping—No Work

Motoring Now All Pleasure

THIS great car performs all the labor itself—electrically self-started—electric lights and ignition, tire pumping and the automatic regulation of fuel consumption.

For the first time in the history of the automobile, electricity plays its *real part* in the entire mechanism. The Inter-State Electric System is really the *nerve system* commanding the energy and motion of the powerful steel muscles that make the Inter-State such a masterpiece of construction. Every conceivable accessory and feature is built into or included in the Inter-State. The Inter-State is truly the *only complete car* in this country or abroad —and this statement is made advisedly.

The Only Complete Car—Equipment and Features Unequalled

INTER-STATE AUTOMOBILE COMPANY, Dept. X, Muncie, Indiana
Boston Branch: 153 Massachusetts Avenue   *Omaha Branch:* 310 South 18th Street

21. Auto Horn.

Source 22 from 1884 and 1908 advertisements.

22. Stove (1884) and Washer and Wringer (1908).

ASK YOUR DEALER FOR THE
"GLENWOOD"

WITH PATENT MAGIC GRATE.

There is nothing more essential to the healthy happy
home than well cooked food—which you may always be
sure of by using the Glenwood Range. 100 styles!
Illustrated Circular and Price List sent free.

WEIR STOVE CO., Taunton, Mass.

The Electric Washer and Wringer

YOU can now have your washings done by electricity.
The 1900 Electric Washer Outfit (Washer, Wringer and Motor complete) does all the heavy work of washing and wrings out the clothes.

Any electric light current furnishes the power needed. You connect up the washer the same way you put an electric light globe into its socket. Then all there is to do to start the washer is—turn on the electricity. The motion of the tub (driven by the electricity) and the water and soap in the tub wash the clothes clean. Washing is done quicker and easier, and more thoroughly and economically this way than ever before.

Washing

30 Days' FREE Trial—Freight Prepaid

Wringing

Servants will stay contented—laundry bills will be saved—clothes will last twice as long—where there is a 1900 Electric Washer to do the washing.

These washers save so much work and worry and trouble, that they *sell themselves.* This is the way of it—

We ship you an Electric Washer and *prepay the freight.*

Use the washer a month. Wash your linens and laces—wash your blankets and quilts—wash your rugs.

Then—when the month is up, if you are not convinced the washer is all we say—don't keep it. Tell us you don't want the washer and that will settle the matter. We won't charge anything for the use you have had of it.

This is the *only* washer outfit that does *all* the drudgery of the washing—*washes* and *wrings* clothes—saves them from wear and tear—and keeps your servants contented.

Our Washer Book tells how our washers are made and how they work. Send for this book today.

Don't mortgage your pleasure in life to dread of wash-day and wash-day troubles with servants. Let the 1900 Electric Washer and Wringer shoulder your wash-day burden—save your clothes and money, and keep your servants contented.

Write for our Washer Book at once. Address—

The 1900 Washer Co. 3133 Henry Street, Binghamton, N. Y. *(If you live in Canada, write to the Canadian 1900 Washer Co., 355 Yonge Street, Toronto, Ont.)*

Why stir up the Dust Demon to Frenzy like this?

The Man

always wonders why some way of cleaning can't be found without tormenting him with choking clouds of dust.

The Woman

thinks she is performing praiseworthy and necessary work in an unavoidable manner.

You can Escape all this for $25

EVERY MAN AND WOMAN

should now realize that such laborious and tormenting "cleaning" methods, not only are absolutely unnecessary, but are a *relic of barbarism*, a *mockery and a farce*. "Cleaning" with broom and carpet-sweeper merely scatters more of the dirt over a wider area. Old dirt has to be *rehandled again and again*. The house is never thoroughly clean. Disease germs are left to multiply, then are sent flying to infect all those whose powers of resistance may be lowered.

THE IDEAL VACUUM CLEANER

(Fully Protected by Patents)

Operated by Hand puts no tax on the strength.

Price $25

"IT EATS UP THE DIRT"

literally sucks out all the dust, grit, germs, moths and eggs of vermin that are *on* the object as well as *in* it—gobbles them down into its capacious maw, never to trouble you again.

Or by Electric Motor, at a cost of 2 cents per hour.

Price $55 or $60

This machine places in your hands a method of cleaning carpets, rugs, curtains, upholstery, wall decorations, etc., that hitherto has been limited to the very rich. It does exactly the same work as the Vacuum Cleaning systems that cost from $500 up—*and does it better and with more convenience.* **The Ideal Vacuum Cleaner is the perfection of the Vacuum Cleaning principle.**

OPERATED BY HAND

Weighs only 20 pounds. Anybody can use it. Everybody can afford it. Compared with sweeping

It is ease itself.

It is absolutely dustless. Every machine guaranteed.

Our free Illustrated Booklet tells an interesting story of a remarkable saving in money, time, labor, health, and strength. Send for it to-day.

The American Vacuum Cleaner Company
225 Fifth Avenue, New York City

The Noiselessness of the Siwelclo Is an Advantage Found in No Other Similar Fixture.

This appeals particularly to those whose sense of refinement is shocked by the noisy flushing of the old style closet. The Siwelclo was designed to prevent such embarrassment and has been welcomed whenever its noiseless feature has become known. When properly installed it cannot be heard outside of its immediate environment.

SIWELCLO Noiseless Siphon Jet CLOSET

Every sanitary feature has been perfected in the Siwelclo—deep water seal preventing the passage of sewer gas, thorough flushing, etc.

The Siwelclo is made of Trenton Potteries Co. Vitreous China, with a surface that actually repels dirt like a china plate. It is glazed at a temperature 1000 degrees higher than is possible with any other material.

The most sanitary and satisfactory materials for all bathroom, kitchen and laundry fixtures are Trenton Potteries Co. Vitreous China and Solid Porcelain. Your architect and plumber will recommend them. If you are planning a new house or remodeling, you ought to see the great variety and beauty of design such as are shown in our new free booklet S18 "**Bathrooms of Character.**" Send for a copy now.

The Trenton Potteries Co.
Trenton, N.J., U.S.A.

The largest manufacturers of sanitary pottery in the U.S.A.

Source 24 from an 1882 advertisement.

24. Musical Organ.

"LIBRARY ORGAN."

Containing the Celebrated Carpenter Organ Action.

Something Entirely New! The Æsthetic Taste Gratified!

THIS IS ONLY ONE OF ONE HUNDRED DIFFERENT STYLES.

THIS effective and beautiful design in the modern Queen Anne Style is intended to meet the demands of those desiring an instrument of special elegance, and in harmony with the fittings and furnishings of the Study or Library Room, combining as it does, in a substantial and tasteful manner, the Organ, the Library cases, and the cabinet for bric-a-brac and articles of virtu.

It is well adapted to find favor in homes of culture and refinement, and will be championed by the music lover and connoisseur.

The composition is one of well balanced proportions, chaste subordination of ornamentation, and of artistic arrangement in constructive details, imparting to the design a rich simplicity and substantial worth

This beautiful organ contains the Celebrated Carpenter Organ Action. The action is to an Organ what the works are to a watch. The merits of the Carpenter Organ were fully proved on page 158 of the YOUTH'S COMPANION of April 20th, to which special attention is directed.

A beautiful 80-page Catalogue, the finest of its kind ever published, is now ready and will be sent free to all applying for it.

Nearly all reliable dealers sell the Carpenter Organs, but if any do not have them to show you, write to us for a Catalogue and information where you can see them. DO NOT BUY ANY ORGAN UNTIL YOU HAVE EXAMINED "THE CARPENTER." In writing for a Catalogue always state that you saw this advertisement, in the *Youth's Companion.*

Address or call on E. P. CARPENTER, Worcester, Mass., U. S. A.

25. Reed and Rattan Furniture.

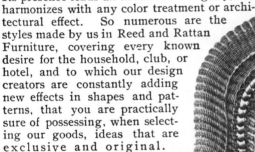

ESTABLISHED 1826

Heywood-Wakefield

TRADE MARK

FACSIMILE OF OUR TAG

THE name *Heywood-Wakefield* appearing on Reed and Rattan Furniture signifies quality, style, and workmanship, that individualizes our brands of goods and has made them world-renowned. The best in Rattan Furniture is *not* the best unless it bears the tag *Heywood-Wakefield*

Our furniture enhances the beauty of any home. Its presence lends an influence of dignity, comfort, and artisticness that harmonizes with any color treatment or architectural effect. So numerous are the styles made by us in Reed and Rattan Furniture, covering every known desire for the household, club, or hotel, and to which our design creators are constantly adding new effects in shapes and patterns, that you are practically sure of possessing, when selecting our goods, ideas that are exclusive and original.

We are also producers of the well-known line of

Heywood *Wakefield*

go-carts and baby carriages. Made in every conceivable style, including our celebrated collapsible, room-saving go-carts.

We have prepared attractive illustrated catalogs showing and describing our Reed and Rattan Furniture. Before purchasing, *write for catalog G*.

We also furnish, free, interesting catalog of our go-carts and baby carriages. If interested, *write for catalog 7*.

Write to our nearest store.

HEYWOOD BROTHERS AND WAKEFIELD COMPANY

BOSTON, BUFFALO, NEW YORK, PHILADELPHIA, BALTIMORE, CHICAGO, SAN FRANCISCO, LOS ANGELES, PORTLAND, ORE.

J. C. PLIMPTON & CO., Agts.
LONDON AND LIVERPOOL, ENG.

Style 6830 B

Source 26 from 1887 and 1892 advertisements.

26. Houses in New York (1887) and Tennessee (1892). Exterior View and Floor Plan.

* * * This marvelous house has been built more than 300 times from our plans; *it is so well planned* that it affords ample room even for a large family. 1st floor shown above; on 2d floor are 4 bedrooms and in attic 2 more. Plenty of Closets. The whole warmed by one chimney.

Large illustrations and full description of the above as well as of 39 other houses, ranging in cost from $400 up to $6,500, may be found in "SHOPPELL'S MODERN LOW-COST HOUSES," a large quarto pamphlet, showing also how to select sites, get loans, &c. Sent postpaid on receipt of 50c. Stamps taken, or send $1 bill and we will return the change. Address, BUILDING PLAN ASSOCIATION. (Mention this paper.) 24 Beekman St. (Box 2702,) N. Y.

27. Advice for Couples Buying a Home.

This is the house the young couple saved and paid for in five years.

A Young Couple
Were Married 5 Years Ago

He had a moderate salary. They started simply and saved. But they didn't skimp. They gave little dinners and heard the best lectures. In five years they had saved enough to pay for the house at the head of this page.

Another Young Couple Were Married, Too

They put by $7 a week, and the house at the bottom of this page is now theirs, —entirely paid for. A third young couple's income was $16 per week. They saved $8 of it, and bought and paid for the house at the bottom of this page.

How these and 97 others did it, step by step, dollar by dollar, is all told in the great series, "*How We Saved For a Home,*"— 100 articles by 100 people who saved for and now own their own homes on an

Average Salary of $15 a Week: None Higher Than $30

This great series will run for an entire year in

The Ladies' Home Journal

For ONE DOLLAR, for a year's subscription, you get the whole series.

THE CURTIS PUBLISHING COMPANY, PHILADELPHIA, PA.

This is the house saved for on $7 a week and now all paid for.

This is the house paid for out of a salary of $16 per week, saving $8.

Sources 28 through 31 from *Palliser's Model Homes*, 1878.

28. Cottage for a Mill Hand at Chelsea, Mass. (Cost $1,200).

This is a very attractive design, and intended to give ample accommodation at a low cost for an ordinary family.

The cellar is placed under the Kitchen and Hall, which was thought in this instance to be sufficient to meet all requirements, though it is generally considered, in the Eastern States at least, to be poor economy not to have a cellar under the whole house, as it only requires about one foot in depth of additional stone work to secure a cellar, it being necessary to put down the stone work in any case, so that it will be beyond the reach of frost. The Kitchen is without a fire-place, the cooking to be done by a stove, which, if properly contrived, is a very effective ventilator, and preferred by many housekeepers for all Kitchen purposes.

The Parlor and Dining-room or general Living-room are provided with the healthy luxury of an open fire-place, and we know of no more elegant, cleanly and effective contrivance for this purpose than the one adopted in this instance; they are built of buff brick, with molded jambs and segment arch, and in which a basket grate or fire dogs can be placed for the desired fire, and in this way large rooms are kept perfectly comfortable in cold weather without heat from any other source. These fire-places are also provided with neat mantels constructed of ash, and which are elegant compared with the marbelized slate mantel, which is a sham, and repulsive to an educated taste.

On entering nearly every house in the land we find the same turned walnut post at the bottom of the stairs with tapering walnut sticks all the way up, surmounted with a flattened walnut rail having a shepherd's crook at the top; however, in this instance it is not so, but the staircase is surmounted with an ash rail, balusters and newel of simple, though unique design; and now that people are giving more attention to this important piece of furniture, we may look for a change in this respect.

This house is supplied with a cistern constructed with great care, the Kitchen sink being supplied with water by a pump, and there is no more easy method of procuring good water for all purposes of the household.

For a compact, convenient Cottage with every facility for doing the work with the least number of steps, for a low-priced elegant Cottage, we do not know of anything that surpasses this. Cost, $1,200.

Mr. E. A. Jones of Newport, Ohio, is also erecting this Cottage with the necessary changes to suit points of compass. Such a house as this if taste-fully furnished, and embellished with suitable surroundings, as neat and well-kept grounds, flowers, etc., will always attract more attention than the uninviting, ill-designed buildings, no matter how much money may have been expended on them.

It is not necessary that artistic feeling should have always a large field for its display; and in the lesser works and smaller commissions as much art may find expression as in the costly façades and more pretentious structures.

29. Floor Plan of Cottage for a Mill Hand.

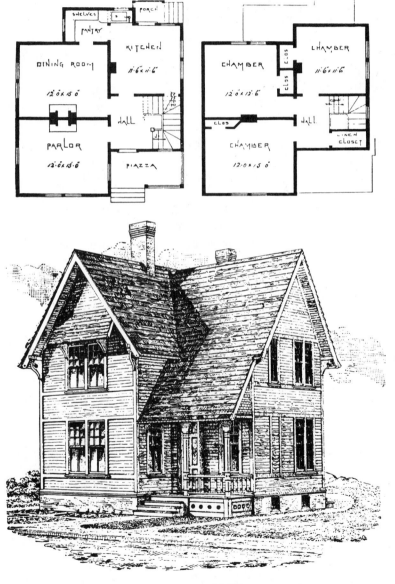

30. Residence of Rev. Dr. Marble, Newtown, Conn. (Cost $2,925).

This house commands a particularly fine view from both sides and the front, and is situated in one of the pleasantest country towns in New England, the hotels of this town being crowded during the summer months with people from the cities.

The exterior design is plain, yet picturesque, and at once gives one an idea of ease and comfort. The roofing over the Hall and Sitting-room is a particularly fine feature, and the elevation of the rear is very striking, the roof over the porch being a part of the main roof.

The interior arrangements are very nice, the Hall being very spacious, and in it we have a very easy and handsome stair-case of plain design, constructed of Georgia pine; the newel extends up to ceiling of first floor, while the other two posts extend up to ceiling of second floor. In all country houses one of the first things to be aimed at is to secure ample stair-cases, and until a man can afford space for an easy ascent to a second floor he should stay below; and to-day we find in houses, where there is no necessity for it, stairs that are little better than step-ladders, making a pretence of breadth at the bottom with swelled steps, and winding the steps on approaching the floor above, thus making a trap for the old and for the children.

The corner fire-place between Parlor and Dining-room is a feature we indulge in to a great extent in these days of economy, sliding doors and fire-places, although we sometimes have clients who object to this, thinking it would not look as well as when placed in center of side wall; but when they are asked how this and that can be provided for with the best and most economical results, they readily give in.

There is no water-closet in the house, but an Earth-Closet is provided in the rear Hall, which is thoroughly ventilated.

The Dining-room is a very cheerful room and the Kitchen is reached through a passage also connecting with side veranda. The pantry is lighted with a window placed above press; each fire-place is furnished with a neat hard-wood mantel, and the Hall is finished in Georgia pine, the floor being laid with this material, and finished in natural color.

The exterior is painted as follows: Ground, light slate; trimmings, buff, and chamfers, black. Cost, $2,925.

The sight of this house in the locality in which it is built is very refreshing, and is greatly in advance of the old styles of rural box architecture to be found there. When people see beautiful things, they very naturally covet them, and they grow discontented in the possession of ugliness. Handsome houses, other things equal, are always the most valuable. They sell quickest and for the most money. Builders who feign a blindness to beauty must come to grief.

31. Floor Plan of a Clergyman's Residence.

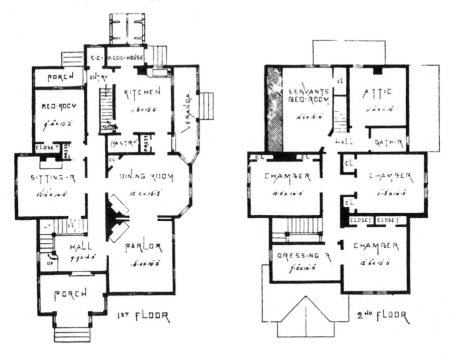

32. Perspective View and Floor Plans for a Suburban Middle-Class Home (Cost $3,600).

PERSPECTIVE.

DESCRIPTION.

For explanation of all symbols (* † etc.) see supplement page 120.

GENERAL DIMENSIONS: Width, including veranda, 43 ft.; depth, including veranda, 49 ft. 6 ins.

HEIGHTS OF STORIES : Cellar, 7 ft.; first story, 10 ft.; second story, 9 ft.; attic, 8 ft.

EXTERIOR MATERIALS: Foundation, brick; first story, clapboards; second story, gables, roofs and lower portion of veranda railing, shingles.

INTERIOR FINISH: Two coat plaster for papering; plaster, cornices and centers in hall, parlor and dining-room. Soft wood flooring and trim throughout. Main stairs, ash. Kitchen and bath-room, wainscoted. Chair-rail in dining-room. Picture molding in hall, parlor and dining-room. All interior woodwork grain filled and finished with hard oil.

COLORS: All clapboards, first story, Colonial yellow. Trim, including water-table, corner boards, casings, cornices, bands, veranda posts and rails, outside doors, conductors, etc., ivory white. Veranda floor and ceiling, oiled. Shingles on side walls and gables stained dark yellow. Roof shingles, dark red.

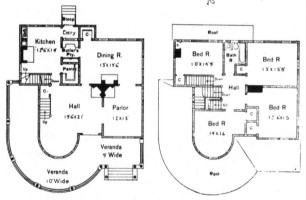

FIRST FLOOR.   SECOND FLOOR.

ACCOMMODATIONS: The principal rooms, and their sizes, closets, etc., are shown by the floor plans. Cellar under whole house with inside and outside entrances and concrete floor. One room finished in attic, remainder of attic floored for storage. Double folding doors between parlor and hall and parlor and dining-room. Direct communication from hall with dining-room, parlor and kitchen. Bathroom, with complete plumbing, in second story. Open fire-places in dining-room, parlor and hall. Wide veranda. Bay-window in hall and bedroom over. Two stationary wash-tubs in cellar under kitchen.

COST: $3,600, including mantels, range and heater. The estimate is based on † New York prices for labor and materials.

Price of working plans, specifications, detail drawings, etc., $35.
Price of †† bill of materials, ... 10.

FEASIBLE MODIFICATIONS: General dimensions, materials and colors may be changed. Cellar may be decreased in size or wholly omitted. Sliding doors may be used in place of folding doors. Portable range may be used instead of brick-set range. Servants' water-closet could be introduced in cellar. Fireplaces may be reduced in number.

The price of working plans, specifications, etc., for a modified design, varies according to the alterations required and will be made known upon application to the Architects.

Address, CO-OPERATIVE BUILDING PLAN ASSOCIATION, Architects, 203 Broadway and 164-6-8 Fulton Street, New York, N. Y.

ᘡ QUESTIONS TO CONSIDER ᘡ

For convenience, the evidence is divided into two sections. Sources 1 through 25 are advertisements from popular magazines and the 1897 and 1902 Sears Roebuck & Co. catalogues. The prices probably seem ridiculously low to you, but these items were reasonably priced and affordable—although not really cheap—for most middle-class Americans in cities and towns and on farms. Sources 26 through 32 all deal with houses and buying a house, including house plans readily available by mail and through pattern books. Again, the prices seem very low, but working-class homes could be built for less than one thousand dollars (excluding the cost of the land) and middle-class homes for as little as two thousand dollars during this period.

As you read each advertisement, you will find it helpful to jot down notes. First, try to determine the message of the ad. What is the advertiser trying to sell? What emotion(s) does the ad appeal to? What fears? What hopes? Then ask what the ad tells you about society during that time. Does it tell you anything about men's roles? About women's roles? About the relationships between men and women? Does it tell you anything about children or young people? About adults' concerns about young people? About old people? Finally, do you see any changes occurring during the time period—for example, in the two ads for the Gramophone and the Victrola (Source 19) or in the ads for automobiles (Source 20)? If so, what do these changes tell you about the roles of men, women, and young people between the 1880s and 1917?

Source 26 includes two advertisements for houses. Source 27 is an advertisement for a magazine series giving advice on how to buy a home. What do they tell you about people's needs and wants with regard to housing? What advice is offered to young married people? What values are emphasized by these advertisements for housing? The remaining evidence (Sources 28 through 32) consists of house plans and descriptions from architectural pattern books, arranged chronologically from 1878 to 1900. Look carefully at the exterior features of these houses. How would you describe them to a student who had not seen the pictures? Next, look at the interior rooms and their comparative sizes. What use or uses would each room probably have had? What rooms did these houses have that our own modern houses do not have? Do modern houses have rooms that these houses lacked? What similarities do you find in all the houses, from the mill hand's cottage ($1,200) to the suburban middle-class home ($3,600)? What differences are there? Finally, what kinds of things seemed to be important to the owners of these houses? What kind of impression did they wish to make on other people?

To conclude, consider what you have learned as a whole from the evidence of both sections. Can you describe how white middle-class Americans lived during this period? What do you know about their values, hopes, and fears during this era of rapid changes?

⚭ EPILOGUE ⚭

Of course, not all Americans could live like the middle-class families you just studied. The poor and the immigrants who lived in the cities were crowded into windowless, airless tenement buildings that often covered an entire block. Poor rural black and white sharecroppers in the South lived in one- or two-room shacks, and many farmers in the western plains and prairies could afford to build only sod houses. During the Great Depression of the 1930s, many people, including middle-class families, lost their homes entirely through foreclosure, and the 1960s and 1970s saw the price of houses increase so rapidly that many families were priced out of the housing market. Even today, the problem of the homeless has not been solved.

The early twentieth century saw the captains of industry come under attack for what many came to believe were their excesses. Evidence of their disdain for and defiance of the public good, as well as of their treatment of workers, their political influence, and their ruthless business practices, came more and more to light due to the efforts of reformers and muckraking journalists. The society that once had venerated the industrial barons began to worry that they had too much power and came to believe that such power should be restricted.

Architecture also was undergoing a rapid transformation. Neoclassical, Georgian, Colonial, and bungalow styles signaled a shift toward less ostentation and increased moderation in private dwellings. Perhaps the most striking work was done by Chicago architect Frank Lloyd Wright, who sought to give functional and social meaning to his designs and to make each structure blend into its unique landscape. According to Wright's concepts, there was no standard design for the "perfect house." Wright's ideas formed the basis for a series of movements that ultimately changed the perspective and direction of American architecture.

Progressive muckrakers also criticized advertising, particularly the claims of patent medicine advertisements. Such salesmanship, however, was described as "the brightest hope of America" by the 1920s. Bruce Barton, a talented salesman and founder of a huge advertising agency, even discovered "advertisements" in the Bible, which he described as the first "best seller." Although its image was slightly tarnished by the disillusionment accompanying the Great Depression, advertising helped "sell" World War II to the American public by encouraging conservation of scarce resources, and it emerged stronger and more persuasive than ever in the 1950s. Americans were starved for consumer goods after wartime rationing, and their rapid acceptance of a new entertainment medium—television—greatly expanded advertising opportunities.

But advertising still had (and has) its critics. Writing in 1954, historian David Potter characterized advertising as the basic "institution of abundance." Advertising, he maintained, had become as powerful as religion or education had been in earlier eras. Advertising, he said, now actually *created* the standards and values of our society. Because advertising lacked social goals or social responsibility, however, he believed that its power was dangerous. We must not forget, Potter warned, "that it ultimately regards man as a consumer and defines its own mission as one of stimulating him to consume."

CHAPTER 4

JUSTIFYING AMERICAN IMPERIALISM: THE LOUISIANA PURCHASE EXPOSITION, 1904

 THE PROBLEM

From the formal end of Reconstruction in 1877 to the United States' entry into the First World War in 1917, Americans appeared to fall in love with world's fairs. Between 1876 and 1916, various United States cities hosted fourteen international expositions that were attended by nearly 100 million eager visitors.[1] Intended to stimulate economic development in the host cities as well as provide opportunities for manufacturers to show their newest products to millions of potential consumers, these expositions or world's fairs also acquainted provincial Americans with machines and technology (the Corliss engine, electric lights, the air brake, refrigeration, the dynamo, x-rays, the telephone), new delights (the Ferris wheel, ice cream cones, the hoochie-koochie dance), and spectacular architecture, art, and historical artifacts (the Liberty Bell was brought from Philadelphia to both the New Orleans and Atlanta expositions). As President William McKinley commented at the 1901 Pan-American Exposition in Buffalo (where he was soon after assassinated), "Expositions are the timekeepers of progress."

1. The first international exposition was held in London's Crystal Palace in 1851. Between 1876 and 1916, American expositions were held in Philadelphia, New Orleans, Chicago, Atlanta, Nashville, Buffalo, Charleston, St. Louis, Jamestown, Portland, Seattle, San Francisco, and San Diego. Numerous regional expositions and fairs also were held.

Visitors to the Louisiana Purchase Exposition in St. Louis in 1904[2] saw all this and more. More than 19 million people[3] attended the largest world's fair ever held (1,272 acres, 75 buildings, 70,000 exhibits).[4] Visitors could examine a display of 100 automobiles or watch demonstrations of totally electric cooking. But the highlight of the St. Louis Exposition was its Anthropology Department, headed by the pre-eminent Smithsonian Institution ethnologist W. J. McGee. The department brought to St. Louis representatives of "all the races of the world," who lived on the fairgrounds in villages designed to reproduce their "native habitats." For example, 1,200 people were brought from the Philippine Islands, an area acquired from Spain in the Spanish-American War of 1898 and where American soldiers recently (1902) had subdued a Filipino rebellion. On a 47-acre site, 6 villages were constructed for these people, where American visitors could observe them and their customs.

In this chapter, you will be analyzing several photographs taken at the 1904 Louisiana Purchase Exposition in St. Louis. As noted earlier, in 1898 the United States had acquired a colonial empire from Spain as a result of the Spanish-American War. How did the exhibits at the 1904 St. Louis Exposition attempt to justify America's rise as an imperialist power? How do you think American visitors might have reacted to these exhibits?

⦶ BACKGROUND ⦷

Until the late nineteenth century, the United States' transoceanic foreign policy clearly had been of minor concern to the nation's citizens. Westward expansion and settlement, the slavery controversy and the Civil War, postwar reconstruction of the republic, and industrialization and urbanization had alternately captured the attention of Americans and pushed foreign affairs into the background. But beginning in the latter part of the nineteenth century, several factors prompted Americans to look beyond their own shores, and by the end of the century, the United States had become

2. The St. Louis Exposition commemorated the acquisition of the Louisiana Territory from France. The treaty between the United States and France was signed in Paris on April 30, 1803; the United States Senate ratified the treaty on October 20; and the United States took formal possession of the Louisiana Territory on December 20, 1803.
3. Nineteen million people (the official count; others were lower) represented 23.1 percent of the total U.S. population in 1904. Of course, not all visitors were Americans, and some people visited the exposition more than once and thus were counted more than once in the total figure.
4. In terms of acreage, the St. Louis Exposition remains the largest world's fair ever held. The 1939–1940 New York World's Fair covered 1,217 acres and the 1967 Montreal World's Fair 1,000 acres.

CHAPTER 4

JUSTIFYING
AMERICAN
IMPERIALISM:
THE LOUISIANA
PURCHASE
EXPOSITION,
1904

a world power complete with a modest empire.

Initially, the American business community opposed this drift toward expansion and colonialism, believing that American industry would do well just meeting the needs of the rapidly growing population and fearing that a colonial empire would mean large armies and navies, increased government expenses, and the possibility of the nation's involvement in war. However, by the mid-1890s, American business leaders were beginning to have second thoughts. The apparent cycle of economic depressions (1819, 1837, 1857, 1873, 1893) made some businessmen believe that American prosperity could be maintained only by selling surpluses of manufactured goods in foreign markets. Business leaders also were constantly looking for areas in which to invest their surplus capital. Investments beyond the borders of the United States, they believed, would be more secure if the American government would act to stabilize the areas in which they invested. In 1895, the newly organized National Association of Manufacturers sounded both those chords at its convention, where the keynote speaker was soon-to-be-president William McKinley, an Ohio governor with decided expansionist leanings.

Yet it would be wrong to see American expansion and colonialism strictly as a scheme to better the nation's industrial and commercial interests. A number of other intellectual currents dovetailed with American commercial interests to create a powerful and popular urge toward imperialism. For example, those who advocated military growth (especially of a large, steam-powered navy) saw in American expansion a perfect justification for their position. Their interests were represented by increasingly influential lobbies in Washington. Especially important was Captain Alfred Thayer Mahan, whose book *The Influence of Sea Power Upon History* (published in 1890) argued persuasively that national self-preservation depended on international trade protected by a large and powerful navy with worldwide bases and refueling stations. Two of Mahan's disciples, Theodore Roosevelt and Henry Cabot Lodge, eventually achieved positions whereby they could put Mahan's philosophy to work.

Another current influencing American expansion was the dramatic increase in religious missionary zeal in the late nineteenth century. Working through both individual denominations and powerful congressional lobbies, missionaries argued that it was their duty to "Christianize" the world.[5] In the United States, Methodists, Baptists, Presbyterians, and Congregationalists were especially active, giving money and attention to their denominational missionary boards as well as to those who went out to convert the "heathen." In large part, these missionaries were selfless, committed men and women. Some, however, attempted to westernize as well

5. Because the majority of Filipinos were Roman Catholics (making the Philippines the only Christian "nation" in Asia), obviously American missionaries to the Philippines after 1899 meant *Protestantize* when they said "Christianize."

as Christianize their flocks, often denigrating or destroying indigenous cultures and traditions even as they brought modern health and educational institutions with them. All argued for the United States government to more actively protect the missionaries and open up other areas around the world to missionary work.

Accompanying this religious zeal were two other intellectual strains that in some ways were contradictory but that both justified American expansion. The first was that of Social Darwinism. An application of Charles Darwin's theories of biological evolution to human affairs, Social Darwinism taught that peoples, like species, were engaged in a life-or-death struggle to determine the "survival of the fittest." Those classes or nations that emerged triumphant in this struggle were considered the best suited to carry on the evolution of the human race. Therefore, the subjugation of weak peoples by strong ones was not only in accordance with the laws of nature, but it was bound to result in a more highly civilized world as well. Most celebrated among the Social Darwinists was the Englishman Herbert Spencer, a diminutive and eccentric writer who became a worldwide celebrity through his writings. (A letter was once addressed to him, "Herbert Spencer. England. And if the postman doesn't know the address, he ought to." It was delivered.)

Although Spencer himself disapproved of imperialism, it is easy to see how his writings could be used as a justification for empire building, not only in the United States but in Western Europe as well (which at this time

was furiously engaged in imperialistic adventures). One reflection of the intellectual strain of Social Darwinism was reflected in the writings of the American author Josiah Strong. As he predicted in his book *Our Country: Its Possible Future and Its Present Crisis* (1885),

> this race of unequaled energy . . . will spread itself over the earth. If I read not amiss, this powerful race will move down upon Mexico, down upon Central and South America, out upon the islands of the sea, over upon Africa and beyond. And can anyone doubt that the result of this competition of races will be the "survival of the fittest"?

Paralleling this notion of struggle for survival between the "fittest" and the "unfit" (a doctrine with strong racist overtones) was the concept of the "White Man's Burden." This concept held that it was the duty of the "fittest" not so much to destroy the "unfit" as to "civilize" them. White people, according to this view, had a responsibility to educate the rest of the world to the norms of Western society. As racist as Social Darwinism, the belief in the White Man's Burden downplayed the idea of a struggle for survival between peoples and emphasized the "humanitarian" notion of bringing the benefits of "civilization" to the "uncivilized." Using this argument, many in the West justified imperialism as an obligation, a sacrifice that God had charged the "fittest" to make. Although the doctrine differs in tone from that of Social Darwinism, one can see that its practical results might well be the same.

CHAPTER 4

JUSTIFYING
AMERICAN
IMPERIALISM:
THE LOUISIANA
PURCHASE
EXPOSITION,
1904

All these ideological impulses (economic, military, religious, "scientific," paternalistic) rested on one common assumption: that the world was a great competitive battlefield and that those nations that did not grow and expand would wither and die. Indeed, this "growth mania," or fascination with growth and the measurement of growth, was perhaps the most powerful intellectual strain in all of American society. For those who accepted such an assumption, the world was a dangerous, competitive jungle in which individuals, races, religions, nations, corporations, and cities struggled for domination. Those that grew would continue to exist; those that did not grow would die.

The convergence of these intellectual strains in the late nineteenth century prompted Americans to view the outside world as an area into which the United States' influence should expand. This expansionist strain was not an entirely new phenomenon; it had been an almost regular feature of American life nearly since the nation's beginning. Yet except for the purchase of Alaska, this was the first time that large numbers of Americans seemed to favor the extension of United States influence into areas that would not be settled subsequently by Americans and would not eventually become states of the Union. In that sense, the American imperialism of the late nineteenth century was a new phenomenon, different from previous expansionist impulses. Instead, it more nearly resembled the "new" imperialism that engulfed European nations in the late nineteenth and early twentieth centuries, in which those nations rushed to carve out colonies or spheres of influence in Africa and Asia.

The Spanish-American War of 1898 was the event that helped the various impulses for United States expansion and colonization to converge. When Cubans began a revolt to secure their independence from Spain in 1895, most Americans were genuinely sympathetic toward the Cuban underdogs. Those genuine feelings were heightened by American newspaper reporters and editors, some of whom wrote lurid (and knowingly inaccurate) accounts of the Spanish "monsters" and the poor, downtrodden Cubans. President William McKinley tried to pressure Spain into making concessions and sent the American battleship *Maine* to Havana on a "courtesy call," an obvious move to underscore the United States' position toward Spain. But on February 15, 1898, the *Maine* blew up in Havana harbor. Although we now know (as a result of a 1976 study) that the explosion on the *Maine* was an internal one, almost surely the result of an accident, at the time many Americans, fired up by the press, were convinced that the Spanish had been responsible. Yet war with Spain did not come immediately and, in the opinion of some, was not inevitable, even after the *Maine* incident. However, on April 11, 1898, after two months of demands, negotiations, and arguments in which it sometimes appeared that war might be avoided, McKinley asked Congress for authorization to intervene in Cuba "in the name of humanity and civilization." On April 20, Congress granted authorization, and the Spanish-American War began.

If the Spanish-American War had not begun as an imperialistic venture, the convergence of the economic, military, religious, and racist impulses mentioned previously and the prostrate condition of Spain gave American leaders the opportunity to use the war and victory for expansionist purposes.

Once the United States had achieved a comparatively bloodless[6] victory against nearly impotent Spain, a general debate began over whether the United States should demand from Spain the surrender of its colonial empire, the jewels of which were Cuba and the Philippine Islands. Although President McKinley admitted that he had to consult a globe to find out where the Philippine Islands were, he was never in doubt that they should become a part of a new American empire. McKinley thus pressured the Spanish to include the surrender of their empire in the peace treaty (signed in Paris on December 10, 1898) and submitted that treaty to the United States Senate on January 4, 1899. After a brisk debate in which opponents of acquisition charged that acquiring colonies went against America's history and morality, that acquiring the Philippines would embroil the United States in future wars, and that Filipinos would be able to migrate to the United States, where they would compete with American labor, on February 6, 1899, the Senate ratified the treaty by a vote of 57–27, just one vote more than the two-thirds necessary for ratifying a treaty.[7] Learning of the vote, an exultant McKinley boasted that the Philippines would become

a land of plenty and increasing possibilities; a people redeemed from savage and indolent habits, devoted to the arts of peace, in touch with commerce and trade of all nations, enjoying the blessings of freedom, of civil and religious liberty, of education, and of homes, and whose children's children shall for ages hence bless the American republic because it emancipated their fatherland, and set them in the pathway of the world's best civilization.

The Senate vote, however, did not end the debate over whether the United States should become a colonial power. Two days before the Senate voted, fighting broke out between United States troops and Filipinos under Emilio Aguinaldo, who had helped American soldiers overthrow the Spanish and who expected the United States to grant the Philippines immediate independence. Before the United States broke Aguinaldo's insurrection, approximately 125,000 American troops served in the Philippines, 4,200 were killed in action, and 2,800 were wounded, but an alleged 220,000 Filipinos died in battle, from disease and famine, and through torture. Government censors kept war-related atrocities from the American

---

6. The Spanish-American War lasted less than 3 months. The United States suffered only 362 battle or battle-related deaths (an additional 5,100 died of either disease or food poisoning), and the war cost only $250 million.

7. Outside the Senate, opponents of imperialism included Carl Schurz, William James, Mark Twain, Andrew Carnegie, Charles Francis Adams, Jane Addams, and William Jennings Bryan.

CHAPTER 4

JUSTIFYING
AMERICAN
IMPERIALISM:
THE LOUISIANA
PURCHASE
EXPOSITION,
1904

people. By 1902, the Philippine insurrection had been broken.

In 1900, Democratic presidential nominee William Jennings Bryan campaigned against McKinley on an anti-imperialist platform. The incumbent won easily (probably because of the fairly widespread prosperity that American voters enjoyed in 1900), but Bryan carried 45.5 percent of the vote, a better showing for a loser than in all but four presidential elections from 1900 to the present. By the time the St. Louis Exposition opened in 1904, anti-imperialist rhetoric had lost much of its appeal, but the issue was far from dead.

At the St. Louis Exposition, the "Philippine Reservation" was sponsored almost totally by the United States government. (It cost approximately $1 million.) Undoubtedly, this delighted the exposition's organizers, for they knew that similar attractions (called ethnological villages) had been extremely popular at the Paris Exposition of 1889, the Columbian Exposition of 1893, and the Pan-American Exposition of 1901. Former civil governor of the Philippines William Howard Taft (who in 1904 became secretary of war) supported the Philippine Reservation completely, as did Pedro A. Paterno, president of the Philippine Senate, who hoped that such an exhibit would attract investment capital to the islands. Federal agents scoured the Philippines, collecting materials to exhibit and "inviting" various Filipinos to journey to St. Louis. Those who agreed to come were allowed to make money by diving for coins, selling handicrafts, demonstrating their prowess with bows and arrows, and having their photographs taken with visitors to the exposition.

As expected, the Philippine Reservation was one of the highlights of the St. Louis Exposition. How did the Philippine Reservation seek to justify American imperialism? How do you think visitors might have reacted to what they saw? According to a 1904 *Harper's* magazine article, the St. Louis Exposition "fills a visitor full of pictures . . . that keep coming up in his mind for years afterwards." What were those pictures?

THE METHOD

According to historian Robert W. Rydell, who wrote an excellent book about American international expositions in the late nineteenth and early twentieth centuries, expositions "propagated the ideas and values of the country's political, financial, corporate, and intellectual leaders and offered these ideas as the proper interpretation of social and political reality."[8] In other words, the millions of Americans who visited exhibits the Anthropology Department had created at the 1904 exposition saw what someone else wanted them to see. At

8. Robert W. Rydell, *All the World's a Fair: Visions of Empire at American International Expositions, 1876–1916* (Chicago: University of Chicago Press, 1984), p. 3.

the Philippine Reservation, visitors made their way through six Filipino villages erected by the United States government in which representatives of "all the races of the Philippine Islands" could be "studied" by scientists and where most Americans had their only opportunity to see Filipinos with their own eyes. This allowed the American government to use the Reservation to justify its imperialistic ventures in the Philippines and elsewhere. Through photographs taken by official exposition photographers, you will be able to see some of what the fair's visitors saw.

As you examine the photographs in this chapter's Evidence section, keep in mind that you are seeing what someone else wants you to see. The Philippine Islands in 1904 contained an enormous diversity of peoples, from the most "primitive" to the most technologically and culturally sophisticated. About seventy-five linguistic groups were represented, as well as a plethora of Western and non-Western religious (under Spanish rule, most Filipinos had become Roman Catholics) and social customs. Yet of the many peoples who inhabited the Philippine Islands, the United States government selected only six groups to inhabit the Reservation's villages. Five of the six groups are photographically depicted in the Evidence section.[9] Why do you think each group was selected to go to St. Louis? What impressions do you think each group left in the minds of American visitors?

A second problem you will confront is the photographer's bias. As do journalists, photojournalists have a particular point of view or bias toward or against their subjects. These biases often affect the *way* subjects are presented to the viewers of the photographs. As you examine each photograph, think about the photographer's bias, including whether the subjects are presented in a favorable or an unfavorable light.

Although you are not used to thinking of photographs as historical evidence, photographs and other visual documents (drawings, paintings, movies) often can yield as much information as more traditional sources. As Charles F. Bryan, Jr., and Mark V. Wetherington note,

> Through the eye of the camera, the researcher can examine people and places "frozen" in time. . . . Photographs can tell us much about the social preferences and pretensions of their subjects, and can catch people at work, at play, or at home. In fact, you can "read" a photograph in much the same manner as any other historical document.[10]

When a historian "reads" a photograph, it means that he or she puts the photograph into words, describing it in terms of its intent, specific details about it, and the overall impression it makes.

For you to read the photographs, you will have to subject each one to

9. Negro pygmies (or Negritos), Igorots, Tagalos, Bontocs, and Visayans. The sixth group was the Moros.

10. Charles F. Bryan, Jr., and Mark V. Wetherington, *Finding Our Past: A Guidebook for Group Projects in Community History* (Knoxville: East Tennessee Historical Society, 1983), p. 26.

CHAPTER 4

JUSTIFYING
AMERICAN
IMPERIALISM:
THE LOUISIANA
PURCHASE
EXPOSITION,
1904

the following questions (take notes as you go):

1. What "message" is the photographer attempting to convey? How does the photographer convey that message (there may well be more than one way)?
2. Is the photographer biased in any way? How? What is the purpose of the photograph?
3. Are there buildings in the photograph? What impressions of these buildings does the photographer intend that viewers should get? How does the photograph seek to elicit those impressions?
4. Are there people in the photograph? Are they posed or "natural"? How has the photographer portrayed these people? What are the people doing (if anything)? What impressions of these people does the photographer intend that viewers of the photograph should retain?
5. Examine the people in more detail. What about their clothing? Their facial expressions? *Note:* Because photographers expected their subjects to strike artificial poses in order to be photographed, many of the pictures appear rigid and posed. Indeed, they were. If you have an old family album, see how similar some of the poses are to those in these photographs.

After you have examined each photograph, look at all the photographs together. What "message" is the photographer (or photographers) intending to convey? Most professional photographers judge whether a photograph is good or poor by the responses it evokes in the viewer's mind. What is the relationship between the responses you imagine these photographs might have elicited with America's justification for imperialism?

❧ THE EVIDENCE ❧

Source 1 from Robert W. Rydell, *All the World's a Fair: Visions of Empire at American International Expositions, 1876–1916* (Chicago: University of Chicago Press, 1984), p. 158.

1. The Sunken Gardens.

CHAPTER 4

JUSTIFYING
AMERICAN
IMPERIALISM:
THE LOUISIANA
PURCHASE
EXPOSITION,
1904

Source 2 from J. W. Buel, ed., *Louisiana and the Fair: An Exposition of the World, Its People, and Their Achievements* (St. Louis: World's Progress Publishing Co., 1904), Vol. V, frontispiece.

2. Types and Development of Man.

Source 3 from Rydell, *All the World's a Fair*, p. 175.

3. Negrito Tribesman from the Philippines (Exposition Officials Named This Man "Missing Link").

[113]

Source 4 from *The World's Fair, Comprising the Official Photographic Views of the Universal Exposition Held in Saint Louis, 1904* (St. Louis: N. D. Thompson Publishing Co., 1903), p. 149.

4. Igorots from the Philippines.

Source 5 from Rydell, *All the World's a Fair,* p. 173.

5. Igorot Tribesmen and Visitors.

Source 6 from *The World's Fair, Comprising the Official Photographic Views,*
p. 174.

6. Igorot Men and Women.

7. Tagalo Women Washing.

8. Igorots Performing a Festival Dance.

CHAPTER 4

JUSTIFYING
AMERICAN
IMPERIALISM:
THE LOUISIANA
PURCHASE
EXPOSITION,
1904

Source 9 from Rydell, *All the World's a Fair,* p. 174.

9. Igorot Dance and Spectators.

10. Igorots Preparing a Feast of Dog.

Source 11 from *The World's Fair, Comprising the Official Photographic Views,* p. 169.

11. Bontoc Head-Hunters from the Philippines.

Source 12 from Rydell, *All the World's a Fair*, p. 176.

12. Reproduction of an American School in the Philippines.

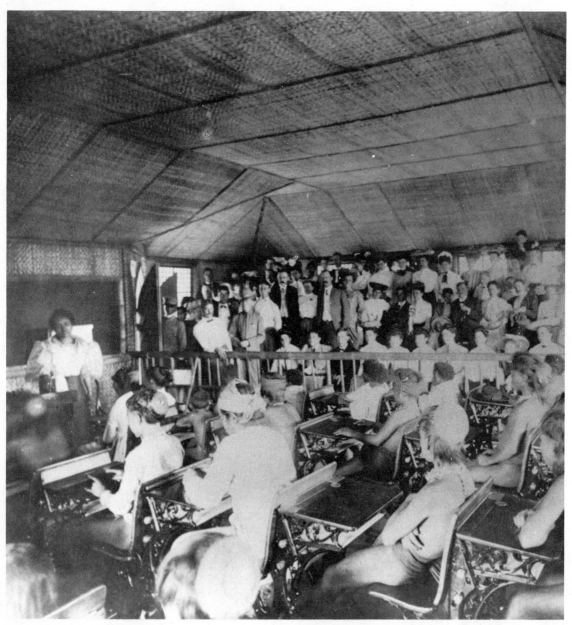

Sources 13 through 15 from *The World's Fair, Comprising the Official Photographic Views,* pp. 161, 163, 152–153.

13. Visayan Mothers with Their Children (Two of Whom Were Born at the Exposition).

CHAPTER 4

JUSTIFYING
AMERICAN
IMPERIALISM:
THE LOUISIANA
PURCHASE
EXPOSITION,
1904

14. A Visayan Troupe of Singers, Dancers, and Orchestra.

15. Filipino Soldiers (with American Officers) Who Fought with the Americans During the Philippine Insurrection (1899–1902).

CHAPTER 4

JUSTIFYING
AMERICAN
IMPERIALISM:
THE LOUISIANA
PURCHASE
EXPOSITION,
1904

 QUESTIONS TO CONSIDER

As you examine the photographs, first look for the photographer's intent and biases in each one. What "message" was the photographer trying to communicate? How might that message be used as a justification for American imperialism in the Philippines? For example, examine Source 1, which shows the impressive sunken gardens and surrounding buildings at the exposition. Who built these things? What impressions (amusement, awe, disgust) might viewers have of this scene? Now compare the structures in Source 1 to those in Sources 4 through 6 and 8. What "message" did photographers want viewers to receive?

The caption for Source 2 (from the official history of the Louisiana Purchase Exposition) reads in part, "The photogravure herewith is from an excellent specially prepared drawing which very accurately illustrates, as nearly as the science of ethnology is able to do, the characteristic types of mankind arranged in a progressive order of development from primitive or prehistoric man to the highest example of modern civilization." How does this photograph of a painting (which was on display at the exposition) help you assess the intent of all the photographers?

Sources 3 through 11 are of posed Philippine men and women from the Negrito, Igorot, Tagalo, and Bontoc tribes. These groups were among the most "primitive" of all Filipinos. Why did United States government officials select these people to appear at the St. Louis Exposition? How are these peo-

ples portrayed by photographers? How are they dressed? What are they doing? What impressions might visitors or viewers of the photographs have had of these peoples? When there are American visitors in the photographs (as in Sources 5, 9, and 12), what are they doing? Why did photographers place them in these pictures?

Source 12 is a photograph depicting a replica of an American school for Filipinos in the Philippines. What was the purpose of the photographer who took this picture? What is the photograph's message? What impressions would viewers have had?

Sources 13 and 14 are photographs of Visayans, a people quite different from the Negritos, Igorots, Tagalos, and Bontocs. What was different about them? How might you account for these differences?[11] How might American visitors to the village and viewers of these photographs have reacted to the Visayans as compared to other Filipino peoples at the exposition? What impressions would the Visayans have made? How might the Visayans have been used to justify American imperialism in the Philippines?

Source 15 is of a detachment of Filipino soldiers nicknamed the "Little Macs," who fought with the Americans during the Philippine insurrec-

11. *Note:* The Visayans were Roman Catholics, whereas all the other Filipinos brought to St. Louis practiced non-Western religions or held on to native Filipino religious customs. What does this tell you about the Visayans?

tion. How are these men depicted? Was the impression likely to be favorable or unfavorable? Do you think it is significant that the officers for this detachment were Americans? Why? How might the Little Macs be used to justify American imperialism in the Philippines?

Once you have examined the photographs individually, analyze them collectively. What was their collective message? How does that message relate to American actions in the Philippines from 1898 to the exposition in 1904? Could these photographs or word descriptions of them have been used to justify American imperialism in the Philippines? How? Refer to specific photographs to prove your points.

∽ EPILOGUE ∾

At the Louisiana Purchase Exposition in 1904, American visitors saw countless exhibits that communicated very strong messages. Arranged and erected by the nation's corporate, intellectual, and political leaders, the exhibits nevertheless were what Americans wanted to see. These exhibits trumpeted America's own scientific, technological, and cultural prowess while at the same time offering living proof that it was the United States' economic, political, and moral duty to become a colonial power. In addition to Filipino villages, villages had been set up for American Indians and Alaskan Eskimos, who, like the Filipinos, were wards of the United States. It was as powerful a visual justification for American imperialism as could possibly have been contrived.

Once the Philippine revolt was broken in 1902, the United States invested considerable time and energy in trying to Americanize the Filipinos, largely through education and giving Filipinos an increasing voice in their own affairs. In 1913, President Wood-row Wilson appointed Francis B. Harrison governor general of the Philippines, with the explicit instructions to prepare the Filipinos for their ultimate independence (a promise Congress gave its assent to in 1916, noting that independence would be granted "as soon as a stable government can be established"). Schools were set up throughout the islands, and by the 1930s, almost 50 percent of the population was literate. Gradually, American officials increased the percentage of Filipinos in the civil service, from 49 percent in 1903 to 94 percent in 1923. Elections were held for a Philippine legislature, although the real power remained in the hands of Americans.

In economic matters, the Americans' record in the Philippines was not so impressive. Economic power remained in the hands of a small, native Philippine landed elite, who, with the cooperation of Americans, continued to dominate the Philippine economy. Between 1900 and 1935, poverty became more widespread, real wages ac-

CHAPTER 4

JUSTIFYING
AMERICAN
IMPERIALISM:
THE LOUISIANA
PURCHASE
EXPOSITION,
1904

tually declined, and sharecropping (like that in the American South) doubled. This was the situation when the Japanese attacked the Philippine Islands on December 8, 1941.

With the defeat of Japan in 1945, the United States moved quickly to grant independence to the Philippines (which occurred on July 4, 1946), although America's economic and military presence in the new nation remained strong. Favorable leases on military and naval bases were negotiated, and the Central Intelligence Agency closely monitored Philippine elections and on occasion secretly backed candidates for office.

In 1965, campaigning against widespread government corruption and favoritism to the landed elite, Ferdinand Marcos was elected president of the Philippines. A much-lauded war hero, Marcos had entered politics in 1949, when he had become the youngest person ever elected to the Philippine Congress. As president, however, Marcos increased the power of his office to virtual one-man rule, largely by hobbling or eradicating the other branches of government and by a brutal policy of political repression, with more than fifty thousand political prisoners and numerous reported incidents of assassinations and torture. Even so, Marcos's rule was insecure. In the nation's economic expansion, profits went to a very few, usually Marcos's associates (in 1972, the poorest 20 percent of Filipinos received only 4.4 percent of the nation's income), and a population boom (2.5 percent per year) increased poverty and unemployment.

Things began coming apart for Marcos on August 21, 1983, when his principal political rival, Benigno Aquino,

was shot and killed at the Manila airport as he was returning to the Philippines to lead an anti-Marcos political movement. Public opinion in both the Philippines and the United States was that Marcos had been responsible for Aquino's death. By 1984, opinion polls in the Philippines showed a serious erosion of support for the Marcos government.

In 1986, Marcos was challenged for the presidency by Corazon Aquino, the widow of the killed opposition leader. The election results were clouded by charges of fraud, and both Marcos and Aquino claimed victory. By this time, the aging and ill Marcos had become increasingly isolated from the people, as he and his wife, Imelda, remained cloistered in the presidential palace. In February 1986, a general strike by Aquino supporters, the army's turning against the government, and the increasing displeasure of the Reagan administration finally toppled Marcos, who fled the Philippines for American protection in Hawaii. Corazon Aquino became president, to face the nation's severe economic and political problems. Her term expired in 1992, and she did not seek re-election, having survived numerous coup attempts. She left a nation that was more democratic but still economically and politically unstable.

Filipinos were not the only people "displayed" at the St. Louis Exposition. Indeed, the same economic, political, and intellectual strains that supported America's overseas imperialism also was evident in the conquest and subjugation of Native Americans, the growing efforts to exclude certain immigrants (the Chinese Exclusion Act of 1882, for example), the rising tide of American nativism, and the successful legal and extralegal methods southern whites used to deprive African Americans of their economic and civil rights. Not surprisingly, both Geronimo and Chief Joseph were extremely popular "attractions" at the exposition, as were the Sioux men and women pictured in Source 16. What similarities can you see between Source 16 and the photographs of Filipinos? Undoubtedly, ethnologist W. J. McGee, head of the exposition's Anthropology Department, spoke for most white Americans when he remarked that "*white* and *strong* are synonymous terms."

In one sense, the Louisiana Purchase Exposition of 1904 marked the high point of Americans' interest in international expositions and world's fairs. As Americans became less pro-

Source 16 from *The World's Fair, Comprising the Official Photographic Views*, p. 137.

16. Sioux Men and Women.

CHAPTER 4

JUSTIFYING
AMERICAN
IMPERIALISM:
THE LOUISIANA
PURCHASE
EXPOSITION,
1904

vincial, especially after the introduction of modern communications media, attendance at such events declined. As a result, such expositions became smaller (as opposed to the St. Louis Exposition, which covered 1,272 acres, the Knoxville, Tennessee, world's fair of 1982 was held on less than 70 acres). Moreover, the purpose of American expositions changed. Rather than being celebrations of the nation's technological might or justifications for American imperialism, world's fairs were viewed by their backers as massive urban renewal projects, in which the city government would come into possession of valuable acreage to be used for economic development. Such was the goal of recent fairs in Portland, Knoxville, and New Orleans. Finally, increased costs and lower attendance figures meant that such expositions were not economical. The New Orleans World's Fair lost millions of dollars. As a result, Chicago, which had planned to host an international exposition in 1992, had second thoughts.

In 1904, however, millions of Americans came to St. Louis to visit the Louisiana Purchase Exposition, a massive reinforcement of their own ideas about American superiority and the rectitude of Euro-American world domination. At the same time, the ideas that spurred and justified imperialism similarly spurred and justified increasingly harsh treatment of American Indians, African Americans, Hispanics, Asian Americans, and recent immigrants from southern and eastern Europe. In a nation and a world filled with opportunities, few Americans realized that their own ideology and attitudes not only did not carry them forward but in many ways actually held them back.

CHAPTER 5

HOMOGENIZING A PLURALISTIC CULTURE: PROPAGANDA DURING WORLD WAR I

∽ THE PROBLEM ∽

One week after Congress approved the war declaration that brought the United States into World War I, President Woodrow Wilson signed Executive Order 2594, which created the Committee on Public Information, designed to mobilize public opinion behind the war effort. Apparently there was considerable worry in the Wilson administration that the American public, which had supported neutrality and noninvolvement, would not rally to the war effort.

Wilson selected 41-year-old journalist and political ally George Creel to head the Committee on Public Information. Creel rapidly established voluntary press censorship, which made the committee essentially the overseer of all war and war-related news. The committee also produced films, engaged some 75,000 lecturers (called "Four Minute Men") who delivered approximately 7.5 million talks, commissioned posters intended to stir up support for the war and sell war bonds (700 poster designs were submitted, and more than 9 million posters were printed in 1918 alone), and engaged in numerous other activities to blend this ethnically and ideologically diverse nation into a homogeneous nation in support of the country's war effort and to discredit any potential opposition to America's entry into the war.

In this chapter, you will analyze the propaganda techniques of a modern nation at war. The evidence contains material sponsored or commissioned by the Committee on Public Information (posters, newspaper advertisements, selections of speeches by Four

CHAPTER 5

HOMOGENIZING
A PLURALISTIC
CULTURE:
PROPAGANDA
DURING WORLD
WAR I

Minute Men) as well as privately produced works (musical lyrics and commercial films) that tended to parallel the committee's efforts. Essentially, the question you are to answer is this: how did the United States mobilize public opinion in support of the nation's participation in World War I? In addition, what were the consequences, positive and negative, of this mobilization of public opinion?

On a larger scale, you should be willing to ponder other questions as well, although they do not relate directly to the evidence you will examine. To begin with, is government-sponsored propaganda during wartime a good thing? When it comes into conflict with the First Amendment's guarantees of freedom of speech, which should prevail? Finally, is there a danger that government-sponsored propaganda can be carried too far? Do you think that was the case during World War I?

BACKGROUND

By the early twentieth century, the United States had worldwide economic interests and even had acquired a modest colonial empire, but many Americans wanted to believe that they were insulated from world affairs and impervious to world problems. Two great oceans seemed to protect the nation from overseas threats, and the enormity of the country and comparative weakness of its neighbors appeared to secure it against all dangers. Let other nations waste their people and resources in petty wars over status and territory, Americans reasoned. The United States should stand above such greed or insanity, and certainly should not wade into foreign mud puddles.

To many Americans, European nations were especially suspect. For centuries, European nations had engaged in an almost ceaseless round of armed conflicts—wars for national unity, territory, or even religion or empire.

Moreover, in the eyes of many Americans, these bloody wars appeared to have solved little or nothing, and the end of one war seemed to be but a prelude to the next. Ambitious kings and their plotting ministers seemed to make Europe the scene of almost constant uproar, an uproar that many Americans saw as devoid of reason and morality. Nor did it appear that the United States, as powerful as it was, could have any effect on the unstable European situation.

For this reason, most Americans greeted news of the outbreak of war in Europe in 1914 with equal measures of surprise and determination not to become involved. They applauded President Wilson's August 4 proclamation of neutrality, his statement (issued two weeks later) urging Americans to be impartial in thought as well as in deed, and his insistence that the United States continue neutral commerce with all the belligerents. Few Americans protested German violation of Belgian neutrality. Indeed, most Americans (naively, as it turned out) believed that the United States both should and could remain aloof from the conflict in Europe.

But many factors pulled the United States into the conflict that later became known as World War I. America's economic prosperity to a large extent rested on commercial ties with Europe. United States trade with the Allies (England, France, Russia) exceeded $800 million in 1914, whereas trade with the Central Powers (Germany, Austria, Turkey) stood at approximately $170 million in that same year. Much of the trade with Great Britain and France was financed through loans from American banks, something President Wilson and Secretary of State William Jennings Bryan openly discouraged because both men believed that those economic interests might eventually draw the United States into the conflict. Indeed, Wilson and Bryan probably were correct. Nevertheless, American economic interests were closely tied to those of Great Britain and France. Thus a victory by the Central Powers might damage United States trade. As Wilson drifted to an acceptance of this fact, Bryan had to back down.

A second factor pulling the United States into the war was the deep-seated feelings of President Wilson himself. Formerly a constitutional historian (Wilson had been a college professor and university president before entering the political arena as a reform governor of New Jersey), Wilson had long admired the British people and their form of government. Although technically neutral, the president strongly, though privately, favored the Allies and viewed a German victory as unthinkable. Moreover, many of Wilson's key advisers and the people close to him were decidedly pro-British. Such was the opinion of the president's friend and closest adviser, Colonel Edward House, as well as that of Robert Lansing (who replaced Bryan as secretary of state)[1] and Walter Hines Page (ambassador to England). These men and others helped strengthen Wilson's strong political opinions and influence the president's changing position toward the war in Europe. Hence, although Wilson asked Americans to be neutral in thought as well as in deed, in fact he and his principal advisers were neither. More than once, the president chose to ignore British violations of America's neutrality. Finally, when it appeared that the Central Powers might outlast their enemies, Wilson was determined to intercede. It was truly an agonizing decision for the president, who had worked so diligently to keep his nation out of war.

A third factor affecting the United States' neutrality was the strong ethnic ties of many Americans to the Old World. Many Americans had been born in Europe, and an even larger number were the sons and daughters of European immigrants (Tables 1 and

---

1. Bryan resigned in 1915, in protest over what he considered Wilson's too sharp note to Germany over the sinking of the passenger liner *Lusitania*. Wilson called the act "illegal and inhuman." Bryan sensed that the Wilson administration was tilting away from neutrality.

CHAPTER 5

HOMOGENIZING
A PLURALISTIC
CULTURE:
PROPAGANDA
DURING WORLD
WAR I

1. Foreign-Born Population, by Country of Birth*

Country of Birth	Total Foreign Born
England	813,853
Scotland	254,570
Ireland	1,037,234
Germany	1,686,108
Austria	575,627
Hungary	397,283
Russia	1,400,495
Italy[2]	1,610,113

*Both this and Table 2 were compiled from the United States census of 1920, the closest census to America's entrance into World War I (1917). The figures on Ireland include Northern Ireland, and the figures on Russia include the Baltic States.

2. Native-Born Population of Foreign or Mixed Parentage, by Country of Origin

Country of Origin of Parents	Total Native-Born Children
England and Wales	1,864,345
Scotland	514,436
Ireland	3,122,013
Germany	5,346,004
Austria	1,235,097
Hungary	538,518
Russia	1,508,604
Italy	1,751,091

2). Although these people considered themselves to be, and were, Americans, some retained emotional ties to

2. Italy entered the war in 1914 on the side of the Central Powers. In March 1915, however, Italy switched sides, declaring war on Austria-Hungary in March 1915 and on Germany the next year.

Europe that they sometimes carried into the political arena—ties that could influence America's foreign policy.

Finally, as the largest neutral commercial power in the world, the United States soon became caught in the middle of the commercial warfare of the belligerents. With the declaration of war, Great Britain and Germany both threw up naval blockades. Great Britain's blockade was designed to cut the Central Powers off from war materiel. American commercial vessels bound for Germany were stopped, searched, and often seized by the British navy. Wilson protested British policy many times, but to no effect. After all, giving in to Wilson's protests would have deprived Britain of its principal military asset: the British navy.

Germany's blockade was even more dangerous, partly because the vast majority of American trade was with England and France. In addition, however, Germany's chief method of blockading the Allies was the use of the submarine, a comparatively new weapon in 1914. Because of the nature of the submarine (lethal while underwater, not equal to other fighting vessels on the surface), it was difficult for the submarine to remain effective and at the same time adhere to international law, such as the requirement that sufficient warning be given before sinking an enemy ship.[3] In 1915, hoping to terrorize the British into making peace, Germany unleashed its submarines in the Atlantic with orders to

3. International laws governing warfare at sea, as well as neutral shipping during wartime, were written in the mid-eighteenth century, more than one hundred years before the submarine became a potent seagoing weapon.

sink all ships flying Allied flags. In March, a German submarine sank the British passenger ship *Falaba.* Then on May 7, 1915, the British liner *Lusitania* was sunk with a loss of more than 1,000 lives, 128 of them American. Although Germany had published warnings in American newspapers specifically cautioning Americans not to travel on the *Lusitania,* and although it was ultimately discovered that the *Lusitania* had gone down so fast (in only eighteen minutes) because the British were shipping ammunition in the hold of the passenger ship, Americans were shocked by the Germans' actions on the high seas. Most Americans, however, continued to believe that the United States should stay out of the war and approved of Wilson's statement, issued three days after the *Lusitania* went to the bottom, that "there is such a thing as a man being too proud to fight."

Yet a combination of economic interests, German submarine warfare, and other events gradually pushed the United States toward involvement. In early February 1917, Germany announced a policy of unrestricted submarine warfare against all ships—belligerent and neutral alike. Ships would be sunk without warning if found to be in what Germany designated forbidden waters. Later that month, the British intercepted a secret telegram intended for the German minister to Mexico, stationed in Mexico City. In that telegram, German foreign secretary Arthur Zimmermann offered Mexico a deal: Germany would help Mexico retrieve territory lost to the United States in the 1840s if Mexico would make a military alliance with Germany and declare war on the United States in the event that the United States declared war on Germany. Knowing the impact that such a telegram would have on American public opinion, the British quickly handed the telegram over to Wilson, who released it to the press. From that point on, it was but a matter of time before the United States would become involved in World War I.

On March 20, 1917, President Wilson called his cabinet together at the White House to advise him on how to proceed in the deteriorating situation with Germany. Wilson's cabinet officers unanimously urged the president to call Congress into session immediately and ask for a declaration of war against Germany. When the last cabinet member had finished speaking, Wilson said, "Well, gentlemen, I think there is no doubt as to what your advice is. I thank you," and dismissed the meeting without informing the cabinet of his own intentions.

Yet even though Wilson had labored so arduously to keep the United States out of the war in Europe, by March 20 (or very soon thereafter) his mind was made up: the United States must make war on Germany. Typing out his war message on his own Hammond portable typewriter, Wilson was out of sorts and complained often of headaches. The president, devoted to peace and Progressive reform, was drafting the document he had prayed he would never have to write.

On April 2, 1917, President Wilson appeared in person before a joint session of Congress to deliver his war message. Congress was ready. On April 4, the Senate approved a war declaration (the vote was 82–6). The

CHAPTER 5

HOMOGENIZING
A PLURALISTIC
CULTURE:
PROPAGANDA
DURING WORLD
WAR I

House of Representatives followed suit two days later (with a vote of 373–50).[4]

At the outset of America's entry into the war, many government officials feared (incorrectly, as it turned out) that large blocs of Americans would not support the war effort. In 1917, the Bureau of the Census had estimated that approximately 4,662,000 people living in the United States had been born in Germany or in one of the other Central Powers.[5] As Tables 1 and 2 show, the United States also contained a large number of Irish Americans, many of whom were vehemently anti-British and hence emotionally sided with the Central Powers. Could this heterogeneous society be persuaded voluntarily to support the war effort? Could Americans of the same ethnic stock as the enemies be rallied to the cause?

Furthermore, there had been no decisive event to prompt the war declaration (some even thought the Zimmermann telegram was a British hoax). Would Americans support such a war with sufficient unanimity? No firing on Fort Sumter or blowing up of the battleship *Maine* had forced America's entrance into World War I. The *Lusitania* sinking had occurred two years before the war declaration. Without the obvious threat of having been attacked, would the American people stand together to defeat the faraway enemy? Could American isolationist and noninterventionist opinion, very strong as late as the presidential election of 1916, be overcome? To solidify the nation behind the war, Wilson created the Committee on Public Information.

THE METHOD

For George Creel and the Committee on Public Information, the purposes of propaganda were very clear:

1. Unite a multiethnic, pluralistic society behind the war effort

2. Attract a sufficient number of men to the armed services and elicit universal civilian support for those men

3. Influence civilians to support the war effort by purchasing war bonds or by other actions (such as limiting personal consumption or rolling bandages)

4. Influence civilians to put pressure on other civilians to refrain from

4. The fifty-six votes in the Senate and House against the declaration of war essentially came from three separate groups: senators and congressmen with strong German and Austrian constituencies, isolationists who believed the United States should not become involved on either side, and some Progressive reformers who maintained that the war would divert America's attention from political, economic, and social reforms.

5. No census had been taken since 1910, so this was a very rough guess. As shown in Table 1, the bureau's 1917 estimate was much too high, almost double the actual number of people living in the United States who had been born in Germany or in one of the other Central Powers.

antiwar comments, strikes, anti-draft activities, unwitting dispersal of information to spies, and other public acts that could hurt the war effort

To achieve these ends, propaganda techniques had to be used with extreme care. For propaganda to be effective, it would have to contain one or more of the following features:

1. Portrayal of American and Allied servicemen in the best possible light
2. Portrayal of the enemy in the worst possible light
3. Portrayal of the American and Allied cause as just and the enemy's cause as unjust
4. Message to civilians that they were being involved in the war effort in important ways
5. Communication of a sense of urgency to civilians

In this chapter, you are given the following six types of World War I propaganda to analyze, some of it produced directly by the Committee on Public Information and some produced privately but examined and approved by the committee:

1. Popular songs performed in music halls or vaudeville houses. Although the Committee on Public Information did not produce this material, it could have discouraged performances of "unpatriotic" material.
2. Newspaper and magazine advertisements produced directly by the Committee on Public Information.

3. Posters, approved by the committee and used for recruiting, liberty loans, and other purposes.
4. An editorial cartoon, produced privately but generally approved by the committee.
5. A selection of speeches by Four Minute Men, volunteers engaged by the committee to speak in theaters, churches, and other gathering places. Their speeches were not to exceed four minutes in length—hence, their name. The committee published a newsletter that offered suggestions and material for speaking topics.
6. A review of the documentary film *Pershing's Crusaders* (1918) and some advertising suggestions to theater owners concerning the film *Kultur.* The film industry was largely self-censored, but the committee could—and did—stop the distribution of film that, in its opinion, hurt the war effort. *Pershing's Crusaders* was a committee-produced film, whereas *Kultur* was a commercial production.

As you examine the evidence, you will see that effective propaganda operates on two levels. On the surface, there is the logical appeal for support to help win the war. On another level, however, certain images and themes are used to excite the emotions of the people for whom the propaganda is designed. As you examine the evidence, ask yourself the following questions:

1. For whom was this piece of propaganda designed?
2. What was this piece of propaganda trying to get people to think? To do?

CHAPTER 5

HOMOGENIZING
A PLURALISTIC
CULTURE:
PROPAGANDA
DURING WORLD
WAR I

3. What logical appeal was being made?
4. What emotional appeals were being made?
5. What might have been the results, positive and negative, of these kinds of appeals?

In songs, speeches, advertisements, and film reviews, are there key words or important images? Where there are illustrations (advertisements, posters, cartoons), what facial expressions and images are used? Finally, are there any common logical and emotional themes running through American propaganda during World War I? How did the United States use propaganda to mobilize public opinion during World War I? What were some of the consequences, positive and negative, of this type of propaganda?

⬭ THE EVIDENCE ⬭

Source 1 is a popular song by George M. Cohan, 1917.

1. "Over There."

Johnnie, get your gun,
Get your gun, get your gun,
Take it on the run,
On the run, on the run.
Hear them calling you and me,
Every son of liberty.
Hurry right away,
No delay, no delay.
Make your daddy glad
To have had such a lad.
Tell your sweetheart not to pine,
To be proud her boy's in line.

Chorus (repeat chorus twice)
Over there, over there,
Send the word, send the word over there—
That the Yanks are coming,
The Yanks are coming,
The drums rum-tumming
Ev'rywhere.
So prepare, say a pray'r,
Send the word, send the word to beware.
We'll be over, we're coming over,
And we won't come back till it's over
Over there.

Source 2 from Alfred E. Cornbise, *War as Advertised: The Four Minute Men and America's Crusade, 1917–1918* (Philadelphia: American Philosophical Society, 1984), p. 70.

2. Untitled Popular Song. [*To be sung to a variation of "My Country Tis of Thee."*]

Come, freemen of the land,
Come meet the great demand,
True heart and open hand,
 Take the loan!

For the hopes that prophets saw,
For the swords your brothers draw,
For liberty and law
 Take the loan!

CHAPTER 5

HOMOGENIZING
A PLURALISTIC
CULTURE:
PROPAGANDA
DURING WORLD
WAR I

Sources 3 through 5 from James R. Mock and Cedric Larson, *Words That Won the War: The Story of the Committee on Public Information* (Princeton: Princeton University Press, 1939), pp. 64, 169, 98.

3. Advertisement Urging Americans to Report the Enemy.

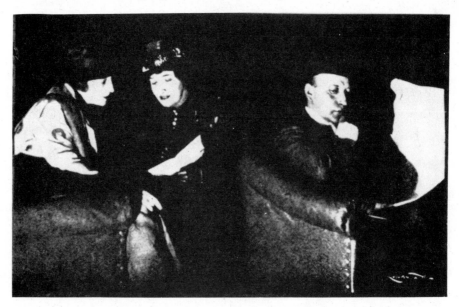

Spies *and* Lies

German agents are everywhere, eager to gather scraps of news about our men, our ships, our munitions. It is still possible to get such information through to Germany, where thousands of these fragments — often individually harmless — are patiently pieced together into a whole which spells death to American soldiers and danger to American homes.

But while the enemy is most industrious in trying to collect information, and his systems elaborate, he is *not* superhuman — indeed he is often very stupid, and would fail to get what he wants were it not deliberately handed to him by the carelessness of loyal Americans.

Do not discuss in public, or with strangers, any news of troop and transport movements, or bits of gossip as to our military preparations, which come into your possession.

Do not permit your friends in service to tell you — or write you — "inside" facts about where they are, what they are doing and seeing.

Do not become a tool of the Hun by passing on the malicious, disheartening rumors which he so eagerly sows. Remember he asks no better service than to have you spread his lies of disasters to our soldiers and sailors, gross scandals in the Red Cross, cruelties, neglect and wholesale executions in our camps, drunkenness and vice in the Expeditionary Force, and other tales certain to disturb American patriots and to bring anxiety and grief to American parents.

And do not wait until you catch someone putting a bomb under a factory. Report the man who spreads pessimistic stories, divulges — or seeks — confidential military information, cries for peace, or belittles our efforts to win the war.

Send the names of such persons, even if they are in uniform, to the Department of Justice, Washington. Give all the details you can, with names of witnesses if possible — show the Hun that we can beat him at his own game of collecting scattered information and putting it to work. The fact that you made the report will not become public.

You are in contact with the enemy today, just as truly as if you faced him across No Man's Land. In your hands are two powerful weapons with which to meet him — discretion and vigilance. *Use them.*

COMMITTEE   ON   PUBLIC   INFORMATION
8 JACKSON PLACE, WASHINGTON, D. C.

George Creel, Chairman
The Secretary of State
The Secretary of War
The Secretary of the Navy

Contributed through Division of Advertising  *United States Gov't Comm. on Public Information*

4. Advertisement for Fighting the Enemy by Buying Liberty Bonds.

Bachelor of Atrocities

IN the vicious guttural language of Kultur, the degree A. B. means Bachelor of Atrocities. Are you going to let the Prussian Python strike at your Alma Mater, as it struck at the University of Louvain?[4]

The Hohenzollern[5] fang strikes at every element of decency and culture and taste that your college stands for. It leaves a track so terrible that only whispered fragments may be recounted. It has ripped all the world-old romance out of war, and reduced it to the dead, black depths of muck, and hate, and bitterness.

You may soon be called to fight. But you are called upon right now to buy Liberty Bonds. You are called upon to economize in every way. It is sometimes harder to live nobly than to die nobly. The supreme sacrifice of life may come easier than the petty sacrifices of comforts and luxuries. You are called to exercise stern self-discipline. Upon this the Allied Success depends.

Set aside every possible dollar for the purchase of Liberty Bonds. Do it relentlessly. Kill every wasteful impulse, that America may live. Every bond you buy fires point-blank at Prussian Terrorism.

BUY U. S. GOVERNMENT BONDS FOURTH LIBERTY LOAN

Contributed through Division of Advertising

United States Gov't Comm. on Public Information

This space contributed for the Winning of the War by
A. T SKERRY, '84, and CYRILLE CARREAU, '04.

6. The University of Louvain, in Belgium, was pillaged and partially destroyed by German troops. Some professors were beaten and others killed, and the library (containing 250,000 books and manuscripts, some irreplaceable) was totally destroyed. The students themselves were home for summer vacation.

7. Hohenzollern was the name of the German royal family since the nation's founding in 1871. It had been the Prussian royal family since 1525.

CHAPTER 5

HOMOGENIZING
A PLURALISTIC
CULTURE:
PROPAGANDA
DURING WORLD
WAR I

5. Advertisement Contrasting the American Idea with the German Idea.

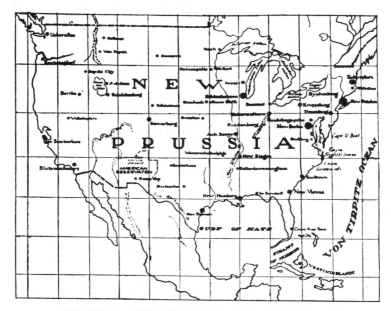

THE GERMAN IDEA

SHALL this war make Germany's word the highest law in the world? Read what she expects. Here are the words of her own spokesmen. Then ask yourself where Germany would have the United States stand after the war.

Shall we bow to Germany's wishes--assist German ambition?

No. The German idea must be so completely crushed that it will never again rear its venomous head.

It's a fight, as the President said, "to the last dollar, the last drop of blood."

THE AMERICAN IDEA

The President's Flag Day Speech, With Evidence of Germany's plans. 32 pages.

The War Message and the Facts Behind It. 32 pages.

The Nation in Arms. 16 pages.

Why We Fight Germany.

War, Labor and Peace.

THE GERMAN IDEA

Conquest and Kultur. 160 pages.

German War Practices. 96 pages.

Treatment of German Militarism and German Critics.

The German War Code.

COMMITTEE ON PUBLIC INFORMATION
8 JACKSON PLACE, WASHINGTON, D. C.

Contributed through Division of Advertising, United States Governm't Committee on Public Information

George Creel, Chairman
The Secretary of State
The Secretary of War
The Secretary of the Navy

This space contributed for the Winning of the War by

The Publisher of *Publisher*

Source 6 from *The James Montgomery Flagg Poster Book,* introduction by Susan E. Meyer (New York: Watson-Guptill Publications, 1975). Courtesy of the Library of Congress.

6. The Famous Uncle Sam Poster.

CHAPTER 5

HOMOGENIZING
A PLURALISTIC
CULTURE:
PROPAGANDA
DURING WORLD
WAR I

Source 7 from Peter Stanley, *What Did You Do in the War, Daddy?* (Melbourne: Oxford University Press, 1983), p. 55.

7. Poster Portraying Germany as a Raging Beast.

Sources 8 through 10 from *The James Montgomery Flagg Poster Book.*

8. Recruiting Poster.

9. Poster Depicting Our Relationship with Our Ally, England.

CHAPTER 5

HOMOGENIZING
A PLURALISTIC
CULTURE:
PROPAGANDA
DURING WORLD
WAR I

10. Poster Urging Americans to Buy Liberty Bonds.

Source 11 from Stanley, *What Did You Do in the War, Daddy?*, p. 65.

THE EVIDENCE

11. Poster for the Fourth Liberty Bond Campaign.

CHAPTER 5

HOMOGENIZING
A PLURALISTIC
CULTURE:
PROPAGANDA
DURING WORLD
WAR I

Source 12 from Joseph Darracott, ed., *The First World War in Posters* (New York: Dover Publications, 1974), p. 30.

12. Poster with Boy Scout Motto Promoting Liberty Bonds.

Source 13 from Darracott, *The First World War in Posters*, p. 30.

13. Promotional Poster for the Red Cross.

Source 14 from Anthony Crawford, *Posters in the George C. Marshall Research Foundation* (Charlottesville: University of Virginia Press, 1939), p. 30.

14. Poster Targeting American Women.

CHAPTER 5

HOMOGENIZING
A PLURALISTIC
CULTURE:
PROPAGANDA
DURING WORLD
WAR I

Sources 15 and 16 from Walton Rawls, *Wake Up, America! World War I and the American Poster* (New York: Abbeville Press, 1988), pp. 232, 129.

16. Our Boys Need Sox.

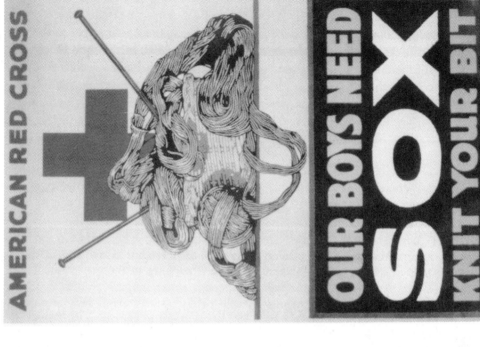

15. Americans All!

Source 17 from John Higham, *Strangers in the Land: Patterns of American Nativism,* 1860–1925 (New Brunswick, N.J.: Rutgers University Press, 1955), p. 210.

17. Editorial Cartoon. German American Dr. Karl Muck, Conductor of the Boston Symphony Orchestra, Needed a Police Escort When He Conducted a Concert in March 1918 in New York City.

CHAPTER 5

HOMOGENIZING
A PLURALISTIC
CULTURE:
PROPAGANDA
DURING WORLD
WAR I

Sources 18 through 21 from Cornbise, *War as Advertised: The Four Minute Men and America's Crusade,* pp. 72–73, 122, 60, 27.

18. Speech by a Four Minute Man.

Ladies and Gentlemen:

I have just received the information that there is a German spy among us—a German spy watching *us.*

He is around here somewhere, reporting upon you and me—sending reports about us to Berlin and telling the Germans just what we are doing with the Liberty Loan. From every section of the country these spies have been getting reports over to Potsdam[8]—not general reports but details—where the loan is going well and where its success seems weak, and what people are saying in each community.

For the German government is worried about our great loan. Those Junkers[9] fear its effect upon the German *morale.* They're raising a loan this month, too.

If the American people lend their billions now, one and all with a hip-hip-hurrah, it means that America is united and strong. While, if we lend our money half-heartedly, America seems weak and autocracy remains strong.

Money means everything now; it means quicker victory and therefore less bloodshed. We are *in* the war, and now Americans can have but *one* opinion, only *one* wish in the Liberty Loan.

Well, I hope these spies are getting their messages straight, letting Potsdam know that America is *hurling back* to the autocrats these answers:

For treachery here, attempted treachery in Mexico, treachery everywhere—*one billion.*

For murder of American women and children—*one billion more.*

For broken faith and promise to murder more Americans—*billions and billions more.*

And then we will add:

In the world fight for Liberty, our share—*billions and billions and billions and endless billions.*

Do not let the German spy hear and report that *you* are a slacker.

8. Potsdam (a suburb of Berlin) was where the kaiser lived.
9. Junkers were the Prussian nobility.

19. Part of a Speech by a Four Minute Man.

German agents are telling the people of this . . . race[10] through the South that if they will not oppose the German Government, or help our Government, they will be rewarded with Ford automobiles when Germany is in control here. They are told that 10 negroes are being conscripted to 1 white man in order that the Negro race may be killed off; and that the reason Germany went into Belgium was to punish the people of that country for the cruel treatment of the negroes in the Congo.

20. Poem Read by Four Minute Men: "It's Duty Boy."

My boy must never bring disgrace to his immortal sires—
At Valley Forge and Lexington they kindled freedom's fires,
John's father died at Gettysburg, mine fell at Chancellorsville;
While John himself was with the boys who charged up San Juan Hill.
And John, if he was living now, would surely say with me,
"No son of ours shall e'er disgrace our grand old family tree
By turning out a slacker when his country needs his aid."
It is not of such timber that America was made.
I'd rather you had died at birth or not been born at all,
Than know that I had raised a son who cannot hear the call
That freedom has sent round the world, its precious rights to save—
This call is meant for you, my boy, and I would have you brave;
And though my heart is breaking, boy, I bid you do your part,
And show the world no son of mine is cursed with craven heart;
And if, perchance, you ne'er return, my later days to cheer,
And I have only memories of my brave boy, so dear,
I'd rather have it so, my boy, and know you bravely died
Than have a living coward sit supinely by my side.
To save the world from sin, my boy, God gave his only son—
He's asking for MY boy, to-day, and may His will be done.

10. At the front lines in France, Germans barraged America's African American soldiers with leaflets urging them to desert (none did). One of those propaganda leaflets said, in part, "Do you enjoy the same rights as the white people do in America . . . or are you rather not treated over there as second-class citizens?" As to the charge of discrimination against African Americans by draft boards, there were numerous complaints that African Americans found it almost impossible to get exemptions from military service. In the end, about 31 percent of the African Americans who registered were called into service, as opposed to 26 percent of the registered whites. To counteract German propaganda, prominent African Americans were sent to France to lecture to the African American troops.

CHAPTER 5

HOMOGENIZING
A PLURALISTIC
CULTURE:
PROPAGANDA
DURING WORLD
WAR I

21. Poem Read by Four Minute Men.

Attention, Mr. Farmer Man, and listen now to me,
and I will try and show to you what I can plainly see.
Your Uncle Sam, the dear old man who's been so good to you,
is needing help and watching now to see what you will do.
Your Uncle's in the great world war and since he's entered in
it's up to every one of us to see that he shall win.
He's trying hard to "speed things up" and do it with a dash,
and so just now he's asking you to aid him with your cash.
Remember, all he asks of you is but a simple loan,
and every patriot comes across without a single moan.
Should Uncle Sammy once get mad (he will if you get lax),
he then will exercise his right, and make you pay a tax.
Should Kaiser Bill and all his hordes, once get across the Pond,
d'ye think he'll waste his time on you, and coax to take a bond?
Why no, siree. He'd grab and hold most everything he saw.
He'd take your farm, your stock and lands, your wife and babies all.
He'd make you work, he'd make you sweat, he'd squeeze you till you'd
groan.
So be a man, and come across. Let Uncle have that loan.

Source 22 from *Literary Digest,* June 8, 1918 (film review of *Pershing's
Crusaders*).

22. Seeing Our Boys "Over There."

Multiform are the war-activities of Uncle Sam. Whoever would have
thought of him a year ago as an *impresario* in moving pictures? In a small
way this has been one of his war-activities, but now he boldly challenges
competition with the biggest and launches his "Pershing's Crusaders" for
the benefit of the American Army, the American Navy, and the Allied War-
Relief. The initial performance at the Lyric Theater, New York, brought
out an audience that might have swelled to the dimensions of a Metropolitan Opera crowd if capacity had permitted. Mr. E. H. Sothern and our
former Ambassador to Germany, Mr. James W. Gerard, were present to
speak, but the pictures of the boys at the front were the thing, and the
country will eagerly await the sight of her sons in their present environ-

ment here and "over there." As described by the *New York Tribune,* we learn that—

> Whoever took the pictures have not depended on the popularity of the subject alone, for they show a fine attention to detail that is most satisfying, when everything connected with the boys at the front is of vital interest.

The pictures show "the mailed fist of the world," and altho this is merely symbolic, it is such a telling hit that it is impossible not to mention it. Germany and France are shown as tho modeled in clay, and then slowly, out of the center of Germany, rises a volcano, and a huge mailed fist appears scattering mud and sand and lava over France.

The first part of the picture shows how plots, fires, strikes, etc., were fomented by German agents in America; how America is putting her hand to the plow to feed the Allies; the huge cantonments which have sprung up to house the Army; cutting the khaki clothes by machinery. Other subjects are: What American women are doing; how the army shoes are made; feeding America's Army; mighty ships in the building; supremacy in the air will strike down the German vultures; our Navy; camouflage of the sea; our own submarines; in the aviation camps; baptizing the boys ordered to the front; tenderness and skill at the dressing-stations; the sniper's job; the victor of yesterday and the victor of to-morrow, and Pershing's crusaders and their Allies, who will get the Kaiser.

CHAPTER 5

HOMOGENIZING
A PLURALISTIC
CULTURE:
PROPAGANDA
DURING WORLD
WAR I

Source 23 from *The Moving Picture World,* September 28, 1918.

23. Promotional Tips to Theater Managers.

ADVERTISING AIDS FOR BUSY MANAGERS

"KULTUR."

William Fox Presents Gladys Brockwell in a Typical Example of the Brutality of the Wilhelmstrasse to Its Spy-slaves.

Cast.

Countess Griselda Von Arenburg,
                     Gladys Brockwell
Eliska ....Georgia Woodthorpe
René de Bornay ....William Scott
Baron von Zeller ....Willard Louis
Archduke Franz Ferdinand ....Charles Clary
Danilo ....Nigel de Brullier
The Kaiser ....William Burress
Emperor Franz Josef.........Alfred Fremont

Directed by Edward J. Le Saint.

The Story: The Kaiser decides that the time is ripe for a declaration of war, and sends word to his vassal monarch of Austria. René de Bornay is sent by France to discover what is being planned. He meets the Countess, who falls in love with him. She sickens of the spy system and declares that she is done with it, but is warned that she cannot withdraw. She is told to secure René's undoing, but instead procures his escape and in her own boudoir is stood against the wall and shot for saving the man whom she loves better than her life.

Feature Gladys Brockwell as Countess Griselda Von Arenburg and William Scott as René de Bornay.

Program and Advertising Phrases: Gladys Brockwell, Star of Latest Picture, Exposing Hun Brutality and Satanic Intrigue.
How An Austrian Countess Gave Her All for Democracy.
She Was an Emperor's Favorite Yet She Died for World Freedom.
Story of an Emperor's Mistress and a Crime That Rocked the World.
Daring Exposure of Scandals and Crimes in Hun Court Circles.
Astonishing Revelations of Hun Plots to Rape Democracy.

Advertising Angles: Do not offer this as a propaganda story, but tell that it is one of the angles of the merciless Prussian spy system about which has been woven a real romance. Play up the spy angle heavily both in your newspaper work and through window cards with such lines as "even the spies themselves hate their degradation." Miss Brockwell wears some stunning and daring gowns in this play, and with these special appeal can be made to the women.

∽ QUESTIONS TO CONSIDER ∽

Sources 1 and 2 are songs that were popular during World War I. Each song should be analyzed for its message. What was "Over There" urging young men to do? How would that song have appealed to the home front? What emotions were the lyrics trying to arouse? The untitled song was intended exclusively for the home front. What sacrifices were expected of Americans who did not go to war? How did the song appeal to these people?

The next evidence consists of three advertisements (Sources 3 through 5) produced by the Committee on Public Information. How are the Germans portrayed in "Spies and Lies"? In "Bachelor of Atrocities"? In "The German Idea"? How could Americans counteract Germans and their actions? Were there any dangers inherent in the kinds of activities the committee was urging on patriotic Americans?

In some ways, poster art, which follows in the Evidence section, is similar to editorial cartoons, principally because the artist has only one canvas or frame in which to tell his or her story. Yet the poster must be more arresting than the cartoon, must convey its message rapidly, and must avoid ambiguities or confusion. Posters were an extremely popular form of propaganda during World War I. Indeed, so popular were the posters of James Montgomery Flagg (1877–1960) that, along with other artists and entertainers, Flagg helped sell $1,000 liberty bonds by performing (in his case, painting posters) in front of the New

York Public Library. The well-known "Tell That to the Marines!" (Source 8) was created there.

As you examine the three posters[11] in Sources 6 through 8, determine their intended audience. What emotional appeal did each poster make? What feelings did each poster seek to elicit? The poster in Source 9 ("Side by Side") is quite different from its predecessors in this exercise. How is it different? What appeal was it making? The next two posters, Sources 10 and 11 ("Halt the Hun!" and "Remember Belgium"), were intended to encourage American civilians to buy Liberty Bonds. What logical and emotional appeals were being made? How are the two posters similar? How did they use innuendos to make their point?

The three posters in Sources 12 through 14 were each intended to elicit a different reaction from those who saw them. Yet they are remarkably similar in their logical and emotional appeals. What do these posters have in common? How are women portrayed in Sources 13 and 14?

Source 15 is a most interesting poster, given the role assigned to the Committee on Public Information and the government's fears. What emotion did this extraordinary work attempt to elicit? How does that poster appear to address the government's fears?

11. The first poster "I Want YOU for U.S. Army") by Flagg is the most famous American poster ever created. The idea was taken from a British poster by Alfred Leete, and Flagg drew himself as Uncle Sam. The poster is still used by the United States Army.

CHAPTER 5

HOMOGENIZING
A PLURALISTIC
CULTURE:
PROPAGANDA
DURING WORLD
WAR I

Source 16 was addressed to the home front. As opposed to posters urging Americans to buy Liberty Bonds (Sources 10, 11, and 12) or make similar financial contributions to the war effort (Sources 13 and 14), this poster made another demand on American women. Why do you think this poster was especially effective?

The editorial cartoon from the *New York Herald* (Source 17) is self-explanatory. What emotions does the cartoon elicit? What actions, intended or unintended, might have resulted from those emotions?

Sources 18 through 21, by the Four Minute Men, are from the Committee on Public Information's *Bulletin,* which was distributed to all volunteer speakers (they also received a letter of commendation and a certificate from President Wilson after the war). What logical and emotional appeals are made in each selection?

No sound films were produced in the United States before 1927. Until that time, a small orchestra or (more prevalent) a piano accompanied a film's showing. What dialogue there was—and there was not much—was done in subtitles. Therefore, the best means we have to learn about these films, short of actually viewing them, is to analyze movie reviews. The review presented in Source 22 is of the film *Pershing's Crusaders,* a documentary produced by the Committee on Public Information in 1918.[12] Can you tell from the review what logical and emotional appeals were made in the film?

The advertising aids for the film *Kultur* (Source 23) suggest a number of phrases and angles designed to attract audiences. What are the strongest emotional appeals suggested to theater owners? Do those same appeals also appear in the other evidence?

You must now summarize your findings and return to the central questions: How did the United States use propaganda to mobilize public opinion in support of our participation in World War I? What were the consequences, positive and negative, of the mobilization of public opinion?

∽ EPILOGUE ∾

The creation of the Committee on Public Information and its subsequent work show that the Wilson administration had serious doubts concerning whether the American people, multiethnic and pluralistic as they were, would support the war effort with unanimity. And, to be sure, there was opposition to American involvement in the war, not only from socialist Eugene Debs and the left but also from reformers Robert La Follette, Jane Addams, and others. As it turned out, however, the Wilson administration's worst fears proved groundless. Americans of all ethnic backgrounds overwhelmingly supported the war effort,

12. *Pershing's Crusaders* is in the National Archives in Washington, D.C.

sometimes rivaling each other in patriotic ardor. How much of this unanimity can be attributed to patriotism and how much to the propaganda efforts of the Committee on Public Information will never really be known. Yet, for whatever reason, it can be said that the war had a kind of unifying effect on the American people. Women sold Liberty Bonds, worked for agencies such as the Red Cross, rolled bandages, and cooperated in the government's effort to conserve food and fuel. Indeed, even African Americans sprang to the colors, reasoning, as did the president of Howard University, that service in the war might help them achieve long-withheld civil and political rights.

However, this homogenization was not without its price. Propaganda was so effective that it created a kind of national hysteria, sometimes with terrible results. Vigilante-type groups often shamefully persecuted German Americans, lynching one German American man of draft age for not being in uniform (the man was physically ineligible, having only one eye) and badgering German American children in and out of school. Many states forbade the teaching of German in schools, and a host of German words were purged from the language (sauerkraut became liberty cabbage, German measles became liberty measles, hamburgers became liberty steaks, frankfurters became hot dogs). The city of Cincinnati even banned pretzels from saloons. In such an atmosphere, many Americans lived in genuine fear of being accused of spying or of becoming victims of intimidation or violence. In a society intent upon homogenization, being different could be dangerous.

During such hysteria, one would expect the federal government in general and the Committee on Public Information in particular to have attempted to dampen the more extreme forms of vigilanteism. However, it seemed as if the government had become the victim of its own propaganda. The postmaster general (Albert Burleson), empowered to censor the mail, looking for examples of treason, insurrection, or forcible resistance to laws, used his power to suppress all socialist publications, all anti-British and pro-Irish mail, and anything that he believed threatened the war effort. One movie producer, Robert Goldstein, was sentenced to ten years in prison for releasing his film *The Spirit of '76* (about the American Revolution) because it portrayed the British in an unfavorable light.[13] Socialist party leader Eugene Debs was given a similar sentence for criticizing the war in a speech in Canton, Ohio.[14] The left-wing Industrial Workers of the World (IWW) was broken. Freedom of speech, press, and assembly were violated countless times, and numerous lynchings, whippings, and tar-and-featherings occurred. Excesses by both government and private individuals were as effective in *forcing* homogeneity as were the voluntary efforts of American people of all backgrounds.

13. This gave rise to a court case with the improbable title *United States v. The Spirit of '76*.
14. Debs was indicted the day before he made his speech. He spent two years in prison.

CHAPTER 5

HOMOGENIZING
A PLURALISTIC
CULTURE:
PROPAGANDA
DURING WORLD
WAR I

Once the hysteria had begun, it is doubtful whether even President Wilson could have stopped it. Yet Wilson showed no inclination to do so, even stating that dissent was not appreciated by the government. Without the president to reverse the process, the hysteria continued unabated.

Before the outbreak of World War I, anti-immigrant sentiment had been growing, although most Americans seem to have believed that the solution was to Americanize the immigrants rather than to restrict their entrance. But the drive toward homogenization that accompanied America's war hysteria acted to increase cries for restricting further immigration and to weaken champions of the "melting pot." As restriction advocate Madison Grant wrote in 1922, "The world has seen many such [racial] mixtures and the character of a mongrel race is only just beginning to be understood at its true value. . . . Whether we like to admit it or not, the result of the mixture of two races . . . gives us a race reverting to the more ancient, generalized and lower type." Labor leaders, journalists, and politicians called for immigration restrictions, and a general immigration restriction (called the National Origins Act) became law in 1924.

This insistence on homogenization also resulted in the Red Scare of 1919, during which Attorney General A. Mitchell Palmer violated many people's civil liberties in a series of raids, arrests, and deportations directed largely against recent immigrants. As

seen, the efforts to homogenize a pluralistic nation could have an ugly side.

As Americans approached the Second World War, some called for a revival of the Committee on Public Information. Yet President Franklin Roosevelt rejected this sweeping approach. The Office of War Information was created, but its role was a restricted one. Even so, Japanese Americans were subjected to relocation and humiliation in one of the more shameful episodes of recent American history. And although propaganda techniques were sometimes more subtle, they nevertheless displayed features that would cause Americans to hate their enemies and want to destroy them. Japanese especially were portrayed as barbaric. A good example is Source 24. In general, however, a different spirit pervaded the United States during World War II, a spirit generally more tolerant of American pluralism and less willing to stir Americans into an emotional frenzy.

And yet the possibility that propaganda will create mass hysteria and thus endanger the civil rights of some Americans is present in every national crisis, especially in wartime. In the "total wars" of the twentieth century, in which civilians played as crucial a role as fighting men (in factories, in training facilities for soldiers, and in shipping soldiers and materiel to the front), the mobilization of the home front was a necessity. But could that kind of mobilization be carried too far?

Source 24 from Stanley, *What Did You Do in the War, Daddy?*, p. 99.

24. United States Army Poster from World War II.

CHAPTER 6

THE "NEW" WOMAN OF THE 1920s:
IMAGE AND REALITY

∽ THE PROBLEM ∾

With the publication of his novel *Main Street* in 1920, American author Sinclair Lewis produced the first of several best sellers. This novel was especially popular among college students, perhaps because many of them identified with the young protagonist, Carol, a so-called new woman of the early twentieth century—college educated, young, attractive, idealistic, ambitious, and "modern." The novel begins as Carol, who has graduated from a coeducational college in the Midwest and then drifted into library school in Chicago, returns to St. Paul, Minnesota, as a librarian. Bored, lonely, and dissatisfied with her job, she soon meets Dr. Will Kennicott, more than twelve years her senior. After a brief courtship, they marry and return to his hometown of Gopher Prairie.

In the small town of Gopher Prairie, the young bride finds narrow-mindedness, conformity, vicious gossip, and rigid insistence on traditional male and female roles. None of her efforts to improve her situation—town beautification plans, a community theater, a reading and discussion group—is successful. With the birth of a child, Carol feels more trapped and desperate. Finally, determined to find a better life, she separates from her husband and moves to Washington, D.C., with her young son. There she works as a government clerk, rents an apartment, and makes a lively new circle of friends. After a year, her husband comes to visit her, and five months later, pregnant again, she returns to Gopher Prairie for good.

At the end of the novel, Carol Kennicott passionately defends her rebellion and her aspirations for women, crying out that she may have failed, but she tried her best. "Sure. . . . feels like it might snow tomorrow," her husband replies. "Have to be thinking about putting up the storm windows pretty soon."

Was there a "new" woman who came of age in the 1920s? Were young women liberated from outmoded expectations based on gender? In this chapter, the central question asks you to analyze both the images and the realities of the new woman as portrayed in best sellers and nonfiction from the 1920s.

BACKGROUND

The 1920s have caught the imaginations of both historians and the general public, who have, nevertheless, found the period difficult and elusive to characterize. Marked at its beginning by the conclusion of the Great War (which we now call World War I) and at its end by the disastrous stock market crash of 1929, this decade seemed special even to those people living at the time. Many of them called it the Jazz Age. It was in some ways an era of incredibly rapid changes, most noticeably in the economic and cultural aspects of American life. Some of these changes raised very real questions about the values and assumptions of an older, more rural way of life. Indeed, one useful way to examine the decade is in terms of the strains and conflicts between pre–World War I attitudes, beliefs, and behaviors and those of twentieth-century modernism.

Economically, after some postwar dislocations in 1920 and 1921, the country seemed to be enjoying enormous prosperity. Mass production of new goods fed consumer demand fueled by seductive advertising, and personal worth increasingly became identified with possessing up-to-date material goods. Business practices and values were widely admired, imitated, and accepted by the general public, as corporate mergers and the development of chain stores standardized and homogenized the goods and services available to customers in all sections of the country. Like Henry Ford, corporate leaders soon came to understand that better-paid workers could buy more products and that more satisfied workers produced more. Management transformed its hostility toward organized labor into "corporate paternalism," an approach to labor relations that reduced labor union membership during the decade. Technological breakthroughs in both pure and applied science, as well as in medicine, seemed to promise better and healthier lives for all Americans. That farmers, miners, and a few other sectors of the economy were not sharing in this prosperity did not seem very important.

Continuity rather than change characterized the politics of the decade. With the exception of the presidential election of 1928, which pitted old stock American, Protestant, "dry," Republican, rural, small-town candidate Herbert Hoover against Democrat Alfred Smith, who seemed to represent the newer, ethnic, Catholic, "wet" immigrants from urban areas, American politics was business as usual. The three conservative Republican presidents—Warren Harding, Calvin Coolidge, and Herbert Hoover—in theory opposed intervening in the economy but in practice were pro-business in their actions. From the scandalous, graft-ridden administration of Warren Harding, the farm bill veto and strikebreaking activities of Calvin Coolidge, and the anti-Progressive decisions of the United States Supreme Court, to the short-lived flurry of hope for a new Progressive party under the leadership of Senator Robert La Follette, little positive change was achieved.

What seemed most obvious to the majority of people were the rapid cultural changes taking place in American society. Urbanization, along with the radio and movies, made possible the rise of a truly national mass culture. Radio listeners in all parts of the country could enjoy the new music, especially jazz, and the new spectator sports, such as baseball and football. Even small cities had movie theaters. In Muncie, Indiana (population thirty-five thousand in 1920), there were nine theaters that showed more than twenty different films every week. Because of the rapidity of communication, such varied individuals as baseball player George Herman "Babe" Ruth, aviator Charles Lindbergh, and

English Channel swimmer Gertrude Ederle became widely admired national heroes. The proliferation and popularity of mass-circulation magazines for both middle- and working-class readers were paralleled by the success of the new middle-class book clubs, which created instant best sellers, both in fiction and nonfiction. Some serious writers of the Lost Generation left the country; others stayed home and wrote critically of the materialism and values of the era. And in the Harlem Renaissance, a new generation of African American authors found their voice and wrote about the strengths of their heritage.

Perhaps the single most important factor in changing the way Americans lived in this era was the automobile. When asked about changes that had taken place in his lifetime, one long-time Muncie resident replied, "I can tell you what's happening in just four letters: A-U-T-O!" The automobile offered the freedom to live farther away from one's place of work, visit other nearby towns, and go away for a vacation. For young people, access to an automobile meant freedom from chaperons or curious neighbors, as serious courtship was replaced by casual dating. By the 1920s, the automobile also had become an important status symbol for both youths and their parents.

Such sweeping changes were not without opposition, and the twenties witnessed a series of reactions against the forces of modernism. Feeling overwhelmed by the late nineteenth- and early twentieth-century influx of poorer immigrants from southern and eastern Europe, Congress established a temporary and then a permanent quota system to bar them. These laws marked the abandonment of the traditional American policy of welcoming those who immigrated for economic opportunity.

The twenties also saw the rise of a new Ku Klux Klan, for the first time popular in urban areas and outside the South, dedicated to "100 percent Americanism" and devoted to enforcing the values of a nineteenth-century rural America. Two famous trials of the decade, the Sacco and Vanzetti case against Italian anarchists convicted of committing a murder during a payroll robbery and the Scopes case in which a teacher was found guilty of breaking Tennessee law by teaching about evolution, highlighted the social and cultural strains inherent in the conflict between the older values of rural, small-town America and modernism.

Perhaps nowhere were these strains more evident than in the heated debates of the decade about the proper place and roles of women. There was no doubt in the minds of contemporary observers that women's roles were changing. The Nineteenth Amendment, granting women the vote, had been ratified in 1920, setting off wild speculations about the impact women voters might have on politics. Transforming their organization into the League of Women Voters, the leaders of the National American Woman's Suffrage Association urged citizenship education and took a neutral, bipartisan position on candidates. Thus voting patterns did not change much. Social feminists did successfully lobby for the Sheppard-Towner maternal and infant health care bill, although

their efforts to ratify the Child Labor Amendment met with defeat. The more radical feminists of the National Woman's Party surveyed the remaining legal discriminations against women and, in 1923, proposed an Equal Rights Amendment (ERA), which would have required that all laws apply equally to men and women. Those women who favored protective labor laws for women opposed the ERA, however, and feminists, all of whom wanted to expand women's opportunities and choices, were once again divided over goals and strategies.

Economically, women continued to enter the work force but were clustered in "women's jobs." Approximately one in four women worked for pay. Most women workers were young and unmarried, although more married women were taking paid employment during the twenties. Openings for women in the service sector expanded, as did clerical jobs and a limited number of professional positions. But women in general were not taken seriously as workers. Employers believed that they worked only to earn "pin money" for unnecessary purchases and that they would quit their jobs as soon as they could. Married women who worked carried the double burden of paid employment and unpaid housework and often faced public disapproval as well. In spite of unequal pay and limited employment opportunities, many "new" women of the twenties worked diligently and expected to rise to higher positions on the basis of their merit. This was especially true of women with high school and college educations.

Culturally, there were noticeable changes in the appearance and behavior of younger women. The new woman had begun to emerge well before World War I, but in the 1920s, popularized by the media and the cartoons of John Held, Jr., a single stereotype began to dominate: the flapper. The flapper, so called because of the short-lived fad of wearing unbuckled galoshes that flapped when one walked, had short "bobbed" hair and wore cosmetics, short skirts, and dangling beads. She often smoked and even drank in public, and she presented herself as a "good sport" and "pal" to men of her own age. Flirting with and dating many different young men, she often seemed to care only about dancing and having fun. Older Americans were appalled by the appearance and outraged by the behavior of this 1920s woman. Worried and upset about the practice of "petting" (engaging in sexual intimacies that usually stopped just short of sexual intercourse), Americans complained that the new woman was completely immoral.

Of course, as historian Paul Carter has pointed out, there was another side to the twenties, and only a small minority of women were flappers. Nevertheless, fashion responded to the flapper style, middle-aged married women adopted variations of it, and even mail-order catalogues intended for rural and small-town consumers featured models with short hair and skimpy skirts. Films, novels, nonfiction, mass-circulation magazines, and advertisements all portrayed the new woman, investigated the dilemmas she faced, and reached conclusions about her life based on their own presuppositions and value judgments.

In this chapter, you will be analyzing both best-selling fiction and some selected nonfiction to determine the degree to which there was a new woman who came of age in the 1920s. To do so, you will need to compare the image of the new woman with some of the realities of her life.

⌒ THE METHOD ⌒

Historians must always be aware of the possibility that an *image*—how a person or a particular time appeared—may be quite different from its historical *reality*—how that person or era actually was. The independent ethical cowboy, the docile happy slave, and the passive oppressed Victorian wife and mother are all examples of historically inaccurate images. Such images are usually culturally constructed.

Sometimes, as in the case of the new woman of the 1920s, the image is created by contemporaries who are attempting to understand their own times. The image may also be created at a later time. For example, the story of George Washington, who was so honest that he would not lie about chopping down his father's cherry tree, is a consciously developed and accepted image created by Americans who were seeking national heroes in an uncertain and difficult period of history.

The image of the new woman of the 1920s came from many sources including journalism, films, and advertising. In this problem, you will be using only two kinds of evidence, fiction and nonfiction, to determine both the image of the new woman—how she was portrayed—and the reality—how different from previous women she actually was.

Since the nineteenth century, women have provided the bulk of the readership for popular novels, often those written by other women. In the 1920s, book clubs patronized by middle-class subscribers chose book-of-the-month selections on the basis of their potential appeal to club members and, in the process, helped to create widely read and discussed best sellers. Another phenomenon of the 1920s was the influx of students on college campuses. Certain books became fads, and most students read them. The excerpts from the novels that you will be analyzing here are examples of these kinds of popular fiction. Describe the image of the new woman portrayed in each novel: How does she look? What do others think about her? How does she feel about herself? What does she do? What happens to her?

When a resident of Muncie submitted a story to *Live Stories*, the magazine rejected it, stating that "stories should embody picturesque settings for action; they should also present situations of high emotional character, rich in sentiment. A moral conclusion is essential." Although our own modern fiction often does not contain a "moral conclusion" or message, popular fiction in the 1920s almost always did. When you analyze the excerpts from the best-selling novels of the twenties, also ask yourself questions about the conclusions: Who wins? Who loses? Why?

It would be a mistake, however, to depend solely on fiction to understand the past. In this exercise, you will also be reading three nonfiction excerpts from two books and an article. Reformers, especially Progressives of the late nineteenth and early twentieth centuries, used nonfiction and documentary photographs extensively to educate the public about problems created by rapid industrialization and urbanization. By the 1920s, there was a large middle-class audience for nonfiction. Serious books such as H. G. Wells's *Outline of History* and Will Durant's *The Story of Philosophy* each sold over a million copies. These books were obviously educational. Other nonfiction, such as *Woman and the New Race*, tried to persuade readers to support a particular course of action. *Middletown* documented conditions and attitudes through direct field research and "Feminist—New Style" sought to explain the times in which its readers were living. Nonfiction should be both compared to and contrasted with fiction from the same historical period to provide a more complete understanding of our history.

⚬ **THE EVIDENCE** ⚬

FICTION

Source 1 from E. M. Hull, *The Sheik* (Boston: Small, Maynard and Company, 1921), pp. 1–2, 4, 10–11, 35, 259, 272–273, 275.

1. Excerpts from E. M. Hull's *The Sheik*.

[*The novel begins at a hotel in French Africa, where a farewell dance is being held for the young Diana Mayo, a "new" woman who is about to leave on a month-long trip through the desert. Lady Conway is talking with a young man about Diana's proposed trip.*]

. . . "I thoroughly disapprove of the expedition of which this dance is the inauguration. I consider that even by contemplating such a tour alone into the desert with no chaperon or attendant of her own sex, with only native camel drivers and servants, Diana Mayo is behaving with a recklessness and impropriety that is calculated to cast a slur not only on her own reputation, but also on the prestige of her country. I blush to think of it. . . . The girl herself seemed, frankly, not to understand the seriousness of her position, and was very flippant and not a little rude. I wash my hands of the whole affair. . . ."

[*Diana, who has a reputation for arrogance, is there with her older brother, who looks bored.*]

. . . By contrast, the girl at his side appeared vividly alive. She was only of medium height and very slender, standing erect with the easy, vigorous carriage of an athletic boy, her small head poised proudly. Her scornful mouth and firm chin showed plainly an obstinate determination, and her deep blue eyes were unusually clear and steady. The long, curling black lashes that shaded her eyes and the dark eyebrows were a foil to the thick crop of loose, red-gold curls that she wore short, clubbed about her ears. . . .

[*At the dance, one of Diana's admirers begs her not to take the trip, confessing that he is in love with her and worried about her safety because she is so beautiful. When he tries to hold her hand, she pulls away.*]

. . . "Please stop. I am sorry. We have been good friends, and it has never occurred to me that there could be anything beyond that. I never thought that you might love me. I never thought of you in that way at all. . . . I am very content with my life as it is. Marriage for a woman means the end of independence, that is marriage with a man who is a man, in spite of all that the most modern woman may say. I have never obeyed any one in my life; I do not wish to try the experiment. I am very sorry to have hurt you. You've been a splendid pal, but that side of life does not exist for me. . . . A man to me is just a companion with whom I ride or shoot or fish; a pal, a comrade, and that's just all there is to it." . . .

[*In spite of everyone's objections, Diana sets off on horseback with an Arab guide and servants she has hired. Before they have gone very far, a large caravan passes them.*]

. . . One of two of the camels carried huddled figures, swathed and shapeless with a multitude of coverings, that Diana knew must be women. The contrast between them and herself was almost ridiculous. It made her feel stifled even to look at them. . . . The thought of those lives filled her with aversion. . . .

[*When night falls, Diana's party is attacked by a group of Arabs, and she is kidnapped and taken to their camp, where Sheik Ahmed Ben Hassan, who masterminded the kidnapping, has sex with her against her will. In spite of herself, she gradually falls in love with him during the next two months. But she pretends to be cold and uncaring for fear he will get tired of her and leave her. Out for a ride with a servant, she is captured by the Sheik's enemy, and when the Sheik tries to rescue her, he is badly wounded. While the Sheik is still unconscious, Diana learns that he is not really an Arab but the son of an English aristocrat and a Spanish noblewoman, adopted by the Arabs after his mother died in the desert.*]

. . . He must live, even if his life meant death to her hopes of happiness; that was nothing compared with his life. She loved him well enough to sacrifice anything for him. If he only lived she could even bear to be put out of his life. It was only he that mattered, his life was everything. . . . If she could only die for him. . . .

[*The Sheik recovers. Convinced that he has grown tired of her, Diana gives in to depression.*]

She wondered numbly what would become of her. It did not seem to matter much. Nothing mattered now that he did not want her any more. The old life was far away, in another world. She could never go back to it. She did not care. It was nothing to her. It was only here in the desert, in Ahmed Ben Hassan's arms, that she had become alive, that she had learned what life really meant, that she had waked both to happiness and sorrow. . . . If she could have had the promise of a child. . . . A child that would be his and hers, a child—a boy with the same passionate dark eyes, the same crisp brown hair, the same graceful body, who would grow up as tall and strong, as brave and fearless as his father. Surely he must love her then. . . . Beside her love, everything dwindled into nothingness. He was her life, he filled her horizon. Honour itself was lost in the absorbing passion of her love. He had stripped it from her and she was content that it should lie at his feet. He had made her nothing, she was his toy, his plaything, waiting to be thrown aside. . . .

[*At the end of the novel, after Diana tries to kill herself rather than be sent back, the Sheik admits that he loves her.*]

Source 2 from Percy Marks, *The Plastic Age* (New York: The Century Company, 1924), pp. 157, 174, 212–213, 216–217, 223–224, 244–245, 248–249, 265, 288, 320, 322.

2. Excerpts from Percy Marks's *The Plastic Age.*

[*The novel begins as Hugh Carver, a high school track star and likable, clean-cut young man, arrives for his freshman year at the all-male college of Sanford. He pledges the same fraternity to which his father belonged, studies just enough to get by with average grades, and spends endless hours discussing life and "girls" with his friends. When one of the upperclassmen suggests that if they went out with "cheap women" it would take their minds off sex, another student disagrees.*]

. . . "The old single standard fight," he said, propping his head on his hand. "I don't see any sense in scrapping about that any more. We've got a single standard now. The girls go just as fast as the fellows."

"Oh, that's not so," Hugh exclaimed. "Girls don't go as far as fellows."

Ferguson smiled pleasantly at Hugh and drawled; "Shut up, innocent; you don't know anything about it. I tell you the old double standard has gone all to hell." . . .

[*In his sophomore year, Hugh—who has just started drinking alcohol—and his room-mate, Carl, get drunk and go into town, where two prostitutes try to pick them up.*]

. . . They were crude specimens, revealing their profession to the most casual observer. If Hugh had been sober they would have sickened him, but he wasn't sober; he was joyously drunk and the girls looked very desirable. . . .

[*A football player prevents Hugh from going with the prostitutes, but Carl goes anyway. A few weeks later, Carl and seven others are diagnosed with venereal disease and expelled from Sanford. Hugh's next adventure takes place at a fraternity dance. He doesn't have a date, but he sees a young woman, Hester, whom he has met. He dances with her.*]

"Hot stuff, isn't it?" she asked lazily.

Hugh was startled. Her breath was redolent of whisky. . . .

As the evening wore on he danced with a good many girls who had whisky breaths. One girl clung to him as they danced and whispered, "Hold me up, kid; I'm ginned." He had to rush a third, a dainty blond child, to the porch railing. She wasn't a pretty sight as she vomited into the garden; nor did Hugh find her gasped comment, "The seas are rough to-night," amusing. Another girl went sound asleep in a chair and had to be carried up-stairs and put to bed. . . .

[*Later that evening, Hester drags Hugh into the darkened dining room of the fraternity house and tells him she wants to pet. Going to get one of the chaperon's coats, he walks in on a couple in bed. Disgusted, he leaves the dance.*]

He thought of Hester Sheville, of her whisky breath, her lascivious pawing—and his hands clenched. "Filthy little rat," he said aloud, "the stinkin', rotten rat."

Then he remembered that there had been girls there who hadn't drunk anything, girls who somehow managed to move through the whole orgy calm and sweet. His anger mounted. It was a hell of a way to treat a decent girl, to ask her to a dance with a lot of drunkards and soused rats.

[*The summer of his junior year, Hugh visits his friend Norry Parker, whose family has a cottage on Long Island. There Hugh meets lots of "new" women.*]

. . . They flirted with him, perfected his "petting" technique, occasionally treated him to a drink, and made no pretense of hiding his attraction for them.

At first Hugh was startled and a little repelled, but he soon grew to like the frankness, the petting, and the liquor; and he was having a much too exciting time to pause often for criticism of himself or anybody else. . . .

[*Just before he leaves, Hugh meets Cynthia Day and falls in love with her.*]

. . . Suddenly Hugh was attracted by a girl he had never seen before. She wore a red one-piece bathing-suit that revealed every curve of her slender, boyish figure. . . . Her hair was concealed by a red bathing-cap, but Hugh guessed that it was brown; at any rate, her eyes were brown and very large. She had an impudent little nose and full red lips. . . .

[*After returning to college that fall, Hugh and Cynthia write to each other regularly, and she accepts his invitation to come to Sanford for prom week.*]

When Hugh eventually saw Cynthia standing on a car platform near him, he shouted to her and held his hand high in greeting. She saw him and waved back, at the same time starting down the steps.

She had a little scarlet hat pulled down over her curly brown hair, and she wore a simple blue traveling-suit that set off her slender figure perfectly. Her eyes seemed bigger and browner than ever, her nose more impudently tilted, her mouth more supremely irresistible. Her cheeks were daintily rouged, her eyebrows plucked into a thin arch. She was New York from her small pumps to the expensively simple scarlet hat. . . .

[*Later, Norry Parker has a talk with Hugh.*]

"I never expected you to fall in love with Cynthia, Hugh," he said in his gentle way. "I'm awfully surprised. . . ."

Hugh paused in taking off his socks. "Why not?" he demanded. "She's wonderful."

"You're so different."

"How different? . . ."

Norry was troubled. "I don't think I can explain exactly," he said slowly. "Cynthia runs with a fast crowd, and she smokes and drinks—and you're —well, you're idealistic."

Hugh pulled off his underclothes and laughed as he stuck his feet into slippers and drew on a bathrobe. "Of course, she does. All the girls do now. She's just as idealistic as I am." . . .

[*That night at the prom, Hugh and Cynthia dance to a "hot" jazz band, get drunk, and go back to Norry's dorm room. Just as they are about to make love, Norry comes in and escorts Cynthia back to her room. Hugh is ashamed and hung over the next morning; Cynthia decides to return to New York. When she asks if he loves her, Hugh says yes, but she knows that he's lying.*]

"I'm twenty and lots wiser about some things than you are. I've been crazy about you—I guess I am kinda yet—and I know that you thought you were in love with me. I wanted you to have hold of me all this time. That's all that mattered. It was—was your body, Hugh. You're sweet and fine, and I respect you, but I'm not the kid for you to run around with. I'm too fast. I woke up early this morning, and I've done a lot of thinking since. You know what we came near doing last night? Well, that's all we want each other for. We're not in love." . . .

[*After prom week, Hugh goes into training for a big track meet and applies himself to his studies. Elected to the prestigious senior council, Hugh begins to plan for his future: graduate school at Harvard and teaching. When Norry returns from Christmas holidays, he tells Hugh that he saw Cynthia and that she looked terrible.*]

. . . "What's the matter? Is she sick?"

Norry shook his head. "No, I don't think she is exactly sick," he said gravely, "but something is the matter with her. You know, she has been going an awful pace, tearing around like crazy. I told you that, I know, when I came back in the fall. Well, she's kept it up, and I guess she's about all in. I couldn't understand it. Cynthia's always run with a fast bunch, but she's never had a bad name. She's beginning to get one now." . . .

[*After this conversation, Hugh writes a brief note to Cynthia asking what's wrong. She replies that she loves him and had tried to give him up because she knew she was bad for him. Confused, Hugh continues to correspond with her and just before graduation asks her to meet him in New York. He can stay only two hours, so they go to a coffee shop to talk. Hugh asks her to marry him, then changes his mind. They discuss prom night, and Hugh tells Cynthia that he has not been drunk at all since then and has regained his self-respect. Cynthia thinks about her own partying.*]

She did not say that she knew that he did not love her; she did not tell him how much his quixotic chivalry moved her. Nor did she tell him that she knew only too well that she could lead him to hell, as he said, but that that was the only place she could lead him. . . .

[*Again, Hugh asks her to marry him after he has completed his graduate education and become established. She refuses his offer, lying and saying that she does not love him. She also points out that he shouldn't marry her if he doesn't love her.*]

"Of course not." He looked down in earnest thought and then said softly, his eyes on the table, "I'm glad that you feel that way, Cynthia." She bit her lip and trembled slightly. "I'll confess now that I don't think that I love you either. You sweep me clean off my feet when I'm with you, but when I'm away from you I don't feel that way. I think love must be something more than we feel for each other." He looked up and smiled boyishly. "We'll go on being friends anyhow, won't we?"

Somehow she managed to smile back at him. "Of course," she whispered, and then after a brief pause added: "We had better go now. Your train will be leaving pretty soon." . . .

NONFICTION

Source 3 from Margaret Sanger, *Woman and the New Race* (New York: Brentano's 1920), pp. 93–95.

3. Excerpt from Margaret Sanger's *Woman and the New Race.*

The problem of birth control has arisen directly from the effort of the feminine spirit to free itself from bondage. Woman herself has wrought that bondage through her reproductive powers and while enslaving herself has enslaved the world. The physical suffering to be relieved is chiefly woman's. Hers, too, is the love life that dies first under the blight of too prolific breeding. Within her is wrapped up the future of the race—it is hers to make or mar. All of these considerations point unmistakably to one fact—it is woman's duty as well as her privilege to lay hold of the means of freedom. Whatever men may do, she cannot escape the responsibility. For ages she has been deprived of the opportunity to meet this obligation. She is now emerging from her helplessness. Even as no one can share the suffering of the overburdened mother, so no one can do this work for her. Others may help, but she and she alone can free herself.

The basic freedom of the world is woman's freedom. A free race cannot be born of slave mothers. A woman enchained cannot choose but give a measure of that bondage to her sons and daughters. No woman can call herself free who does not own and control her body. No woman can call herself free until she can choose consciously whether she will or will not be a mother.

It does not greatly alter the case that some women call themselves free because they earn their own livings, while others profess freedom because they defy the conventions of sex relationship. She who earns her own living gains a sort of freedom that is not to be undervalued, but in quality and in quantity it is of little account beside the untrammeled choice of mating or not mating, of being a mother or not being a mother. She gains food and clothing and shelter, at least, without submitting to the charity of her companion, but the earning of her own living does not give her the development of her inner sex urge, far deeper and more powerful in its outworkings than any of these externals. In order to have that development, she must still meet and solve the problem of motherhood.

Source 4 from Robert S. Lynd and Helen M. Lynd, *Middletown: A Study in American Culture* (New York: Harcourt, Brace and Company, 1929), pp. 256–257, 112, 114–117, 120–121, 123, 131, 241, 266–267.

4. Excerpts from Robert S. and Helen M. Lynd's *Middletown*.

The general attitude reflected in such characteristic school graduation essays of the 1890 period as "Woman Is Most Perfect When Most Womanly" and "Cooking, the Highest Art of Woman" contrasts sharply with the idea of getting one's own living current among the Middletown high school girls of today: 89 per cent. of 446 girls in the three upper classes in 1924 stated that they were planning to work after graduation, and 2 per cent. more were "undecided"; only 3 per cent. said definitely that they did not expect to work.

But the married woman in business or industry finds herself much less readily accepted than her unmarried sister. As late as 1875 the Supreme Court of the state held that a wife's earnings were the property of her husband, and even today there is a widespread tendency to adhere to the view of a generation ago that the employment of married women involves an "ethical" problem. Wives who do not themselves work may grumble that married women who work displace men and lower wages, and that they neglect their children or avoid the responsibility of child-bearing, while through their free and easy association with men in the factory they encourage divorce. Many husbands, in their turn, oppose their wives' working as a reflection upon their ability as "good providers." These objections are, however, in the main, back-eddies in a current moving in the other direction. The Federal Census for 1920 showed that approximately twenty-eight women in every hundred women gainfully employed in Middletown were married, and among those employed in "manufacturing and mechanical industries," thirty-three in every hundred. . . .

A heavy taboo, supported by law and by both religious and popular sanctions, rests upon sexual relationships between persons who are not married. There appears to be some tentative relaxing of this taboo among the younger generation, but in general it is as strong today as in the county-seat of forty years ago. There is some evidence that in the smaller community of the eighties in which everybody knew everybody else, the group prohibition was outwardly more scrupulously observed than today. A man who was a young buck about town in the eighties says, "The fellows nowadays don't seem to mind being seen on the street with a fast woman, but you bet we did then!" . . .

. . . Theoretically, it is the mysterious attraction of two young people for each other and that alone that brings about a marriage, and actually most of Middletown stumbles upon its partners in marriage guided chiefly by "romance." Middletown adults appear to regard romance in marriage as something which, like their religion, must be believed in to hold society together. Children are assured by their elders that "love" is an unanalyzable mystery that "just happens"—"You'll know when the right one comes along," they are told with a knowing smile. . . .

And yet, although theoretically this "thrill" is all-sufficient to insure permanent happiness, actually talks with mothers revealed constantly that, particularly among the business group, they were concerned with certain other factors; the exclusive emphasis upon romantic love makes way as adolescence recedes for a pragmatic calculus. Mothers of the business group give much consideration to encouraging in their children friendships with the "right" people of the other sex, membership in the "right" clubs, deftly warding off the attentions of boys whom they regard it as undesirable for their daughters to "see too much of," and in other ways interfering with and directing the course of true love.

Among the chief qualifications sought by these mothers, beyond the mutual attraction of the two young people for each other, are, in a potential husband, the ability to provide a good living, and, in a wife of the business class, the ability, not only to "make a home" for her husband and children, but to set them in a secure social position. In a world dominated by credit this social function of the wife becomes, among the business group, more subtle and important; the emphasis upon it shades down as we descend in the social scale until among the rank and file of the working class the traditional ability to be a good cook and housekeeper ranks first.

"Woman," as Dorothy Dix says, "makes the family's social status. . . . The old idea used to be that the way for a woman to help her husband was by being thrifty and industrious, by . . . peeling the potatoes a little thinner, and . . . making over her old hats and frocks. . . . But the woman who makes of herself nothing but a domestic drudge . . . is not a help to her husband. She is a hindrance . . . and . . . a man's wife is the show window where he exhibits the measure of his achievement. . . . The biggest deals are put across over luncheon tables; . . . we meet at dinner the people who can push our fortunes. . . . The woman who cultivates a circle of worth-while people, who belongs to clubs, who makes herself interesting and agreeable . . . is a help to her husband. . . ."

Not unrelated to this social skill desired in a wife is the importance of good looks and dress for a woman. In one of Marion Harland's *Talks*, so popular in Middletown in the nineties, one reads, "Who would banish from our midst the matronly figures so suggestive of home, comfort, and motherly love?" Today one cannot pick up a magazine in Middletown without seeing in advertisements of everything from gluten bread to reducing tablets instructions for banishing the matronly figure and restoring "youthful beauty." "Beauty parlors" were unknown in the county-seat of the nineties; there are seven in Middletown today.

"Good looks are a girl's trump card," says Dorothy Dix, though she is quick to add that much can be done without natural beauty if you "dress well and thereby appear 50 per cent. better-looking than you are . . . make yourself charming," and "cultivate bridge and dancing, the ability to play jazz and a few outdoor sports."

Emphasis upon the function of the man in marriage as "a good provider" and of the woman as home-maker, child-rearer, and, among the bulk of the business group, social pace-setter, is far-reaching as affecting the attitude of the sexes toward each other. In general, "brains" tend to be regarded as of small importance in a wife; as one of the city's most "two-fisted" young business men announced to the high school seniors at a Rotary high school "chapel," "The thing girls get from high school is the ability to know how to choose a 'real one' from a 'near one.' When a girl gets around eighteen or so I begin to expect her to get married."

Middletown husbands, when talking frankly among themselves, are likely to speak of women as creatures purer and morally better than men but as relatively impractical, emotional, unstable, given to prejudice, easily hurt, and largely incapable of facing facts or doing hard thinking. "You simply cannot criticize or talk in general terms to a woman," emphatically agreed a group of the city's most thoughtful men. "There's something about the female mind that always short-circuits a general statement into a personal criticism." A school official, approached regarding the possibility of getting a woman on the school board, replied that "with only three people on the board there isn't much place for a woman." . . .

Traditionally this institution of marriage is indissoluble. "What God hath joined together let no man put asunder," commands the religious marriage ritual. But the trend toward secularization noted in the performance of the marriage ceremony appears even more clearly in the increased lifting of the taboo upon the dissolution of marriage. With an increase, between 1890 and 1920, of 87 per cent. in the population of the county in which Middletown is located, the number of recorded divorces for the four years 1921–24 has increased 622 per cent. over the number of divorces in the county in the four years 1889–92.

The frequency of divorces and the speed with which they are rushed through have become commonplaces in Middletown. "Anybody with $25 can get a divorce" is a commonly heard remark. Or as one recently divorced man phrased it, "Any one with $10 can get a divorce in ten minutes if it isn't contested. All you got to do is to show non-support or cruelty and it's a cinch." . . .

Traditionally, voluntary control of parenthood is strongly tabooed in this culture, as is all discussion of sexual adjustment involved in mating, but this prohibition is beginning to be somewhat lifted, a fact perhaps not unrelated to the increasing secularization of marriage noted above. The widely divergent habits of different persons in regard to control of parenthood reveal strikingly the gap found in so many cases to exist between the habits of different groups of people living together in the same community. All of the twenty-seven women of the business class who gave information on this point used or believed in the use of some method of birth control and took it for granted. Only one woman spoke of being uncertain as to whether she had been wise in limiting her family as she had. Of the seventy-seven wives of workers from whom information was secured on this subject, only thirty-four said that they used any means of birth control. . . .

Child-bearing and child-rearing are regarded by Middletown as essential functions of the family. Although the traditional religious sanction upon "fruitfulness" has been somewhat relaxed since the nineties, and families of six to fourteen children, upon which the grandparents of the present generation prided themselves, are considered as somehow not as "nice" as families of two, three, or four children, child-bearing is nevertheless to Middletown a moral obligation. Indeed, in this urban life of alluring alternate choices, in which children are mouths instead of productive hands, there is perhaps a more self-conscious weighting of the question with moral emphasis; the prevailing sentiment is expressed in the editorial dictum by the leading paper in 1925 that "married persons who deliberately refuse to take the responsibility of children are reasonable targets for popular opprobrium." But with increasing regulation of the size of the family, emphasis has shifted somewhat from child-bearing to child-rearing. The remark of the wife of a prosperous merchant, "You just can't have so many children now if you want to do for them. We never thought of going to college. Our children never thought of anything else," represents an attitude almost universal today among business class families and apparently spreading rapidly to the working class.

Although, according to the city librarian, increased interest in business and technical journals has been marked, as in its reading of books Middletown appears to read magazines primarily for the vicarious living in fictional form they contain. Such reading centers about the idea of romance underlying the institution of marriage; since 1890 there has been a trend toward franker "sex adventure" fiction. It is noteworthy that a culture which traditionally taboos any discussion of sex in its systems of both religious and secular training and even until recently in the home training of children should be receiving such heavy diffusion of this material through its periodical reading matter. The aim of these sex adventure magazines, diffusing roughly 3,500 to 4,000 copies monthly throughout the city, is succinctly stated. . . .

. . . "Middletown is amusement hungry," says the opening sentence in a local editorial; at the comedies Middletown lives for an hour in a happy sophisticated make-believe world that leaves it, according to the advertisement of one film, "happy convinced that Life is very well worth living."

Next largest are the crowds which come to see the sensational society films. The kind of vicarious living brought to Middletown by these films may be inferred from such titles as: "*Alimony*—brilliant men, beautiful jazz babies, champagne baths, midnight revels, petting parties in the purple dawn, all ending in one terrific smashing climax that makes you gasp"; "*Married Flirts—Husbands*: Do you flirt? Does your wife always know where you are? Are you faithful to your vows? *Wives*: What's your hubby doing? Do you know? Do you worry? Watch out for *Married Flirts*." So fast do these flow across the silver screen that, e.g., at one time *The Daring Years, Sinners in Silk, Women Who Give*, and *The Price She Paid* were all running synchronously, and at another "*Name the Man*—a story of betrayed womanhood," *Rouged Lips*, and *The Queen of Sin*. While Western "action" films and a million-dollar spectacle like *The Covered Wagon* or *The Hunchback of Notre Dame* draw heavy houses, and while managers lament that there are too few of the popular comedy films, it is the film with burning "heart interest," that packs Middletown's motion picture houses week after week. Young Middletown enters eagerly into the vivid experience of *Flaming Youth*: "neckers, petters, white kisses, red kisses, pleasure-mad daughters, sensation-craving mothers, by an author who didn't dare sign his name; the truth bold, naked, sensational"—so ran the press advertisement—under the spell of the powerful conditioning medium of pictures presented with music and all possible heightening of the emotional content, and the added factor of sharing this experience with a "date" in a darkened room. Meanwhile, *Down to the Sea in Ships*, a costly spectacle of whaling adventure, failed at the leading theater "because," the exhibitor explained, "the whale is really the hero in the film and there wasn't enough 'heart interest' for the women."

Source 5 from Dorothy Dunbar Bromley, "Feminist—New Style," *Harper's Monthly*, October 1927, pp. 552, 554–556, 558–559.

5. Excerpts from Dorothy Dunbar Bromley's "Feminist—New Style."

Is it not high time that we laid the ghost of the so-called feminist?

"Feminism" has become a term of opprobrium to the modern young woman. For the word suggests either the old school of fighting feminists who wore flat heels and had very little feminine charm, or the current species who antagonize men with their constant clamor about maiden names, equal rights, woman's place in the world, and many another cause . . . *ad infinitum*. Indeed, if a blundering male assumes that a young woman is a feminist simply because she happens to have a job or a profession of her own, she will be highly—and quite justifiably insulted: for the word evokes the antithesis of what she flatters herself to be. . . .

. . . Why, then, does the modern woman care about a career or a job if she doubts the quality and scope of women's achievement to date? There are three good reasons why she cares immensely: first, she may be of that rare and fortunate breed of persons who find a certain art, science, or profession as inevitable a part of their lives as breathing; second, she may feel the need of a satisfying outlet for her energy whether or no she possesses creative ability; third, she may have no other means of securing her economic independence. And the latter she prizes above all else, for it spells her freedom as an individual, enabling her to marry or not to marry, as she chooses—to terminate a marriage that has become unbearable, and to support and educate her children if necessary. . . .

But even though Feminist—New Style may not see her own course so clearly marked out before her, and even if she should happen to have an income, she will make a determined effort to fit her abilities to some kind of work. For she has observed that it is only the rare American of either sex who can resist the mentally demoralizing effect of idleness. She has seen too many women who have let what minds they have go to seed, so that by the time they are forty or forty-five they are profoundly uninteresting to their husbands, their children, and themselves. . . .

. . . Nor has she become hostile to the other sex in the course of her struggle to orient herself. On the contrary, she frankly likes men and is grateful to more than a few for the encouragement and help they have given her. . . .

When she meets men socially she is not inclined to air her knowledge and argue about woman's right to a place in the sun. On the contrary, she either talks with a man because he has ideas that interest her or because she finds it amusing to flirt with him—and she will naturally find it doubly amusing if the flirtation involves the swift interplay of wits. She will not waste many engagements on a dull-witted man, although it must be admitted that she finds fewer men with stagnant minds than she does women. . . .

. . . As for "free love," she thinks that it is impractical rather than immoral. With society organized as it is, the average man and woman cannot carry on a free union with any degree of tranquillity.

Incidentally, she is sick of hearing that modern young women are cheapening themselves by their laxity of morals. As a matter of fact, all those who have done any thinking, and who have any innate refinement, live by an aesthetic standard of morals which would make promiscuity inconceivable. . . .

. . . She readily concedes that a husband and children are necessary to the average woman's fullest development, although she knows well enough that women are endowed with varying degrees of passion and of maternal instinct. Some women, for instance, feel the need of a man very intensely, while others want children more than they want a husband, want them so much, in fact, that they vow they would have one or two out of wedlock if it were not for the penalty that society would exact from the child, and if it were not for the fact that a child needs a father as much as a mother.

But no matter how much she may desire the sanction of marriage for the sake of having children, she will not take any man who offers. First of all a man must satisfy her as a lover and a companion. And second, he must have the mental and physical traits which she would like her children to inherit. . . .

. . . But even while she admits that a home and children may be necessary to her complete happiness, she will insist upon *more freedom and honesty within the marriage relation.*

She considers that the ordinary middle-class marriage is stifling in that it allows the wife little chance to know other men, and the husband little chance to know other women—except surreptitiously. It seems vital to her that both should have a certain amount of leisure to use exactly as they see fit, without feeling that they have neglected the other. . . .

Feminist—New Style would consider it a tragedy if she or her husband were to limit the range of each other's lives in any way. Arguing from the fact that she herself can be interested in other men without wanting to exchange them for her husband, she assumes that she has something to give him that he may not find in other women. But if the time should come when it was obvious that he preferred another woman to her or that he preferred to live alone, she would accept the fact courageously, just as she would expect him to accept a similar announcement from her; although she would hope that they would both try to preserve the relationship if it were worth preserving, or if there were children to be considered. But if the marriage should become so inharmonious as to make its continuation a nightmare, she would face the tragedy, and not be submerged by it. For life would still hold many other things—and people—and interests.

∽ QUESTIONS TO CONSIDER ∽

The first part of the evidence (Sources 1 and 2) consists of excerpts from two best sellers: the enormously popular novel *The Sheik* (1921), which went into fifty printings in the first year of its publication and was later made into an equally popular film starring Rudolf Valentino, and *The Plastic Age* (1924), a novel that became a fad on college campuses across the country. How are the "new" women in these novels portrayed? What do people think about them? How do they feel about themselves? What happens to them? Are there any moral messages contained in the ways these novels conclude?

The second part of the evidence (Sources 3 through 5) is from two nonfiction books widely discussed by middle-class readers and an article by a "new" woman published in the middle-class magazine *Harper's Monthly*. Because of the social purity laws of the late nineteenth and early twentieth centuries, birth control information and devices were illegal in many states. Through women's clinics, pam-

phlets, and books, Margaret Sanger struggled to make birth control legal and acceptable. What did she want women to do? Why did she believe that access to birth control was so important for women?

In 1925, sociologists Robert and Helen Lynd, along with three female field researchers, conducted in-depth interviews in a medium-size city they called Middletown (Muncie, Indiana). They were interested in the changes that had occurred since the 1890s, particularly the changes in the way people lived and what they believed. These interviews (Source 4) have become a valuable resource for social historians and were of great interest to people living at the time. What trends did the Lynds identify with respect to working women? What did people think about women who worked outside the home? What were the attitudes of the residents toward premarital sex? Marriage? Divorce? Birth control? Child rearing? How did the citizens react to the new emphasis on sex and sexuality in mass culture?

Dorothy Bromley's article is an attempt to describe the young women whom she called "New Style" feminists. According to Bromley, why didn't young women like to be called feminists? In what ways were they independent? What were their attitudes toward men? Toward marriage and children? What were their goals for themselves?

Now you are ready to answer this chapter's central questions: From the fiction and nonfiction you have read, how would you describe the image of the new woman of the 1920s? How would you describe the realities that affected her—the limits of her freedom? Finally, to what degree was the young woman of the 1920s actually new or different from women of the previous generation?

⧼ EPILOGUE ⧽

For all practical purposes, the stock market crash of 1929 and the deep depression that lasted throughout the 1930s ended the fascination with the new woman and replaced it with sympathy and concern for the "forgotten man." Women who worked, especially married women, were perceived as taking jobs away from unemployed men who desperately needed to support their families. In hard times, people clung to traditional male and female roles: men should be the breadwinners, and women should stay home and take care of the family. Women's fashions changed just as dramatically. Clothing became more feminine, hemlines dropped, and hair styles were no longer short and boyish.

Yet women, including married women, continued to move into paid employment throughout the 1930s, and with the United States' entry into World War II, millions of women who had never held paying jobs before went to work in factories and shipyards, motivated by patriotism and a desire to aid the war effort. By the 1950s, women workers, having been replaced by returning veterans, were once again being urged to stay at home and fulfill their destinies as wives and mothers. Women's educational achievements and age at marriage dropped, while the white middle-class birth rate nearly doubled. Women were still entering the work force, but in feminized clerical and retail jobs and in professions such as elementary school teaching and nursing. Fashions changed from knee-length tailored suits and dresses and "Rosie the Riveter" slacks to puff-sleeved, tiny-waisted, full-skirted, ankle-length dresses.

The problem of image versus reality, so prominent in the 1920s, was also present in the 1960s. By the mid-1960s, another new woman was emerging. Wearing jeans, T-shirts, jewelry, and long hair, young women were dressing like young men. New feminist organizations were founded, a revised version of the ERA was passed by Congress (but not ratified by the states), and millions of women entered universities, paid jobs, and professions. Older Americans expressed a dislike for unisex clothing, were concerned about the easy birth control available with the pill, and objected to the morality of young women and the popularity of primitive-sounding music. Films, best-selling novels, nonfiction, and advertising all portrayed images of these newest "new" women, but almost never analyzed the realities of their lives.

CHAPTER 7

DOCUMENTING THE DEPRESSION: THE FSA PHOTOGRAPHERS AND RURAL POVERTY

∽ THE PROBLEM ∽

On a cold, rainy afternoon in the spring of 1936, Dorothea Lange was driving home from a month-long field trip to central California. One of several young photographers hired by the Historical Section of the Farm Security Administration (FSA), Lange had been talking with migrant laborers and taking photographs of the migrants' camps.

After passing a hand-lettered road sign that read PEA PICKERS CAMP, Lange drove on another twenty miles. Then she stopped, turned around, and went back to the migrant camp. The pea crop had frozen, and there was no work for the pickers, but several families were still camped there. She approached a woman and her daughters, talked with them briefly, asked to take a few pictures, and left ten minutes later. The result was one of the most famous images of the Great Depression, "Migrant Mother." This photograph and others like it moved Americans deeply and helped to create support for New Deal legislation and programs to aid migrant workers, sharecroppers, tenant farmers, and small-scale farmers.

In this chapter, you will be analyzing some of the documentary photographs from the FSA to determine how and why they were so effective in creating support for New Deal legislation.

CHAPTER 7

DOCUMENTING
THE
DEPRESSION:
THE FSA
PHOTOGRAPHERS
AND RURAL
POVERTY

☙ BACKGROUND ☙

In 1930, President Herbert Hoover was at first bewildered and then defensive about the rapid downward spiral of the nation's economy. Hoover, like many other Americans, believed in the basic soundness of capitalism, advocated the values of individualism, and maintained that the role of the federal government should be limited. Nevertheless, Hoover was a compassionate man. As private relief sources dried up, he authorized public works projects and some institutional loans, at the same time vetoing other relief bills and trying to convince the nation that prosperity would return soon. The media, especially newspapers and middle-class magazines, followed Hoover's lead.

Americans turned out at the polls in record numbers for the election of 1932—and voted for the Democratic candidate, Franklin D. Roosevelt, in equally record numbers. As unemployment increased dramatically along with bank and business failures, Congress reacted by rapidly passing an assortment of programs collectively known as the New Deal. Calling together a group of experts (mainly professors and lawyers) to form a "brain trust," the newly elected president acted quickly to try to restore the nation's confidence. In his fireside radio chats, as well as in his other speeches, Roosevelt consistently reassured the American public that the country's economic institutions were sound.

Like her husband, Eleanor Roosevelt was tireless in her efforts to mitigate the effects of the depression. With boundless energy, she traveled throughout the country, observing conditions firsthand and reporting back to her husband. One of the few New Dealers deeply committed to civil rights for African Americans, she championed both individuals and the civil rights movement whenever she could. Although she was criticized and ridiculed for her nontraditional behavior as first lady, to millions of Americans, Eleanor Roosevelt was the heart of the New Deal. In fact, during the depression, more than 15 million Americans wrote directly to the president and first lady about their personal troubles and economic difficulties.

In an emergency session early in 1933, Congress began the complicated process of providing immediate relief for the needy and legislation for longer-term recovery and reform. Banking, business, the stock market, unemployed workers, farmers, and young people were targets of this early New Deal legislation.

The New Deal administration soon realized that the problems of farmers were going to be especially difficult to alleviate. To meet the unusual European demand for farm products during World War I, many American farmers had overexpanded. They had mortgaged their farms and borrowed money to buy expensive new farm equipment, but most had not shared in the profits of the so-called prosperous decade of the 1920s.

Unfortunately, the New Deal's Agricultural Adjustment Act (AAA) benefited only relatively large, prosperous farmers. Intended to reduce farm production and thus improve the prices farmers received for their goods, the AAA unintentionally encouraged large farmers to accept payment for reducing their crops, use the money to buy machinery, and evict the sharecroppers and tenants who had been farming part of their land. Explaining to Dorothea Lange why his family was traveling to California, one farmer simply said they had been "tractored out." With no land of their own to farm, sharecroppers and tenants packed their few belongings and families into old trucks and cars and took to the road looking for seasonal agricultural work in planting, tending, or picking produce.

In so doing, they joined thousands of other American farm families who lived in the Dust Bowl—the plains and prairie states where unwise agricultural practices and a long drought had combined to create terrifying dust storms that blotted out the sun, blew away the topsoil, and actually buried some farms in dust. These Dust Bowl refugees, along with former tenants and sharecroppers, joined Mexican Americans already working as migrant laborers in California. For those left behind, especially in the poverty-stricken areas of the rural Midwest and South, conditions were almost as terrible as in the migrant camps.

It was to aid these displaced farmers that President Roosevelt created the Resettlement Administration (RA), which two years later became the Farm Security Administration (FSA). The RA was headed by Rexford Tugwell, an economics professor from Columbia University. A former Progressive, Tugwell was an optimist who believed that if the public was educated about social and economic problems, they would support legislation to correct whatever was wrong. To accomplish this task, he hired Roy Stryker, a former graduate student of his, to direct the Historical Section of the agency.

Stryker in turn hired a small group of photographers to travel around the country and take photos illustrating the difficulties faced by small farmers, tenants, and sharecroppers and, to a lesser extent, the FSA projects intended to ameliorate these problems. Hoping to mobilize public opinion in support of FSA-funded projects such as model migrant camps, rural cooperatives, health clinics, and federal relief for the poorest families, Stryker made the photographs widely available to national middle-class magazines and local newspapers. The Historical Section also organized traveling exhibits and encouraged authors to use the photographs in their books.

How did Americans feel when they saw these images? What qualities did the photographs portray? Why were they so effective in creating support for New Deal legislation?

CHAPTER 7

DOCUMENTING
THE
DEPRESSION:
THE FSA
PHOTOGRAPHERS
AND RURAL
POVERTY

THE METHOD

By the end of the nineteenth century, technological advances had made using cameras and developing photographs easier, but both the equipment and the developing methods were still cumbersome and primitive by today's standards. Nevertheless, people were fascinated by photography, and many talented amateurs, such as E. Alice Austen, spent hours taking pictures of their families, friends, and homes. Indeed, these photographs are an important source of evidence for social historians trying to reconstruct how Americans lived in the past.

Documentary photography, however, has a different purpose: reform. During the Progressive era of the late nineteenth and early twentieth centuries, middle-class Americans increasingly became concerned about the growing number of poor families who depended on the labor of their children to supplement their meager standard of living. First Jacob Riis, the author of *How the Other Half Lives* (1890), and then Lewis Hine, in his work for the National Child Labor Committee, photographed the living and working conditions of young children and documented the ill effects of child labor. These photographs were used to persuade the public to support the abolition of child labor. In states that were unwilling to end child labor completely, the pictures were used to convince people to support the strict regulation of young people's work. Although this effort was successful in some states, it failed on the national level when the United States Supreme Court struck down a federal law regulating child labor in 1919 (*Hammer v. Dagenhart*).

Roy Stryker was impressed by the power of such photographs and had used many of Hine's images to illustrate Rexford Tugwell's reform-oriented economics textbook in the 1920s. The dozen or so talented photographers whom Stryker hired to work for the Historical Section of the FSA were relatively young (most were in their twenties or thirties) and came from a variety of backgrounds. Most, like Dorothea Lange, Walker Evans, Jack Delano, Carl Mydans, John Collier, Marion Post (Wolcott), and Theodor Jung, were already either established professionals or serious amateurs. Others took their first professional photographs for the Historical Section: Ben Shahn and Russell Lee had been painters, and Arthur Rothstein and John Vachon were unemployed college students. All the photographers were white, except Gordon Parks, a twenty-nine-year-old African American fashion photographer who joined the Historical Section in 1941. Parks never photographed farmers while at the FSA; instead, he sensitively documented the lives of African Americans and racial discrimination in Washington, D.C.

Stryker himself was not a photographer but an able administrator who planned the field trips, developed background reading lists for the photographers, and wrote "shooting scripts" to guide them once they were in the field. "As you are driving through the agricultural areas . . . ," Stryker wrote to Dorothea Lange in California, "would you take a few shots of various types of farm activities such as your picture showing the lettuce workers?" But beyond these kinds of general suggestions, Stryker gave his photographers remarkable freedom while he concentrated on co-ordinating their activities, promoting the wide use of their photos, and defending the Historical Section against congressional criticism and budget cuts.

When analyzing these pictures, you must remember that documentary pho-tographs are not intended to pre-sent a balanced or an unbiased view. Instead, these photographs are in-tended to appeal to viewers' emotions and motivate viewers to work for and support change. As a student looking at these photographs, you will need to be specific about *what* you feel and then try to determine *why* the photo-graph makes you feel that way. Fi-nally, try to make some connections between the photographs and the fed-eral programs sponsored by the RA and the FSA.

CHAPTER 7

DOCUMENTING
THE
DEPRESSION:
THE FSA
PHOTOGRAPHERS
AND RURAL
POVERTY

⌔ THE EVIDENCE ⌔

Sources 1 through 17 from United States Farm Security Administration, Historical Division, Library of Congress, Washington, D.C.

1. Abandoned Farm Home, Ward County, North Dakota, 1940 (John Vachon).

2. "Tractored-Out" Farm, Hall County, Texas, 1938 (Dorothea Lange).

3. Skull, South Dakota Badlands, 1936 (Arthur Rothstein).

CHAPTER 7

DOCUMENTING
THE
DEPRESSION:
THE FSA
PHOTOGRAPHERS
AND RURAL
POVERTY

4. Farmer and Sons in Dust Storm, Cimarron County, Oklahoma, 1936 (Arthur Rothstein).

5. Family Moving to Krebs, Oklahoma, from Idabel, Oklahoma, 1939 (Dorothea Lange).

6. Migrant Family Living in a Shack Built on an Abandoned Truck Bed, Highway 70, Tennessee, 1936 (Carl Mydans).

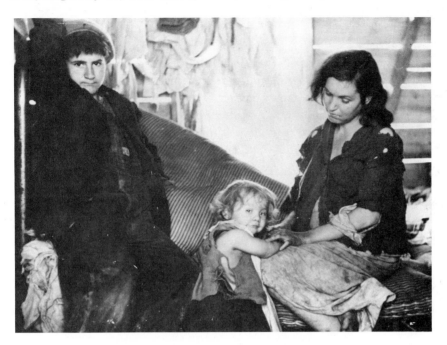

7. Migrants from Oklahoma, Blyth, California, 1936 (Dorothea Lange).

CHAPTER 7

DOCUMENTING
THE
DEPRESSION:
THE FSA
PHOTOGRAPHERS
AND RURAL
POVERTY

8. Migrant Mother, Nipomo, California, 1936 (Dorothea Lange).

9. Mexican Migrant Worker's Home, Imperial Valley, California, 1937 (Dorothea Lange).

10. Living Quarters of Fruit-Packing House Workers, Berrien, Michigan, 1940 (John Vachon).

11. Plantation Owner and Field Hands, Clarksdale, Mississippi, 1936 (Dorothea Lange).

CHAPTER 7

DOCUMENTING
THE
DEPRESSION:
THE FSA
PHOTOGRAPHERS
AND RURAL
POVERTY

12. Cotton Pickers, Pulaski County, Arkansas, 1935 (Ben Shahn).

13. Owner of the General Store, Bank, and Cotton Gin, Wendell, North Carolina, 1939 (Marion Post Wolcott).

14. FSA Client and His Family, Beaufort, South Carolina, 1936 (Carl Mydans).

15. Mule Dealer, Creedmoor, North Carolina, 1940 (Arthur Rothstein).

CHAPTER 7

DOCUMENTING
THE
DEPRESSION:
THE FSA
PHOTOGRAPHERS
AND RURAL
POVERTY

16. Bud Fields and His Family, Tenant Farmers, Hale County, Alabama, 1936 (Walker Evans).

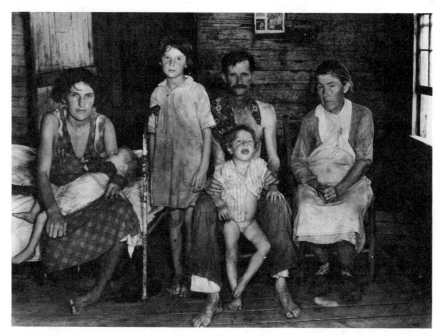

17. Christmas Dinner, Tenant Farmer's Home, Southeastern Iowa, 1936 (Russell Lee).

∽ QUESTIONS TO CONSIDER ∾

Sources 1 through 4 are photographs taken to illustrate what had happened to the once-fertile farmlands of the plains and prairies. How would you describe these pictures to someone who could not see them? What had happened to the land? How do these photos make you feel?

Sources 5 through 8 are photographs of farm families who were on the road. They had left or been evicted from the farms where they had lived and were looking for jobs as migrant workers. How would middle-class Americans have felt when they saw these pictures? Which photograph do you think is the most effective? Why?

Sources 9, 10, 12, 14, 16, and 17 show the living and working conditions at migrant camps and for the tenant and sharecropper families who did not leave their homes. What do you notice most when you look at these photographs? How do these pictures make you feel? Why? In contrast, Sources 11, 13, and 15 are of men who were relatively well-off during the depression. How are they portrayed? How do you feel about these men? Why?

Finally, think about the photographs as a whole. What messages did they send to the middle-class Americans who saw them in newspapers, magazines, books, or traveling exhibits? What major problems did the photographs portray, and what kinds of programs did the FSA propose to try to aid the poorer farmers? Why do you think these documentary photographs were so effective in creating sympathy and support for aid to these farmers?

∽ EPILOGUE ∾

By 1941, the FSA photographs were well-known to millions of Americans, and the Historical Section had justified its existence. That year also saw the publication of the classic book *Let Us Now Praise Famous Men: Three Tenant Families*, written by James Agee and illustrated with photos by FSA photographer Walker Evans. After the Japanese attack on Pearl Harbor in December 1941 and the United States' subsequent entry into World War II, the direction of the Historical Section changed. The build-up of defense industries and the effects of the war on everyday Americans dominated the photographers' assignments. Eventually, the Historical Section was moved to the Office of War Information, and in 1943, after transferring more than 130,000 FSA photographs to the Library of Congress, Roy Stryker resigned from government service.

America's participation in World War II finally brought an end to the Great Depression—and an end to the New Deal as well. Stryker spent the

CHAPTER 7

DOCUMENTING
THE
DEPRESSION:
THE FSA
PHOTOGRAPHERS
AND RURAL
POVERTY

next decade working for Standard Oil of New Jersey, and most of the former FSA photographers did free-lance work, taught courses, or found permanent jobs in photojournalism with magazines such as *Life* and *Look*. Ben Shahn went back to his first love, painting, and became a well-known artist. Marion Post (Wolcott) got married and raised a family, returning to photography only when she was in her sixties. The plight of the rural poor was once again forgotten, and middle-class materialism and conformity dominated the cold war years of the 1950s.

Yet a whole new generation was soon to rediscover the work of the FSA photographers. In 1962, Edward Steichen, head of the photography department at the New York Museum of Modern Art and a photographer himself, mounted a major exhibition of the FSA images called "The Bitter Years, 1935–1941." By the end of the 1960s, young Americans also had rediscovered some of the same problems the New Deal photographers had captured in their pictures: rural poverty, racial discrimination, and social injustice. Once again, Americans demanded reform, especially during the presidencies of John F. Kennedy and Lyndon Johnson.

CHAPTER 8

THE BURDENS OF POWER: THE DECISION TO DROP THE ATOMIC BOMB, 1945

∽ THE PROBLEM ∾

At 2:45 A.M. on August 6, 1945, three B-29 bombers took off from an American air base in the Marianas, bound for Japan. Two of the airplanes carried cameras and scientific instruments; the third carried an atomic bomb, a new type of weapon with the destructive power of 20,000 tons of TNT.

In the Japanese city of Hiroshima, residents were so undisturbed by the sight of so few enemy planes that most did not bother to go to air raid shelters. When the bomb exploded 2,000 feet above the city, 80,000 people were killed instantly, and at least that many died soon afterward of radiation poisoning.[1] More than 80 percent of Hi-

roshima's buildings were destroyed, and the flash of light was so intense that shadowlike "silhouettes" of people who disappeared were "photographed" onto the walls of buildings and rubble.

The decision to drop the atomic bomb on Hiroshima ultimately rested with President Harry S Truman, who had been in office only 116 days when

---

1. The actual number of bomb-related deaths at Hiroshima has been the subject of much dispute. The U.S. Strategic Bombing Survey estimated the number of people who were killed instantly at 80,000. An August 1946 survey placed the total number killed (instantly and soon after, from radiation poisoning) at more than 122,000. A 1961 Japanese study contended that the true figure was about 166,000. In the late 1970s, a careful estimate by Japanese officials placed the total bomb-related deaths (as of November 1945) at 130,000. The total population of Hiroshima at the time the bomb was dropped was 300,000.

CHAPTER 8

THE BURDENS
OF POWER: THE
DECISION TO
DROP THE
ATOMIC BOMB,
1945

the bomb was dropped and, indeed, had known of its existence only since April 25. The war in Europe ended with the surrender of Nazi Germany in early May of 1945. But Japan was still to be conquered, and there was enormous hostility against the Japanese in the United States. Truman's military advisers told him that an invasion of the Japanese mainland could cost the United States between 500,000 and 1,000,000 casualties. At the same time, however, the situation in Europe was grave, as it was becoming increasingly clear that the wartime alliance between the United States and the Soviet Union was rapidly deteriorating. As for President Truman, he had been suspicious of the Russians since 1941, and the eroding alliance confirmed his worst fears. To what extent might the dropping of the atomic bomb on Hiroshima have been used to threaten the Soviets with American military prowess in the postwar years? Moreover, at the Yalta Conference, Soviet premier Joseph Stalin promised to enter the war against Japan approximately three months after the fall of Germany. To what ex-

tent was the atomic bomb used to end the war in the Pacific before the Russians could become involved and thus increase the Soviet Union's power in Asia?

In this chapter, you will be analyzing the evidence to answer four major questions: (1) Why did President Truman decide to drop the atomic bomb on Hiroshima? (2) What principal factors went into that decision? (3) Were there any alternatives to using the atomic bomb? If so, why did President Truman not choose one of the alternatives? (4) Who were the key figures who helped President Truman make up his mind? Why did he heed the words of some advisers but not others?

Even though you will have to go beyond the evidence provided here, you also should be willing to ponder the important question of whether President Truman's decision to use the atomic bomb on Hiroshima was the proper one. To answer that question (a controversial one even today), you will have to combine the evidence with material in the Background section of this chapter and with other reading.

⌘ BACKGROUND ⌘

In 1918, New Zealand physicist Ernest Rutherford was criticized for his failure to attend a meeting of a British committee of scientists trying to create a defense against German submarines during World War I. Rutherford's excuse for his absence shocked his fellow scientists: "Talk softly,

please. I have been engaged in experiments which suggest that the atom can be artificially disintegrated. If it is true, it is of far greater importance than a war."

By the 1920s, separate research centers investigating the splitting of the atom had been established at Göttingen (Germany), Cambridge (England), and Copenhagen (Denmark). Physicists and chemists from all over the Western world came to these centers to study and perform research, encouraging each other and sharing their ideas in what was, briefly, a true international community of scientists. Experiments were carried out using comparatively crude equipment as scientists groped in the dark for the essence of matter itself and how that matter could be transformed. Some researchers had used alpha particles[2] to bombard atoms of nitrogen, thereby changing the atoms into oxygen and hydrogen. When others asked the scientists the practical usefulness of their work, most of them simply shrugged; they did not know. Yet they felt that they were on the brink of an important scientific breakthrough in unlocking the riddles of the universe.

In 1932, scientists at Cambridge discovered the neutron,[3] a subatomic particle that could be used to bombard and split atoms. That important discovery speeded up atomic research considerably. Neutrons were used to split atoms in Paris, Cambridge, Rome, Zurich, and Berlin. In 1934, building on those experiments, scientists in Rome created the first chain reaction, in which the split atoms themselves released neutrons, which in turn split other atoms. In late 1938,

two German physicists at Berlin's Kaiser Wilhelm Institute used neutrons to split atoms of uranium. That type of uranium (U-235) was a highly unstable element that, when split by neutrons, created significant amounts of radioactivity.

At this point, politics entered the realm of science. In early 1933, Adolf Hitler came to power in Germany as an avowed nationalist, expansionist, and anti-Semite. Czechoslovakia, occupied by Germany in 1938, was the only place in Europe that held large stocks of high-grade uranium. Although Hitler himself was cool toward atomic research, officers in the German War Department recognized that a chain reaction of uranium could produce an extremely powerful weapon and urged scientists in Berlin to push forward. Interestingly, those scientists purposely slowed down their work, fearing the uses Hitler might make of such an atomic device. Scientists working in Germany who were unsympathetic to or fearful of Hitler fled the country, principally to England and the United States. One such person was Leo Szilard, a Hungarian who recognized that a possible race over the production of atomic weapons might develop between Germany and other nations. At Columbia University in New York, Szilard urged upon his fellow émigrés a self-imposed moratorium on publishing the results of their atomic research in scientific journals. At the same time, in October 1939, Szilard was instrumental in getting world-famous mathematician and scientist Albert Einstein to write a letter to President Roosevelt proposing a speed-up of American atomic research.

2. Alpha particles are positively charged composite particles consisting of two protons and two neutrons that are indistinguishable from the nucleus of a helium atom.
3. Rutherford predicted the existence of the neutron in 1915. Fittingly, it was his laboratory that proved his theoretical hunch correct.

CHAPTER 8

THE BURDENS
OF POWER: THE
DECISION TO
DROP THE
ATOMIC BOMB,
1945

Roosevelt gave his vague go-ahead, although funds were not made available to the scientists, most of whom were centered at Columbia University, until December 6, 1941 (ironically, one day before the Japanese attacked Pearl Harbor).

Once the United States was officially in World War II, President Roosevelt gave his full support to the top-secret project to develop atomic weaponry, a project that in the end cost more than $2 billion (carefully hidden from Congress). In 1942, British and United States scientists merged their efforts to create the Manhattan Project, the code name for the building of an atomic bomb.

To direct the Manhattan Project, Roosevelt chose General Leslie Groves, forty-eight years old in 1942 and a career military officer well-known for his skill in administration. An FBI investigation of Groves showed only that he had an incredible weakness for chocolate (he stored his private supply of chocolate in the same safe that contained some of the world's most vital nuclear secrets). He often called the scientists "my crackpots" but was an able administrator who provided his "crackpots" with everything they desired. Ultimately, the Manhattan Project employed more than 150,000 people (only a dozen or so of whom knew of the whole operation) who worked at the University of Chicago, Oak Ridge (Tennessee), Hanford (Washington), and Los Alamos (New Mexico).[4]

The Manhattan Project was given its urgency by the fear that Hitler would have his hands on the atomic bomb before the Allies. As noted, what the scientists of the West did not know was that German physicists, because they hated Hitler and feared nuclear weaponry, had purposely slowed down their efforts. In 1944, soldiers of American general George Patton's advancing armies captured the papers of one of the German scientists engaged in nuclear research. These papers showed that Germany was at least two years behind the West in the development of atomic weapons.

This fact presented American scientists with a real dilemma. The entire goal of the Manhattan Project was to beat Hitler to the atomic bomb, but now it was clear that nuclear research, purposely retarded by German physicists, was years away from building a successful nuclear device for the Third Reich. As Albert Einstein said, "If I had known that the Germans would not succeed in constructing the atomic bomb, I would never have lifted a finger." Several other scientists agreed with Einstein and hoped that, even if the bomb was developed, it would never be used.

Yet, as seen above, political and military considerations rarely were far from nuclear research. Even with Nazi

4. Columbia University scientists were transferred to the University of Chicago, away from the coast, where they continued their experiments and calculations. Oak Ridge was a city built by the Manhattan Project in an isolated area of eastern Tennessee; there U-235 was extracted from the more passive U-238. Hanford was where plutonium (used in the bomb dropped on Nagasaki) was produced, a new element that Chicago scientists discovered by using neutrons to bombard U-238. Los Alamos was where the bombs were assembled and tested.

Germany close to defeat, President Truman, who assumed the presidency upon Roosevelt's death on April 12, 1945, looked upon a world filled with dangers. Japan remained unconquered, and Truman's military advisers predicted a fearful toll if the Japanese mainland was invaded. Relations with the Soviet Union, an ally in the war against Germany, also were deteriorating rapidly. To what extent might Truman have seen the atomic bomb as the military and political solution to both these problems?

It is important to note that what eventually became the cold war between the Soviet Union and the West actually had its origins in World War II itself, long before it was known that the atomic bomb would work. In many ways, the only factor that brought the Soviet Union and the West together as allies was their mutual enemy, Hitler's Germany. Soviet premier Joseph Stalin, whose nation had been invaded twice by Germany in the twentieth century, viewed the West as a constant threat. To Stalin, the Soviet Union had carried the burden of the fight against Hitler since 1941 (until the 1944 Allied landing at Normandy, in France, to create a "second front" against Germany), had suffered staggering casualties, and had seen whole areas of the Soviet Union utterly devastated.[5] To guard against another

such invasion, Stalin believed that the Soviet Union must dominate the nations of eastern Europe and not let a strong Germany emerge from World War II. Increasingly suspicious of Great Britain and the United States, Stalin believed that he needed to keep those nations as unaware as possible of his country's economic and military vulnerability, a belief that resulted in a policy of secrecy toward the West.

Many policymakers in Great Britain and the United States were as suspicious of the Soviet Union as Stalin was of them. Britain's prime minister Winston Churchill had distrusted the Russians since the Bolshevik Revolution of 1917, believed that Russian communists had a master plan for world domination, and urged that a hard line be taken against Stalin. On the other hand, President Franklin Roosevelt, although harboring few illusions about the Soviet Union, hoped that by making some concessions he could lessen Stalin's fears and gain the Soviet premier's cooperation in the postwar world and in forming the United Nations. At the Yalta Conference in February 1945, Roosevelt, Churchill, and Stalin agreed that the postwar governments of eastern Europe would be freely elected but pro-Russian. The three powers also agreed on the temporary partition of Germany into three zones of occupation to be governed cooperatively by the three victorious powers, who eventually would merge these

---

5. Russian military deaths are estimated to have exceeded 7 million. In contrast, Germany suffered approximately 3.5 million military deaths, China 2.2 million, Japan 1.3 million, Great Britain and the Commonwealth 500,000, and the United States 350,000. Indeed, when civilian deaths are added to military deaths, the Soviet Union

lost a total of 40 percent of all people killed in World War II, or approximately 20 of 50 million.

CHAPTER 8

THE BURDENS
OF POWER: THE
DECISION TO
DROP THE
ATOMIC BOMB,
1945

zones into one reconstructed and re-formed German state. The city of Berlin, well within the projected Soviet zone, likewise would be divided into three administrative sectors. In addition, the Soviet Union was given the right to exact heavy reparations from a defeated Germany, which ultimately amounted to the dismantling of German industry within the Russian zone for shipment to the Soviet Union. Stalin agreed to enter the war against Japan three months after the fall of Germany and also promised to conclude a treaty with China's Chiang Kai-shek, the person the United States hoped would lead China after the defeat of Japan. Even amid these joint declarations for unity at Yalta, however, considerable distrust remained.

Roosevelt's death brought Truman to the presidency. Truman's views of the Soviet Union were closer to those of Churchill than to Roosevelt's. Although Truman honored agreements [on reparations, the partitioning of Germany and Berlin, and the return of Russian "traitors" (deserters) to the Soviet government] and ordered the United States Army (which had advanced beyond the line Roosevelt, Churchill, and Stalin had agreed on earlier) to draw back, in other ways he made it clear that his policy toward the Soviet Union would be different from that of Roosevelt. Immediately after the surrender of Germany, Truman cut off aid to the Soviet Union, reasoning that the war in Europe had ended and that further assistance was unnecessary. Stalin was outraged. Furthermore, at the Potsdam Conference, Truman demanded that free elections be held immediately in eastern Europe, a demand that Stalin unhesitatingly rejected. Also at Potsdam, Truman informed Stalin that the United States had developed a new weapon of enormous destructive power, a fact Stalin probably already knew through espionage.

Thus it is evident that even before the end of World War II, the alliance between the Soviet Union and the West had eroded badly. Deep suspicions and distrust on both sides caused leaders of the United States and the Soviet Union to view the other as a dangerous threat to peace and stability. As Truman confronted his first weeks in office and considered whether to use the atomic bomb against Japan, he faced other difficult decisions with regard to the Soviet Union. Should the bomb be used on Japan to save American lives? Could the bomb's secrets be used as a "bargaining chip" with the Soviet Union?

⚭ THE METHOD ⚭

Although personal memoirs are sometimes written several years after a particular event has occurred, historians nevertheless treat them as *primary sources* (evidence that is contemporary to the event being analyzed), principally because the authors of these memoirs were present when the event was taking place. Indeed, as seen in this chapter, some of those people were more than mere eyewitnesses—some were key figures in the event itself. Therefore, personal memoirs can be invaluable tools for those seeking to understand the past, a particular decision someone made in the past, and the factors that went into the making of that decision.

Yet one always must be cautious when using personal diaries, memoirs, and reminiscences. The historian must keep in mind that each memoir is only one person's view or perspective of the event or decision. Was the author in a good position to see how a particular event unfolded or how a particular decision was made? Was the author aware of all the factors and people involved? Was the author trying to make himself or herself "look good" to future generations (as British prime minister Winston Churchill clearly tried to do in his history of the Second World War)? Generally, the farther away from the event or decision the author was, the less reliable that author's memories are considered to be. Therefore, as you examine each piece of evidence, ask yourself this question: Was the person in a good position to see what she or he is reporting?

The next thing you must look for is the author's *intent* in writing down recollections in the first place. Does the author of the memoir have a bias? If so, what is it? Is the author seeking to justify, defend, attack, or exonerate? Does the author magnify or minimize his or her role in the decision? Why? Be alert for the author's intent, stated or hidden, and possible biases.

Sometimes authors of memoirs either accidentally or purposely omit vital information or distort the facts. Did any of the authors of the memoirs in this chapter do so? How can you tell? Aside from simple forgetfulness or having a poor vantage point, can you think of any other reasons why this might have been done?

As you read each selection carefully, keep a chart like the one below to help you recall the main points. And as you examine each piece of evidence, keep the central questions you are to answer firmly in mind:

1. Why did President Truman decide to drop the atomic bomb on Hiroshima?
2. What principal factors went into that decision?

Author	Position	What Author Should Be Expected to Know	Biases?	Agreement or Disagreement with Other Memoirs (Omissions?)

[205]

CHAPTER 8

THE BURDENS
OF POWER: THE
DECISION TO
DROP THE
ATOMIC BOMB,
1945

3. Were there any alternatives to using the atomic bomb? If so, why didn't President Truman choose one of them?

4. Who were the key figures who helped Truman with his decision? Why did he heed the words of some advisers but not those of others?

5. Do you think the decision President Truman made to drop the atomic bomb on Hiroshima was the proper one?

Keep in mind that alternatives to dropping an atomic bomb on Japan were open to President Truman. Those alternatives included urging Japan to surrender and offering a guarantee that the emperor would retain his throne; an American invasion of the Japanese mainland; the continued (or increased) use of conventional bombs; a joint United States–Soviet Union assault on Japan; and inviting Japanese government and military leaders to witness a test demonstration of an atomic bomb in the hope that it would convince Japan to surrender. As you examine the evidence, you might well get a clearer picture of why Truman ultimately made the decision he did if you keep in mind the alternatives open to him. As you will see in the evidence, many of these alternatives were advocated by others.

⟋ THE EVIDENCE ⟍

Source 1 from Harry S Truman, *Memoirs: Year of Decisions* (Garden City, N.Y.: Doubleday and Company, 1955), pp. 10–11, 416–423.

1. Harry S Truman (President of the United States, April 12, 1945–January 1953).[6]

My own knowledge of these developments had come about only after I became President, when Secretary Stimson had given me the full story. He had told me at that time that the project was nearing completion and that a bomb could be expected within another four months. It was at his suggestion, too, that I had then set up a committee of top men and had asked

6. We have rearranged Truman's recollections to put events closer to chronological order.

them to study with great care the implications the new weapon might have for us. . . .[7]

[Here Truman identifies the eight-man Interim Committee, chaired by Secretary of War Stimson and composed of leading figures in government, business, and education. Truman then names the three scientists from the Manhattan Project who would consult with the committee and reports that the Interim Committee's recommendations were brought to him by Stimson on June 1, 1945.]

It was their recommendation that the bomb be used against the enemy as soon as it could be done. They recommended further that it should be used without specific warning and against a target that would clearly show its devastating strength. I had realized, of course, that an atomic bomb explosion would inflict damage and casualties beyond imagination. On the other hand, the scientific advisers of the committee reported, "We can propose no technical demonstration likely to bring an end to the war; we see no acceptable alternative to direct military use." It was their conclusion that no technical demonstration they might propose, such as over a deserted island, would be likely to bring the war to an end. It had to be used against an enemy target.

The final decision of where and when to use the atomic bomb was up to me. Let there be no mistake about it. I regarded the bomb as a military weapon and never had any doubt that it should be used. The top military advisers to the President recommended its use, and when I talked to Churchill he unhesitatingly told me that he favored the use of the atomic bomb if it might aid to end the war.

In deciding to use this bomb I wanted to make sure that it would be used as a weapon of war in the manner prescribed by the laws of war. That meant that I wanted it dropped on a military target. I had told Stimson that the bomb should be dropped as nearly as possible upon a war production center of prime military importance. . . .

[Here Truman describes how the four potential targets of Hiroshima, Kokura, Niigata, and Nagasaki were chosen by Truman, Stimson, and the president's military advisers. The Strategic Air Forces were given the latitude to choose from among those four cities the one where the first atomic bomb would be dropped, with weather as the primary consideration.]

A month before the test explosion of the atomic bomb the service Secretaries and the Joint Chiefs of Staff had laid their detailed plans for the

---

7. This was the Interim Committee, referred to below and in other memoirs.

CHAPTER 8

THE BURDENS
OF POWER: THE
DECISION TO
DROP THE
ATOMIC BOMB,
1945

defeat of Japan before me for approval. There had apparently been some differences of opinion as to the best route to be followed, but these had evidently been reconciled, for when General Marshall had presented his plan for a two-phase invasion of Japan, Admiral King[8] and General Arnold had supported the proposal heartily.

The Army plan envisaged an amphibious landing in the fall of 1945 on the island of Kyushu, the southernmost of the Japanese home islands. This would be accomplished by our Sixth Army, under the command of General Walter Krueger. The first landing would then be followed approximately four months later by a second great invasion, which would be carried out by our Eighth and Tenth Armies, followed by the First Army transferred from Europe, all of which would go ashore in the Kanto plains area near Tokyo. In all, it had been estimated that it would require until the late fall of 1946 to bring Japan to her knees.

This was a formidable conception, and all of us realized fully that the fighting would be fierce and the losses heavy. But it was hoped that some of Japan's forces would continue to be preoccupied in China and others would be prevented from reinforcing the home islands if Russia were to enter the war.

There was, of course, always the possibility that the Japanese might choose to surrender sooner. Our air and fleet units had begun to inflict heavy damage on industrial and urban sites in Japan proper. Except in China, the armies of the Mikado had been pushed back everywhere in relentless successions of defeats.

Acting Secretary of State Grew had spoken to me in late May[9] about issuing a proclamation that would urge the Japanese to surrender but would assure them that we would permit the Emperor to remain as head of the state. Grew backed this with arguments taken from his ten years' experience as our Ambassador in Japan, and I told him that I had already given thought to this matter myself and that it seemed to me a sound idea. Grew had a draft of a proclamation with him, and I instructed him to send it by the customary channels to the Joint Chiefs and the State-War-Navy Coordinating Committee in order that we might get the opinions of all concerned before I made my decision.

On June 18 Grew reported that the proposal had met with the approval of his Cabinet colleagues and of the Joint Chiefs. The military leaders also

8. Admiral Ernest J. King (1878–1956) was chief of naval operations. He favored using the bomb on Hiroshima.
9. This was the important May 28 meeting. See Joseph C. Grew, *Turbulent Era: A Diplomatic Record of Forty Years, 1904–1945,* ed. Walter Johnson (Boston: Houghton Mifflin Company, 1952), Vol. II, pp. 1421–1428.

discussed the subject with me when they reported the same day. Grew, however, favored issuing the proclamation at once, to coincide with the closing of the campaign on Okinawa, while the service chiefs were of the opinion that we should wait until we were ready to follow a Japanese refusal with the actual assault of our invasion forces.

It was my decision then that the proclamation to Japan should be issued from the forthcoming conference at Potsdam. This, I believed, would clearly demonstrate to Japan and to the world that the Allies were united in their purpose. By that time, also, we might know more about two matters of significance for our future effort: the participation of the Soviet Union and the atomic bomb. We knew that the bomb would receive its first test in mid-July. If the test of the bomb was successful, I wanted to afford Japan a clear chance to end the fighting before we made use of this newly gained power. If the test should fail, then it would be even more important to us to bring about a surrender before we had to make a physical conquest of Japan. General Marshall told me that it might cost half a million American lives to force the enemy's surrender of his home grounds. . . .

At Potsdam, as elsewhere, the secret of the atomic bomb was kept closely guarded. We did not extend the very small circle of Americans who knew about it. Churchill naturally knew about the atomic bomb project from its very beginning, because it had involved the pooling of British and American technical skill.

On July 24 I casually mentioned to Stalin that we had a new weapon of unusual destructive force. The Russian Premier showed no special interest. All he said was that he was glad to hear it and hoped we would make "good use of it against the Japanese." . . .

On July 28 Radio Tokyo announced that the Japanese government would continue to fight. There was no formal reply to the joint ultimatum of the United States, the United Kingdom, and China. There was no alternative now. The bomb was scheduled to be dropped after August 3 unless Japan surrendered before that day.

On August 6, the fourth day of the journey home from Potsdam, came the historic news that shook the world. I was eating lunch with members of the *Augusta's* crew when Captain Frank Graham, White House Map Room watch officer, handed me the following message:

TO THE PRESIDENT
FROM THE SECRETARY OF WAR
Big bomb dropped on Hiroshima August 5 at 7:15 P.M. Washington time. First reports indicate complete success which was even more conspicuous than earlier test.

CHAPTER 8

THE BURDENS
OF POWER: THE
DECISION TO
DROP THE
ATOMIC BOMB,
1945

I was greatly moved. I telephoned Byrnes aboard ship to give him the news and then said to the group of sailors around me, "This is the greatest thing in history. It's time for us to get home." . . .

Source 2 from Henry L. Stimson and McGeorge Bundy, *On Active Service in Peace and War* (New York: Harper and Brothers, 1948), pp. 613–633.

2. Henry L. Stimson (Secretary of War, 1941–1945).[10]

The policy adopted and steadily pursued by President Roosevelt and his advisers was a simple one. It was to spare no effort in securing the earliest possible successful development of an atomic weapon. The reasons for this policy were equally simple. The original experimental achievement of atomic fission had occurred in Germany in 1938, and it was known that the Germans had continued their experiments. In 1941 and 1942 they were believed to be ahead of us, and it was vital that they should not be the first to bring atomic weapons into the field of battle. Furthermore, if we should be the first to develop the weapon, we should have a great new instrument for shortening the war and minimizing destruction. At no time, from 1941 to 1945, did I ever hear it suggested by the President, or by any other responsible member of the government, that atomic energy should not be used in the war. All of us of course understood the terrible responsibility involved in our attempt to unlock the doors to such a devastating weapon; President Roosevelt particularly spoke to me many times of his own awareness of the catastrophic potentialities of our work. But we were at war, and the work must be done. I therefore emphasize that it was our common objective, throughout the war, to be the first to produce an atomic weapon and use it. The possible atomic weapon was considered to be a new and tremendously powerful explosive, as legitimate as any other of the deadly explosive weapons of modern war. The entire purpose was the production of a military weapon; on no other ground could the wartime expenditure of so much time and money have been justified. The exact circumstances in which that weapon might be used were unknown to any of us until the middle of 1945, and when that time came, as we shall presently see, the military use of atomic energy was connected with larger questions of national policy. . . .

10. Parts of this chapter appeared earlier as "The Decision to Use the Atomic Bomb" in the February 1947 issue of *Harper's* magazine.

As time went on it became clear that the weapon would not be available in time for use in the European theater, and the war against Germany was successfully ended by the use of what are now called conventional means. But in the spring of 1945 it became evident that the climax of our prolonged atomic effort was at hand. By the nature of atomic chain reactions, it was impossible to state with certainty that we had succeeded until a bomb had actually exploded in a full-scale experiment; nevertheless it was considered exceedingly probable that we should by midsummer have successfully detonated the first atomic bomb. This was to be done at the Alamogordo Reservation in New Mexico. It was thus time for detailed consideration of our future plans. What had begun as a well-founded hope was now developing into a reality.

On March 15, 1945 I had my last talk with President Roosevelt. . . .

I did not see Franklin Roosevelt again. The next time I went to the White House to discuss atomic energy was April 25, 1945, and I went to explain the nature of the problem to a man whose only previous knowledge of our activities was that of a Senator who had loyally accepted our assurance that the matter must be kept a secret from him. Now he was President and Commander-in-Chief, and the final responsibility in this as in so many other matters must be his. President Truman accepted this responsibility with the same fine spirit that Senator Truman had shown before in accepting our refusal to inform him. . . .

[*Here Stimson summarizes his report to Truman and reproduces a nine-point memorandum on postwar atomic policy, the high points of which were Stimson's belief that atomic bomb secrets should not be shared with any other nation and his corresponding fear that eventual nuclear proliferation constituted a serious threat to civilization. Stimson then summarizes the work and recommendations of the Interim Committee, which agree with Truman's recollections on page 207.*]

In reaching these conclusions the Interim Committee carefully considered such alternatives as a detailed advance warning or a demonstration in some uninhabited area. Both of these suggestions were discarded as impractical. They were not regarded as likely to be effective in compelling a surrender of Japan, and both of them involved serious risks. Even the New Mexico test would not give final proof that any given bomb was certain to explode when dropped from an airplane. Quite apart from the generally unfamiliar nature of atomic explosives, there was the whole problem of exploding a bomb at a predetermined height in the air by a complicated mechanism which could not be tested in the static test of New Mexico. Nothing would have been more damaging to our effort to obtain surrender than a warning or a demonstration followed by a dud—and this was a real

CHAPTER 8

THE BURDENS
OF POWER: THE
DECISION TO
DROP THE
ATOMIC BOMB,
1945

possibility. Furthermore, we had no bombs to waste. It was vital that a sufficient effect be quickly obtained with the few we had. . . .

The principal political, social, and military objective of the United States in the summer of 1945 was the prompt and complete surrender of Japan. Only the complete destruction of her military power could open the way to lasting peace.

Japan, in July, 1945, had been seriously weakened by our increasingly violent attacks. It was known to us that she had gone so far as to make tentative proposals to the Soviet Government, hoping to use the Russians as mediators in a negotiated peace. These vague proposals contemplated the retention by Japan of important conquered areas and were therefore not considered seriously. There was as yet no indication of any weakening in the Japanese determination to fight rather than accept unconditional surrender. If she should persist in her fight to the end, she had still a great military force. . . .

[*Here Stimson summarizes the military strength of the Japanese, which was believed to include an armed force of 5 million men and 5,000 suicide aircraft. Stimson then recalls that his military advisers estimated that an assault on the Japanese mainland would result in more than 1 million casualties to American forces alone. With those considerations in mind, Stimson wrote a memorandum to President Truman on July 2 reporting that Japan might be close to surrender and that a properly worded call to Japan to lay down its arms (and including an American promise that Emperor Hirohito could remain on his throne) might avoid the inevitably bloody combat on the Japanese mainland. The atomic bomb, untested as of July 2, was not mentioned in the memorandum for security reasons.*]

The adoption of the policy outlined in the memorandum of July 2 was a decision of high politics; once it was accepted by the President, the position of the atomic bomb in our planning became quite clear. I find that I stated in my diary, as early as June 19, that "the last chance warning . . . must be given before an actual landing of the ground forces in Japan, and fortunately the plans provide for enough time to bring in the sanctions to our warning in the shape of heavy ordinary bombing attack and an attack of S-1." S-1 was a code name for the atomic bomb.

There was much discussion in Washington about the timing of the warning to Japan. The controlling factor in the end was the date already set for the Potsdam meeting of the Big Three. It was President Truman's decision that such a warning should be solemnly issued by the U.S. and the U.K. from this meeting, with the concurrence of the head of the Chinese Government, so that it would be plain that *all* of Japan's principal enemies were in entire unity. This was done, in the Potsdam Ultimatum of July 26, which very closely followed the above memorandum of July 2, with the exception that it made no mention of the Japanese Emperor.[11]

On July 28 the Premier of Japan, Suzuki, rejected the Potsdam ultimatum by announcing that it was "unworthy of public notice." In the face of this rejection we could only proceed to demonstrate that the ultimatum had meant exactly what it said when it stated that if the Japanese continued the war, "the full application of our military power, backed by our resolve, will mean the inevitable and complete destruction of the Japanese armed forces and just as inevitably the utter devastation of the Japanese homeland." . . .

As I read over what I have written, I am aware that much of it, in this year of peace, may have a harsh and unfeeling sound. It would perhaps be possible to say the same things and say them more gently. But I do not think it would be wise. As I look back over the five years of my service as Secretary of War, I see too many stern and heartrending decisions to be willing to pretend that war is anything else than what it is. The face of war is the face of death; death is an inevitable part of every order that a wartime leader gives. The decision to use the atomic bomb was a decision that brought death to over a hundred thousand Japanese. No explanation can change that fact and I do not wish to gloss it over. But this deliberate, premeditated destruction was our least abhorrent choice. The destruction of Hiroshima and Nagasaki put an end to the Japanese war. It stopped the fire raids, and the strangling blockade; it ended the ghastly specter of a clash of great land armies. . . .

Source 3 from Dwight D. Eisenhower, *The White House Years: Mandate for Change, 1953–1956* (Garden City, N.Y.: Doubleday and Company, 1963), pp. 312–313.

3. General Dwight D. Eisenhower (Supreme Commander, Allied Military Forces in Europe).

. . . The incident took place in 1945 when Secretary of War Stimson, visiting my headquarters in Germany, informed me that our government was preparing to drop an atomic bomb on Japan. I was one of those who felt that there were a number of cogent reasons to question the wisdom of such an act. I was not, of course, called upon, officially, for any advice or counsel

11. Keep this point in mind, for it will be very important later.

CHAPTER 8

THE BURDENS
OF POWER: THE
DECISION TO
DROP THE
ATOMIC BOMB,
1945

concerning the matter, because the European theater, of which I was the commanding general, was not involved, the forces of Hitler having already been defeated. But the Secretary, upon giving me the news of the successful bomb test in New Mexico, and of the plan for using it, asked for my reaction, apparently expecting a vigorous assent.

During his recitation of the relevant facts, I had been conscious of a feeling of depression and so I voiced to him my grave misgivings, first on the basis of my belief that Japan was already defeated and that dropping the bomb was completely unnecessary, and secondly because I thought that our country should avoid shocking world opinion by the use of a weapon whose employment was, I thought, no longer mandatory as a measure to save American lives. It was my belief that Japan was, at that very moment, seeking some way to surrender with a minimum loss of "face." The Secretary was deeply perturbed by my attitude, almost angrily refuting the reasons I gave for my quick conclusions. . . .

Source 4 from William D. Leahy, *I Was There* (New York: Whittlesey House, 1950), pp. 440–442.

4. Admiral William D. Leahy (Chief of Staff to Presidents Roosevelt and Truman).

In the spring of 1945 President Truman directed Mr. Byrnes to make a special study of the status and prospects of the new atomic explosive on which two billion dollars already had been spent. Byrnes came to my home on the evening of June 4 to discuss his findings. He was more favorably impressed than I had been up to that time with the prospects of success in the final development and use of this new weapon.

Once it had been tested, President Truman faced the decision as to whether to use it. He did not like the idea, but was persuaded that it would shorten the war against Japan and save American lives. It is my opinion that the use of this barbarous weapon at Hiroshima and Nagasaki was of no material assistance in our war against Japan. The Japanese were already defeated and ready to surrender because of the effective sea blockade and the successful bombing with conventional weapons.

It was my reaction that the scientists and others wanted to make this test because of the vast sums that had been spent on the project. Truman knew that, and so did the other people involved. However, the Chief Executive made a decision to use the bomb on two cities in Japan. We had only produced two bombs at that time. We did not know which cities would be the targets, but the President specified that the bombs should be used against military facilities. . . .

One of the professors associated with the Manhattan Project told me that he had hoped the bomb wouldn't work. I wish that he had been right. . . .

Source 5 from Joseph C. Grew, *Turbulent Era: A Diplomatic Record of Forty Years, 1904–1945,* ed. Walter Johnson (Boston: Houghton Mifflin Company, 1952), Vol. II, pp. 1421–1428.

5. Joseph C. Grew (Former Ambassador to Japan and in 1945 Under Secretary of State and Briefly Acting Secretary of State).

For a long time I had held the belief, based on my intimate experience with Japanese thinking and psychology over an extensive period, that the surrender of the Japanese would be highly unlikely, regardless of military defeat, in the absence of a public undertaking by the President that unconditional surrender would not mean the elimination of the present dynasty if the Japanese people desired its retention. I furthermore believed that if such a statement could be formulated and issued shortly after the great devastation of Tokyo by our B-29 attacks on or about May 26, 1945, the hands of the Emperor and his peace-minded advisers would be greatly strengthened in the face of the intransigent militarists and that the process leading to an early surrender might even then be set in motion by such a statement. Soviet Russia had not then entered the war against Japan, and since the United States had carried the major burden of the war in the Pacific, and since the President had already publicly declared that unconditional surrender would mean neither annihilation nor enslavement, I felt that the President would be fully justified in amplifying his previous statement as suggested. My belief in the potential effect of such a statement at that particular juncture was fully shared and supported by those officers in the Department of State who knew Japan and the Japanese well. . . .

In my own talk with the President on May 28, he immediately said that his own thinking ran along the same lines as mine, but he asked me to discuss the proposal with the Secretaries of War and Navy and the Chiefs of Staff and then to report to him the consensus of that group. A conference was therefore called and was held in the office of the Secretary of War in the Pentagon Building on May 29, 1945, and the issue was discussed for an hour. According to my memorandum of that meeting it became clear in the course of the discussion that Mr. Stimson, Mr. Forrestal, and General Marshall (Admiral King was absent) were all in accord with the principle

CHAPTER 8

THE BURDENS
OF POWER: THE
DECISION TO
DROP THE
ATOMIC BOMB,
1945

of the proposal but that for certain military reasons, not then divulged, it was considered inadvisable for the President to make such a statement at that juncture. It later appeared that the fighting on Okinawa was still going on, and it was felt that such a declaration as I proposed would be interpreted by the Japanese as a confession of weakness. The question of timing was the nub of the whole matter, according to the views expressed. I duly reported this to the President, and the proposal for action was, for the time being, dropped.

When Mr. Byrnes became Secretary of State over a month later, I endeavored to interest him in the importance and urgency of a public statement along the lines proposed, but during those few days he was intensely occupied in preparing for the Potsdam Conference, and it was only on the morning of his departure for Potsdam that I was able to hand him a draft on which a declaration might be based. This was the draft I had shown to the President. Mr. Byrnes was already on his way out of his office to drive to the airport, and his last action before leaving was to place our draft in his pocket. Mr. Stimson was then already in Europe and I urged Jack McCloy, Assistant Secretary of War, when he met him over there, to tell Mr. Stimson how strongly I felt about the matter.

Mr. Stimson did take energetic steps at Potsdam to secure the decision by the President and Mr. Churchill to issue the proclamation. In fact, the opinion was expressed to me by one American already in Potsdam, that if it had not been for Mr. Stimson's wholehearted initiative, the Potsdam Conference would have ended without any proclamation to Japan being issued at all. But even Mr. Stimson was unable to have included in the proclamation a categorical undertaking that unconditional surrender would not mean the elimination of the dynasty if the Japanese people desired its retention.

The main point at issue historically is whether, if immediately following the terrific devastation of Tokyo by our B-29s in May, 1945,[12] "the President had made a public categorical statement that surrender would not mean the elimination of the present dynasty if the Japanese people desired its retention, the surrender of Japan could have been hastened.

"That question can probably never be definitively answered but a good deal of evidence is available to shed light on it. From statements made by a number of the moderate former Japanese leaders to responsible Americans after the American occupation, it is quite clear that the civilian advisers to the Emperor were working toward surrender long before the Potsdam Proclamation, even indeed before my talk with the President on

12. The following quotation is taken from a letter from Grew to Stimson, February 12, 1947.

May 28, for they knew then that Japan was a defeated nation. The stumbling block that they had to overcome was the complete dominance of the Japanese Army over the Government, and even when the moderates finally succeeded in getting a decision by the controlling element of the Government to accept the Potsdam terms, efforts were made by the unreconciled elements in the Japanese Army to bring about nullification of that decision. The Emperor needed all the support he could get, and in the light of available evidence I myself and others felt and still feel that if such a categorical statement about the dynasty had been issued in May, 1945, the surrender-minded elements in the Government might well have been afforded by such a statement a valid reason and the necessary strength to come to an early clear-cut decision.

"If surrender could have been brought about in May, 1945, or even in June or July, before the entrance of Soviet Russia into the war and the use of the atomic bomb, the world would have been the gainer.

"The action of Prime Minister Suzuki in rejecting the Potsdam ultimatum by announcing on July 28, 1945, that it was 'unworthy of public notice' was a most unfortunate if not an utterly stupid step.[13] Suzuki, who was severely wounded and very nearly assassinated as a moderate by the military extremists in 1936, I believe from the evidence which has reached me was surrender-minded even before May, 1945, if only it were made clear that surrender would not involve the downfall of the dynasty. That point was clearly *implied* in Article 12 of the Potsdam Proclamation that 'the occupying forces of the Allies shall be withdrawn from Japan as soon as . . . there has been established in accordance with the freely expressed will of the Japanese people a peacefully inclined and responsible government.' This however was not, at least from the Japanese point of view, a categorical undertaking regarding the dynasty, nor did it comply with your [Henry L. Stimson's] suggestion that it would substantially add to the chances of acceptance if the ultimatum should contain a statement that we would not exclude a constitutional monarchy under the present dynasty. Suzuki's reply was typical of oriental methods in retaining his supposed bargaining position until he knew precisely what the Potsdam Proclamation meant in that respect. The Asiatic concern over the loss of assumed bargaining power that might arise from exhibiting what might be interpreted as a sign of weakness is always uppermost in Japanese mental processes. He can seldom be made to realize that the time for compromise has passed if it ever existed. This explains but certainly does not excuse Suzuki's reply, and the result of his reply was to release the atom bomb to fulfill its appointed purpose.

13. See Truman memoirs, p. 209, and Stimson memoirs, p. 212.

CHAPTER 8

THE BURDENS
OF POWER: THE
DECISION TO
DROP THE
ATOMIC BOMB,
1945

Yet I and a good many others will always feel that had the President issued as far back as May, 1945, the recommended categorical statement that the Japanese dynasty would be retained if the Japanese people freely desired its retention, the atom bomb might never have had to be used at all. . . ."

Source 6 from John L. McCloy, *The Challenge to American Foreign Policy* (Cambridge, Mass.: Harvard University Press, 1953), pp. 40–44.

6. John L. McCloy (Assistant Secretary of War, 1941–1945).

[*McCloy was present at the meeting of Truman and his military advisers in late June. As he recalled, the "prospect of an attack on the main Japanese islands, even at that late date, was not too attractive." Nevertheless, the Joint Chiefs of Staff unanimously recommended an amphibious assault on the islands of Kyushu and Honshu, and Truman gave his tentative approval, even though the president had been sobered by the estimates of American casualties.*]

After the President's decision had been made and the conference was breaking up, an official, not theretofore participating,[14] suggested that serious attention should be given to a political attempt to end the war. The meeting fell into a tailspin, but after control was recovered, the idea appealed to several present. It appealed particularly to the President, and to one member of the Joint Chiefs of Staff, who, by the way, was the one member of that body who had no responsibility to a particular service.

It was also at this meeting that the suggestion was first broached that warning be given the Japanese of our possession of the bomb before we dropped it. Although all present were "cleared," the uninhibited mention of the "best-kept secret of the war" caused a sense of shock, even among that select group.

Now this incident indicates that at that time everyone was so intent on winning the war by military means that the introduction of political considerations was almost accidental. It cannot be charged against the military that they did not initially put forward the suggestion of political action. It was not their job to do so. Nor did any one of them oppose the thought of political action, though several of the Chiefs were not too happy about it. Not one of the Chiefs nor the Secretary thought well of a bomb warning, an effective argument being that no one could be certain, in spite of the assurances of the scientists, that the "thing would go off." At that time, we had not yet had the benefit of the Alamogordo test.

14. As it turns out, "an official" was McCloy himself. See Forrestal memoirs, p. 223.

As a result of the meeting, a rather hastily composed paper was drawn up. It embodied the idea which later formed the basis of the appeal to the Japanese to surrender. That proposal, it will be recalled, was refused brusquely by the Japanese Government. Yet, as we now know, it did provoke considerable discussion and divergence of opinion among the Japanese military leaders and politicians. It is interesting to speculate whether, better prepared, this proposal might not have included statements of the policy which we put into effect in Japan almost immediately after the war ended. Such a proposal might well have induced surrender without the use of the bomb. What effect that might have had on postwar developments is a subject worthy of conjecture.

Although no one from the State Department was present at the conference which has been described, Mr. Joseph Grew for some time had been most energetically urging a political approach to the Japanese, but his thoughts never seemed effectively to have gotten to the White House, at least prior to the June meeting. . . .

Source 7 from James F. Byrnes, *All in One Lifetime* (New York: Harper and Brothers, 1958), pp. 282–287, 290–291, 300–301.

7. James F. Byrnes (Secretary of State, 1945–1947).

[Byrnes was Truman's personal representative on the Interim Committee, and Truman soon would name him secretary of state. Byrnes's recollections begin with the formation and work of the Interim Committee.]

As I heard these scientists and industrialists predict the destructive power of the weapon, I was thoroughly frightened. I had sufficient imagination to visualize the danger to our country when some other country possessed such a weapon. Thinking of the country most likely to become unfriendly to us, I asked General Marshall and some of the others at the meeting how long it would take the Soviets to develop such a bomb. The consensus was that they would have the secret in two or three years, but could not actually produce a bomb in less than six or seven years. One or two expressed the opinion that Soviet progress would depend upon whether or not they had taken German scientists and production experts as prisoners of war for the purpose of having them work on such weapons. No one seemed too alarmed at the prospect because it appeared that in seven years we should be far ahead of the Soviets in this field; and, of course, in 1945 we could not believe that after their terrible sacrifices, the Russians would think of making war for many years to come.

CHAPTER 8

THE BURDENS
OF POWER: THE
DECISION TO
DROP THE
ATOMIC BOMB,
1945

A few days after the committee was appointed, President Truman referred to me a letter addressed to President Roosevelt by Dr. Albert Einstein, dated March 25, which was in President Roosevelt's office at the time of his death at Warm Springs. In it Dr. Einstein requested the President to receive Dr. L. Szilard,[15] "who proposes to submit to you certain considerations and recommendations." After citing Dr. Szilard's reputation in the scientific field, Dr. Einstein went on to say that Dr. Szilard was concerned about the lack of adequate contact between the atomic scientists and the Cabinet members who were responsible for determining policy. Dr. Einstein concluded with the hope that the President would give his personal attention to what Dr. Szilard had to say.

President Truman asked me to see Szilard, who came down to Spartanburg, bringing with him Dr. H. C. Urey and another scientist. As the Einstein letter had indicated he would, Szilard complained that he and some of his associates did not know enough about the policy of the government with regard to the use of the bomb. He felt that scientists, including himself, should discuss the matter with the Cabinet, which I did not feel desirable. His general demeanor and his desire to participate in policy making made an unfavorable impression on me, but his associates were neither as aggressive nor apparently as dissatisfied. . . .

[*Here Byrnes recalls that, with the exception of Robert Oppenheimer, Szilard was critical of the scientific consultants to the Interim Committee, presumably because of what Szilard feared was their overenthusiasm to use the bomb. Byrnes reported to General Leslie Groves (director of the Manhattan Project) the visit of Szilard and his colleagues, whereby Groves replied that he already knew of the meeting, because he had had the scientists followed. Byrnes then summarizes the recommendations of the Interim Committee, recalls plans to cover up the test firing of the atomic bomb at Alamogordo, New Mexico, voices his concern about the estimated losses an assault on the Japanese mainland would inflict, and remembers Stimson arguing at Potsdam for an ultimatum to the Japanese before either an assault or the dropping of an atomic bomb.*]

On our arrival[16] we were informed that Stalin, who traveled by train for health reasons, would be delayed for a day. However, the Prime Minister

15. Leo Szilard was a physicist working on the Manhattan Project. According to Szilard's reminiscences, Byrnes was especially concerned about the Soviet Union's postwar behavior and believed that a show of America's nuclear power would frighten the Soviets and make them "more manageable" after the war was over. Szilard recalled that he was "flabbergasted" by Byrnes's "rattling the bomb" as a diplomatic weapon. See Leo Szilard, "Reminiscences," in *The Intellectual Migration: Europe and America, 1930–1960*, ed. Donald Fleming and Bernard Bailyn (Cambridge, Mass.: Harvard University Press, 1969), pp. 122–133.
16. At the Potsdam Conference, July 1945.

was already in residence; his quarters, about a mile away, he had designated as "10 Downing Street, Potsdam," this address appearing on the dinner menus when he entertained. Stalin's quarters were more remote, located in the vast wooded park surrounding Cecilienhof Palace, where the meetings were to be held. Though we received official invitations to visit his quarters on several occasions, it was obvious that their location was a well-guarded secret to the Conference personnel generally.

We spent a morning with our military advisers, and in the afternoon the President, Admiral Leahy, and I drove into Berlin. Here we saw what remained of the German Chancellery and other relics of the broken regime. But our small party had no monopoly on sightseeing. On our return I heard from Will Clayton and Ed Pauley (our representative on the reparations Committee) that they had seen machinery from a manufacturing plant which had been moved from the U.S. zone of Germany into the Soviets' shortly before our arrival. It was now standing in an open field. They also had heard stories of all kinds of materials and even herds of cattle being taken to Russia. We knew that in our quarters the original bath fixtures had vanished, others having been hurriedly substituted for our use, and there was plain evidence that the Soviets were unilaterally awarding themselves reparations, both in large and small quantities.

About noon the next day, July 17, Stalin called on the President. It was, of course, their first meeting. Molotov accompanied him and from that moment things began to happen. For more than an hour the four of us remained in conference, Chip Bohlen and Pavlov doing the interpreting. After an exchange of greetings, and some remarks on his long and tiresome train journey, Stalin launched into a discussion of Russia's entry into the Japanese war. He reported that the Japanese had already made overtures to him to act as mediator, to which he had given no definite reply since they did not provide for an unconditional surrender. But he left me with the distinct impression that he was not anxious to see an end to the fighting until Soviet entry into the war could help secure the concessions he expected of China. He said he had not yet reached an agreement with the Chinese Premier, T. V. Soong, on certain matters, and that this was necessary before he could declare war. Negotiations had been halted until after the Potsdam meeting, he said, and mentioned, among other unsettled questions, arrangements for the Port of Dairen. The President commented that the United States wanted to be certain that Dairen was maintained as an open port, and Stalin said that would be its status, should the Soviets obtain control of it.

CHAPTER 8
THE BURDENS
OF POWER: THE
DECISION TO
DROP THE
ATOMIC BOMB,
1945

Not having been at Yalta on the day the so-called secret agreement was arrived at, and having been out of government service for three months, I could make no statement of my own knowledge, but having heard a few days before that there had been an understanding between President Roosevelt and Stalin that Dairen should be an open port, I supported the President's statement in a general way, saying that our people understood that at Yalta President Roosevelt had taken the same position. Stalin merely repeated that that would be its status under Soviet control. Nevertheless, I was disturbed about what kind of bargain he might coerce China into making, for the very fact that they had not reached agreement made me suspect that Stalin was increasing his demands. The President told Stimson that night that "he had clinched the Open Door in Manchuria." I was encouraged but not quite that confident. However, the President and I felt that, without appearing to encourage Chiang to disregard any pledges made by Roosevelt at Yalta, we should let him know that the United States did not want him to make additional concessions to the Soviets. Then the President received from Chiang a cable stating that China had gone the limit to fulfill the Yalta agreement. I prepared a message which the President approved and on the 23rd sent to Chiang Kai-shek: "I asked that you carry out the Yalta agreements, but I have not asked that you make any concessions in excess of that agreement. If you and Generalissimo Stalin differ as to the correct interpretation of the Yalta agreement, I hope you will arrange for Soong to return to Moscow and continue your efforts to reach complete understanding."

Our purpose was stated in the first sentence. The second sentence was to encourage the Chinese to continue negotiations after the adjournment of the Potsdam Conference. I had some fear that if they did not, Stalin might immediately enter the war, knowing full well that he could take not only what Roosevelt and Churchill, and subsequently Chiang, had agreed to at Yalta, but—with China divided and Chiang seeking Soviet support against Chinese Communists—whatever else he wanted. On the other hand, if Stalin and Chiang were still negotiating, it might delay Soviet entrance and the Japanese might surrender. The President was in accord with that view. . . .

The President and I discussed whether or not we were obligated to inform Stalin that we had succeeded in developing a powerful weapon and shortly would drop a bomb in Japan. Though there was an understanding that the Soviets would enter the war with Japan three months after Germany surrendered, which would make their entrance about the middle of August, with knowledge of the Japanese peace feeler and the successful bomb test in New Mexico, the President and I hoped that Japan would surrender before then. However, at luncheon we agreed that because it was uncertain, and because the Soviets might soon be our allies in that war, the President should inform Stalin of our intention, but do so in a casual way.

He then informed the British of our plan, in which they concurred. Upon the adjournment of the afternoon session, when we arose from the table, the President, accompanied by our interpreter, Bohlen, walked around to Stalin's chair and said, substantially, "You may be interested to know that we have developed a new and powerful weapon and within a few days intend to use it against Japan." I watched Stalin's expression as this was being interpreted, and was surprised that he smiled blandly and said only a few words. When the President and I reached our car, he said that the Generalissimo had replied only, "That's fine. I hope you make good use of it against the Japanese."

I did not believe Stalin grasped the full import of the President's statement, and thought that on the next day there would be some inquiry about this "new and powerful weapon," but I was mistaken. I thought then and even now believe that Stalin did not appreciate the importance of the information that had been given him; but there are others who believe that in the light of later information about the Soviets' intelligence service in this country, he was already aware of the New Mexico test, and that this accounted for his apparent indifference. . . .

Source 8 from James Forrestal, *The Forrestal Diaries,* ed. Walter Millis and E. S. Duffield (New York: Viking Press, 1951), pp. 55, 70–71, 74–78, 80–81.

8. James Forrestal (Secretary of the Navy).

[*Forrestal recalls a meeting that took place on May 11, 1945, between himself, a few high-ranking naval officers, and United States ambassador to the Soviet Union Averell Harriman, the main topic of which was the threat of the Soviet Union's postwar power in Asia. There was some talk of making a separate peace with Japan before the Soviets entered the Pacific war (as they had promised to do at Yalta). The fear that a weak postwar China would be an invitation to the Russians to "move in quickly" also was expressed.*]

8 March 1947   *Meeting with McCloy*
. . . McCloy recalled the meeting with President Truman at the White House at which the decision was taken to proceed with the invasion of Kyushu. He said this for him illustrated most vividly the necessity for the civilian voice in military decisions even in time of war. He said that what

CHAPTER 8

THE BURDENS
OF POWER: THE
DECISION TO
DROP THE
ATOMIC BOMB,
1945

he had to say was pertinent not merely to the question of the invasion of the Japanese mainland but also to the question of whether we needed to get Russia in to help us defeat Japan. At this particular meeting, which occurred in the summer of 1945, before the President went to Potsdam, where, under the pressure of Secretary Byrnes, he states his principal mission would be to get the Russians into the war against the Japs, the President made the rounds of his military advisers and asked them to tell him whether the Japanese mainland invasion was necessary. They all agreed it was. He finally left it that they would proceed with the plannings for the invasion of Kyushu but that they were to raise the question with him again before its execution and he would reserve decision on whether or not the attack should be carried into the Tokyo plan [plain?].

As the meeting broke up, McCloy said he had not been asked but wanted to state his views.[17] (Neither Stimson nor I was at this meeting.) He said that he thought before the final decision to invade Japan was taken or it was decided to use the atomic bomb political measures should be taken; the Japanese should be told of what had happened to Germany, particularly in view of the fact that some of their people who had been in Germany were back in Japan and would be able to report on the destruction and devastation which they had witnessed; that the Japs should be told, furthermore, that we had another and terrifyingly destructive weapon which we would have to use if they did not surrender; that they would be permitted to retain the Emperor and a form of government of their own choosing. He said the military leaders were somewhat annoyed at his interference but that the President welcomed it and at the conclusion of McCloy's observations ordered such a political offensive to be set in motion.

13 July 1945   *Japanese Peace Feeler*

The first real evidence of a Japanese desire to get out of the war came today through intercepted messages from Togo, Foreign Minister, to Sato, Jap Ambassador in Moscow, instructing the latter to see Molotov if possible before his departure for the Big Three meeting [the Potsdam Conference], and if not then, immediately afterward, to lay before him the Emperor's strong desire to secure a termination of the war. This he said arose not only out of the Emperor's interest in the welfare of his own subjects but out of his interest toward mankind in general. He was anxious, he said, to see cessation of bloodshed on both sides. Togo said to convey to the Russians the fact that they wanted to remain at peace with Russia, that the Japanese did not desire permanent annexation of any of the territories they had

17. See McCloy memoirs, p. 218.

conquered in Manchuria. Togo said further that the unconditional surrender terms of the Allies was about the only thing in the way of termination of the war and he said that if this were insisted upon, of course the Japanese would have to continue the fight.

Sato's response . . . was to protest that the proposals were quite unrealistic; looked at objectively it was clear that there was no chance now of dividing Russia from the other Allies.

15 July 1945   *Japanese Peace Feeler*

Messages today on Japanese–Russian conversations. Togo, Foreign Minister, insisted that Sato present to Molotov the request of the Emperor himself. Sato's replies insistently pointed out the lack of reality in Togo's apparent belief that there is a chance of persuading Russia to take independent action on the Eastern war. He stated very bluntly and without any coating how fantastic is the hope that Russia would be impressed by Japanese willingness to give up territory which she had already lost. . . . Throughout Sato's message ran a note of cold and realistic evaluation of Japan's position; and he said that the situation was rapidly passing beyond the point of Japan's and Russia's cooperating in the security of Asia but [that the question was] rather whether there would be any Manchukuo or even Japan itself left as entities. The gist of his final message was that it was clear that Japan was thoroughly and completely defeated and that the only course open was quick and definite action recognizing such fact. . . .

It is significant that these conversations began before there could have been much effect from the thousand-plane raids of the Third Fleet and several days before the naval bombardment of Kamaishi.

24 July 1945   *Japanese Peace Feeler*

. . . Finally, on the first of July, Sato sent a long message outlining what he conceived to be Japan's position, which was in brief that she was now entirely alone and friendless and could look for succor from no one. . . . He strongly advised accepting any terms, including unconditional surrender, on the basis that this was the only way of preserving the entity of the Emperor and the state itself. . . .

The response to his message was that the Cabinet in council had weighed all the considerations which he had raised and that their final judgment and decisions was that the war must be fought with all the vigor and bitterness of which the nation was capable so long as the only alternative was the unconditional surrender.

CHAPTER 8

THE BURDENS
OF POWER: THE
DECISION TO
DROP THE
ATOMIC BOMB,
1945

28 July 1945

. . . Talked with Byrnes [now at Potsdam as American Secretary of State, having succeeded Mr. Stettinius on the conclusion of the San Francisco Conference]. . . . Byrnes said he was most anxious to get the Japanese affair over with before the Russians got in, with particular reference to Dairen and Port Arthur. Once in there, he felt, it would not be easy to get them out. . . .

29 July 1945

. . . On the way back to our headquarters we passed the equipment of an American armored division drawn up alongside the road. It included tanks and light armored vehicles and must have extended for about three miles. Commodore Schade said the Russians were much impressed by it. There came back to my mind the President's remark about Stalin's observation about the Pope: When Churchill suggested that the Pope would still be a substantial influence in Europe, Stalin snorted and said, "How many divisions has the Pope got?" . . .

QUESTIONS TO CONSIDER

The selections begin with the memoirs of President Harry S Truman because he ultimately had to make the decision to drop the atomic bomb on Hiroshima. According to Truman, what figures were most influential in his thinking? What alternatives did Truman himself think he had?

Truman's July 26 proclamation calling on the Japanese to surrender is a crucial piece of evidence. According to Truman (based on his conversations with Acting Secretary of State Joseph Grew), what was the nature of the proclamation to be? Did Truman offer any more details about that proclamation? Keep these points in mind because they will be of some importance later. Secretary of War Henry Stimson was

one of Truman's key advisers. How did Stimson enhance Truman's memories with regard to the April 25 meeting (where the president received his first full briefing on the bomb)? Did Stimson add important information about the Interim Committee?

Stimson's recollection of the July 26 proclamation to Japan (he called it the Potsdam Ultimatum) adds one vital piece of information Truman does not mention. What is it? How important was this piece of information? How important was its omission by Truman?

The memoirs of Eisenhower and Leahy were included to give you the views of two military men concerning the detonation of the atomic bomb. Both men seem to have been opposed.

Why? According to Eisenhower, what was Stimson's reaction? Why? According to Leahy, who was "pushing" the bomb? Why?

Joseph Grew probably knew Japanese thinking better than anyone in Truman's inner circle, having been ambassador to Japan for several years. According to Grew, what was the situation in Japan in early July 1945? In his view, would Japan have surrendered if the atomic bomb had *not* been dropped? What did Grew think of the July 26 Potsdam Ultimatum (it was, after all, his idea)?

According to John McCloy, how did the Potsdam Ultimatum originate? McCloy calls the document a "rather hastily composed paper." Why? Did McCloy see any alternatives? More important, how influential did McCloy think Grew was in Truman's "inner circle"? Why? In a larger sense, what point was McCloy trying to make?

James Byrnes was Truman's personal observer on the Interim Committee and soon after his secretary of state. What apparently was one of Byrnes's important concerns with regard to dropping the bomb? How influential would you say this view was?

Byrnes's meeting with scientist Leo Szilard and H. C. Urey apparently went badly, a fact corroborated by Szilard's reminiscences. Why? What does this tell you about Byrnes?

According to Byrnes, what were the United States' alternatives in July 1945? Reporting on the Potsdam Conference, how did Byrnes portray Stalin? Furthermore, Byrnes raised a key point with regard to the Soviet Union's entrance into the war against Japan. It had been agreed earlier that the Soviets would reach an agreement with the Chinese *before* entering the war. How did Byrnes view these negotiations? Why did he hope the Soviets and the Chinese would take a long time in reaching an agreement? What does this tell you about Byrnes's thinking? His biases? How does Forrestal's diary help us understand Byrnes's thinking? How did Forrestal clarify the situation in Japan? Did he offer any clues as to how United States officials believed the Soviet Union should be dealt with?

Now return to the central questions. Why did President Truman decide to drop the atomic bomb on Hiroshima? What factors went into his decision? Were there any alternatives to dropping the bomb? If so, why did Truman not pursue them? What advisers were and were not influential with Truman? Finally, do you think Truman's decision was the proper one?

⊙⊃ EPILOGUE ⊂⊙

Two days after the United States dropped the uranium bomb on Hiroshima, the Soviet Union declared war on Japan and invaded Manchuria. Meanwhile, Japanese scientists, realizing the magnitude of what had

CHAPTER 8

THE BURDENS
OF POWER: THE
DECISION TO
DROP THE
ATOMIC BOMB,
1945

happened at Hiroshima, begged their government to surrender. Japanese military leaders stubbornly refused. Therefore, the next day (August 9), the United States dropped a second atomic bomb (this one using plutonium instead of uranium) on Nagasaki, with equally devastating results. On August 10, the Japanese emperor asserted himself against the military and agreed to surrender on the terms announced in the Potsdam Ultimatum of July 26. On September 2, the formal surrender took place, and the Second World War came to an end, with a total loss of life of approximately 50 million military personnel and civilians.

The scientists who worked on the Manhattan Project were of two minds concerning Hiroshima and Nagasaki. American physicist Robert Brode probably spoke for the majority when he said, "But if I am to tell the whole truth I must confess that our relief was really greater than our horror," principally because the war at last was over. Yet American electronics specialist William Higinbotham spoke for others when he wrote to his mother, "I am not a bit proud of the job we have done . . . perhaps this is so devastating that man will be forced to be peaceful." As for Robert Oppenheimer, the director of the Los Alamos operation and popularly known as the "father of the bomb," he feared that Hiroshima and Nagasaki were only the beginning and that a nuclear arms race between the United States and the Soviet Union was almost inevitable.

Most other Americans also were of two minds about the bomb. Even as they enthusiastically celebrated the end of the war, at the same time the atomic bomb frightened them and made their collective future insecure. A few years later, when *Time* magazine asked an eight-year-old boy what he wanted to be when he grew up, the boy replied, "Alive!"

Some Americans criticized Truman's decision to drop atomic bombs on Hiroshima and Nagasaki. Several African American newspaper editors were especially critical, claiming that no such horrible device would ever have been dropped on "white" Germans and that Japanese were victims because they were not Caucasians. For example, the *Chicago Defender,* a weekly newspaper with a national circulation primarily to African American readers, reacted angrily to a public opinion poll that reported a 12 to 1 margin in favor of dropping more atomic bombs on Japan: "Would the people . . . have voted 12 to 1 for the use of the bomb against Germany or any other white race?" the newspaper asked. For the most part, however, African Americans were more worried about keeping their newly won jobs once white veterans returned from the war. And, like white Americans, African Americans rejoiced at the war's end, even as they feared the weapon that had ended it.

Oppenheimer was prophetic that the postwar years would witness a nuclear arms race between the United States and the Soviet Union. Both nations had scooped up as many German scientists as they could to supplement their own atomic weapons research.

Moreover, the Soviet Union tried to pierce American atomic secrecy through espionage. Neither side seems to have been fully committed to international control (through the United Nations) of atomic research. The Soviets rejected such a plan in 1946,[18] and in 1947 President Truman issued his "loyalty order," which placed government employees, including nuclear scientists, under rigid scrutiny.

In August 1949, a United States Air Force "flying laboratory" picked up traces of radioactive particles in the atmosphere in East Asia, a clear indication that the Soviet Union had detonated an atomic device. In January 1950, Truman gave orders for the United States to proceed with the development of a hydrogen bomb, nicknamed "Super" by some scientists. That bomb was tested on November 1, 1952. By 1953, however, the Soviet Union had announced that it, too, possessed such a bomb. The nuclear arms race was well under way, given even more urgency by the cold war mentality that gripped both superpowers in the late 1940s and 1950s.[19]

By the 1980s, several other nations possessed atomic devices, thus in-

creasing world tensions. Yet the two superpowers appeared to be acting more responsibly, gradually moving toward arms limitation treaties and agreements providing for the elimination of certain weapons in their nuclear arsenals. In December 1987, President Ronald Reagan and Soviet premier Mikhail Gorbachev signed a historic treaty that eliminated enough medium- and short-range nuclear missiles to have destroyed Hiroshima thirty-two thousand times. Moreover, the successors to these two men, President George Bush and Russian president Boris Yeltsin, acted with equal responsibility in decreasing nuclear arms, even in the face of political opposition (in Bush's case, a negative reaction by conservatives in his own party; in Yeltsin's case opposition from a strong but frustrated military establishment).

In spite of those initiatives, tensions remain. The collapse of the Soviet Union has created the troubling possibility that nuclear scientists from the former superpower might sell their technology, secrets, and services to less responsible nations, thereby heightening the threat of nuclear proliferation. Indeed, the concern that Iraq was close to developing a nuclear device was one of the major factors behind Operation Desert Storm in early 1991.

President Truman's decision to drop an atomic bomb on Hiroshima would have far-reaching consequences for all peoples who inhabited the earth during the second half of the twentieth century, and very likely far beyond that. What factors went into that

18. The plan, conceived by the United States, forbade the Soviet Union from developing its own atomic weapon and would have created an international agency to control nuclear raw materials.
19. Robert Oppenheimer had opposed the development of the hydrogen bomb. In late 1953, he was accused of having had "associations" with Communists and of being disloyal. A closed-door hearing (April 12 to May 6, 1954) ended with Oppenheimer's security clearance being removed.

CHAPTER 8

THE BURDENS
OF POWER: THE
DECISION TO
DROP THE
ATOMIC BOMB,
1945

momentous decision? What alternatives, if any, did Truman have?[20] Why

has this event continued to be so controversial?

20. The argument continues as to whether Japan would have surrendered without the detonation of the two atomic bombs or a massive and costly amphibious assault. We do know that Grew's appeal that the Japanese be guaranteed the retention of their emperor was not pursued in the Potsdam Ultimatum of July 26, 1945. After the war, the United States wrote a constitution that the defeated Japanese were forced to accept. In that constitution, the dynasty was retained, and Emperor Hirohito continued to sit on the throne until his death in January 1989.

CHAPTER 9

THE SECOND RED SCARE:
HUAC VS. HOLLYWOOD, 1947

⌘ THE PROBLEM ⌘

On October 20, 1947, Congressman J. Parnell Thomas, chairman of the House Committee on Un-American Activities (HUAC), called to order what perhaps were the most sensational hearings in the committee's long and checkered history. Since 1945, the committee had promised to investigate communist infiltration into the American film industry, largely centered in Hollywood, California. At that time, Congressman John E. Rankin (D, Miss.), a committee member, promised that the HUAC would uncover in Hollywood "one of the most dangerous plots ever instigated for the overthrow of the government." When open hearings finally were convened in October 1947, popular and press interest was fanned by a series of famous witnesses (including Walt Disney, Robert Taylor, Gary Cooper, and Ronald Reagan), as well as by the number of Hollywood personalities who either attended one session of the hearings or spoke vigorously against them (Lauren Bacall, Humphrey Bogart, Gene Kelly, Jane Wyatt, Danny Kaye, Judy Garland, Frank Sinatra, Henry Fonda, John Houseman, Gregory Peck, Kirk Douglas, Groucho Marx, and many others).

The HUAC investigations of Hollywood took place in an atmosphere of considerable fear and anxiety. The wartime alliance of the United States and the Soviet Union had completely deteriorated and was replaced by what many referred to as the cold war between the two postwar superpowers. Each side regarded the other as a potential threat against which constant vigilance must be maintained. In such an atmosphere, many Americans be-

CHAPTER 9

THE SECOND
RED SCARE:
HUAC vs.
HOLLYWOOD,
1947

came convinced that Soviet spies and agents had infiltrated the federal government as well as many American institutions. Hence, as the HUAC began its investigations of alleged communist infiltration of the film industry, some people, caught up in the suspicion and distrust that marked the cold war, were willing to believe that Communists were using moving pictures to disseminate anti-American propaganda.

In this chapter, you will be reading and analyzing selections from those October 1947 hearings and then answering the following four questions:

1. Based on the evidence at your disposal, to what extent did Communists in Hollywood constitute (in the words of Congressman Rankin) "the greatest hotbed of subversive activities in the United States?" In other words, based on the evidence in this chapter, was the communist threat to America's film industry a genuine one?
2. Based on excerpts from the hearings, how much hard evidence was there that supported charges of communist infiltration of Hollywood? What was the nature of the evidence presented?
3. What effects did the October 1947 HUAC hearings have on the Hollywood film community?
4. What does the evidence in this chapter tell you about the nature and character of the second Red Scare of the late 1940s and 1950s?

Finally, you should be willing to go beyond the evidence provided to answer the following two questions:

5. In your opinion, did the members of the HUAC act responsibly in their investigations of communist infiltration of the film industry?
6. Should the constitutional rights of Americans who are Communists be protected and ensured the same way as rights of Americans who are not Communists? Why or why not?

The answers to questions 5 and 6 will be *value judgments,* statements of beliefs that cannot be proven or disproven using facts as evidence.

✧ BACKGROUND ✧

The years immediately following the end of the First World War in 1918 were filled with tension and anxiety for the American people. More than 112,000 American soldiers, sailors, and marines had died to (in President Woodrow Wilson's words) "make the world safe for democracy."[1] Yet the treaties that formally brought the war to an end were harsh, a far cry from the idealism Wilson had whipped up

1. The United States suffered approximately 49,000 battle-related deaths. The remainder of the troop deaths were due to disease, pri-

among the American people. The result was a cynical aftertaste, a spirit that dominated much of American life in the 1920s.

At the same time, many in the West viewed the Bolshevik Revolution of 1917 in Russia and the call by the Communist International (Comintern) for a worldwide Bolshevik revolution as a direct threat to their governments and way of life. In response, several nations—including the United States—sent troops to Russia in an attempt to support the Russian enemies of Bolshevism. The United States contributed approximately five thousand soldiers to this effort, but foreign intervention in the Russian civil war ultimately was unsuccessful. Western European nations and the United States feared the spread of Bolshevism. Thus World War I ended not with solutions to international problems but with more problems.

At home, conversion to a peacetime economy resulted in high unemployment rates and inflation of prices. A wave of postwar strikes—3,600 in 1919 alone—idled more than 4 million workers, including shipyard employees, steelworkers, and the Boston police force. Violence against African Americans in the South increased dramatically, with 78 recorded lynchings in 1919 alone. Yet African Americans who had abandoned the South for opportunities in northern cities also faced antiblack violence. In Chicago in July 1919, the killing of an African American youth who was swimming

in an area of Lake Michigan traditionally reserved for whites touched off 5 days of rioting in which 38 people lost their lives. More than two dozen other cities experienced racial violence in that year as well. Simultaneously, the end of the war brought a resumption of the wave of immigrants, mostly from southern and eastern Europe, who arrived on American shores. To many Americans, inflation, unemployment, strikes, racial violence, and the resumption of immigration were threats to their hopes of returning to their safe and ordered prewar world, a world that in fact no longer existed.

The Bolshevik Revolution gave many Americans a convenient scapegoat for their postwar troubles. A few Americans were involved in radical activities, as evidenced by the discovery of numerous mail bombs intended for thirty-six prominent government leaders. Americans, however, identified communist conspirators as the cause of all their postwar difficulties. The result was the first Red Scare, fueled by the politically ambitious attorney general A. Mitchell Palmer. Under Palmer's direction, raids were staged against radical organizations. Thousands were arrested and denied their civil liberties, and some three hundred were deported. At the same time, a revived Ku Klux Klan gained enormous popularity in the South and Midwest, principally by emphasizing its nativist, anti-immigrant and anti–African American dogmas. The first Red Scare ended sometime in the early 1920s, when the Palmer-incited hysteria and the strength of the Ku Klux Klan began declining.

marily the Spanish influenza epidemic of 1918–1919, which killed roughly 25 million people worldwide.

CHAPTER 9

THE SECOND
RED SCARE:
HUAC vs.
HOLLYWOOD,
1947

In many ways, the period following the end of World War II in 1945 was similar to the years after World War I. The return of approximately 16 million servicemen to civilian life (more than 10 percent of the nation's total population) was accomplished more smoothly than after World War I, principally because pent-up consumer demand for housing, automobiles, and other products stimulated the national economy. Nevertheless, a large portion of the 6 million women who had entered the labor force during the war were expected to turn over their jobs to the returning servicemen, whether they wanted to or not. Similar to the post–World War I period, consumer demand produced a rapid inflation rate, which was not brought under control until the early 1950s. Also, labor unrest was widespread as unions pushed for wage increases they had not demanded during the wartime emergency. By the end of 1946, roughly 5 million workers had gone on strike. In response, President Harry Truman threatened to draft striking railroad workers into the army and briefly seized control of the nation's coal mines when the United Mine Workers went on strike.

For African Americans, the years after World War II were ones of opportunity and challenge. Almost 900,000 African Americans, both men and women, had served in the armed forces, and more than 1 million blacks had migrated from the South to take industrial jobs in other sections of the nation. By 1945, roughly one-third of the nation's African American population lived outside the South,[2] were

voting for the first time, and were beginning to push for political and social rights to complement their economic gains.

Probably the greatest similarity to the post–World War I epoch, however, was the advent of another Red Scare. The United States had emerged from the war as the world's industrial and military leader, and many Americans were anxious that the country not retreat into isolationism but use its power to build a better postwar world. As President Franklin Roosevelt's close adviser Harry Hopkins remembered, "We really believed in our hearts that this was the dawn of the new day we had all been praying for and talking about for so many years."

This optimism, however, was soon tempered by the realities of the postwar world. Two major superpowers emerged from World War II: the United States and the Soviet Union. The total defeat of the Axis powers (Germany, Italy, and Japan) and the wartime devastation of much of Western Europe created power vacuums in Western and Central Europe and parts of Asia. In time, each postwar superpower came to believe that the other was trying to take advantage of that unstable situation for its own purposes. Soviet premier Joseph Stalin feared that the West would learn how economically and militarily vulnerable the Soviet Union actually was and

---

2. In 1940, five years earlier, the percentage of African Americans living outside the South was 23 percent. In 1970, the Bureau of the Census reported that for the first time, more than 50 percent of the nation's African Americans lived outside the South.

quickly move into those power vacuums. To counter this potential threat, Stalin was determined to dominate the nations of Eastern Europe, especially Poland, and to make Soviet influence felt in Central Europe as well, especially in Germany. At the same time, many Americans, including President Harry Truman, believed that Russian Communists were dedicated to the overthrow of capitalism and democracy and intent on world domination. As a result, the American government became increasingly committed to propping up the pro-American governments of Western Europe and Asia, determined that the Soviets would not swoop into these power vacuums. And as both the Soviet Union and the United States became more suspicious and secretive in their dealings with one another, both powers resorted to widespread espionage activities.

The year 1947 witnessed an increase in international tensions and a heightening of cold war hysteria. In February 1947, a financially desperate Great Britain informed the United States that it was unable to maintain support to the government of Greece, itself beset with economic problems and besieged by communist guerrillas.[3] Truman responded almost immediately with the Truman Doctrine, which promised United States support to "free peoples who are resisting attempted subjugation by armed minorities or outside pressures." In May, a bipartisan Congress backed Truman

3. Contrary to American beliefs, Stalin was not supporting the communist guerrillas in Greece and even disapproved of their actions.

with a $400 million aid package to Greece and Turkey. The United States had issued a challenge to Stalin. The world waited nervously for the next events of the cold war.

Meanwhile, Americans were becoming increasingly convinced of the danger of Soviet spies and agents in the United States. On March 22, 1947, Truman issued an executive order (known as the Loyalty Order) that required investigations of federal employees in the executive branch. This hunt for "subversives" was put into effect in August.

On June 5, in his commencement address to graduates of Harvard University, Secretary of State George Marshall unveiled what became known as the Marshall Plan. The plan was to provide American funds for the economic recovery of European countries whose postwar economic problems made them vulnerable to communism. The Soviet Union denounced the Marshall Plan and accused the United States of warmongering.

Thus by the time the HUAC investigations of Hollywood convened in Washington in October 1947, the world was filled with cold war tensions and the United States had entered into the second Red Scare.

The second Red Scare affected almost every aspect of Americans' behavior and collective thought. Most states joined the federal government in requiring loyalty oaths and establishing loyalty review boards, many of which flagrantly disregarded the constitutional safeguards of those under suspicion. Worse, a growing number of private individuals (some historians

CHAPTER 9

THE SECOND
RED SCARE:
HUAC vs.
HOLLYWOOD,
1947

have called them "loyalty sleuths") added to the alarm by hunting subversives on their own. Almost anyone was a potential target.[4]

What caused someone to be accused of subversion? In 1947, United States attorney general Tom C. Clark issued a list of "subversive organizations" thought to be dominated by or sympathetic to Communists. Although most of the listed organizations conformed to neither criterion (several were leftist but not communist), membership or former membership in any of them could be the basis for suspicion. For example, both the Southern Conference for Human Welfare and the Highlander Center (in eastern Tennessee), advocates of civil rights for African Americans, were labeled as subversive and subjected to investigations, and their members were harassed—in spite of the fact that one leader of the Southern Conference for Human Welfare was Dr. Frank P. Graham, the widely respected president of the University of North Carolina.

In the 1930s, during the depths of the depression and the rise of fascism in Europe, many Americans, many of them idealistic college students, joined leftist organizations. During World War II, when the American government purposely was cultivating sentiment for its Russian allies against Hitler (amid much publicity, First Lady Eleanor Roosevelt cut the cake at a birthday party honoring the Red Army), these men and women rarely made a secret of these affiliations. Most abandoned those organizations after World War II, when many came to believe that Stalin was not fulfilling their idealistic hopes. Former memberships, however, often returned to haunt people during the second Red Scare. People having friends or associates who had been accused of subversion and people who obstructed, criticized, or refused to cooperate with anticommunist investigations also came under suspicion. In short, a person could be accused on the most trivial and insubstantial "evidence."

In such an atmosphere, when accusations could cost people their jobs, ruin careers, or alienate friends, it is not surprising that people generally embraced extreme patriotism, conformity, and a collective mentality that strongly encouraged a "don't be different, don't make waves" approach to living. A few people resisted, but the majority went along, afraid of either a communist menace or being destroyed by someone's accusation against them, no matter how groundless. Government employees and teachers were but two groups under continual investigation. Everyone— from businesspeople to actors, actresses, and writers—were deeply affected and afraid. And because both Republicans and Democrats participated in this hysteria, there was little political objection to its excesses.

4. Young screen actress Nancy Davis was rumored to be the subject of such an investigation. She appealed for help to Screen Actors Guild president Ronald Reagan, claiming that there was no truth to the accusations against her. Reagan offered her the assistance of his office. Later, Nancy Davis became Mrs. Ronald Reagan. More recently, the story of their first meeting has been disputed. See Jon Wiener, *Professor, Politics, and Pop* (London: Verson, 1991), pp. 333–335.

The period of the second Red Scare was a confusing one for the American film industry, largely centered in Hollywood, California. On one hand, filmmakers traditionally had opposed censorship from outside the industry, preferring instead to let Hollywood police itself as to language, sexual material, and sociopolitical opinions. On the other hand, many people in the film community felt strongly that leftists within that community were such a threat to the United States and to the independence of the film industry that these people must be rooted out by any means possible. Therefore, when the HUAC undertook an investigation of communism in Hollywood in 1947, the film community was deeply divided. Some members of that community resented what they considered political intrusion into the creative arts, but others cooperated with the committee, offering examples of leftist activity in the film industry and names of men and women thought to have communist affiliations.

The HUAC, formed in 1938 as a temporary committee to investigate fascist and communist activities in the United States, had long been eager, according to one member, "to track down the footprints of Karl Marx in movieland." Republican victories in the 1946 congressional elections gave Republicans control of both the House of Representatives and the Senate, and, as a result, the chairs of all congressional committees. The chairmanship of the HUAC fell to J. Parnell Thomas of New Jersey, a man determined to purge Hollywood of all communist and leftist influence. Under Thomas, the committee held closed hearings in Los Angeles in May 1947, and, amid much ballyhoo, open hearings in Washington in October.

The evidence in this chapter is taken from those October hearings. Read the evidence carefully and answer the questions posed at the beginning of the chapter.

⌇ THE METHOD ⌇

The exclusive purpose of hearings by congressional committees or subcommittees is to gather information to use in drafting legislation. Occasionally, however, congressional committees and subcommittees stray from that purpose. As you examine the evidence, ask yourself whether the HUAC's investigation of Hollywood strayed from the purpose of hearings. In other words, why do you think the hearings were held in the first place? Note that a good deal of the HUAC's attention focused on the federal government's wartime role in Hollywood. Does this concern give you a clue as to one reason why the HUAC conducted these hearings? (The statement read by Albert Maltz, one of the witnesses, provides an excellent clue.)

CHAPTER 9

THE SECOND
RED SCARE:
HUAC vs.
HOLLYWOOD,
1947

Almost immediately, you will recognize two things about these HUAC hearings. First, the witnesses can be classified as "friendly" (that is, those willing to cooperate with the HUAC) or "unfriendly." In all, the committee called a total of forty witnesses, twenty-five of them decidedly friendly (willing to testify about a communist threat in Hollywood and/or willing to name people thought to be Communists), eleven decidedly unfriendly (ten of whom had been named as Communists either in these hearings or earlier), and four who cannot be classified as either. It helps to classify the witnesses in this way. Did the committee treat the friendly and unfriendly groups differently? If so, in what ways?

Second, although congressional hearings are not trials, the two events share certain traits. Committee members try to build a case, much like trial attorneys, by arranging evidence and witnesses to suit their aims. Also like attorneys, congressional committee members sometimes try to get both friendly and unfriendly witnesses to say things that the witnesses do not want to say. Can you see the similarities in the October 1947 hearings? More important, do you think the case the HUAC built is convincing? Why or why not? In other words, did Communists in Hollywood constitute a serious threat to the film industry? How much hard evidence was there in the hearings that proved such a threat existed? As you come across what you consider to be such evidence, be sure to note it for later use.

To answer questions 3 and 4, you will have to exercise some historical imagination. As in any community, the film community was made up of people who held all sorts of opinions but who were required to work together to produce a product. And as in other communities, people in the film community were not merely coworkers but neighbors who socialized with one another and whose children often went to school and played together. They attended churches and synagogues together, served on local charitable groups and PTAs, and dined at each other's homes. As you read the evidence, imagine what effects the HUAC hearings might have had on the film community.

Finally, you can gain a great deal of understanding about the *style* and *nature* of the second Red Scare by examining the evidence. As you read the selections from the hearings, can you think of some adjectives to describe the second Red Scare? How would you go about proving that those adjectives are accurate?

Questions 5 and 6 require that you combine material from the Evidence and Background sections of this chapter with your other reading. As noted earlier, the answers to these questions will be *value judgments,* statements of opinion that cannot be proven or disproven with facts but that instead are grounded in the value system of the person making the statements. Beware of people who claim that their value judgments are supported by hard evidence when in fact this "evidence" is merely another statement of opinion. For example, someone might argue that accused Communists in Hollywood should have been jailed, citing as "evidence" that "they constituted a threat to America." The latter statement, as you can see, is not evidence at all but merely another statement of opinion. Remember that value judgments rarely can be proven or disproven by using facts.

⟋ THE EVIDENCE ⟋

Sources 1 through 15 from House of Representatives, Committee on Un-American Activities, *Hearings Regarding the Communist Infiltration of the Motion Picture Industry,* October 20–30, 1947 (Washington, D.C.: U.S. Government Printing Office, 1947), pp. 1–3, 10–12, 17, 38–39, 55, 58–59, 70–76, 92–94, 100, 103–104, 106–107, 109–112, 128–130, 138, 165–169, 214, 217, 219–224, 282–284, 289–295, 306–309, 364–366, 522.

COMMITTEE ON UN-AMERICAN ACTIVITIES

J. PARNELL THOMAS, New Jersey, *Chairman*

KARL E. MUNDT, South Dakota

JOHN MCDOWELL, Pennsylvania

RICHARD M. NIXON, California

RICHARD B. VAIL, Illinois

JOHN S. WOOD, Georgia

JOHN E. RANKIN, Mississippi

J. HARDIN PETERSON, Florida

HERBERT C. BONNER, North Carolina

ROBERT E. STRIPLING, *Chief Investigator*

BENJAMIN MANDEL, *Director of Research*

1. J. Parnell Thomas, Chairman (Opening Remarks).

. . . The committee is well aware of the magnitude of the subject which it is investigating. The motion-picture business represents an investment of billions of dollars. It represents employment for thousands of workers, ranging from unskilled laborers to high-salaried actors and executives. And even more important, the motion-picture industry represents what is probably the largest single vehicle of entertainment for the American public— over 85,000,000 persons attend the movies each week.

However, it is the very magnitude of the scope of the motion-picture industry which makes this investigation so necessary. We all recognize,

CHAPTER 9

THE SECOND
RED SCARE:
HUAC vs.
HOLLYWOOD,
1947

certainly, the tremendous effect which moving pictures have on their mass audiences, far removed from the Hollywood sets. We all recognize that what the citizen sees and hears in his neighborhood movie house carries a powerful impact on his thoughts and behavior.

With such vast influence over the lives of American citizens as the motion-picture industry exerts, it is not unnatural—in fact, it is very logical—that subversive and undemocratic forces should attempt to use this medium for un-American purposes.

I want to emphasize at the outset of these hearings that the fact that the Committee on Un-American Activities is investigating alleged Communist influence and infiltration in the motion-picture industry must not be considered or interpreted as an attack on the majority of persons associated with this great industry. I have every confidence that the vast majority of movie workers are patriotic and loyal Americans.

This committee, under its mandate from the House of Representatives, has the responsibility of exposing and spotlighting subversive elements wherever they may exist. As I have already pointed out, it is only to be expected that such elements would strive desperately to gain entry to the motion-picture industry, simply because the industry offers such a tremendous weapon for education and propaganda. That Communists have made such an attempt in Hollywood and with considerable success is already evident to this committee from its preliminary investigative work. . . .

I cannot emphasize too strongly the seriousness of Communist infiltration, which we have found to be a mutual problem for many, many different fields of endeavor in the United States. Communists for years have been conducting an unrelentless "boring from within" campaign against America's democratic institutions. While never possessing a large numerical strength, the Communists nevertheless have found that they could dominate the activities of unions or other mass enterprises in this country by capturing a few strategic positions of leadership. . . .

There is no question that there are Communists in Hollywood. We cannot minimize their importance there, and that their influence has already made itself felt has been evidenced by internal turmoil in the industry over the Communist issue. Prominent figures in the motion-picture business have been engaged in a sort of running battle over Communist infiltration for the last 4 or 5 years and a number of anti-Communist organizations have been set up within the industry in an attempt to combat this menace.

The question before this committee, therefore, and the scope of its present inquiry, will be to determine the extent of Communist infiltration in the Hollywood motion-picture industry. We want to know what strategic positions in the industry have been captured by these elements, whose loyalty is pledged in word and deed to the interests of a foreign power.

The committee is determined that the hearings shall be fair and impartial. We have subpoenaed witnesses representing both sides of the question. All we are after are the facts.

Now, I want to make it clear to the witnesses, the audience, the members of the press, and other guests here today that this hearing is going to be conducted in an orderly and dignified manner at all times. But if there is anyone here today or at any of the future sessions of this hearing who entertains any hopes or plans for disrupting the proceedings, he may as well dismiss it from his mind.

2. Jack L. Warner, Vice President, Warner Bros. Studios.

. . . Ideological termites have burrowed into many American industries, organizations, and societies. Wherever they may be, I say let us dig them out and get rid of them. My brothers and I will be happy to subscribe generously to a pest-removal fund. We are willing to establish such a fund to ship to Russia the people who don't like our American system of government and prefer the communistic system to ours.

That's how strongly we feel about the subversives who want to overthrow our free American system.

If there are Communists in our industry, or any other industry, organization, or society who seek to undermine our free institutions, let's find out about it and know who they are. Let the record be spread clear, for all to read and judge. The public is entitled to know the facts. And the motion-picture industry is entitled to have the public know the facts.

Our company is keenly aware of its responsibilities to keep its product free from subversive poisons. With all the vision at my command, I scrutinize the planning and production of our motion pictures. It is my firm belief that there is not a Warner Bros. picture that can fairly be judged to be hostile to our country, or communistic in tone or purpose.

Many charges, including the fantasy of "White House pressure" have been leveled at our wartime production Mission to Moscow.[5] In my previous

5. *Mission to Moscow* is the film adaptation of the best-selling memoirs of former United States ambassador to the Soviet Union (1936–1938) Joseph E. Davies. Davies was an admirer of Stalin, and his memoirs show the Soviet Union in a highly favorable light.

CHAPTER 9

THE SECOND
RED SCARE:
HUAC vs.
HOLLYWOOD,
1947

appearance before members of this committee, I explained the origin and purposes of Mission to Moscow.

That picture was made when our country was fighting for its existence, with Russia as one of our allies. It was made to fulfill the same wartime purpose for which we made such other pictures as Air Force, This Is the Army, Objective Burma, Destination Tokyo, Action in the North Atlantic, and a great many more.

If making Mission to Moscow in 1942 was a subversive activity, then the American Liberty ships which carried food and guns to Russian allies and the American naval vessels which convoyed them were likewise engaged in subversive activities. The picture was made only to help a desperate war effort and not for posterity.

The Warner Bros. interest in the preservation of the American way of life is no new thing with our company. Ever since we began making motion pictures we have fostered American ideals and done what we could to protect them.

Not content with merely warning against dangers to our free system, Warner Bros. has practiced a policy of positive Americanism. We have gone, and will continue to go, to all possible lengths to iterate and reiterate the realities and advantages of America.

Good American common sense is the determining factor in judging motion-picture scripts before they are put in production and motion-picture scenes after they are photographed. We rely upon a deep-rooted, pervading respect for our country's principles.

One of those American principles is the right to gripe and criticize in an effort to improve. That right to gripe is not enjoyed under communistic dictatorships. To surrender that privilege under pressure would betray our American standards.

Freedom of expression, however, does not, under our Constitution and laws, include a license to destroy. . . .

[In response to questions from Stripling and Thomas, Warner admitted that he had discovered that some of his scriptwriters had tried to insert "un-American" lines in Warner films and that those writers were not rehired. In the closed hearings in Hollywood, Warner supplied the committee with the names of those writers.]

MR. STRIPLING. Well, is it your opinion now, Mr. Warner, that Mission to Moscow was a factually correct picture, and you made it as such?

MR. WARNER. I can't remember.

MR. STRIPLING. Would you consider it a propaganda picture?

MR. WARNER. A propaganda picture——

MR. STRIPLING. Yes.

MR. WARNER. In what sense?

MR. STRIPLING. In the sense that it portrayed Russia and communism in an entirely different light from what it actually was?

MR. WARNER. I am on record about 40 times or more that I have never been in Russia. I don't know what Russia was like in 1937 or 1944 or 1947, so how can I tell you if it was right or wrong?

MR. STRIPLING. Don't you think you were on dangerous ground to produce as a factually correct picture one which portrayed Russia——

MR. WARNER. No; we were not on dangerous ground in 1942, when we produced it. There was a war on. The world was at stake.

MR. STRIPLING. In other words——

MR. WARNER. We made the film to aid in the war effort, which I believe I have already stated.

MR. STRIPLING. Whether it was true or not?

MR. WARNER. As far as I was concerned, I considered it true to the extent as written in Mr. Davies' book.

MR. STRIPLING. Well, do you suppose that your picture influenced the people who saw it in this country, the millions of people who saw it in this country?

MR. WARNER. In my opinion, I can't see how it would influence anyone. We were in war and when you are in a fight you don't ask who the fellow is who is helping you.

MR. STRIPLING. Well, due to the present conditions in the international situation, don't you think it was rather dangerous to write about such a disillusionment as was sought in that picture?

MR. WARNER. I can't understand why you ask me that question, as to the present conditions. How did I, you, or anyone else know in 1942 what the conditions were going to be in 1947? I stated in my testimony our reason for making the picture, which was to aid the war effort—anticipating what would happen.

MR. STRIPLING. I don't see that this is aiding the war effort, Mr. Warner—with the cooperation of Mr. Davies or with the approval of the Government—to make a picture which is a fraud in fact.

MR. WARNER. I want to correct you, very vehemently. There was no cooperation of the Government.

MR. STRIPLING. You stated there was.

MR. WARNER. I never stated the Government cooperated in the making of it. If I did, I stand corrected. And I know I didn't.

MR. STRIPLING. Do you want me to read that part, Mr. Chairman?

CHAPTER 9
THE SECOND
RED SCARE:
HUAC vs.
HOLLYWOOD,
1947

THE CHAIRMAN. No; I think we have gone into this Mission to Moscow at some length. . . .

3. Samuel G. Wood, Producer and Director.

. . . MR. STRIPLING. Will you tell the committee of the efforts that you are aware of on the part of the Communists to infiltrate the Screen Directors Guild?

MR. WOOD. There is a constant effort to get control of the guild. In fact, there is an effort to get control of all unions and guilds in Hollywood. I think our most serious time was when George Stevens was president; he went in the service and another gentleman took his place, who died, and it was turned over to John Cromwell. Cromwell, with the assistance of three or four others, tried hard to steer us into the Red river, but we had a little too much weight for that.

MR. STRIPLING. Will you name the others?

MR. WOOD. Irving Pichel, Edward Dmytryk, Frank Tuttle, and—I am sorry, there is another name there. I forget.

MR. STRIPLING. If you think of it, will you give it for the record?

MR. WOOD. Yes. . . .

MR. STRIPLING. Is it your opinion that there are Communist writers in the motion-picture industry?

MR. WOOD. Oh, yes. It is not my opinion, I know positively there are.

MR. STRIPLING. Would you care to name any that you know yourself to be Communists?

MR. WOOD. Well, I don't think there is any question about Dalton Trumbo; any question about Donald Ogden Stewart. The reporter asked the question of a great many writers, "Are you a member of the Communist Party," or "Are you a Communist?"

MR. STRIPLING. Did they deny it?

MR. WOOD. They didn't answer it.

MR. STRIPLING. Was John Howard Lawson one of those persons?

MR. WOOD. Oh, yes; he is active in every piece of Communist work going on.

MR. STRIPLING. Is there any question in your mind that John Howard Lawson is a Communist?

MR. WOOD. If there is, then I haven't any mind. I suppose there are 19 gentlemen back there that say I haven't.

MR. STRIPLING. When did you first notice this effort on the part of the Communists to enter Hollywood or to exert influence in the motion-picture industry?

MR. WOOD. Well, I think they really started working around 1930, some, I forget the exact time. I think we were very conscious of it, had been for some time, but like everyone else we probably hadn't done anything, because it is quite an effort and you get quite smeared, and a lot of people would like to duck that. It is fun to play bridge, for instance, rather than to check on something like that. We felt it more, I think, just previously [sic] to our organization in 1944.

MR. STRIPLING. That was the reason, in other words, that you formed your organization, was to combat the increased activity on the part of the Communists in the industry?

MR. WOOD. Yes, sir; we felt there was a great danger, and it was in the interest of self-defense on our business, because we felt a normal responsibility for our business. It has been very kind to a lot of us, and we want to protect it.

MR. STRIPLING. Now, Mr. Wood, would you give the committee some of these examples in which the Communists have exerted influence in the motion-picture industry? In other words, how do they go about it, what is the mechanics of it?

MR. WOOD. There are a number of ways. I think the thing that is very important, and the thing I was most anxious about, is the pride of Americans in working. They are pretty subtle. For instance, a man gets a key position in the studio and has charge of the writers. When you, as a director or a producer, are ready for a writer you ask for a list and this man shows you a list. Well, if he is following the party line his pets are on top or the other people aren't on at all. If there is a particular man in there that has been opposing them they will leave his name off the list. Then if that man isn't employed for about 2 months they go to the head of the studio and say, "Nobody wants this man." The head is perfectly honest about it and says, "Nobody wants to use him, let him go." So a good American is let out. But it doesn't stop there. They point that out as an example and say, "You better fall in line, play ball, or else." And they go down the line on it.

MR. STRIPLING. That is true in the case of writers. Would you say it is true in any other branch of the industry?

MR. WOOD. I don't think in any part of the business, they will use a party who is opposed to their ideas, if they can avoid it, and they can usually avoid it.

CHAPTER 9

THE SECOND
RED SCARE:
HUAC vs.
HOLLYWOOD,
1947

MR. STRIPLING. They operate as cliques, in other words?

MR. WOOD. Oh, yes; they have their meetings every night. They are together; they work for one purpose.

MR. STRIPLING. What is that purpose, Mr. Wood?

MR. WOOD. Well, I think they are agents of a foreign country myself.

MR. STRIPLING. I see. . . .

4. Louis B. Mayer, Head, Metro-Goldwyn-Mayer Studios.

. . . During my 25 years in the motion-picture industry I have always sought to maintain the screen as a force for public good.

The motion-picture industry employs many thousands of people. As is the case with the newspaper, radio, publishing, and theater businesses, we cannot be responsible for the political views of each individual employee. It is, however, our complete responsibility to determine what appears on the motion-picture screen.

It is my earnest hope that this committee will perform a public service by recommending to the Congress legislation establishing a national policy regulating employment of Communists in private industry. It is my belief they should be denied the sanctuary of the freedom they seek to destroy.

Communism is based upon a doctrine inconsistent with American liberty. It advocates destruction of the system of free enterprise under which our industry has achieved popularity among the freedom-loving peoples of the world.

Our hatred of communism is returned in full measure. The Communists attack our screen as an instrument of capitalism. Few, if any, of our films ever reach Russia. It hates us because it fears us. We show too much of the American way of life, of human dignity, of the opportunity and the happiness to be enjoyed in a democracy.

More than any other country in the world, we have enjoyed the fullest freedom of speech in all means of communication. It is this freedom that has enabled the motion picture to carry the message to the world of our democratic way of life.

The primary function of motion pictures is to bring entertainment to the screen. But, like all other industries, we were lending every support to our Government in the war effort, and whenever a subject could be presented as entertaining, we tried, insofar as possible, to cooperate in building morale. . . .

There were a number of representatives of the Government who made periodical visits to the studios during the war. They discussed with us from time to time the types of pictures which they felt might assist the war effort. They were coordinators and at no time did they attempt to tell us what we should or should not do. We made our own decisions on production. We are proud of our war efforts and the results speak for themselves.

Mention has been made of the picture Song of Russia, as being friendly to Russia at the time it was made. Of course it was. It was made to be friendly. In 1938 we made Ninotchka, and shortly thereafter Comrade X, with Clark Gable and Hedy Lamarr—both of these films kidded Russia.

It was in April of 1942 that the story for Song of Russia came to our attention. It seemed a good medium of entertainment and at the same time offered an opportunity for a pat on the back for our then ally, Russia. It also offered an opportunity to use the music of Tschaikovsky. We mentioned this to the Government coordinators and they agreed with us that it would be a good idea to make the picture.

According to research I have made, our newspapers were headlining the desperate situation of the Russians at Stalingrad at that time. Admiral Standley, American Ambassador to the Soviet Union, made a vigorous plea for all-out aid. He pleaded for assistance second only to the supplies being provided the United States Fleet, and emphasized that the best way to win the war was to keep the Russians killing the Germans, and that the most effective way was to give them all the help they needed.

The United States Army Signal Corps made The Battle of Stalingrad, released in 1943, with a prolog expressing high tribute from President Roosevelt, our Secretaries of State, War, and Navy, and from Generals Marshall and MacArthur.

The final script of Song of Russia was little more than a pleasant musical romance—the story of a boy and girl that, except for the music of Tschaikovsky, might just as well have taken place in Switzerland or England or any other country on the earth.

I thought Robert Taylor ideal for the leading male role in Song of Russia, but he did not like the story. This was not unusual as actors and actresses many times do not care for stories suggested to them.

At the time, Taylor mentioned his pending commission in the Navy, so I telephoned the Secretary of the Navy, Frank Knox, and told him of the situation, recalling the good that had been accomplished with Mrs. Miniver and other pictures released during the war period. The Secretary called back and said he thought Taylor could be given time to make the film before being called to the service. Accordingly, Taylor made the picture.

CHAPTER 9

THE SECOND
RED SCARE:
HUAC vs.
HOLLYWOOD,
1947

Since 1942 when the picture was planned, our relationship with Russia has changed. But viewed in the light of the war emergency at the time, it is my opinion that it could not be construed as anything other than for the entertainment purpose intended and a pat on the back for our then ally, Russia. . . .

H. A. SMITH (COMMITTEE INVESTIGATOR). Are there any Communists, to your knowledge, in Metro-Goldwyn-Mayer?

[*Responding to questions, Mayer testified that he had been told that Dalton Trumbo and Lester Cole were Communists. Mayer also stated that his attorneys advised him that he should not fire a person who had been accused of being a Communist, fearing a lawsuit for damages, but that he would dismiss such a person if there was sufficient proof of communist activities.*]

MR. SMITH. Going back to the picture Song of Russia, I notice in your statement, Mr. Mayer, you state:

The final script of Song of Russia was little more than a pleasant musical romance—the story of a boy and girl that, except for the music of Tschaikovsky, might just as well have taken place in Switzerland or England or any other country on the earth.

Is that your definite opinion on that particular picture?

MR. MAYER. Basically, yes.

MR. SMITH. Don't you feel the picture had scene after scene that grossly misrepresented Russia as it is today, or as it was at that time?

MR. MAYER. I never was in Russia, but you tell me how you would make a picture laid in Russia that would do any different than what we did there?

MR. SMITH. Don't you feel from what you have read, and from what you have heard from other people, that the scenes just did not depict Russia in one iota?

MR. MAYER. We did not attempt to depict Russia; we attempted to show a Russian girl entreating this American conductor to conduct a concert in her village where they have a musical festival every year and as it inevitably happens this girl fell in love with the conductor, and he with her. Then we showed the attack of the Germans on the Russians and the war disrupted this union.

MR. SMITH. The original story was written by whom, Mr. Mayer!

MR. MAYER. I don't recall now. . . .

MR. SMITH. Did you read the first script, Mr. Mayer?

MR. MAYER. Yes, sir.

MR. SMITH. What was your opinion at that time?

MR. MAYER. They had farm collectivism in it and I threw it out and said, "This will not be made until they give me the story they told me originally when I approved the making of it."

MR. SMITH. In other words, the first script, in your opinion, was not producible?

MR. MAYER. Not the first.

MR. SMITH. Why not?

MR. MAYER. Because I will not preach any ideology except American, and I don't even treat that. I let that take its own course and speak for itself.

MR. SMITH. That showed an ideology or condition, so far as Russia is concerned, that you did not approve of?

MR. MAYER. I wouldn't have it.

MR. SMITH. As to the last script then, was the script, in your opinion, satisfactorily cleaned up?

MR. MAYER. I think so; yes, sir.

MR. SMITH. Who was responsible, if you know, for taking the collectivism and other things out of the script?

MR. MAYER. I ordered it out, and the producer said it would all be rewritten, and it was. That is why Taylor was delayed getting into the service.

THE CHAIRMAN. May I ask a question right there?

MR. SMITH. Yes, sir.

THE CHAIRMAN. Mr. Mayer, you say the main reason why Taylor was delayed getting into the service was because the first script had these foreign ideologies in it and was not acceptable to you, so there was this delay?

MR. MAYER. Yes, sir.

MR. SMITH. Did a Government representative ever come to you, Mr. Mayer, about that picture, as to the making of it?

MR. MAYER. I don't recall anybody coming about the making of it. I think I told them about it or discussed it with them. So much happened in that period, coming and going. They had an office out there—War Information, I think they called themselves.

MR. SMITH. Have you seen the picture recently, Mr. Mayer?

MR. MAYER. Yes, sir.

MR. SMITH. What are your feelings about the picture, as to the damage it might cause to the people in the United States, that is, misleading them as to conditions in Russia?

CHAPTER 9

THE SECOND
RED SCARE:
HUAC vs.
HOLLYWOOD,
1947

MR. MAYER. What scenes are you referring to?

MR. SMITH. Do you recall scenes in there at the night club when everybody was drinking?

MR. MAYER. They do in Moscow.

MR. SMITH. Do you feel that that represents Russia as it is today?

MR. MAYER. I didn't make it as it is today. I made it when they were our ally in 1943. . . .

5. Adolphe Menjou, Screen Actor.

. . . MR. STRIPLING. Do you consider that the Communist Party members in this country are engaged in treasonable activities?

MR. MENJOU. Definitely.

MR. STRIPLING. Mr. Menjou, this committee also has a legislative function as well as an investigative function. During this session there were two bills introduced which sought to outlaw the Communist Party. Do you think that the Communist Party should be outlawed by legislation?

MR. MENJOU. I believe that the Communist Party in the United States should be outlawed by the Congress of the United States. It is not a political party. It is a conspiracy to take over our Government by force, which would enslave the American people, as the Soviet Government— 14 members of the Politburo—hold the Russian people in abject slavery. Any one of a dozen books will prove it. This is not hearsay. Dozens of other testimony will prove what horrors are going on in Russia today, so horrible that you cannot read them without becoming ill.

Now, we don't want that here.

MR. STRIPLING. Now, Mr. Menjou, there has been quite a bit said and written in the Communist publications and certain left-wing organizations have circulated pamphlets to the effect that this committee is trying to bring about thought control.

MR. MENJOU. Well, I also have heard many other words—"witch-hunting." I am a witch-hunter if the witches are Communists. I am a Red-baiter. I make no bones about it whatsoever. I would like to see them all back in Russia. I think a taste of Russia would cure many of them. . . .

MR. VAIL. Mr. Menjou, do you think there is justification for the action of this committee in its instituting an investigation of Communist activities in Hollywood?

MR. MENJOU. Do I think so? Certainly.

MR. VAIL. In the daily papers in the past few days I noticed a statement that was signed by a number of prominent Hollywood actors and actresses deploring the investigation and describing it as a smear. What is your impression of the people who were signatory to that statement?

MR. MENJOU. I am just as shocked and amazed—which I believe were their words—as they said they were shocked and amazed. I don't believe any of them has ever made a serious study of the subject. I believe they are innocent dupes; that is my impression of them, innocent dupes.

I guarantee not one of them could name four men on the Politburo; I guarantee not one of them could name a date or an action against Russia or a violation of the antiaggression pacts which Mr. Stalin violated. If these people will only read and read and read and read, they will wake up. I have all the sympathy in the world for them; I am sorry for them.

MR. VAIL. I have no more questions.

THE CHAIRMAN. Mr. Nixon.

MR. NIXON. Mr. Menjou, from what you have said to charge a person with being a Communist is a very serious thing?

MR. MENJOU. Yes, sir.

MR. NIXON. You would not want that charge made?

MR. MENJOU. Without substantiation, that is right. That is playing right into the Communists' hands.

MR. NIXON. In answer to a question by Mr. Stripling you indicated that although you might not know whether a certain person was a Communist, I think you said he certainly acted like a Communist.

MR. MENJOU. If you belong to a Communist-front organization and you take no action against the Communists, you do not resign from the organization when you still know the organization is dominated by Communists, I consider that a very, very dangerous thing.

MR. NIXON. Have you any other tests which you would apply which would indicate to you that people acted like Communists?

MR. MENJOU. Well, I think attending any meetings at which Mr. Paul Robeson[6] appeared and applauding or listening to his Communist songs in America, I would be ashamed to be seen in an audience doing a thing of that kind. . . .

6. Paul Robeson (1898–1976) was an African American who earned degrees at Rutgers University (he was a Phi Beta Kappa) and Columbia Law School (1923) but who chose to become a world-famous actor and concert singer. His championship of African American rights and controversial causes and his many trips to the Soviet Union caused him to be branded a Communist and blacklisted.

CHAPTER 9

THE SECOND
RED SCARE:
HUAC vs.
HOLLYWOOD,
1947

THE CHAIRMAN. It has been said in the press by certain individuals in the United States that these hearings now being held by the Un-American Activities Committee are a censorship of the screen. What have you to say about that?

MR. MENJOU. I think that is juvenile.

THE CHAIRMAN. So anybody that would make such a statement would be considered as such?

MR. MENJOU. It is perfectly infantile to say this committee is trying to control the industry. How could they possibly control the industry! They wouldn't know anything about it. You wouldn't know how to make a picture or anything else. I don't see how that could be said by any man with the intelligence of a louse. . . .

I would move to the State of Texas if it [Communism] ever came here because I think the Texans would kill them on sight. . . .

6. John Charles Moffitt, Film Critic for *Esquire* Magazine, Former Screenwriter.

. . . MR. STRIPLING. Did you ever join any organizations while you were in Hollywood in connection with being a writer for the motion-picture industry?

MR. MOFFITT. Yes, sir; I did. In 1937, shocked by the conduct of the Fascists in Spain, I joined an organization known as the Hollywood Anti-Nazi League. Both my wife and I became members of that organization. We contributed considerable sums of money—for us—to what we supposed was the buying of ambulances and medical supplies for the assistance of the Loyalists in Spain.

After we had been in that organization some months we were invited to what turned out to be a more or less star chamber meeting, an inner corps meeting. It took place in the home of Mr. Frank Tuttle, a director. Mr. Herbert Biberman, who had been responsible for my being in the Anti-Nazi League, was there, as was his wife, Miss Gail Sondergaard, an actress. Donald Ogden Stewart was also one of those present.

[Moffitt then related that he and his wife were shocked to learn at that meeting that the leaders of the Anti-Nazi League were Communists. In addition to Biberman and Stewart, Moffitt named John Howard Lawson as one of the league's leaders.]

MR. STRIPLING. We will go back to your activities in the Anti-Nazi League.

MR. MOFFITT. During the period I referred to, the period between the time I discovered that this was a Communist front organization and the period some 6 weeks later, there, when I resigned, I had several conversations with Mr. Biberman, Mr. Lawson, and others of that organization.

During the course of it Mr. Lawson made this significant statement: He said:

As a writer do not try to write an entire Communist picture.

He said:

The producers will quickly identify it and it will be killed by the front office.

He said:

As a writer try to get 5 minutes of the Communist doctrine, 5 minutes of the party line in every script that you write.

He said:

Get that into an expensive scene, a scene involving expensive stars, large sets or many extras, because—

He said:

Then even if it is discovered by the front office the business manager of the unit, the very watchdog of the treasury, the very servant of capitalism, in order to keep the budget from going too high, will resist the elimination of that scene. If you can make the message come from the mouth of Gary Cooper or some other important star who is unaware of what he is saying, by the time it is discovered he is in New York and a great deal of expense will be involved to bring him back and reshoot the scene.

If you get the message into a scene employing many extras it will be very expensive to reshoot that scene because of the number of extras involved or the amount of labor that would be necessary to light and reconstruct a large set.

That was the nucleus of what he said at that time.

I later heard another statement by Mr. Lawson. That was made in the summer of 1941 when some young friends of mine who were attending what was purported to be a school for actors in Hollywood—I think it was on Labrea Boulevard—asked me to go over and hear one of the lectures, instructions on acting.

I went over on this night and Mr. Lawson was the lecturer. During the course of the evening Mr. Lawson said this—and I think I quote it

CHAPTER 9

THE SECOND
RED SCARE:
HUAC vs.
HOLLYWOOD,
1947

practically verbatim—Mr. Lawson said to these young men and women
who were training for a career of acting, he said:

It is your duty to further the class struggle by your performance.

He said—

If you are nothing more than an extra wearing white flannels on a country
club veranda do your best to appear decadent, do your best to appear
to be a snob; do your best to create class antagonism.

He said—

If you are an extra on a tenement street do your best to look downtrodden,
do your best to look a victim of existing society. . . .

7. Ruppert Hughes, Screenwriter.

[*Hughes testified that John Howard Lawson and others had made the Screen Writers
Guild "an instrument of communist power." In response, Hughes and others founded
the Screen Playwrights in 1935 or 1936. Under attack from the Screen Writers Guild
as Fascists and a company union, the Screen Playwriters were forced to disband.
Hughes then testified how Biberman and others had refused to attack Hitler when
Germany was allied with the Soviet Union.*]

MR. HUGHES. That is the way I tell a Communist, a man who never says a
word against the bloodiest butcher in history, Stalin, and who says
violent words against the most modest American. That is my test.

MR. STRIPLING. Mr. Hughes, do you consider the Screen Writers Guild to be
under Communist domination at the present time?

MR. HUGHES. Weakeningly so. It was absolutely under Communist domination when the authority was put to use. It was voted for something
like 310 to 7 and the poor 7 were hissed and booed. It was revived,
then the last vote was something like 225 to 125. The anti-Communists
are trying to take it back and I have some hopes they will succeed. It
has been, up to the present, strongly dominated by Communists.

MR. STRIPLING. Do you think the Communists in Hollywood at the present
time are on the defensive or the offensive?

MR. HUGHES. I think they are on the defensive now because they are losing
a great many of those fashion followers who thought it was smart to
be Communists and who now find it is unpopular and are deserting
them. . . .

THE CHAIRMAN. The Chair would like to say . . . this committee has made
a very thorough investigation of Communist personnel in Hollywood.

We have a very complete record on at least 79 persons active out in Hollywood. The time will come in these hearings when this documented evidence will be presented, so I just want to let you know now you cannot make the kind of investigation we can, but we have made a very thorough investigation, and that material will be presented at this public hearing either some time this week or some time next week. . . .

8. Robert Taylor, Film Actor.

. . . MR. STRIPLING. During the time you have been in Hollywood has there been any period during which you considered that the Communist Party or the fellow travelers of the Communist Party were exerting any influence in the motion-picture industry?

MR. TAYLOR. Well, of course, I have been looking for communism for a long time. I have been so strongly opposed to it for so many years; I think in the past 4 or 5 years, specifically, I have seen more indications which seemed to me to be signs of communistic activity in Hollywood and the motion-picture industry.

MR. STRIPLING. In any particular field?

MR. TAYLOR. No, sir. I suppose the most readily determined field in which it could be cited would be in the preparation of scripts—specifically, in the writing of those scripts. I have seen things from time to time which appeared to me to be slightly on the pink side, shall we say; at least, that was my personal opinion.

MR. STRIPLING. Could we have a little better order?

THE CHAIRMAN (pounding gavel). Please come to order.

MR. STRIPLING. Mr. Taylor, in referring to the writers, do you mean writers who are members of the Screen Writers Guild?

MR. TAYLOR. I assume that they are writers of the Screen Writers Guild. There seem to be many different factions in skills in Hollywood. I don't know just who belongs to what sometimes, but I assume they are members of the guild.

MR. STRIPLING. Are you a member of any guild?

MR. TAYLOR. I am a member of the Screen Actors Guild; yes, sir.

MR. STRIPLING. Have you ever noticed any elements within the Screen Actors Guild that you would consider to be following the Communist Party line?

CHAPTER 9

THE SECOND
RED SCARE:
HUAC vs.
HOLLYWOOD,
1947

MR. TAYLOR. Well, yes, sir; I must confess that I have. I am a member of the board of directors of the Screen Actors Guild. Quite recently I have been very active as a director of that board. It seems to me that at meetings, especially meetings of the general membership of the guild, there is always a certain group of actors and actresses whose every action would indicate to me that if they are not Communists they are working awfully hard to be Communists. I don't know. Their tactics and their philosophies seem to me to be pretty much party-line stuff. . . .

MR. STRIPLING. Mr. Taylor, these people in the Screen Actors Guild who, in your opinion follow the Communist Party line, are they a disrupting influence within the organization?

MR. TAYLOR. It seems so to me. In the meetings which I have attended, at least on issues in which apparently there is considerable unanimity of opinion, it always occurs that someone is not quite able to understand what the issue is and the meeting, instead of being over at 10 o'clock or 10:30 when it logically should be over, probably winds up running until 1 or 2 o'clock in the morning on such issues as points of order, and so on.

[*In response to questions, Taylor named Howard DaSilva and Karen Morley as "disruptive" but refused to call them Communists.*]

MR. STRIPLING. Mr. Taylor, have you ever participated in any picture as an actor which you considered contained Communist propaganda?

MR. TAYLOR. I assume we are now referring to Song of Russia. I must confess that I objected strenuously to doing Song of Russia at the time it was made. I felt that it, to my way of thinking at least, did contain Communist propaganda. However, that was my personal opinion. A lot of my friends and people whose opinions I respect did not agree with me.

When the script was first given me I felt it definitely contained Communist propaganda and objected to it upon that basis. I was assured by the studio that if there was Communist propaganda in that script it would be eliminated. I must admit that a great deal of the things to which I objected were eliminated.

Another thing which determined my attitude toward Song of Russia was the fact that I had recently been commissioned in the Navy and was awaiting orders. I wanted to go ahead and get in the Navy. However, it seems at the time there were many pictures being made to more or less strengthen the feeling of the American people toward Russia.

I did Song of Russia. I don't think it should have been made. I don't think it would be made today.

MR. STRIPLING. Mr. Taylor, in connection with the production of Song of Russia, do you know whether or not it was made at the suggestion of a representative of the Government?

MR. TAYLOR. I do not believe that it was made at the suggestion of a Government representative; no, sir. I think the script was written and prepared long before any representative of the Government became involved in it in any way.

MR. STRIPLING. Were you ever present at any meeting at which a representative of the Government was present and this picture was discussed?

MR. TAYLOR. Yes, sir; in Mr. L. B. Mayer's office. One day I was called to meet Mr. Mellett whom I met in the company of Mr. Mayer and, as I recall, the Song of Russia was discussed briefly. I don't think we were together more than 5 minutes.

It was disclosed at that time that the Government was interested in the picture being made and also pictures of that nature being made by other studios as well. As I say, it was to strengthen the feeling of the American people toward the Russian people at that time.

MR. STRIPLING. The Mellett you referred to is Mr. Lowell Mellett?

MR. TAYLOR. Yes, sir.

MR. STRIPLING. He was the Chief of the Bureau of Motion Pictures of the Office of War Information?

MR. TAYLOR. That is right. However, may I clarify something?

MR. STRIPLING. Yes; go right ahead.

MR. TAYLOR. If I ever gave the impression in anything that appeared previously that I was forced into making Song of Russia, I would like to say in my own defense, lest I look a little silly by saying I was ever forced to do the picture, I was not forced because nobody can force you to make any picture.

I objected to it but in deference to the situation as it then existed I did the picture. . . .

[*Taylor then testified that he had seen scripts with communist material and had objected. He then named Lester Cole as a person who was "reputedly a Communist" and added that he would refuse to act in a film with a person he knew to be a Communist.*]

MR. STRIPLING. You definitely consider them to be a bad influence upon the industry?

CHAPTER 9

THE SECOND
RED SCARE:
HUAC vs.
HOLLYWOOD,
1947

MR. TAYLOR. I certainly do; yes, sir.

MR. STRIPLING. They are a rotten apple in the barrel?

MR. TAYLOR. To me they are and I further believe 99.9 percent of the people in the motion-picture industry feel exactly as I do.

MR. STRIPLING. What do you think would be the best way to approach the problem of ridding the industry of the Communists who are now entrenched therein?

[*Taylor's reply, a lengthy one, was that he would discharge all Communists from the motion picture industry. He said he believed most producers would do the same if they were protected by legislation.*]

MR. STRIPLING. Mr. Taylor, do you consider that the motion picture primarily is a vehicle of entertainment and not of propaganda?

MR. TAYLOR. I certainly do. I think it is the primary job of the motion-picture industry to entertain; nothing more, nothing less.

MR. STRIPLING. Do you think the industry would be in a better position if it stuck strictly to entertainment without permitting political films to be made, without being so labeled?

MR. TAYLOR. I certainly do. Moreover, I feel that largely the picture business does stick to entertainment. I do not think they let themselves be sidetracked too much with propaganda films and things of that sort. Every once in a while things do sneak in that nobody catches. If the Communists are not working in the picture business there is no motive for their sneaking things in.

MR. STRIPLING. Mr. Taylor, returning to the picture Song of Russia for a moment, Miss Ayn Rand gave the committee a review of the picture several days ago. In the picture there were several scenes, particularly a wedding scene at which a priest officiated; also several other scenes at which the clergy was present. When you were making this picture were you under the impression that freedom of religion was enjoyed in Russia?

MR. TAYLOR. No, sir; I never was under the impression that freedom of religion was enjoyed in Russia. However, I must confess when it got down to that part of the picture the picture was about two-thirds gone and it didn't actually occur to me until you mentioned it just a minute ago. . . .

9. Ronald Reagan, Actor, President of the Screen Actors Guild.

. . . MR. STRIPLING. As a member of the board of directors, as president of the Screen Actors Guild, and as an active member, have you at any time observed or noted within the organization a clique of either Communists or Fascists who were attempting to exert influence or pressure on the guild?

MR. REAGAN. . . . There has been a small group within the Screen Actors Guild which has consistently opposed the policy of the guild board and officers of the guild, as evidenced by the vote on various issues. That small clique referred to has been suspected of more or less following the tactics that we associate with the Communist Party.

MR. STRIPLING. Would you refer to them as a disruptive influence within the guild?

MR. REAGAN. I would say that at times they have attempted to be a disruptive influence.

MR. STRIPLING. You have no knowledge yourself as to whether or not any of them are members of the Communist Party?

MR. REAGAN. No, sir; I have no investigative force, or anything, and I do not know.

MR. STRIPLING. Has it ever been reported to you that certain members of the guild were Communists?

MR. REAGAN. Yes, sir; I have heard different discussions and some of them tagged as Communists. . . .

Whether the party should be outlawed, I agree with the gentlemen that preceded me that that is a matter for the Government to decide. As a citizen I would hesitate, or not like, to see any political party outlawed on the basis of its political ideology. We have spent 170 years in this country on the basis that democracy is strong enough to stand up and fight against the inroads of any ideology. However, if it is proven that an organization is an agent of a power, a foreign power, or in any way not a legitimate political party, and I think the Government is capable of proving that, if the proof is there, then that is another matter. . . .

CHAPTER 9

THE SECOND
RED SCARE:
HUAC vs.
HOLLYWOOD,
1947

10. Gary Cooper, Film Actor.

. . . MR. SMITH. Are you a member of the Screen Actors Guild?

MR. COOPER. Yes; I have been a member since the guild was organized.

MR. SMITH. During the time that you have been in Hollywood, have you ever observed any communistic influence in Hollywood or in the motion-picture industry?

MR. COOPER. I believe I have noticed some.

MR. SMITH. What do you believe the principal medium is that they use Hollywood or the industry to inject propaganda?

MR. COOPER. Well, I believe it is done through word of mouth——

THE CHAIRMAN. Will you speak louder, please, Mr. Cooper?

MR. COOPER. I believe it is done through word of mouth and through the medium of pamphleting—and writers, I suppose.

MR. SMITH. By word of mouth, what do you mean, Mr. Cooper?

MR. COOPER. Well, I mean sort of social gatherings.

MR. SMITH. That has been your observation?

MR. COOPER. That has been my only observation; yes.

MR. SMITH. Can you tell us some of the statements that you may have heard at these gatherings that you believe are communistic?

MR. COOPER. Well, I have heard quite a few, I think, from time to time over the years. Well, I have heard tossed around such statements as, "Don't you think the Constitution of the United States is about 150 years out of date?" and—oh, I don't know—I have heard people mention that, well, "Perhaps this would be a more efficient Government without a Congress"—which statements I think are very un-American.

[*Cooper then stated that he had turned down "quite a few scripts" because they contained communist ideas, but he could not recall the titles. He added that he turned down one script because it was about a man organizing an army "who would never fight to defend their country."*]

MR. SMITH. Mr. Cooper, have you ever had any personal experience where you feel the Communist Party may have attempted to use you?

MR. COOPER. They haven't attempted to use me, I don't think, because, apparently, they know that I am not very sympathetic to communism. Several years ago, when communism was more of a social chit-chatter in parties for offices, and so on, when communism didn't have the implications that it has now, discussion of communism was more open and I remember hearing statements from some folks to the effect that the communistic system had a great many features that were desirable, one of which would be desirable to us in the motion-picture business in that it offered the actors and artists—in other words, the creative people—a special place in Government where we would be somewhat immune from the ordinary leveling of income. And as I remember, some actor's name was mentioned to me who had a house in Moscow which was very large—he had three cars, and stuff, with his house being quite a bit larger than my house in Beverly Hills at the time— and it looked to me like a pretty phony come-on to us in the picture business. From that time on, I could never take any of this pinko mouthing very seriously, because I didn't feel it was on the level.

[*Evidence was then introduced that Communists in Italy had claimed that Cooper was sympathetic to communism and had advocated communism before an audience of 90,000 in Philadelphia. Cooper replied that he had never been to Philadelphia and understood that "you would have a hard time getting 90,000 people out in Philadelphia for anything."*]

THE CHAIRMAN. Do you believe as a prominent person in your field that it would be wise for us, the Congress, to pass legislation to outlaw the Communist Party in the United States?

MR. COOPER. I think it would be a good idea, although I have never read Karl Marx and I don't know the basis of communism, beyond what I have picked up from hearsay. From what I hear, I don't like it because it isn't on the level. So I couldn't possibly answer that question. . . .

11. Walt Disney, Head of Walt Disney Studios.

. . . MR. SMITH. Have you had at any time, in your opinion, in the past, have you at any time in the past had any Communists employed at your studio?

MR. DISNEY. Yes; in the past I had some people that I definitely feel were Communists.

MR. SMITH. As a matter of fact, Mr. Disney, you experienced a strike at your studio, did you not?

MR. DISNEY. Yes.

MR. SMITH. And is it your opinion that that strike was instituted by members of the Communist Party to serve their purposes?

CHAPTER 9

THE SECOND
RED SCARE:
HUAC vs.
HOLLYWOOD,
1947

MR. DISNEY. Well, it proved itself so with time, and I definitely feel it was a Communist group trying to take over my artists and they did take them over.

THE CHAIRMAN. Do you say they did take them over?

MR. DISNEY. They did take them over.

MR. SMITH. Will you explain that to the committee, please?

[*Disney related the story of the attempt by Herbert Sorrell, whom Disney called a Communist, to shift his employees to another union. Disney demanded an election, and Sorrell countered with a strike. Disney then said he was smeared by "commie front organizations" and publications, which he proceeded to name. In that group he included the League of Women Voters but later apologized, saying his naming of that organization had been an error.*]

12. John Howard Lawson, Screenwriter.

THE CHAIRMAN. Mr. Stripling, the first witness.

MR. CRUM.[7] Mr. Chairman——

MR. STRIPLING. Mr. John Howard Lawson.

MR. CRUM. Mr. Chairman——

THE CHAIRMAN. I am sorry——

MR. CRUM. May I request the right of cross-examination? I ask you to bring back and permit us to cross-examine the witnesses, Adolphe Menjou, Fred Niblo, John Charles Moffitt, Richard Macaulay, Ruppert Hughes, Sam Wood, Ayn Rand, James McGuinness——

THE CHAIRMAN. The request——

MR. CRUM. Howard Rushmore——

(The chairman pounding gavel.)

MR. CRUM. Morrie Ryskind, Oliver Carlson——

THE CHAIRMAN. The request is denied.

MR. CRUM. In order to show that these witnesses lied.

THE CHAIRMAN. That request is denied. Mr. Stripling, the first witness.

MR. STRIPLING. John Howard Lawson.

(John Howard Lawson, accompanied by Robert W. Kenny and Bartley Crum take places at witness table.)

7. Crum was an attorney representing the nineteen Hollywood figures who had been named as Communists.

THE CHAIRMAN. Stand and please raise your right hand. Do you solemnly swear the testimony you are about to give is the truth, the whole truth, and nothing but the truth, so help you God?

MR. LAWSON. I do.

THE CHAIRMAN. Sit down, please.

MR. LAWSON. Mr. Chairman, I have a statement here which I wish to make——

THE CHAIRMAN. Well, all right; let me see your statement.

(Statement handed to the chairman.)

MR. STRIPLING. Do you have a copy of that?

MR. CRUM. We can get you copies.

THE CHAIRMAN. I don't care to read any more of the statement. The statement will not be read. I read the first line.

MR. LAWSON. You have spent 1 week vilifying me before the American public——

THE CHAIRMAN. Just a minute——

MR. LAWSON. And you refuse to allow me to make a statement on my rights as an American citizen.

THE CHAIRMAN. I refuse you to make the statement, because of the first sentence in your statement. That statement is not pertinent to the inquiry.

Now, this is a congressional committee—a congressional committee set up by law. We must have orderly procedure, and we are going to have orderly procedure.

Mr. Stripling, identify the witness.

MR. LAWSON. The rights of American citizens are important in this room here, and I intend to stand up for those rights, Congressman Thomas.

MR. STRIPLING. Mr. Lawson, will you state your full name, please!

MR. LAWSON. I wish to protest against the unwillingness of this committee to read a statement, when you permitted Mr. Warner, Mr. Mayer, and others to read statements in this room.

My name is John Howard Lawson.

MR. STRIPLING. What is your present address?

MR. LAWSON. 9354 Burnett Avenue, San Fernando, Calif.

MR. STRIPLING. When and where were you born?

MR. LAWSON. New York City.

MR. STRIPLING. What year?

MR. LAWSON. 1894.

MR. STRIPLING. Give us the exact date.

CHAPTER 9

THE SECOND
RED SCARE:
HUAC vs.
HOLLYWOOD,
1947

MR. LAWSON. September 25.

MR. STRIPLING. Mr. Lawson, you are here in response to a subpoena which was served upon you on September 19, 1947; is that true?

MR. LAWSON. That is correct. . . .

MR. STRIPLING. What is your occupation, Mr. Lawson?

MR. LAWSON. I am a writer.

MR. STRIPLING. How long have you been a writer?

MR. LAWSON. All my life—at least 35 years—my adult life.

MR. STRIPLING. Are you a member of the Screen Writers Guild?

MR. LAWSON. The raising of any question here in regard to membership, political beliefs, or affiliation——

MR. STRIPLING. Mr. Chairman——

MR. LAWSON. Is absolutely beyond the powers of this committee.

MR. STRIPLING. Mr. Chairman——

MR. LAWSON. But——

(The chairman pounding gavel.)

MR. LAWSON. It is a matter of public record that I am a member of the Screen Writers Guild.

MR. STRIPLING. I ask——

[Applause.]

THE CHAIRMAN. I want to caution the people in the audience: You are the guests of this committee and you will have to maintain order at all times. I do not care for any applause or any demonstrations of one kind or another.

MR. STRIPLING. Now, Mr. Chairman, I am also going to request that you instruct the witness to be responsive to the questions.

THE CHAIRMAN. I think the witness will be more responsive to the questions.

MR. LAWSON. Mr. Chairman, you permitted——

THE CHAIRMAN (pounding gavel). Never mind——

MR. LAWSON (continuing). Witnesses in this room to make answers of three or five hundred words to questions here.

THE CHAIRMAN. Mr. Lawson, you will please be responsive to these questions and not continue to try to disrupt these hearings.

MR. LAWSON. I am not on trial here, Mr. Chairman. This committee is on trial here before the American people. Let us get that straight.

THE CHAIRMAN. We don't want you to be on trial.

MR. STRIPLING. Mr. Lawson, how long have you been a member of the Screen Writers Guild?

MR. LAWSON. Since it was founded in its present form, in 1933.

MR. STRIPLING. Have you ever held any office in the guild?

MR. LAWSON. The question of whether I have held office is also a question which is beyond the purview of this committee.

(The chairman pounding gavel.)

MR. LAWSON. It is an invasion of the right of association under the Bill of Rights of this country.

THE CHAIRMAN. Please be responsive to the question.

MR. LAWSON. It is also a matter——

(The chairman pounding gavel.)

MR. LAWSON. Of public record——

THE CHAIRMAN. You asked to be heard. Through your attorney, you asked to be heard, and we want you to be heard. And if you don't care to be heard, then we will excuse you and we will put the record in without your answers.

MR. LAWSON. I wish to frame my own answers to your questions, Mr. Chairman, and I intend to do so.

THE CHAIRMAN. And you will be responsive to the questions or you will be excused from the witness stand.

MR. LAWSON. I will frame my own answers, Mr. Chairman.

THE CHAIRMAN. Go ahead, Mr. Stripling.

MR. STRIPLING. I repeat the question, Mr. Lawson: Have you ever held any position in the Screen Writers Guild?

MR. LAWSON. I stated that it is outside the purview of the rights of this committee to inquire into any form of association——

THE CHAIRMAN. The Chair will determine what is in the purview of this committee.

MR. LAWSON. My rights as an American citizen are no less than the responsibilities of this committee of Congress.

THE CHAIRMAN. Now you are just making a big scene for yourself and getting all "het up." [Laughter.]

Be responsive to the questioning, just the same as all the witnesses have. You are no different from the rest.

Go ahead, Mr. Stripling.

MR. LAWSON. I am being treated differently from the rest.

THE CHAIRMAN. You are not being treated differently.

MR. LAWSON. Other witnesses have made statements, which included quotations from books, references to material which had no connection whatsoever with the interest of this committee.

THE CHAIRMAN. We will determine whether it has connection.

Now, you go ahead——

CHAPTER 9

THE SECOND
RED SCARE:
HUAC vs.
HOLLYWOOD,
1947

MR. LAWSON. It is absolutely beyond the power of this committee to inquire into my association in any organization.

THE CHAIRMAN. Mr. Lawson, you will have to stop or you will leave the witness stand. And you will leave the witness stand because you are in contempt. That is why you will leave the witness stand. And if you are just trying to force me to put you in contempt, you won't have to try much harder. You know what has happened to a lot of people that have been in contempt of this committee this year, don't you?

MR. LAWSON. I am glad you have made it perfectly clear that you are going to threaten and intimidate the witnesses, Mr. Chairman.

(The chairman pounding gavel.)

MR. LAWSON. I am an American and I am not at all easy to intimidate, and don't think I am.

(The chairman pounding gavel.)

MR. STRIPLING. Mr. Lawson, I repeat the question. Have you ever held any position in the Screen Writers Guild?

MR. LAWSON. I have stated that the question is illegal. But it is a matter of public record that I have held many offices in the Screen Writers Guild. I was its first president, in 1933, and I have held office on the board of directors of the Screen Writers Guild at other times.

MR. STRIPLING. You have been employed in the motion-picture industry; have you not?

MR. LAWSON. I have.

MR. STRIPLING. Would you state some of the studios where you have been employed?

MR. LAWSON. Practically all of the studios, all the major studios.

MR. STRIPLING. As a screen writer?

MR. LAWSON. That is correct.

MR. STRIPLING. Would you list some of the pictures which you have written the script for?

MR. LAWSON. I must state again that you are now inquiring into the freedom of press and communications, over which you have no control whatsoever. You don't have to bring me here 3,000 miles to find out what pictures I have written. The pictures that I have written are very well known. They are such pictures as Action in the North Atlantic, Sahara——

MR. STRIPLING. Mr. Lawson——

MR. LAWSON. Such pictures as Blockade, of which I am very proud and in which I introduced the danger that this democracy faced from the attempt to destroy democracy in Spain in 1937. These matters are all matters of public record.

MR. STRIPLING. Mr. Lawson, would you object if I read a list of the pictures, and then you can either state whether or not you did write the scripts?

MR. LAWSON. I have no objection at all.

MR. STRIPLING. Did you write Dynamite, by M-G-M?

MR. LAWSON. I preface my answer, again, by saying that it is outside the province of this committee, but it is well known that I did.

MR. STRIPLING. The Sea Bat, by M-G-M?

MR. LAWSON. It is well known that I did.

MR. STRIPLING. Success at Any Price, RKO?

MR. LAWSON. Yes; that is from a play of mine, Success Story.

MR. STRIPLING. Party Wire, Columbia?

MR. LAWSON. Yes; I did.

MR. STRIPLING. Blockade, United Artists, Wanger?

MR. LAWSON. That is correct.

MR. STRIPLING. Algiers, United Artists, Wanger?

MR. LAWSON. Correct.

MR. STRIPLING. Earth Bound, Twentieth Century Fox.

MR. LAWSON. Correct.

MR. STRIPLING. Counterattack, Columbia.

MR. LAWSON. Correct.

MR. STRIPLING. You have probably written others; have you not, Mr. Lawson?

MR. LAWSON. Many others. You have missed a lot of them.

MR. STRIPLING. You don't care to furnish them to the committee, do you?

MR. LAWSON. Not in the least interested.

MR. STRIPLING. Mr. Lawson, are you now, or have you ever been a member of the Communist Party of the United States?

MR. LAWSON. In framing my answer to that question I must emphasize the points that I have raised before. The question of communism is in no way related to this inquiry, which is an attempt to get control of the screen and to invade the basic rights of American citizens in all fields.

MR. MCDOWELL. Now, I must object——

MR. STRIPLING. Mr. Chairman——

(The chairman pounding gavel.)

MR. LAWSON. The question here relates not only to the question of my membership in any political organization, but this committee is attempting to establish the right——

(The chairman pounding gavel.)

MR. LAWSON (continuing). Which has been historically denied to any committee of this sort, to invade the rights and privileges and immunity of American citizens, whether they be Protestant, Methodist, Jewish,

CHAPTER 9

THE SECOND
RED SCARE:
HUAC vs.
HOLLYWOOD,
1947

or Catholic, whether they be Republican or Democrats or anything else.

THE CHAIRMAN (pounding gavel). Mr. Lawson, just quiet down again.

Mr. Lawson, the most pertinent question that we can ask is whether or not you have ever been a member of the Communist Party. Now, do you care to answer that question?

MR. LAWSON. You are using the old technique, which was used in Hitler Germany in order to create a scare here——

THE CHAIRMAN (pounding gavel). Oh——

MR. LAWSON. In order to create an entirely false atmosphere in which this hearing is conducted——

(The chairman pounding gavel.)

MR. LAWSON. In order that you can then smear the motion-picture industry, and you can proceed to the press, to any form of communication in this country.

THE CHAIRMAN. You have learned——

MR. LAWSON. The Bill of Rights was established precisely to prevent the operation of any committee which could invade the basic rights of Americans.

Now, if you want to know——

MR. STRIPLING. Mr. Chairman, the witness is not answering the question.

MR. LAWSON. If you want to know——

(The chairman pounding gavel.)

MR. LAWSON. About the perjury that has been committed here and the perjury that is planned.

THE CHAIRMAN. Mr. Lawson——

MR. LAWSON. You permit me and my attorneys to bring in here the witnesses that testified last week and you permit us to cross-examine these witnesses, and we will show up the whole tissue of lie——

THE CHAIRMAN (pounding gavel). We are going to get the answer to that question if we have to stay here for a week.

Are you a member of the Communist Party, or have you ever been a member of the Communist Party?

MR. LAWSON. It is unfortunate and tragic that I have to teach this committee the basic principles of American——

THE CHAIRMAN (pounding gavel). That is not the question. That is not the question. The question is: Have you ever been a member of the Communist Party?

MR. LAWSON. I am framing my answer in the only way in which any American citizen can frame his answer to a question which absolutely invades his rights.

THE CHAIRMAN. Then you refuse to answer that question; is that correct?

MR. LAWSON. I have told you that I will offer my beliefs, affiliations, and everything else to the American public, and they will know where I stand.

THE CHAIRMAN (pounding gavel). Excuse the witness——

MR. LAWSON. As they do from what I have written.

THE CHAIRMAN (pounding gavel). Stand away from the stand——

MR. LAWSON. I have written Americanism for many years, and I shall continue to fight for the Bill of Rights, which you are trying to destroy.

THE CHAIRMAN. Officers, take this man away from the stand——[8]

[Applause and boos.]

THE CHAIRMAN (pounding gavel). There will be no demonstrations. No demonstrations, for or against. Everyone will please be seated. . . .

13. Eric Johnston, Motion Picture Executive, President of the Motion Picture Association of America.

I'm not here to try to whitewash Hollywood, and I'm not here to help sling a tar brush at it, either.

I want to stick to the facts as I see them.

There are several points I'd like to make to this committee.

The first one is this: A damaging impression of Hollywood has spread all over the country as a result of last week's hearings. You have a lot of sensational testimony about Hollywood. From some of it the public will get the idea that Hollywood is running over the Communists and communism.

I believe the impression which has gone out is the sort of scare-head stuff which is grossly unfair to a great American industry. It must be a great satisfaction to the Communist leadership in this country to have people believe that Hollywood Communists are astronomical in number and almost irresistible in power.

Now, what are the facts? Not everybody in Hollywood is a Communist. I have said before that undoubtedly there are Communists in Hollywood, but in my opinion the percentage is extremely small.

I have had a number of close looks at Hollywood in the last 2 years, and I have looked at it through the eyes of an average businessman. I recognize that as the world's capital of show business, there is bound to be a lot of

8. After Lawson had been led from the stand, the committee's investigator produced what he said was Lawson's Communist party membership card.

CHAPTER 9

THE SECOND
RED SCARE:
HUAC vs.
HOLLYWOOD,
1947

show business in Hollywood. There is no business, Mr. Chairman, like show business. But underneath there is the solid foundation of patriotic, hard-working, decent citizens. Making motion pictures is hard work. You just don't dash off a motion picture between social engagements.

The great bulk of Hollywood people put their jobs first. But I can assure you you won't find a community in the country where hearts are any bigger or the purses more open when it comes to helping out worthy endeavors. Take any national campaign for the public good, and you'll find Hollywood people contributing their time and their money.

Every other country in the world is trying to build up its motion-picture industry, and I can verify that, having just traveled in 12 countries in Europe where they are all trying to build up their motion-picture industry. These governments are trying to do it through government subsidies and devices of all kinds. The American motion-picture industry grew by its own efforts. It has rejected subsidies and Government assistance. It wants no hand-out from Government. All it asks is a fair shake and a chance to live and to grow and to serve its country without being unfairly condemned and crucified.

I wind up my first point with a request of this committee. The damaging impression about Hollywood should be corrected. I urge your committee to do so in these public hearings.

There is another damaging impression which should be corrected. The report of the subcommittee said that some of the most flagrant Communist propaganda films were produced as the result of White House pressure. This charge has been completely refuted by the testimony before you.

My second point includes another request of the committee.

The report of your subcommittee stated that you had a list of all pictures produced in Hollywood in the last 8 years which contained Communist propaganda. Your committee has not made this list public. Until the list is made public the industry stands condemned by unsupported generalizations, and we are denied the opportunity to refute these charges publicly.

Again, I remind the committee that we have offered to put on a special showing of any or all of the pictures which stand accused so that you can see for yourselves what's in them. The contents of the pictures constitute the only proof.

Unless this evidence is presented and we are given the chance to refute it in these public hearings, it is the obligation of the committee to absolve the industry from the charges against it.

Now, I come to my third point—a vitally important one to every American and to the system under which we live.

It is free speech.

Now, I've been advised by some persons to lay off it. I've been told that if I mentioned it I'd be playing into the hands of Communists. But nobody has a monopoly on the issue of free speech in this country. I'm not afraid of being right, even if that puts me in with the wrong company. I've been for free speech ever since I first read the lives of great men of the past who fought and died for this principle—and that was in grade school.

There is nothing I can add to what every great American has said on the subject since the founding of the Republic. Our freedoms would become empty and meaningless without the keystone of our freedom arch—freedom of speech—freedom to speak, to hear, and to see.

When I talk about freedom of speech in connection with this hearing, I mean just this: You don't need to pass a law to choke off free speech or seriously curtail it. Intimidation or coercion will do it just as well. You can't make good and honest motion pictures in an atmosphere of fear.

I intend to use every influence at my command to keep the screen free. I don't propose that Government shall tell the motion-picture industry, directly or by coercion, what kind of pictures it ought to make. I am as wholesouledly against that as I would be against dictating to the press or the radio, to the book publishers or to the magazines.

One of the most amazing paradoxes has grown out of this hearing. At one point we were accused of making Communist propaganda by not making pictures which show the advantages of our system. In other words, we were accused of putting propaganda on the screen by keeping it out.

That sort of reasoning is a little staggering, especially when you know the story of American pictures in some foreign countries. We are accused of Communist propaganda at home, but in Communist-dominated countries in Europe our motion-picture films are banned because they contain propaganda for capitalism.

We can't be communistic and capitalistic at one and the same time. I've said it before, but I'd like to repeat it. There is nothing more feared or hated in Communist countries than the American motion picture.

To sum up this point: We insist on our rights to decide what will or will not go in our pictures. We are deeply conscious of the responsibility this freedom involves, but we have no intention to violate this trust by permitting subversive propaganda in our films.

Now, my next point is this:

When I was before this committee last March, I said that I wanted to see Communists exposed. I still do. I'm heart and soul for it. An exposed Communist is an unarmed Communist. Expose them, but expose them in the traditional American manner.

CHAPTER 9

THE SECOND
RED SCARE:
HUAC vs.
HOLLYWOOD,
1947

But I believe that when this committee or any other agency undertakes to expose communism it must be scrupulous to avoid tying a red tag on innocent people by indiscriminate labeling.

It seems to me it is getting dangerously easy to call a man a Communist without proof or even reasonable suspicion. When a distinguished leader of the Republican Party in the United States Senate is accused of following the Communist Party line for introducing a housing bill, it is time, gentlemen, to give a little serious thought to the dangers of thoughtless smearing by gossip and hearsay.

Senator Robert Taft isn't going to worry about being called a Communist. But not every American is a Senator Taft who can properly ignore such an accusation. Most of us in America are just little people, and loose charges can hurt little people. They take away everything a man has—his livelihood, his reputation, and his personal dignity.

When just one man is falsely damned as a Communist in an hour like this when the Red issue is at white heat, no one of us is safe.

Gentlemen, I maintain that preservation of the rights of the individual is a proper duty for this Committee on Un-American Activities. This country's entire tradition is based on the principle that the individual is a higher power than the state; that the state owes its authority to the individual, and must treat him accordingly.

Expose communism, but don't put any American who isn't a Communist in a concentration camp of suspicion. We are not willing to give up our freedoms to save our freedoms.

I now come to my final point:

What are we going to do positively and constructively about combating communism? It isn't enough to be anti-Communist any more than it is to be antismallpox. You can still die from smallpox if you haven't used a serum against it. A positive program is the best antitoxin of the plague of communism.

Communism must have breeding grounds. Men and women who have a reasonable measure of opportunity aren't taken in by the prattle of Communists. Revolutions plotted by frustrated intellectuals at cocktail parties won't get anywhere if we wipe out the potential causes of communism. The most effective way is to make democracy work for greater opportunity, for greater participation, for greater security for all our people.

The real breeding ground of communism is in the slums. It is everywhere where people haven't enough to eat or enough to wear through no fault of their own. Communism hunts misery, feeds on misery, and profits by it.

Freedoms walk hand-in-hand with abundance. That has been the history of America. It has been the American story. It turned the eyes of the world to America, because America gave reality to freedom, plus abundance when it was still an idle daydream in the rest of the world.

We have been the greatest exporter of freedom, and the world is hungry for it. Today it needs our wheat and our fuel to stave off hunger and fight off cold, but hungry and cold as they may be, men always hunger for freedom.

We want to continue to practice and to export freedom.

If we fortify our democracy to lick want, we will lick communism—here and abroad. Communists can hang all the iron curtains they like, but they'll never be able to shut out the story of a land where free men walk without fear and live with abundance.

[Applause.]

(The chairman pounding gavel.) . . .

[*Following Johnston's testimony, nine of the unfriendly witnesses were called: Dalton Trumbo, Albert Maltz, Alvah Bessie, Samuel Ornitz, Herbert Biberman, Edward Dmytryk, Adrian Scott, Ring Lardner, Jr., and Lester Cole. With the exception of Maltz, none was allowed to make a statement; each was forced from the witness stand and then identified by the committee's investigator as having been a card-carrying member of the Communist party. Only later was the authenticity of those cards challenged. Maltz's statement is reproduced below.*]

14. Albert Maltz, Screenwriter.

THE CHAIRMAN. Mr. Maltz, the committee is unanimous in permitting you to read the statement.

MR. MALTZ. Thank you.

I am an American and I believe there is no more proud word in the vocabulary of man. I am a novelist and a screen writer and I have produced a certain body of work in the past 15 years. As with any other writer, what I have written has come from the total fabric of my life— my birth in this land, our schools and games, our atmosphere of freedom, our tradition of inquiry, criticism, discussion, tolerance. Whatever I am, America has made me. And I, in turn, possess no loyalty as great as the one I have to this land, to the economic and social welfare of its people, to the perpetuation and development of its democratic way of life.

CHAPTER 9

THE SECOND
RED SCARE:
HUAC vs.
HOLLYWOOD,
1947

Now at the age of 39, I am commanded to appear before the House Committee on Un-American Activities. For a full week this committee has encouraged an assortment of well-rehearsed witnesses to testify that I and others are subversive and un-American. It has refused us the opportunity that any pickpocket receives in a magistrate's court— the right to cross-examine these witnesses, to refute their testimony, to reveal their motives, their history, and who, exactly, they are. Furthermore it grants these witnesses congressional immunity so that we may not sue them for libel for their slanders.

I maintain that this is an evil and vicious procedure; that it is legally unjust and morally indecent—and that it places in danger every other American, since if the rights of any one citizen can be invaded, then the constitutional guaranties of every other American have been subverted and no one is any longer protected from official tyranny.

What is it about me that this committee wishes to destroy? My writings? Very well, let us refer to them. . . .

[*Here Maltz listed some of his works and awards, including a special award by the Academy of Motion Picture Arts and Sciences and the 1938 O. Henry Award for the best American short story.*]

This, then, is the body of work for which this committee urges I be blacklisted in the film industry—and tomorrow, if it has its way in the publishing and magazine fields also.

By cold censorship, if not legislation, I must not be allowed to write. Will this censorship stop with me? Or with the others now singled out for attack? If it requires acceptance of the ideas of this committee to remain immune from the brand of un-Americanism, then who is ultimately safe from this committee except members of the Ku Klux Klan?

Why else does this committee now seek to destroy me and others? Because of our ideas, unquestionably. In 1801, when he was President of the United States, Thomas Jefferson wrote:

Opinion, and the just maintenance of it, shall never be a crime in my view; nor bring injury to the individual.

But a few years ago, in the course of one of the hearings of this committee, Congressman J. Parnell Thomas said, and I quote from the official transcript:

I just want to say this now, that it seems that the New Deal is working along hand in glove with the Communist Party. The New Deal is either for the Communist Party or it is playing into the hands of the Communist Party.

Very well, then, here is the other reason why I and others have been commanded to appear before this committee—our ideas. In common with many Americans, I supported the New Deal. In common with many Americans I supported, against Mr. Thomas and Mr. Rankin, the antilynching bill. I opposed them in my support of OPA[9] controls and emergency veteran housing and a fair employment practices law. I signed petitions for these measures, joined organizations that advocated them, contributed money, sometimes spoke from public platforms, and I will continue to do so. I will take my philosophy from Thomas Payne;[10] Thomas Jefferson, Abraham Lincoln, and I will not be dictated to or intimidated by men to whom the Ku Klux Klan, as a matter of committee record, is an acceptable American institution.

I state further that on many questions of public interest my opinions as a citizen have not always been in accord with the opinions of the majority. They are not now nor have my opinions ever been fixed and unchanging, nor are they now fixed and unchangeable; but, right or wrong, I claim and I insist upon my right to think freely and to speak freely; to join the Republican Party or the Communist Party, the Democratic or the Prohibition Party; to publish whatever I please; to fix my mind or change my mind, without dictation from anyone; to offer any criticism I think fitting of any public official or policy; to join whatever organizations I please, no matter what certain legislators may think of them. Above all, I challenge the right of this committee to inquire into my political or religious beliefs[11] in any manner or degree, and I assert that not only the conduct of this committee but its very existence are a subversion of the Bill of Rights.

If I were a spokesman for General Franco, I would not be here today. I would rather be here. I would rather die than be a shabby American, groveling before men whose names are Thomas and Rankin, but who now carry out activities in American like those carried out in Germany by Goebbels and Himmler.

9. Office of Price Administration.
10. Thomas Paine, author of *Common Sense*.
11. This was a reference to Rankin's undisguised anti-Semitism.

CHAPTER 9

THE SECOND
RED SCARE:
HUAC vs.
HOLLYWOOD,
1947

The American people are going to have to choose between the Bill of Rights and the Thomas committee. They cannot have both. One or the other must be abolished in the immediate future.

THE CHAIRMAN. Mr. Stripling (pounding gavel). . . .

15. Concluding Statement.

THE CHAIRMAN. The Chair would like to make this statement.

The hearings today conclude the first phase of the committee's investigation of communism in the motion-picture industry. While we have heard 39 witnesses, there are many more to be heard. The Chair stated earlier in the hearing he would present the records of 79 prominent people associated with the motion-picture industry who were members of the Communist Party or who had records of Communist affiliations. We have had before us 11 of these individuals. There are 68 to go. This hearing has concluded itself principally with spotlighting Communist personnel in the industry.

There is, however, an equally dangerous phase of this inquiry which deals with Communist propaganda in various motion pictures and the techniques employed. At the present time the committee has a special staff making an extensive study of this phase of the committee's inquiry. Either the full committee or a subcommittee will resume hearings on this matter in the near future, either in Washington or in Los Angeles, at which time those persons whose Communist records the committee has will be given an opportunity to appear before the committee to confirm or deny those affiliations. We will also have a number of witnesses who will deal with propaganda in the films and the techniques employed.

I want to emphasize that the committee is not adjourning sine die, but will resume hearings as soon as possible. The committee hearings for the past 2 weeks have clearly shown the need for this investigation. Ten prominent figures in Hollywood whom the committee had evidence were members of the Communist Party were brought before us and refused to deny that they were Communists. It is not necessary for the Chair to emphasize the harm which the motion-picture industry suffers from the presence within its ranks of known Communists who do not have the best interests of the United States at heart. The industry should set about immediately to clean its own house and not wait for public opinion to force it to do so.

The hearings are adjourned.

(Whereupon, at 3 p.m., the committee adjourned.)

∽ QUESTIONS TO CONSIDER ∽

Those who attended the first day of the HUAC hearings should have had a good indication of what was to follow. How did HUAC chairman J. Parnell Thomas set the tone for the hearings in his opening remarks? Toward the end of his opening remarks, Thomas said, "All we are after are the facts." Do you think that statement was true?

Jack L. Warner's testimony is typical of that given by friendly witnesses at the hearings. In what way is it typical? How did his opening statement attempt to satisfy the committee and at the same time defend his studio? Was the committee satisfied? What did it attempt to get Warner to say? Was Samuel Wood more cooperative?

Before the hearings began, Thomas claimed on the floor of Congress that the HUAC had a complete list of Hollywood-made films that contained communist propaganda. During the hearings, the committee focused its attention on two films: *Mission to Moscow* and *Song of Russia*. By looking at the testimonies of Jack Warner, Louis B. Mayer, and Robert Taylor, what was the committee trying to get the witnesses to say? To what extent do you think *Mission to Moscow* and *Song*

of Russia were pieces of communist propaganda? Use the evidence to bolster your case. To what extent do you think the federal government encouraged the making of these pictures (the HUAC spent a good deal of time on this question)? If the government did so, why? What was the committee apparently trying to establish?

One of the important things a historian must do is evaluate the validity of testimony. A good question to ask is "Was an individual who gave testimony in a position to know about those things she or he claimed to have known?" Using that criterion, how would you evaluate the validity of the testimonies of Menjou, Moffitt, Hughes, and Reagan? Which ones were in the best positions to know the facts? How does Reagan's testimony "fit" with the others? How does Warner's testimony fit with the others? To what extent does this testimony expose the threat of communist infiltration into the film industry?

Gary Cooper and Walt Disney were extremely well-known figures in Hollywood and in the nation in general. What did their testimony add to the proceedings? Did they add any hard

CHAPTER 9

THE SECOND
RED SCARE:
HUAC vs.
HOLLYWOOD,
1947

evidence to support the HUAC's investigation?

John Howard Lawson was the first unfriendly witness to be called. As you already know, he had been identified previously by a number of witnesses as a Communist. Do you think he was a Communist? Do you think he posed a significant threat to the United States? To the film industry? Did the committee treat Lawson differently than earlier witnesses? On another note, why do you think Lawson (and others) refused to answer when asked if they were Communists? Do you think this tactic was a wise one?

Eric Johnston's statement to the committee was an important part of the hearings. What are its principal points? What do you think of those points? Would you call Johnston a friendly or an unfriendly witness, or neither? For example, do you think Johnston viewed the HUAC's investigation of Hollywood as beneficial or detrimental to the nation's interests? Use his testimony to prove your point.

Maltz was the only one of the ten unfriendly witnesses permitted to read a prepared statement (the committee required each of the witnesses to submit his statement so the committee could decide whether or not it could be read). Why do you think Maltz's statement was approved but the others were not? Do you think Maltz's references to the New Deal played any role in the committee's decision? Why or why not?

J. Parnell Thomas's closing remarks offered a broad hint to motion picture executives who wanted the hearings stopped because of possible unfriendly publicity. What hint did Thomas give? What do you think of the process he suggested?

∽ EPILOGUE ∾

Two days after the HUAC hearings adjourned, the *New York Herald Tribune* commented that they had produced "a good deal of nonsense and very little else." Although at least some of the unfriendly witnesses undoubtedly were Communists, the committee failed to uncover any effective conspiracy to mold American public opinion through the movies. Nevertheless, an aroused public and nervous New York financial interests upon which Hollywood relied demanded that film executives take steps to bar "suspicious" people from the film industry. In November 1947, fifty motion picture executives held a two-day meeting at the Waldorf-Astoria Hotel in New York, at which they established an informal but highly effective *blacklist* that prevented suspicious people from finding jobs in films.[12] No studio would hire a blacklisted writer, director, producer, actor, or actress, nor would any film in which a blacklisted person had taken part be distributed. Some careers were permanently ruined; other men and women

12. The meeting was chaired by Eric Johnston, who was the strongest advocate of the blacklist. See Source 13.

were unable to find work in films for years; still others, like screenwriter Carl Foreman, were forced to leave the United States to continue their film work. As actor and strong anti-Communist John Wayne said, "I'll never regret having helped run [Carl] Foreman out of the country."[13] Also in November 1947, the House of Representatives voted that the ten unfriendly witnesses (by this time dubbed the "Hollywood Ten") were in contempt of Congress, and they were sentenced to prison and fines. After their appeals were exhausted, the ten began serving their prison terms in 1950.

By then, cold war tensions had increased markedly. In 1948, former Communist Whittaker Chambers accused Alger Hiss, once a well-placed figure in the State Department, of being a Communist. Although the case is still a fairly controversial one, Hiss's later conviction for perjury seemed to give weight to Chambers's charges. Moreover, in 1948 to 1949, the crisis in Berlin reached its height when the Soviets blockaded Berlin and the United States and its allies airlifted food and supplies to the city. Then, in 1949, the American-backed Nationalist government in China fell to the Communists, led by Mao Zedong. Nearly hysterical, Americans asked themselves how this tragedy had occurred.

13. Before Foreman was blacklisted and forced to leave Hollywood, he and Stanley Kramer collaborated on the film *High Noon*, considered by many to be a film classic. The film was released early in 1952 and won the New York Film Critics' award for best picture of 1952.

In February 1950, the little-known junior senator from Wisconsin, Joseph McCarthy, provided what for many Americans was an "answer" to that question. China had fallen and communism was growing stronger, McCarthy asserted, because the government was riddled with Communists who, he charged, had burrowed their way into the State Department, the Voice of America, and even the United States Army. In a series of highly publicized investigations, in the end McCarthy actually proved little or nothing. Yet his charges, many of them without any foundation, made Americans even more nervous. The federal government revived the Smith Act (1940) and used the recently enacted McCarren Internal Securities Act to investigate and remove suspicious persons from government service. The careers of several innocent people were permanently damaged.

In June 1950, the cold war suddenly became very hot. On June 25, troops from communist North Korea invaded United States–supported South Korea. Truman responded immediately, sending United States troops to help the beleaguered South Koreans. These forces had turned the tide of battle when Mao Zedong sent Chinese troops into battle on the side of North Korea.

As in the 1920s, however, the Red Scare of the late 1940s and 1950s gradually abated. Senator Joseph McCarthy was discredited in the 1954 Army–McCarthy hearings, was censured by the United States Senate in that same year, and died in 1957. Many believe that the televising of the 1954 Army–McCarthy hearings proved the senator's undoing, a blow

CHAPTER 9

THE SECOND
RED SCARE:
HUAC vs.
HOLLYWOOD,
1947

from which he never recovered. Gradually, Americans came to believe that it was better to try to negotiate with Communists in the Soviet Union, China, and elsewhere than to try to eradicate them. Indeed, even Ronald Reagan, who was a "cold warrior" and who once referred to the Soviet Union as the "evil empire," as president was willing to negotiate with the Soviets on cutbacks in nuclear weapons.

Those who had been blacklisted in Hollywood gradually drifted back into the industry, a few even recapturing their former prominence. Dalton Trumbo and Ring Lardner, Jr., both members of the Hollywood Ten, actually increased in prestige, Trumbo as the screenwriter for *Spartacus* (1960) and Lardner for his work on *The Cincinnati Kid* (1965) and *M*A*S*H* (1970). Carl Foreman, who wrote the script for *High Noon,* remained in England, where he wrote or cowrote the screenplays for *The Bridge on the River Kwai, The Mouse That Roared, The Guns of Navarone,* and *The Victors.* In certain cases, however, his work was uncredited because some major studios still feared repercussions if they openly re-employed blacklisted artists. Hollywood Ten member Herbert Biberman formed a company of blacklisted artists that made the 1954 film *Salt of the Earth,* a powerful and moving picture about a miners' strike in New Mexico. But that film itself was blacklisted and was not generally released until the 1960s. It is now available on videocassette and, because of its history, has become something of a cult classic (also, perhaps, because one of the blacklisted actors in that film, Will Geer, years later appeared as Grandpa

Walton in the television series "The Waltons").[14]

For its part, the HUAC never gave Congress a formal report of its findings from the 1947 hearings on communism in Hollywood, probably because, as you have seen, there was little evidence to support its sensational charges. In 1951, the HUAC once again turned its attention to Hollywood, with equally inconclusive results, although more unfriendly witnesses were blacklisted.

Throughout the 1950s, the HUAC continued its sensational and well-publicized investigations of communism in the United States, most of which uncovered little or nothing. In the 1960s, the committee (in 1969 renamed the House Committee on Internal Security) conducted a series of outlandish investigations of civil rights groups and Vietnam War protesters. In January 1975, the committee was permanently disbanded. By that time, however, it had accumulated information on more than 750,000 Americans, the vast majority of whom had had no affiliation with communism.

In Hollywood itself, the investigations left a residue of bitterness, anger, suspicion, and loss of community cohesion. In that sense, the Hollywood community was a microcosm of America itself during its second Red Scare.

14. "The Waltons" premiered on September 14, 1972. To the surprise of many, the warm family drama about a Depression-era Virginia family was an almost immediate hit and enjoyed high ratings throughout much of the 1970s. In 1973, the show won an Emmy award for most outstanding dramatic series. Geer was a fixture on the program until his death in April 1978, at the age of 76.

CHAPTER 10

connection between V.N. + Cold War

A GENERATION IN WAR AND TURMOIL: THE AGONY OF VIETNAM

⌘ THE PROBLEM ⌘

When the middle-class readers of *Time* magazine went to their mailboxes in January 1967, they were eager to find out who the widely read newsmagazine had chosen as "Man of the Year." To their surprise, they discovered that the "Inheritors"—the whole generation of young people under twenty-five years of age—had been selected as the major newsmakers of the previous year. *Time*'s publisher justified the selection of an entire generation by noting that, in contrast to the previous "silent generation," young people of the late 1960s were dominating history with their distinctive lifestyles, music, and beliefs about the future of the United States.

Those who wrote to the editor about this issue ranged from a writer who thought the selection was a long-overdue honor to one who called it an "outrageous choice," from a correspondent who described contemporary young people as "one of our best generations" to one who believed the choice of a generation was "eloquent nonsense." Furthermore, many writers were frightened or worried about their children, and some middle-aged correspondents insisted that they themselves belonged to the "put-upon" or "beaten" generation.

There is no doubt that there was a generation gap in the late 1960s, a kind of sharp break between the new generation of young people who comprised nearly half the population and their parents. The first segment of the "baby-boom" generation came to adulthood during the mid- to late 1960s,[1] a time marked by the high

1. Although the birthrate began to climb during World War II (from 19.4 births per 1,000 in 1940 to 24.5 in 1945), the term *baby boom* generally is used to describe the increase in the birthrate between 1946 and the early 1960s.

CHAPTER 10

A GENERATION
IN WAR AND
TURMOIL: THE
AGONY OF
VIETNAM

point of the civil rights movement, the rise of a spirit of rebellion on college campuses, and serious divisions in America over the United States' participation in the Vietnam War. For most "baby boomers," white and black alike, the war was the issue that concerned them most immediately, for this was the generation that would be called on to fight or to watch friends, spouses, or lovers called to military service.

Your task in this chapter is to identify and interview at least one member of the baby-boom generation (prefera-

bly born between 1946 and 1956)[2] about his or her experiences during the Vietnam War era. Then, using your interview, along with those of your classmates and those provided in the Evidence section of this chapter, determine the ways in which the baby-boom generation reacted to the Vietnam War. On what issues did baby boomers agree? On what issues did they disagree? Finally, how can a study of birth cohorts (groups of people of the same generation) help historians to understand a particular era in the past?

∽ BACKGROUND ∽

The year 1945 was the beginning of the longest sustained economic boom in American history. Interrupted only a few times by brief recessions, the boom lasted from 1945 to 1973. And although there were still pockets of severe poverty in America's deteriorating inner cities and in some rural areas such as Appalachia, most Americans had good cause to be optimistic about their economic situations.

The pent-up demand of the depression and war years broke like a tidal wave that swept nearly every economic indicator upward. Veterans returning from World War II rapidly made the transition to the civilian work force or used the GI Bill to become better educated and, as a result, secure better jobs than they had held before the war. Between 1950 and 1960, real wages increased by 20 percent, and disposable family income

rose by a staggering 49 percent. The number of registered automobiles more than doubled between 1945 and 1955, and the American automobile industry was virtually unchallenged by foreign competition. At the same time, new home construction soared, as 13 million new homes were built in the 1950s alone—85 percent of them in the new and mushrooming suburbs.[3]

New homes were financed by new types of long-term mortgage loans that required only a small down payment (5 to 10 percent) and low monthly payments (averaging $56 per

2. A person born during the late 1950s and early 1960s would technically be considered a baby boomer but would probably have been too young to remember enough to make an interview useful.
3. There were 114,000 housing starts in 1944. In 1950, housing starts had climbed to 1,692,000.

month for a tract house in the sub-urbs). And these new homes required furniture and appliances, which led to sharp upturns in these industries. Between 1945 and 1950, the amount spent on household furnishings and appliances increased 240 percent, and most of these items were bought "on time" (installments).[4] Perhaps the most coveted appliance was a television set, a product that had been almost nonexistent before the war. In 1950 alone, 7.4 million television sets were sold in the United States, and architects began designing homes with a "family room," a euphemism for a room where television was watched.

This new postwar lifestyle could best be seen in America's burgeoning suburbs. Populated to a large extent by new members of the nation's mushrooming middle class, suburbanites (as they were called) for the most part were better educated, wealthier, and more optimistic than their parents had been. Most men commuted by train, bus, or automobile back to the center city to work, while their wives remained in the suburbs, having children and raising them. It was in these suburbs that a large percentage of baby boomers were born.

Sociologist William H. Whyte called America's postwar suburbs the "new melting pot," a term that referred to the expectation that new middle-class suburbanites should leave their var-ious class and ethnic characteristics behind in the cities they had abandoned and become homogeneous. Men were expected to work their way up the corporate ladder, tend their carefully manicured lawns, become accomplished barbecue chefs, and serve their suburban communities as Boy Scout leaders or Little League coaches. For their part, women were expected to make favorable impressions on their husband's bosses (to aid their husbands in their climb up the corporate ladder), provide transportation for the children to accepted after-school activities (scouts, athletics, music and dance lessons), and make a happy home for the family's breadwinner. Above all, the goal was to fit in with their suburban neighbors. Thus suburbanites would applaud the 1956 musical *My Fair Lady*, which was based on the premise that working-class flower seller Eliza Doolittle would be accepted by "polite society" as soon as she learned to speak properly.

The desire for homogeneity (or conformity) would have a less beneficial side as well. The cold war and the McCarthy era meant that the demand for homogeneity could be enforced by the threat of job loss and ostracism. In addition, many suburban women had met their husbands in college and hence had had at least some college education.[5] But the expectation that

---

4. Between 1946 and 1956, short-term consumer credit rose from $8.4 billion to almost $45 billion, most of it to finance automobiles and home furnishings. The boom in credit card purchases ("plastic money") did not occur until the 1960s.

5. One midwestern women's college boasted that "a high proportion of our graduates marry successfully," as if that was the chief reason for women to go to college in the first place. Indeed, in many cases it was. See Elaine Tyler May, *Homeward Bound: American Families in the Cold War Era* (New York: Basic Books, 1988), p. 83.

CHAPTER 10

A GENERATION
IN WAR AND
TURMOIL: THE
AGONY OF
VIETNAM

they be primarily wives and mothers often meant that they were discouraged from using their education in other ways. As a result, one survey of suburban women revealed that 11 percent of them felt that they experienced a "great deal of emotional disturbance." At the same time, men were expected to be good corporate citizens and good team players at work. It was rumored that IBM employees began each day by gathering together, facing the home office, and singing the praises of IBM and its executive vice president C. A. Kirk (to the tune of "Carry Me Back to Old Virginny"):

Ever we praise our able leaders,
And our progressive C. A. Kirk is one
  of them,
He is endowed with the will to go for-
  ward,
He'll always work in the cause of IBM.

Finally, homogeneity meant that suburbanites would have to purchase new cars, furniture, television sets, and so on to be like their neighbors (it was called "keeping up with the Joneses"), even though monthly payments already were stretching a family's income pretty thin.

There was, however, an underside to the so-called affluent society. Indeed, many Americans did not share in its benefits at all. As middle-class whites fled to the suburbs, conditions in the cities deteriorated. Increasingly populated by the poor—African Americans, Latin American immigrants, the elderly, and unskilled white immigrants—urban areas struggled to finance essential city services such as police and fire protection. Moreover, poverty and its victims could be found

in rural areas, as Michael Harrington pointed out in his classic study *The Other America*, published in 1962. Small farmers, tenants, sharecroppers, and migrant workers were not only poor, but they often lacked any access to even basic educational opportunities and health care facilities.

Young people who lacked the money or who were not brought up with the expectation of earning a college degree tended to continue in more traditional life patterns. They completed their education with high school or before, although others attended a local vocationally oriented community college or trade school for a year or two. They often married younger than their college counterparts, sought stable jobs, and aspired to own their own homes. In other words, they rarely rejected the values of their parents' generation.

The baby boomers began leaving the suburbs for college in the early 1960s. Once away from home and in a college environment, many of these students began questioning their parents' values, especially those concerned with materialism, conformity, sexual mores and traditional sex roles, corporate structure and power, and the kind of patriotism that could support the growing conflict in Vietnam. In one sense, they were seeking the same thing that their parents had sought: fulfillment. Yet to the baby boomers, their parents had chased false gods and a false kind of fulfillment. Increasingly alienated by impersonal university policies and by the actions of authority figures such as college administrators, political leaders, and police officers, many students turned to new forms of religion, music, and dress and to the use of drugs to set themselves apart from the older generation. The term *generation gap* could be heard across the American landscape as bewildered, hurt, and angry parents confronted their children, who (in the parents' view) had "gotten everything." Nor could the children seem to communicate to their confused parents how bankrupt they believed their parents' lives and values actually were. In the midst of this generational crisis, the Vietnam War was becoming a major conflict.

The Japanese defeat of Western colonial powers, particularly Britain and France, in the early days of World War II had encouraged nationalist movements[6] in both Africa and Asia. The final surrender of Japan in 1945 left an almost total power vacuum in Southeast Asia. As Britain struggled with postwar economic dislocation and, within India, the independence movement, both the United States and the Soviet Union moved into this vacuum, hoping to influence the course of events in Asia.

Vietnam had long been a part of the French colonial empire in Southeast Asia and was known in the West as French Indochina. At the beginning of World War II, the Japanese had driven the French from the area. Under the leadership of Vietnamese nationalist (and Communist) Ho Chi Minh, the Vietnamese had cooperated with American intelligence agents and fought a guerilla-style war against the Japa-

nese. When the Japanese were finally driven from Vietnam in 1945, Ho Chi Minh declared Vietnam independent.

The Western nations, however, did not recognize this declaration. At the end of World War II, France wanted to re-establish Vietnam as a French colony. But seriously weakened by war, France could not re-establish itself in Vietnam without assistance. At this point, the United States, eager to gain France as a postwar ally and NATO member, and viewing European problems as being more immediate than problems in Asia, chose to help the French re-enter Vietnam as colonial masters. From 1945 to 1954, the United States gave more than $2 billion in financial aid to France so that it could regain its former colony. United States aid was contingent upon the eventual development of self-government in French Indochina.

Ho Chi Minh and other Vietnamese felt that they had been betrayed. They believed that in return for fighting against the Japanese in World War II, they would earn their independence. Many Vietnamese viewed the re-entry of France, with the United States' assistance, as a broken promise. Almost immediately, war broke out between the French and their westernized Vietnamese allies and the forces of Ho Chi Minh. In the cold war atmosphere of the late 1940s and early 1950s, the United States gave massive aid to the French, who, it was maintained, were fighting against monolithic communism.

The fall of Dien Bien Phu in 1954 spelled the end of French power in Vietnam. The United States secretary of state, John Foster Dulles, tried hard

6. Those in nationalist movements seek independence for their countries.

CHAPTER 10

A GENERATION
IN WAR AND
TURMOIL: THE
AGONY OF
VIETNAM

to convince Britain and other Western allies of the need for "united action" in Southeast Asia and to avoid any use of American ground troops (as President Truman had authorized earlier in Korea). The allies were not persuaded, however. Rather than let the area fall to the Communists, President Eisenhower and his secretary of state eventually allowed the temporary division of Vietnam into two sections—South Vietnam, ruled by westernized Vietnamese formerly loyal to the French, and North Vietnam, governed by the Communist Ho Chi Minh.

Free and open elections to unify the country were to be held in 1956. However, the elections were never held because American policymakers feared that Ho Chi Minh would easily defeat the unpopular but pro–United States Ngo Dinh Diem, the United States' choice to lead South Vietnam. From 1955 to 1960, the United States supported Diem with more than $1 billion of aid as civil war between the South Vietnamese and the Northern Vietminh (later called the Vietcong) raged across the countryside and in the villages.

President Kennedy did little to improve the situation. Facing his own cold war problems, among them the building of the Berlin Wall and the Bay of Pigs invasion,[7] Kennedy simply poured more money and more "military advisers" (close to seventeen

thousand by 1963) into the troubled country. Finally, in the face of tremendous Vietnamese pressure, the United States turned against Diem, and in 1963 South Vietnamese generals, encouraged by the Central Intelligence Agency, overthrew the corrupt and repressive Diem regime. Diem was assassinated in the fall of 1963, shortly before Kennedy's assassination.

Lyndon Johnson, the Texas Democrat who had succeeded Kennedy in 1963 and won election as president in 1964, was an old New Dealer[8] who wished to extend social and economic programs to needy Americans. The "tragedy" of Lyndon Johnson, as one sympathetic historian saw it, was that the president was increasingly drawn into the Vietnam War. Actually, President Johnson and millions of other Americans still perceived Vietnam as a major test of the United States' willingness to resist the spread of communism.

Under Johnson, the war escalated rapidly, and in 1964 the Vietcong controlled almost half of South Vietnam. Thus when two American ships allegedly were attacked by the North Vietnamese that year, Johnson used the occasion to obtain sweeping powers from Congress[9] to conduct the war as he wished. Bombing of North Vietnam and Laos was increased, refugees were moved to "pacification" camps,

---

7. The Berlin Wall was a barricade created to separate East Berlin (Communist) from West Berlin. The Bay of Pigs invasion was a United States–sponsored invasion of Cuba in April 1961 that failed. The American role was widely criticized.

8. Johnson served in Congress during the 1930s and was a strong supporter of New Deal programs.
9. The Tonkin Gulf Resolution gave Johnson the power to "take all necessary measures to repel any armed attack against the forces of the United States and to prevent further aggression."

entire villages believed to be unfriendly were destroyed, chemical defoliants were sprayed on forests to eliminate Vietcong hiding places, and troops increased until by 1968 about 500,000 American men and women were serving in Vietnam.

As the war effort increased, so did the doubts. In the mid-1960s, the chair of the Senate Foreign Relations Committee, J. William Fulbright, raised important questions about whether the Vietnam War was serving our national interest. Several members of the administration and foreign policy experts (including George Kennan, author of the original containment policy) maintained that escalation of the war could not be justified. Television news coverage of the destruction and carnage, along with reports of atrocities such as the My Lai massacre,[10] disillusioned more and more Americans. Yet Johnson continued the bombing, called for more ground troops, and offered peace terms that were completely unacceptable to the North Vietnamese.

Not until the Tet offensive—a coordinated North Vietnamese strike across all of South Vietnam in January 1968, in which the Communists captured every provincial capital and even entered Saigon (the capital of South Vietnam)—did President Johnson change his mind. Two months later, Johnson appeared on national television and announced to a surprised nation that he had ordered an end to most of the bombing, asked North Vietnam to start real peace negotiations, and withdrawn his name from the 1968 presidential race. Although we now know that the Tet offensive was a setback for Ho Chi Minh, in the United States it was seen as a major setback for the West, evidence that the optimistic press releases about our imminent victory simply were not true.

As the United States' role in the Vietnam War increased, the government turned increasingly to the conscription of men for military service (the draft). Early in the war, all college men up to age twenty-six could get automatic deferments, which allowed them to remain in school while noncollege men (disproportionately poor and black) were drafted and sent to Vietnam. As the demand for men increased, however, such deferments became somewhat more difficult to obtain. College students had to maintain good grades, graduate student deferments were ended, and draft boards increasingly were unsympathetic to pleas for conscientious objector status.[11] Even so, the vast majority of college students who did not want to go to Vietnam were able to avoid doing so, principally by using one of the countless loopholes in the system (ROTC [Reserve Officers' Training Corps] duty, purposely failing physical examinations, getting family members to pull strings, obtaining conscientious objector status, and so on).

---

10. This incident occurred in March 1968, when American soldiers destroyed a Vietnamese village and killed many of the inhabitants, including women and children.

11. Conscientious objectors are those whose religious beliefs are opposed to military service (such as the Society of Friends, or Quakers).

CHAPTER 10

A GENERATION
IN WAR AND
TURMOIL: THE
AGONY OF
VIETNAM

Only 12 percent of the college graduates between 1964 and 1973 served in Vietnam (21 percent of high school graduates and an even higher percentage of high school dropouts served).

As the arbitrary and unfair nature of the draft became increasingly evident, President Richard Nixon finally replaced General Lewis Hershey (who had headed the Selective Service System since 1948) and instituted a new system of conscription: a lottery. In this system, draft-age men were assigned numbers and were drafted in order from lowest to highest number until the draft quota was filled. With this action, the very real threat of the draft spread to those who had previously felt relatively safe. Already divided, an entire generation had to come face to face with the Vietnam War.

∽ THE METHOD ∽

Historians often wish they could ask specific questions of the participants in a historical event—questions that are not answered in surviving diaries, letters, and other documents. Furthermore, many people, especially the poor, uneducated, and members of minority groups, did not leave written records and thus often are overlooked by historians.

But when historians are dealing with the comparatively recent past, they do have an opportunity to ask questions by using a technique called oral history. Oral history—interviewing famous and not-so-famous people about their lives and the events they observed or participated in—can greatly enrich knowledge of the past. It can help the historian capture the "spirit of an age" as seen through the eyes of average citizens, and it often bridges the gap between impersonal forces (wars, epidemics, depressions) and personal and individual responses to them. Furthermore, oral history allows the unique to emerge from the total picture: the conscientious objector who would not serve in the army, the woman who did not marry and devote herself to raising a family, and so forth.

Oral history is both fascinating and challenging. It seems easy to do, but it is really rather difficult to do well. There is always the danger that the student may "lead" the interview by imposing his or her ideas on the subject. Equally possible is that the student may be led away from the subject by the person being interviewed.

Still other problems sometimes arise: the student may miss the subtleties in what is being said or may assume that an exceptional person is representative of many people. Some older people like to tell only the "smiling side" of their personal history—that is, they prefer to talk about the good things that happen to them, not the bad things. Others actually forget what happened or are influenced by reading or television. Some older people cannot resist sending a message to younger people by recounting how hard it was in the past, how few luxuries they had when they were young, how far they had to walk to school, and so forth. Yet oral history, when used carefully and judiciously along with other sources, is an invaluable tool that helps one re-create a sense of our past.

Recently, much attention has been paid—and rightly so—to protecting the rights and privacy of human subjects. For this reason, the federal government requires that the interviewee consent to the interview and be fully aware of how the interview is to be used. The interviewer must explain the purpose of the interview, and the person being interviewed must sign a release form (for samples, see Sources 1 through 3). Although these requirements are intended to apply mostly to psychologists and sociologists, historians who use oral history are included as well.

When you identify and interview an individual of the baby-boom generation, you will be speaking with a member of a *birth cohort*. A birth cohort comprises those people born within a few years of one another who form a historical generation. Members of a birth cohort experience the same events—wars, depressions, assassinations, as well as personal experiences such as marriage and childbearing—at approximately the same age and often have similar reactions to them. Sociologist Glen Elder showed that a group of people who were relatively deprived as young children during the Great Depression grew up and later made remarkably similar decisions about marriage, children, and jobs. Others have used this kind of analysis to provide insights into British writers of the post–World War I era and to explain why the Nazi party appealed to a great many young Germans.

Yet even within a birth cohort, people may respond quite differently to the same event(s). *Frame of reference* refers to an individual's *personal background*, which may influence that person's beliefs, responses, and actions. For example, interviews conducted with Americans who lived during the Great Depression of the 1930s reveal that men and women often coped differently with unemployment, that blacks and whites differed in their perceptions of how hard the times were, and that those living in rural areas had remarkably different experiences from city dwellers.

In this chapter, all the interviewees belong to the generation that came of age during the Vietnam War. Thus, as you analyze their frames of reference, age will not give you any clues. However, other factors, such as gender, race, socioeconomic class, family background, values, region, and experiences, may be quite important in determining the interviewees' frames of reference and understanding their responses to the Vietnam War. When a group of people share the same general frame of reference, they are a generational subset who tend to respond similarly to events. In other words, it may be possible to form tentative generalizations from the interviewees about how others with the same general frames of reference thought about and responded to the Vietnam War. To

CHAPTER 10

A GENERATION
IN WAR AND
TURMOIL: THE
AGONY OF
VIETNAM

assist you in conducting your own interview of a member of the baby-boom generation (or birth cohort), we have included some instructions for interviewers and a suggested interview plan.

Instructions for Interviewers

1. Establish the date, time, and place of the interview well in advance. You may wish to call and remind the interviewee a few days before your appointment.
2. Clearly state the purpose of the interview *at the beginning*. In other words, explain why the class is doing this project.
3. Prepare for the interview by carefully reading background information about the 1960s and by writing down and arranging the questions you will be asking to guide the interview.
4. It is usually a good idea to keep most of your major questions broad and general so the interviewee will not simply answer with a word or two ("How did you spend your leisure time?"). Specific questions such as "How much did it cost to go to the movies?" are useful for obtaining more details.
5. Avoid "loaded" questions, such as "Everyone hated President Lyndon Johnson, didn't they?" Instead, keep your questions neutral—"What did you think about President Lyndon Johnson and his Vietnam strategy?"
6. If any of your questions involve controversial matters, it is better to ask them toward the end of the

interview, when the interviewee is more comfortable with you.
7. Always be courteous, and be sure to give the person enough time to think, remember, and answer. Never argue, even if he or she says something with which you strongly disagree. Remember that the purpose of the interview is to find out what *that person* thinks, not what you think.
8. Always take notes, even if you are tape-recording the interview. Notes will help clarify unclear portions of the tape and will be essential if the recorder malfunctions or the tape is accidentally erased.
9. Many who use oral history believe that the release forms should be signed at the beginning of the interview; others insist that this often inhibits the person who is to be interviewed and therefore should not be done until the end of the session. Although students who are using the material only for a class exercise are not always held strictly to the federal requirements, it is still better to obtain a signed release. Without such a release, the tape cannot be heard and used by anyone else (or deposited in an oral history collection), and the information the tape contains cannot be published or made known outside the classroom.
10. Try to write up the results of your interview as soon as possible after completing the interview. Even in rough form, these notes will help you capture the sense of what was said as well as the actual information that was presented.

A Suggested Interview Plan

Remember that the person you have chosen to interview is a *person*, with feelings, sensitivities, and emotions. If you intend to tape-record the interview, ask permission first. If you believe that a tape recorder will inhibit the person you have selected, leave it at home and rely on your ability to take notes.

The following suggestions may help you get started. People usually remember the personal aspects of their lives more vividly than they remember national or international events. That is a great advantage in this exercise because what you are attempting to find out is how this person lived during the 1960s. Begin by getting the following important data on the interviewee:

1. Name
2. Age in 1968
3. Race, sex
4. Where the person lived in the 1960s and what the area was like then
5. Family background (what the interviewee's parents did for a living; number of brothers and sisters; whether the interviewee considered himself or herself rich, middle class, or poor)
6. Educational background

Then move on to the aspects of the person's life that will flesh out your picture of the 1960s and early 1970s.

1. Was the person in college at any time? What was college life like during the period?
2. If the person was not in college, what did he or she do for a living?

Did he or she live at home or away from home?
3. How did the person spend his or her leisure time? If unmarried, did the person go out on dates? What was dating like? Did he or she go to the movies (if so, which ones)? Did he or she watch much television (if so, which shows)?

These questions should give you a fairly good idea of how the person lived during the period. Now move on to connect the interviewee with the Vietnam War.

1. Did the person know anyone who volunteered or was drafted and sent to Vietnam? How did the interviewee feel about that? Did the person lose any relatives or friends in Vietnam? What was his or her reaction to that?
2. (Male) Was the person himself eligible for the draft? Did he volunteer for the service or was he drafted? Was he sent to Vietnam? If so, what were some memorable Vietnam experiences? What did the person's family think of his going to Vietnam? (Female) If you intend to interview a female who went to Vietnam as a nurse, alter the above questions.
3. Was the person a Vietnam War protester? If so, what was that experience like? If not, did the person know any Vietnam War protesters? What did the person think of them?
4. Did the person know anyone who tried to avoid going to Vietnam? What did the person think of that?

Finally, review the national events and people of the Vietnam era and develop some questions to ask your in-

CHAPTER 10

A GENERATION
IN WAR AND
TURMOIL: THE
AGONY OF
VIETNAM

terviewee about these events and people. As you can see, you have guided the interview through three stages, from personal information and background to the interviewee's reactions to a widening sphere of experiences and events.

❦ THE EVIDENCE ❦

Sources 1 and 2 from Collum Davis, Kathryn Back, and Kay MacLean, *Oral History: From Tape to Type* (Chicago: American Library Assn., 1977), pp. 14, 15.

1. Sample Unconditional Release.

Tri-County Historical Society

For and in consideration of the participation by   Tri-County Historical Society   in any programs involving the dissemination of tape-recorded memories and oral history material for publication, copyright, and other uses, I hereby release all right, title, or interest in and to all of my tape-recorded memoirs to   Tri-County Historical Society   and declare that they may be used without any restriction whatsoever and may be copyrighted and published by the said   Society,   which may also assign said copyright and publication rights to serious research scholars.

In addition to the rights and authority given to you under the preceding paragraph, I hereby authorize you to edit, publish, sell and/or license the use of my oral history memoir in any other manner which the   Society   considers to be desirable and I waive any claim to any payments which may be received as a consequence thereof by the   Society.

PLACE   Indianapolis,

Indiana

DATE   July 14, 1975

Harold S. Johnson

(Interviewee)

Jane Rogers

(for   Tri-County Historical Society   )

2. Sample Conditional Release.

Tri-County Historical Society

I hereby release all right, title, or interest in and to all or any part of my tape-recorded memoirs to   Tri-County Historical Society,   subject to the following stipulations:

That my memoirs are to be *closed* until five years following my death.

PLACE   Indianapolis,

Indiana

DATE   July 14, 1975

Harold S. Johnson
(Interviewee)

Jane Rogers
(for   Tri-County Historical Society   )

Source 3 from the University of Tennessee.

3. Form Developed by a Large United States History Survey Class at the University of Tennessee, Knoxville, 1984.

This form is to state that I have been interviewed by——————— on (Interviewer)
——————— on my recollections of the Vietnam War era. I understand that (date)
this interview will be used in a class project at the University of Tennessee, and that the results will be saved for future historians.

Signature

Date

CHAPTER 10

A GENERATION
IN WAR AND
TURMOIL: THE
AGONY OF
VIETNAM

Sources 4 through 10 are from interviews conducted by the authors. Photographs were supplied by the interviewees.

4. Photograph of John and His Family. Left to Right: John's Father, John, John's Mother, and John's Brother.

John

[*John was born in 1951. His father was a well-to-do and prominent physician, and John grew up in a midwestern town that had a major university. He graduated from high school in 1969 and enrolled in a four-year private college. John dropped out of college in 1971 and returned home to live with his parents. He found work in the community and associated with students at the nearby university.*]

My earliest memory of Vietnam must have been when I was in the seventh grade [1962–1963] and I saw things in print and in *Life* magazine. But I really don't remember much about Vietnam until my senior year in high school [1968–1969].

I came from a repressive private school to college. College was a fun place to hang out, a place where you went after high school. It was just expected of you to go.

At college there was a good deal of apprehension and fear about Vietnam—people were scared of the draft. To keep your college deferments, you had to keep your grades up. But coming from an admittedly well-to-do family, I somehow assumed I didn't have to worry about it too much. I suppose I was outraged to find out that it *could* happen to me.

No, I was outraged that it could happen to *anyone*. I knew who was going to get deferments and who weren't going to get them. And even today my feelings are still ambiguous. On one hand I felt, "You guys were so dumb to get caught in that machine." On the other, and more importantly, it was wrong that *anyone* had to go.

Why? Because Vietnam was a bad war. To me, we were protecting business interests. We were fighting on George III's side, on the wrong side of an anticolonial rebellion. The domino theory didn't impress me at all.[12]

I had decided that I would not go to Vietnam. But I wasn't really worried for myself until Nixon instituted the lottery. I was contemplating going to Canada when my older brother got a CO.[13] I tried the same thing, the old Methodist altar boy gambit, but I was turned down. I was really ticked when I was refused CO status. I thought, "Who are you to tell me who is a pacifist?"

My father was conservative and my mother liberal. Neither one intervened or tried to pressure me. I suppose they thought, "We've done the best we could." By this time I had long hair and a beard. My dad had a hard time.

The antiwar movement was an intellectual awakening of American youth. Young people were concentrated on college campuses, where their maturing intellects had sympathetic sounding boards. Vietnam was part of that awakening. So was drugs. It was part of the protest. You had to be a part of it. Young people were waking up as they got away from home and saw the world around them and were forced to think for themselves.

I remember an argument I had with my father. I told him Ho Chi Minh was a nationalist before he was a Communist, and that this war wasn't really against communism at all. It's true that the Russians were also the bad guys in Vietnam, what with their aid and support of the North Vietnamese, but they had no business there either. When people tried to compare Vietnam to World War II, I just said that no Vietnamese had ever bombed Pearl Harbor.

The draft lottery certainly put me potentially at risk. But I drew a high number, so I knew that it was unlikely that I'd ever be drafted. And yet, I

---

12. The domino theory, embraced by Presidents Eisenhower, Kennedy, and Johnson, held that if one nation fell to the Communists, the result would be a toppling of other nations, like dominoes.
13. CO stands for conscientious objector.

CHAPTER 10

A GENERATION
IN WAR AND
TURMOIL: THE
AGONY OF
VIETNAM

wasn't concerned just for myself. For example, I was aware, at least intellectually, that blacks and poor people were the cannon fodder in Vietnam. But I insisted that *no one*, rich or poor, had to go to fight this war.

Actually I didn't think much about the Vietnamese people themselves. The image was of a kid who could take candy from you one day and hand you a grenade the next. What in hell were we doing in that kind of situation?

Nor did I ever actually know anyone who went to Vietnam. I suppose that, to some extent, I bought the "damn baby napalmers" image. But I never had a confrontation with a veteran of Vietnam. What would I think of him? I don't know. What would he think of me?

Kent State was a real shock to me. I was in college at the time, and I thought, "They were students, just like me." It seemed as if fascism was growing in America.

I was part of the protest movement. After Kent State, we shut down the campus, then marched to a downtown park where we held a rally. In another demonstration, later, I got a good whiff of tear gas. I was dating a girl who collapsed because of the gas. I recall a state policeman coming at us with a club. I yelled at him, telling him what had happened. Suddenly he said, "Here, hold this!" and gave me his club while he helped my date to her feet.

But there were other cops who weren't so nice. I went to the counter-inaugural in Washington in June 1973. You could see the rage on the cops' faces when we were yelling, "One, two, three, four, we don't want your f---ing war!" It was an awakening for me to see that much emotion on the subject coming from the other side. I know that I wasn't very open to other opinions. But the other side *really* was closed.

By '72 their whole machine was falling apart. A guy who gave us a ride to the counter-inaugural was a Vietnam vet. He was going there too, to protest against the war. In fact, he was hiding a friend of his who was AWOL,[14] who simply hid rather than go to Vietnam.

Then Watergate made it all worthwhile—we really had those f---ers scared. I think Watergate showed the rest of the country exactly what kind of "Law and Order" Nixon and his cronies were after!

I have no regrets about what I did. I condemn them all—Kennedy, Johnson, Nixon—for Vietnam. They all had a hand in it. And the war was wrong, in every way imaginable. While I feel some guilt that others went and were killed, and I didn't, in retrospect I feel much guiltier that I wasn't a helluva lot more active. Other than that, I wouldn't change a thing. I can still get angry about it.

---

14. AWOL is an acronym for "absent without leave."

How will I explain all that to my sons? I have no guilt in terms of "duty towards country." The *real* duty was to fight *against* the whole thing. I'll tell my sons that, and tell them that I did what I did so that no one has to go.

[*John chose not to return to college. He learned a craft, which he practices today. He married a woman who shared his views ("I wouldn't have known anyone on the other side, the way the country was divided"), had two children, and shared the responsibilities of child care. John and his wife are now divorced.*]

5. Photograph of Mike in Vietnam.

CHAPTER 10

A GENERATION
IN WAR AND
TURMOIL: THE
AGONY OF
VIETNAM

Mike

[*Mike was born in 1948. His family owned a farm in western Tennessee, and Mike grew up in a rural environment. He graduated from high school in 1966 and enrolled in a community college not far from his home. After two quarters of poor grades, Mike left the community college and joined the United States Marine Corps in April 1967. He served two tours in Vietnam, the first in 1967–1969 and the second in 1970–1971.*]

I flunked out of college my first year. I was away from home and found out a lot about wine, women and song but not about much else. In 1967 the old system of the draft was still in effect, so I knew that eventually I'd be rotated up and drafted—it was only a matter of time before they got me.

My father served with Stilwell in Burma and my uncle was career military. I grew up on a diet of John Wayne flics. I thought serving in the military was what was expected of me. The Marines had some good options— you could go in for two years and take your chances on the *possibility* of not going to Vietnam. I chose the two-year option. I thought what we were doing in Vietnam was a noble cause. My mother was against the war and we argued a lot about it. I told her that if the French hadn't helped us in the American Revolution, then we wouldn't have won. I sincerely believed that.

I took my six weeks of basic training at Parris Island [South Carolina]. It was sheer hell—I've never been treated like that in my life. Our bus arrived at Parris Island around midnight, and we were processed and sent to our barracks. We had just gotten to sleep when a drill instructor threw a thirty-two gallon garbage can down the center of the barracks and started overturning the metal bunks. We were all over the floor and he was screaming at us. It was that way for six weeks—no one ever talked to us, they shouted. And all our drill instructors geared our basic training to Vietnam. They were always screaming at us, "You're going to go to Vietnam and you're gonna f--- up and you're gonna die."

Most of the people in basic training with me were draftees. My recruiter apologized to me for having to go through boot camp with draftees. But most of the guys I was with were pretty much like me. Oh, there were a few s--- birds, but not many. We never talked about Vietnam—there was no opportunity.

There were a lot of blacks in the Corps and I went through basic training with some. But I don't remember any racial tension until later. There were only two colors in the Marine Corps: light green and dark green. My parents drove down to Parris Island to watch me graduate from basic training, and they brought a black woman with them. She was from Memphis and was the wife of one of the men who graduated with me.

After basic training I spent thirteen weeks in basic infantry training at Camp Lejeune [North Carolina]. Lejeune is the armpit of the world. And the harassment didn't let up—we were still called "scumbag" and "hairbag" and "whale---." I made PFC [private first class] at Lejeune. I was an 03-11 [infantry rifleman].

From Lejeune [after twenty days' home leave] I went to Camp Pendleton [California] for four-week staging. It was at Pendleton where we adjusted our training at Parris Island and Lejeune to the situation in Vietnam. I got to Vietnam right after Christmas 1967.

It was about this time that I became aware of antiwar protests. But as far as I was concerned they were a small minority of malcontents. They were the *protected*, were deferred or had a daddy on the draft board. I thought, "These people are disloyal—they're selling us down the drain."

We were not prepared to deal with the Vietnamese people at all. The only two things we were told was don't give kids cigarettes and don't pat 'em on the heads. We had no cultural training, knew nothing of the social structure or anything. For instance, we were never told that the Catholic minority controlled Vietnam and they got out of the whole thing—we did their fighting for them, while they stayed out or went to Paris or something. We had a Catholic chaplain who told us that it was our *duty* to go out and kill the Cong, that they stood against Christianity. Then he probably went and drank sherry with the top cats in Vietnam. As for the majority of Vietnamese, they were as different from us as night and day. To be honest, I still hate the Vietnamese SOBs.

The South Vietnamese Army was a mixed bag. There were some good units and some bad ones. Most of them were bad. If we were fighting alongside South Vietnam units, we had orders that if we were overrun by Charley[15] that we should shoot the South Vietnamese first—otherwise we were told they'd turn on us.

I can't tell you when I began to change my mind about the war. Maybe it was a kind of maturation process—you can only see so much death and suffering until you begin to wonder what in hell is going on. You can only live like a nonhuman so long.

I came out of country[16] in January of 1969 and was discharged not too long after that. I came home and found the country split over the war. I thought, "Maybe there *was* something to this antiwar business after all." Maybe these guys protesting in the streets weren't wrong.

15. "Charley" was a euphemism for the Vietcong, also known as the VC.
16. "Country" was Vietnam.

CHAPTER 10

A GENERATION
IN WAR AND
TURMOIL: THE
AGONY OF
VIETNAM

But when I got back home, I was a stranger to my friends. They didn't want to get close to me. I could feel it. It was strange, like the only friends I had were in the Marine Corps. So I re-upped[17] in the Marines and went back to Vietnam with a helicopter squadron.

Kent State happened when I was back in Vietnam. They covered it in *Stars and Stripes*.[18] I guess that was a big turning point for me. Some of the other Marines said, "Hooray! Maybe we should kill more of them!" That was it for me. Those people at Kent State were killed for exercising the same rights we were fighting for for the Vietnamese. But I was in the minority— most of the Marines I knew approved of the shootings at Kent State.

Meanwhile I was flying helicopters into Cambodia every day. I used pot to keep all that stuff out of my mind. Pot grew wild in Vietnam, as wild as the hair on your ass. The Army units would pick it and send it back. The first time I was in Vietnam nobody I knew was using. The second time there was lots of pot. It had a red tinge, so it was easy to spot.

But I couldn't keep the doubts out of my mind. I guess I was terribly angry. I felt betrayed. I would have voted for Lyndon Johnson—when he said we should be there, I believed him. The man could walk on water as far as I was concerned. I would've voted for Nixon in '68, the only time I ever voted Republican in my life. I believed him when he said we'd come home with honor. So I'd been betrayed twice, and Kent State and all that was rattling around in my head.

I couldn't work it out. I was an E5 [sergeant], but got busted for fighting and then again for telling off an officer. I was really angry.

It was worse when I got home. I came back into the Los Angeles airport and was spit on and called a baby killer and a mother raper. I really felt like I was torn between two worlds. I guess I was. I was smoking pot.

I went back to school. I hung around mostly with veterans. We spoke the same language, and there was no danger of being insulted or ridiculed. We'd been damn good, but nobody knew it. I voted for McGovern in '72— he said we'd get out no matter what. Some of us refused to stand up one time when the national anthem was played.

What should we have done? Either not gotten involved at all or go in with the whole machine. With a different attitude and tactics, we could have *won*. But really we were fighting for just a minority of the Vietnamese, the westernized Catholics who controlled the cities but never owned the

---

17. "Re-upped" means re-enlisted.
18. *Stars and Stripes* is a newspaper written and published by the armed forces for service personnel.

backcountry. No, I take that back. There was no way in hell we could have won that damned war and won anything worth winning.

I went to Washington for the dedication of the Vietnam Veterans Memorial. We never got much of a welcome home or parades. The dedication was a homecoming for me. It was the first time I got the whole thing out of my system. I cried, and I'm not ashamed. And I wasn't alone.

I looked for the names of my friends. I couldn't look at a name without myself reflected back in it [the wall].

One of the reasons I went back to school was to understand that war and myself. I've read a lot about it and watched a lot of TV devoted to it. I was at Khe Sanh and nobody could tell about that who wasn't there. There were six thousand of us. Walter Cronkite said we were there for seventy-two days. I kept a diary—it was longer than that. I'm still reading and studying Vietnam, trying to figure it all out.

[Mike returned to college, repeated the courses he had failed, and transferred to a four-year institution. By all accounts, he was a fine student. Mike is now employed as a park ranger. He is married, and he and his wife have a child. He is considered a valuable, respected, and popular member of his community. He rarely speaks of his time in the service.]

CHAPTER 10

A GENERATION
IN WAR AND
TURMOIL: THE
AGONY OF
VIETNAM

6. Photograph of MM, Boot Camp Graduation.

MM[19]

[*MM was born in 1947 and grew up in a midsize southern city. He graduated from high school in 1965. A standout in high school football, he could not get an athletic scholarship to college because of low grades. As a result, he joined the United States Army two months after graduating from high school to take advantage of the educational benefits he would get upon his discharge. He began his basic training in early September 1965.*]

I went into the service to be a soldier. I was really gung ho. I did my basic training at Fort Gordon [Georgia], my AIT [advanced infantry training] at

19. Since MM's first name also is Mike, his initials are used to avoid confusion.

Ford Ord [California], and Ranger school and Airborne at Fort Benning [Georgia].

All of this was during the civil rights movement. I was told that, being black, I had a war to fight at home, not in Vietnam. That got me uptight, because that wasn't what I wanted to do—I'd done some of that in high school.[20] I had one mission accomplished, and was looking for another.

A lot of guys I went into the service with didn't want to go to Nam—they were afraid. Some went AWOL. One guy jumped off the ship between Honolulu and Nam and drowned. Another guy shot himself, trying to get a stateside wound. He accidentally hit an artery and died. Most of us thought they were cowards.

I arrived in Nam on January 12, 1966. I was three days shy of being eighteen years old. I was young, gung ho, and mean as a snake. I was with the Twenty-fifth Infantry as a machine gunner and rifleman. We went out on search and destroy missions.

I did two tours in Vietnam, at my own request. You could make rank[21] faster in Nam and the money was better. I won two silver stars and three bronze stars. For my first silver star, I knocked out two enemy machine guns that had two of our platoons pinned down. They were drawing heavy casualties. The event is still in my mind. Two of the bronze stars I put in my best friend's body bag. I told him I did it for him.

I had a friend who died in my arms, and I guess I freaked a little bit. I got busted[22] seven times. They [the Army] didn't like the way I started taking enemy scalps and wearing them on my pistol belt. I kept remembering my friend.

I didn't notice much racial conflict in Nam. In combat, everybody seemed to be OK. I fought beside this [white] guy for eleven months; we drank out of the same canteen. When I got home, I called this guy's house. His mother said, "We don't allow our son to associate with niggers." In Vietnam, I didn't run into much of that.

The Vietnamese hated us. My first day in Vietnam, Westmoreland[23] told us that underneath every Vietnamese was an American. I thought, "What drug is he on?" But they hated us. When we weren't on the scene, the enemy would punish them for associating with us. They would call out to us, "G.I. Number Ten."[24] They were caught between a rock and a hard place.

20. MM participated in sit-ins to integrate the city's lunch counters and movie theaters.
21. Earn promotions.
22. Demoted.
23. General William Westmoreland, American commander in Vietnam.
24. "Number Ten" meant bad; no good.

CHAPTER 10

A GENERATION
IN WAR AND
TURMOIL: THE
AGONY OF
VIETNAM

We could have won the war several times. The Geneva Convention[25] wouldn't let us, and the enemy had the home court advantage. To win, it would have taken hard soldiering, but we could have done it. America is a weak country because we want to be everybody's friend. We went in there as friends. We gave food and stuff to the Vietnamese and we found it in the hands of the enemy. We just weren't tough enough.

I got out of the Army in 1970. I was thinking about making the Army a career, and was going to re-enlist. But when they wanted me to go back for a third tour in Vietnam, I got out. Hell, everybody told me I was crazy for doing two.

[*MM used his GI Bill benefits to obtain three years of higher education, two years at two four-year colleges and one in a business school. According to him, however, jobs have been "few and far between." He describes himself as "restless" and reports that automobile backfires still frighten him. He has been married and divorced twice.*]

7. Photograph of Eugene (Second from Right) Marching.

25. The Geneva Convention refers to international agreements for the conduct of war and the treatment of prisoners. The agreements began to be drawn up in the 1860s.

Eugene

[Eugene was born in 1948 in a large city on the West Coast. He graduated from high school in June 1967 and was drafted in August. Initially rejected because of a hernia, he had surgery to correct that problem and then enlisted in the Marine Corps.]

It was pretty clear from basic training on, no ifs, ands, or buts, that we were going to Vietnam. The DIs[26] were all Vietnam vets, so we were told what to expect when we got there. They'd tell us what to do and all we had to do was do it.

I got to Vietnam in June of 1968. Over there, the majority of blacks stuck together because they had to. In the field was a different story, but in the rear you really caught it. Blacks would catch hell in the rear—fights and things like that. When we went to the movies with Navy guys, they put us in the worst seats. Sometimes they just wanted to start a fight. My whole time in Vietnam I knew only two black NCOs[27] and none above that.

We were overrun three times. You could tell when we were going to get hit when the Vietnamese in our camp (who cleaned up hooches) disappeared. Usually Charley had informants inside our base, and a lot of info slipped out. They were fully aware of our actions and weapons.

When we were in the rear, we cleaned our equipment, wrote letters home, went to movies, and thought a lot about what we'd do when we got out. I had training in high school as an auto mechanic, and I wanted to start my own business.

You had to watch out for the rookies until they got a feel for what was going on. We told one new L.T.,[28] "Don't polish your brass out here or you'll tip us off for sure." He paid us no mind and Charley knocked out him and our radio man one night.

You could get anything over there you wanted [drugs]. Marijuana grew wild in the bush. Vietnamese kids would come up to you with a plastic sandwich bag of twenty-five [marijuana] cigarettes for five dollars. It was dangerous, but we smoked in the bush as well as out. At the O.P.s,[29] everybody knew when the officer would come around and check. We'd pass the word: "Here comes the Man." That's why a lot of guys who came back were so strung out on drugs. And opium—the mamasans[30] had purple teeth because of it.

---

26. Drill instructors.
27. Noncommissioned officers; sergeants.
28. Lieutenant.
29. Outposts.
30. Old Vietnamese women.

CHAPTER 10

A GENERATION
IN WAR AND
TURMOIL: THE
AGONY OF
VIETNAM

We could have won the war anytime we wanted to. We could have wiped that place off the map. There was a lot of talk that that's what we should have done. But we didn't because of American companies who had rubber and oil interests in Vietnam, and no telling what else. To them, Vietnam was a money-making thing. We were fighting over there to protect those businesses.

It was frustrating. The Army and Marines were ordered to take Hill 881 and we did, but it was costly. A couple of weeks later we just up and left and gave it back.

When I got out [in January 1970], I was a E5.[31] I couldn't find a job. So I talked to an Air Force recruiter. I got a release from the Marines[32] and joined the Air Force. I rigged parachutes and came out in 1975.

I stayed in L.A.[33] until 1977. Then I became a long-distance truck driver. I was doing pretty good when I got messed up in an accident. My truck jackknifed on ice in Pennsylvania and I hit the concrete barrier.

[*Eugene has not worked regularly since the accident. A lawsuit against the trucking company is pending. He is divorced.*]

31. Sergeant.
32. Eugene had four years of reserve obligation.
33. Los Angeles, California.

8. Photograph of Helen at an Army Hospital in Phu Bai, South Vietnam.

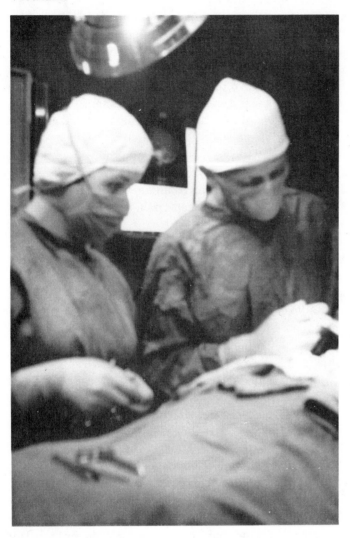

Helen

[*Helen was born in 1942 in Cleveland, Ohio, and grew up there. Since grade school, she had wanted to be a nurse. After graduation from high school, she spent three years in nurses' training to become a registered nurse. She worked for three years in the operating rooms of a major medical facility in Cleveland. In 1966, she joined the United States Navy.*]

CHAPTER 10

A GENERATION
IN WAR AND
TURMOIL: THE
AGONY OF
VIETNAM

I joined the Navy in 1966 and reported to Newport, Rhode Island, for basic training. Our classes consisted of military protocol, military history, and physical education. There was only a passing reference made to our medical assignments and what was expected of us.

I was assigned to the Great Lakes Naval Hospital [outside Chicago]. Although I had been trained and had experience as an operating room surgical nurse, at first I was assigned to the orthopedic wards. It was there that I got my first exposure to mass casualties [from Vietnam]. Depending on the extent of their injuries, we would see patients at Great Lakes about seven to ten days after them being wounded in Vietnam.

I became attached to some of the boys—they were young, scared and badly injured. I remember a Negro who in tears asked for his leg to be taken off—he couldn't stand the smell of it anymore and had been to surgery once too often for the removal of dead tissue. He was in constant pain.

On the wards, we always kept nightlights on. If someone darkened a ward by accident, it produced a sense of terror in the patients. Many were disoriented, and a lot had nightmares.

When I made the decision to go to Vietnam, I volunteered in 1968 and requested duty aboard a hospital ship. It was necessary to extend my time on active duty in order to go. I felt I had a skill that was needed and it was something I felt I personally had to do. I didn't necessarily agree with our policy on being there, but that wasn't the point.

The median age of our troops in Vietnam was nineteen years old. It was like treating our kid brothers. I would have done as much for my own brothers. I know this sounds idealistic, but that's the way I felt then.

The troops got six weeks of staging, preparing them for duty in Vietnam. Most of the nurses were given no preparation, no orientation as to what to expect when you go into a war zone. No one said, "These are the things you'll see," or "These are the things you'll be expected to do."

I was assigned to the U.S.S. *Sanctuary*, which was stationed outside of Da Nang harbor. The *Sanctuary* was a front-line treatment facility. Casualties were picked up in the field combat areas and then brought by Medevac choppers to the ship. During our heaviest months, we logged over seven hundred patient admissions per month. That was at the height of the Tet offensive in January through March, 1968. I had just gotten to Vietnam.

It was terribly intense. There was nothing to shelter you, no one to hold your hand when mass casualties came in. If you had time to think, you'd have thought, "My God, how am I to get through this?" We dealt with multiple amputations, head injuries, and total body trauma. Sometimes injuries were received from our own people caught in crossfires. When all hell breaks loose at night in the jungle, a nineteen-year-old boy under ambush will fire at anything that moves.

How do you insulate yourself against all this? We relaxed when we could, and we put a lot of stock in friendships (the corpsmen were like our kid brothers). We played pranks and sometimes took the launch ashore to Da Nang. Occasionally we were invited to a party ashore and a helicopter came out for the nurses. The men wanted American women at their parties.

There were some people who had the idea that the only reason women were in the service was to be prostitutes or to get a man. Coming back from Vietnam, I was seated next to a male officer on the plane who said to me, "Boy, I bet you had a great time in Vietnam." I had my seat changed. When I got home and was still in uniform I was once mistaken for a police officer.

On the *Sanctuary*, we had Vietnamese patients too. But our guys were distrustful of them, especially children who had been observed planting mines (probably in exchange for a handful of rice). The Vietnamese were often placed under armed guard. I have friends who were nurses in country who harbor a real hatred for the Vietnamese.

I heard a story of a Vietnamese child running up to a chopper that was evacuating casualties and tossing a grenade into it. Everyone on board was killed in a split second; both crew and casualties, because they paused to help a child they thought needed them. A soldier I knew said, "If they're in the fire zone, they get killed." War really takes you to the lowest level of human dignity. It makes you barbaric.

After Vietnam, I was stationed at the Naval Academy in Annapolis to finish out my duty. There I dealt basically with college students—measles and sports injuries. It was a hard adjustment to make.

In Vietnam, nurses had a great deal of autonomy, and we often had to do things nurses normally aren't allowed to do. You couldn't do those things stateside. Doctors saw it as an encroachment on their areas of practice. I'd been a year under extreme surgical conditions in Vietnam, and then in Annapolis someone would ask me, "Are you sure you know how to start an IV?"[34] It was hard to tame yourself down. Also, in the civilian setting, mediocrity was tolerated. I heard people say, "That's not my job." Nobody would have said that in Vietnam. There, the rules were put aside and everybody did what they could. When we got back to the states, there was no one to wind us down, deprogram us, tell us that Vietnam was an abnormal situation. . . . It was as if no one cared, we were just expected to cope and go on with our lives. . . .

I guess the hardest thing about nursing in Vietnam was the different priorities. Back home, if we got multiple-trauma cases from, say, an auto-

34. Intravenous mechanism.

CHAPTER 10

A GENERATION
IN WAR AND
TURMOIL: THE
AGONY OF
VIETNAM

mobile accident, we always treated the most seriously injured first. In Vietnam, it was often the reverse. I remember working on one soldier who was not badly wounded, and he kept screaming for us to help his buddy, who was seriously wounded. I couldn't tell him that his buddy didn't have a good chance to survive, and so we were passing him by. That was difficult for a lot of us, went against all we'd been trained to do. It's difficult to support someone in the act of dying when you're trained to do all you can to save a life. Even today, I have trouble with patients who need amputations or who have facial injuries.

It is most important to realize that there is a great cost to waging war. Many men are living out their lives in veterans' hospitals as paraplegics or quadriplegics, who in World War II or Korea would not have survived. Most Americans will never see these people—they are hidden away from us. But they are alive.

Maybe the worst part of the war for many of these boys was coming home. The seriously wounded were sent to a military hospital closest to their own homes. Our orthopedic ward at Great Lakes Naval Hospital had forty beds, and it was like taking care of forty kid brothers. They joked around and were supportive of each other. But quite a few of them got "Dear John"[35] letters while they were there. Young wives and girlfriends sometimes couldn't deal with these injuries, and parents sometimes had trouble coping too. All these people were "casualties of war," but I believe that these men especially need our caring and concern today, just as much as they did twenty years ago.

[*On her discharge from the United States Navy in August 1969, Helen returned to nursing. She married in 1972. She and her husband, an engineering physicist, have two children. Helen returned to school and received her B.S. degree in nursing. She is now a coordinator of cardiac surgery and often speaks and writes of her Vietnam experience. She also actively participates in a local veteran's organization. Recently, her daughter offered her mother's services to speak on Vietnam to a high school history class, but she was rebuffed by the teacher, who said, "Who wants to hear about that? We lost that war!" Both Helen and her daughter (who is proud of what her mother did) were offended.*]

[*Postscript: On July 29, 1993, a ground-breaking ceremony was held in Washington, D.C., for the Women's Vietnam Memorial. It will be part of the Vietnam Veteran's Memorial and honors the 265,000 women who served in the Vietnam War.*]

35. A "Dear John" letter is one that breaks off a relationship.

9. Photograph of Nick (on Right) with Some Buddies in Vietnam.

Nick

[*Nick was born in 1946 in a midsize southern city. Both his parents were skilled factory workers. Nick graduated from high school in 1964 and wanted to work for the fire department, but he was too young for the civil service. He got a job at the local utility company and got married in 1966. Nick was drafted in 1967.*]

CHAPTER 10

A GENERATION
IN WAR AND
TURMOIL: THE
AGONY OF
VIETNAM

I suppose I could have gotten a deferment, but I didn't know they were available. My wife was pretty scared when I got drafted, but neither of us ever imagined that I would shirk my duty.

I did my boot camp at Fort Benning [Georgia]. About 80 percent of the people in boot camp with me were draftees. A number of the draftees were black. I had worked with blacks before the Army, had many black friends, and never saw any racial problems. We were then sent to Fort Polk, Louisiana, for advanced infantry training. They had built simulated Vietnamese villages that were very similar to what we later encountered in Vietnam. Overall, we were trained pretty well, but we were still pretty scared.

I arrived in Vietnam on December 12, 1967, and was assigned to go out on "search and destroy" missions. Even though I was prepared mentally, I was still very frightened. I was wounded once when we got ambushed while we were setting up an ambush of our own. Another time I got hit with some shrapnel from a 60 mm mortar. That was at 3:00 A.M. and the medics didn't arrive until 7:30.

I'm not proud of everything I did in Vietnam, but I won't run away from it either. You got so hard at seeing friends killed and things like that. We desecrated their dead, just as they did ours. We used to put our unit's shoulder patches on the VC[36] dead (we nailed 'em on) to get credit for it.

I didn't like the Vietnamese themselves. Most of the civilians were VC sympathizers, and the South Vietnamese army just wouldn't fight. I was in some kind of culture shock. Here we were, trying to help these people, and some of them were living in grass huts. Once I asked myself, "What am I doing here?"

The highest rank I made was sergeant, but I was demoted when I caught a guy in my unit asleep on guard duty and busted him with a shotgun. I was demoted for damaging the shotgun, government property.

I got back to the States in December 1968. There were some protesters at the Seattle airport, but they just marched with signs and didn't harass us at all. Over time, I lost my hostility to the antiwar protesters, although at the time I despised them. Except for Jane Fonda (who went too far), I have no bad feelings for them at all. I have a friend who threatened to run his daughter off because she had a Jane Fonda workout tape.

I'm no hero and didn't do anything special. But college students today need to know that the people who fought in that war are no less important than people who fought in World War I, World War II, or Korea.

---

36. The "VC" were the Vietcong.

[Nick returned to his position with the utility company. He and his wife have two sons, born in 1969 and 1972. He never talked about Vietnam and wanted to throw his medals out, but his wife made him keep them. When his sons started asking questions, he told them about Vietnam. They convinced him to bring his medals out and display them. Since returning from Vietnam, he has never voted "and never will. . . . I have no use for politicians at all."]

10. Photograph of Robyn as a College Student.

Robyn

[Robyn was born in 1955 and raised in a Wisconsin farming town of around fifteen hundred people. Her father owned a small construction business and, like many men in town, had proudly served in World War II. Her mother was a high school teacher. Robyn has three sisters and three brothers, none of whom served in Vietnam.]

CHAPTER 10

A GENERATION
IN WAR AND
TURMOIL: THE
AGONY OF
VIETNAM

I remember starting to watch the war on television when I was about ten. I asked my mother, "How come they're killing each other?" She said that America was the land of freedom and that we were in Vietnam to help make the people free. As a teacher, though, she always encouraged us to think for ourselves and find our own answers.

The guys in town started going away [to Vietnam], and, in a town that size, everybody knows. When my ninth-grade algebra teacher suddenly disappeared, no adults would talk about it. Later, we found out that he had received CO status. In my town, that wasn't much different from being a Communist. The peer pressure was tremendous.

I have always believed the United States is the greatest country in the world, but it's not perfect. The more I heard about the war, the more I realized something was wrong. Although only in high school, I felt obligated to let the government know that I thought it was in the wrong. And yet at no time while I was protesting the war was I *ever* against the guys fighting it. My quarrel was with how the government was running the war.

I recall one of my first "protests." I was in the high school band and we were playing "The Star-Spangled Banner" at a basketball game. Although I stood and played with the rest of the band, I turned my back to the flag. When I came home that night, my father hit me for being disrespectful. So much for the right to free speech we were fighting to protect.

When I left for college in 1973, one brother had just gotten a medical deferral, and another would soon be registering for the draft. The war was becoming more and more personal. I skipped classes to attend rallies and antiwar events, and I wrote lots of letters to politicians. When the POW–MIA[37] bracelets came out, I helped sell them. There were quite a few heated discussions with some protesters who thought that wearing a bracelet (my guy is still MIA) was contrary to the cause. In those days, I tended to "discuss" things in decibels.

My second year of college ended with me skipping classes to watch the televised returns of our POWs. I would have loved to hug each one, so this was my way of saying "Welcome home" and to bear witness. I cried the whole time—for them, for their families, and for all the agony we'd all gone through during the war. Then I dropped out of school and just "vegetated" for a year. My idealistic perceptions of humanity had been severely challenged, and I was drained.

After Vietnam, I got involved in some projects that were targets to help Vietnam vets. One of my best and proudest experiences will always be my

37. Prisoners of War and Missing in Action.

work at the Vietnam Veterans Memorial in Washington, D.C. I worked at the wall as a volunteer every week for almost ten years. Unlike past memorials, this one doesn't honor the war. It's the Vietnam *Veterans* Memorial, not War Memorial, and it honors those who fought it.

I have seen firsthand its healing effects on vets and their families. And on me. At the wall, the former protester and the Vietnam veteran share something in common—our great sadness for those who were lost and those who haven't yet returned. Vietnam vets also don't seem to have the glorified view of war that older vets do.

The government's lack of support for Vietnam vets (during and after the war) might be part of the reason. If more people were aware of the other side of war, the side the vets saw, they'd have a lot more incentive to work things out. Instead of seeing war as an alternative solution, people would finally realize that war is simply the result of our failure to find a solution.

[*Robyn returned to college and eventually graduated from law school. She worked in Washington, D.C., for a nonprofit education organization and as a government relations consultant. Robyn now works at a public and government relations firm. She continues to work with Vietnam veterans and, in particular, on the POW–MIA issue.*]

⧼⧽ QUESTIONS TO CONSIDER ⧼⧽

The interviews in this chapter were conducted between 1985 and 1992. As you read through the seven interviews, try to get a sense of the tone and general meaning of each one. Then try to establish the respective frames of reference for each interviewee by comparing and contrasting their backgrounds. From which socioeconomic class does each person come? From what region of the country? What do you know about their parents and friends? What did they think was expected of them? Why?

After high school, all the interviewees' experiences diverged greatly. Eventually, Mike, MM, Eugene, and Helen enlisted in the armed services. What reason did each person give (if any) for enlisting? How different were their reasons? For his part, Nick was drafted. What was his reaction to being drafted?

Both John and Robyn became involved in antiwar protests, but for very different reasons. Why did each become involved? Would John and Robyn have agreed on why the war should have been opposed?

Return to the five veterans. What were their feelings about the Vietnamese people? What did they believe were the reasons for American involvement in the war? What were

CHAPTER 10

A GENERATION
IN WAR AND
TURMOIL: THE
AGONY OF
VIETNAM

their reactions to events of the times—the draft, antiwar protests, Kent State, race relations in the armed services, what they actually did in Vietnam? What did each one think about the situation of returning veterans? Some of the interviewees seem to have made the adjustment to civilian life better than others. Can you think of why that might have been so? Finally, what do you think each person (veterans and civilians alike) learned from his or her personal experiences during the Vietnam War era?

Now look at the photographs carefully. Are they posed or unposed? For whom might they have been intended? What image of each person is projected? How does each person help to create that image?

The majority of the interviewees have never met one another. Do you think they could meet and talk about the Vietnam era today? What might such a conversation be like?

⬭ EPILOGUE ⬭

In the spring of 1971, fifteen thousand antiwar demonstrators disrupted daily activities in the nation's capital by blocking the streets with trash, automobiles, and their own bodies. Twelve thousand were arrested, but the protest movement across the country continued. In June, the Pentagon Papers, a secret 1967 government study of the Vietnam War, was published in installments by the *New York Times*. The Pentagon Papers revealed that government spokespersons had lied to the American public about several important events, particularly about the Gulf of Tonkin incident.

As part of his re-election campaign in 1972, President Nixon traveled first to China and then to the Soviet Union and accelerated the removal of American troops from Vietnam. "Peace," his adviser Henry Kissinger announced, "is at hand." Withdrawal was slow and

painful and created a new group of refugees—those Vietnamese who had supported the Americans in South Vietnam. Nixon became mired in the Watergate scandal and resigned from office in 1974 under the threat of impeachment. The North Vietnamese entered Saigon in the spring of 1975 and began a "pacification" campaign of their own in neighboring Cambodia. Nixon's successors, Gerald Ford and Jimmy Carter, offered amnesty plans that a relatively small number of draft violators used. Many who were reported Missing in Action (MIA) in Vietnam were never found, either dead or alive. The draft was replaced by a new concept, the all-volunteer army.

The Vietnam veterans who never had their homecoming parades and had been alternately ignored and maligned finally got their memorial. A stark, simple, shiny black granite wall engraved with the names of 58,000 war dead, the monument is located on the mall near the Lincoln Memorial in Washington, D.C. The idea came from Jan Scruggs (the son of a milkman), a Vietnam veteran who was wounded and decorated for bravery when he was nineteen years old. The winning design was submitted by twenty-year-old Maya Lin, an undergraduate architecture student at Yale University. A representational statue designed by thirty-eight-year-old Frederick Hart, a former antiwar protester, stands near the wall of names. All one hundred United States senators cosponsored the gift of public land, and the money to build the memorial was raised entirely through 650,000 individual public contributions. Not everyone was pleased by the memorial, and some old emotional wounds were reopened. Yet more than 150,000 people attended the dedication ceremonies on Veterans Day, 1982, and the Vietnam veterans paraded down Constitution Avenue. Millions of Americans have already viewed the monument, now one of Washington's most visited memorials.

As for the baby boomers, many have children old enough to have served in Operation Desert Storm. Many have put their Vietnam-era experiences behind them as they pursue careers, enjoy middle age, and wait for grandchildren (a new birth cohort). For many, however, Vietnam is a chapter in American history that will never be closed.

CHAPTER 11

THE REINVENTION OF AMERICA: WHO "OWNS" OUR HISTORY?

∞ THE PROBLEM ∞

For two years, the students and faculty of Stanford University argued about it, sometimes heatedly. As a student-faculty task force worked deliberately toward some sort of compromise, there were scattered demonstrations on the beautiful campus. United States secretary of education William Bennett was appalled and said so to anyone who would listen. And when civil rights leader and presidential hopeful Jesse Jackson visited Stanford in early 1988 he was greeted by a small group of students chanting, "Hey, Hey, Ho, Ho / Western Culture's got to go." Not confined to Stanford, there were similar debates and demonstrations at the University of Wisconsin, the University of California at Berkeley, the University of Texas, and many other colleges and universities.

What issue had provoked such outbreaks in the usually placid eighties? In fact, these were not conflicts over a foreign war or a government-initiated domestic policy. Rather, these were debates among students and faculty over what was being taught in their classrooms, in many cases in their Western civilization or American history classrooms. Instead of being passive, drowsy note takers, students were arguing over what and who should be included in their history classes. Should history primarily be the story of the shared dominant culture and its leaders, the "major events" of the past? Or should history try to tell the story of *all* people, whether leaders or followers, regardless of race, ethnicity, class, gender, and "importance" in those "major events"?

As in all such debates, there are two sides. At Stanford (where the issue was a required list of core readings in the Western Culture course, all of them "classics" written by white Western males), compromise was reached in 1988. But compromise often is difficult. Those who emphasize the importance of a shared, dominant culture and the centrality of leaders (most of whom are white males) to Western civilization or American history are often characterized as reactionaries by their opponents. On the other hand, those who insist on the significance of diversity and the inclusion of everyone in the historical drama are labeled "radicals" or "P.C.'s" (proponents of political correctness) by their foes.

In this argument over what should be included in a history class, the combatants often lose sight of a very important point. If one were able to visit an American history classroom in, say, 1900, 1920, 1940, or 1960, one would see a very different course from the one most students are enrolled in today. This is because history has never been static and unchanging. Instead, history changes all the time as different generations of teachers and students ask different questions, use different evidence, or come to their classrooms with different points of view. Indeed, the debate at Stanford University in one sense has been going on as long as history courses have existed.

Your task in this chapter is to read five separate accounts of the American Revolution written by historians living in different times. How are these five accounts different? How did each writer attempt to "reinvent" the American past? How can a study of American history that is being written (and taught) today help us to clarify and understand the principal issues of our own times?

⊂⊃ BACKGROUND ⊂⊃

In their twilight years, the men and women who had lived through the American Revolution were almost literally inundated by young people who were not alive when that momentous event took place, an event that some have called the "invention of America." Key figures, such as the signers of the Declaration of Independence, were particularly besieged, causing two of them, Thomas Jefferson and John Adams, to turn increasingly to the subject of the meaning of the American Revolution in their correspondence.[1] Women of the Revolutionary generation passed their remembrances on orally to their children and grandchildren, and one woman, Mercy

1. Jefferson and Adams broke off their friendship during the 1800 presidential contest but renewed it years later when Abigail Adams sent Jefferson a kind letter of sympathy upon the death of one of his daughters. By the time of their deaths, both on July 4, 1826, Jefferson and Adams were once again warm friends.

CHAPTER 11

THE
REINVENTION
OF AMERICA:
WHO "OWNS"
OUR HISTORY?

Otis Warren, wrote a book, *History of the Rise, Progress, and Termination of the American Revolution,* which was published in 1805.[2]

Gradually, however, the men and women of that generation died, and with them died the firsthand accounts of the American Revolution. Indeed, by the time Charles Carroll of Carrollton[3] passed away in 1832 (at the age of ninety-five), the American Revolution was totally in the hands of men and women who could not have remembered it. In a symbolic sense, the first American historians thus were created—men and women who sifted through the letters, diaries, and memoirs of people who had lived through the event so that they could write about something they could not have remembered.

As generation followed generation, historians came to see American history in different ways. Sometimes new evidence was uncovered in attic trunks and dingy cellars. At the same time, each generation of historians was becoming more skilled at using the evidence available to them. By the turn of the twentieth century, a group of trained professional historians had been created. These people taught history classes at colleges and universities and used the evidence they found to write books about America's past.

And yet even as the Revolutionary generation had "invented" America, so each generation of historians seemed to "reinvent" America. Examining the evidence through the prism of their own times, each generation seemed to gaze upon American history with new eyes that saw historical events differently than those of their predecessors. They asked different questions, used evidence in different ways, and (not surprisingly) reached different conclusions. Debates between historians occasionally grew warm, as each claimed that his or her telling of a past event was more nearly correct. As Benjamin R. Barber puts it, "Education is systematic storytelling. No wonder there is such tumult surrounding the attempt to identify the right stories!"[4]

The chapters in this book that you have chosen (or been assigned) to read have shown you a great many things, or at least we hope they have. For one thing, we hope you now appreciate that American history must be the stories of all Americans: leaders and followers; men, women, and children; white, black, red, brown, and yellow; long-time residents and new arrivals; rich and poor; conservatives, moderates, and radicals; the powerful and the powerless. This is not to suggest that all these groups have been equally influential in the shaping (the "reinventing") of America. But it is to say that all have been actors to a

2. Not taking kindly to Warren's treatment of him in her book, John Adams sourly commented, "History is not the Province of the ladies."

3. Charles Carroll of Carrollton (1737–1832) was a signer of the Declaration of Independence who lived long enough to drive the first spike in the building of the Baltimore and Ohio Railroad.

4. Benjamin R. Barber, *An Aristocracy of Everyone: The Politics of Education and the Future of America* (New York: Ballantine Books, 1992), p. 21.

greater or lesser degree in the drama of the American past.

In addition, we hope that you have gained a greater understanding of the varieties of evidence available to historians. What historians refer to as "traditional" evidence (letters, diaries, memoirs, newspapers, court cases and trial records, speeches, and the like) doubtless are of immense value. So also, however, are cartoons, photographs and artworks, architectural drawings, posters, music lyrics, advertisements, statistics, and oral histories, sources often referred to as "nontraditional" evidence. The use of an intelligent combination of traditional and nontraditional evidence often can deepen our understanding of past events as well as give us an appreciation of the perspectives of those individuals or groups who have left no traditional evidence for the historian to examine and analyze.

Finally, we hope that using the evidence yourself has taught you several things. We hope that it has sharpened your skills of analyzing and interpreting the myriad facts (and "pseudofacts") with which you are bombarded almost daily. We hope that the skills you have honed in analyzing the American past are transferable to your lives in the present. Perhaps a bit selfishly, we also hope that you have come to a greater appreciation of how difficult it is to "do history," and certainly how difficult it is to do it well. As you now know, being a historian is hard work!

But why is it necessary to learn history this way? Why not simply find a good and readable book by a historian who has already looked at the evidence—examined it, sifted it, arranged it, analyzed it, and interpreted it? Isn't returning to the evidence itself merely another exercise in "reinventing the wheel"?

To understand why that is not enough, we must understand the important difference between *history* and the *past*. The two words often are used interchangeably, but they really are two significantly different things. The past (defined in the *American Heritage Dictionary* as "the time before the present") is the events of another time *as they actually took place*. History is those events *as they are perceived and written about by others* (historians), most of whom were not alive when the events about which they are writing occurred. History, therefore, is a *study* of the past, but it definitely is *not* the past itself. Unlike natural scientists, historians cannot hope to re-create the experiment (the event) they are studying exactly as that event actually took place. Their view, through the evidence, is never complete.

Another crucial reason why history is not (and cannot ever be) the past is that historians most often are writing in entirely different eras than those in which the events they are studying took place. In the previous chapter, you learned that each historical epoch possesses a different intellectual outlook or point of view. Known as the "climate of opinion," this intellectual outlook (some have referred to it somewhat graphically as a "cultural envelope") strongly influences the way people of the particular generation see the world, ask questions, and perceive the past. Thus each generation possesses a somewhat different climate of opin-

CHAPTER 11

THE
REINVENTION
OF AMERICA:
WHO "OWNS"
OUR HISTORY?

ion and, therefore, peers into the past armed with the questions, concerns, hopes, and fears of the present. Hence, although the past is stationary and unchanging, history is forever fluid, as the study of the past changes to satisfy the climate of the present.

Inevitably, then, historical accounts of a past event differ depending on the time period (and, therefore, the climate of opinion) when they were written. This is especially true of American history textbooks written for college and high school history courses. Not only are the authors of these texts writing in different time periods (climates), but the publishing company itself is afraid that if a textbook is out-of-date (not written in the same climate of opinion as that of its readers), it will be a commercial disaster.

Thus, as the men and women who lived during the American Revolution gradually died, they bequeathed to future generations not only a new nation but also an extremely complex problem. What was the *true nature* of that Revolution? How would people living in different climates of opinion view that momentous event? Finally, how seriously would the past and history ultimately diverge?

∽ THE METHOD ∽

In her excellent study of American history textbooks, Frances FitzGerald has pointed out that in the nineteenth century, "a heavy reliance on textbooks was the distinguishing mark of American education."[5] So different was this from schools in Europe that European observers and educators dubbed this dependence on textbooks "the American system." The principal reason for this reliance on textbooks was that teachers, for the most part, were not particularly well trained or even well educated. Their common teaching tools were textbooks and birch rods, the latter reserved for students who did not read their textbooks. And although college history professors have long since abandoned the textbook as the sole means of instruction, three studies of high school teachers completed in 1976 revealed that most still used the textbook as the dominant instructional tool. Yet, as we have seen, that tool (whether at the college or high school level) is constantly changing, forever in flux.

To illustrate this fact, we have chosen four historical accounts of what is perhaps the most pivotal event in American history: the American Revolution. This event is pivotal because (as we noted earlier) it was the event that "invented" America and it is to that event that historians constantly return in their "reinventions" of America.

5. Frances FitzGerald, *America Revised: History Schoolbooks in the Twentieth Century* (Boston: Atlantic–Little, Brown, 1979), p. 19.

The first selection is from the seventh volume (1858) of George Bancroft's multivolume *History of the United States*. Bancroft (1800–1891) was born in Massachusetts, graduated from Harvard College at the age of seventeen, and spent the next five years studying in Europe (principally in Göttingen and Berlin). Unlike most of his family and fellow New Englanders, he embraced the Democratic party of Andrew Jackson. His many years of work with the Democrats and his support of James K. Polk for the Democratic nomination in 1844 earned him a place in Polk's cabinet as secretary of the navy. In that post, he was responsible for the establishment of the United States Naval Academy at Annapolis. After a brief stint as United States minister to Great Britain, he returned to the United States, purchased a home in New York City (he had a summer place in Newport, Rhode Island), and settled down to complete his *History of the United States*. Although a personal friend of Abraham Lincoln's, he remained a steadfast Democrat, a fact that is reflected in his work. He has often been referred to as the "Father of American History."

The climate of opinion in which Bancroft wrote (and into which he so neatly fit) was that of the rise of American democracy in the 1820s through the 1840s. In that period, many people saw (or believed they saw) an age characterized by conflict between the forces of democracy (the people) and those of aristocracy (the few). Many people, including Bancroft himself, saw the battles over universal suffrage and other political reforms in this light. Finally, people living during that climate of opinion saw America as the unique link between the greatness of past civilizations and unbridled future progress.

The second selection is from *The Rise of American Civilization* (1927) by Charles A. Beard and Mary R. Beard. Charles Beard (1874–1948) was born into a family that, to say the least, marched to a series of different drummers. His grandfather once hid fugitive slaves on his North Carolina farm, and his father was forced to flee to Indiana because of his Unionist sentiments. Charles himself was graduated from DePauw University and then went to England to pursue graduate work at Oxford. While in England, he became deeply involved in working-class movements. Returning to the United States, he earned his Ph.D. in history from Columbia University in 1904 and then joined the Columbia faculty. In 1913, his book *An Economic Interpretation of the Constitution of the United States* created a sensation when it asserted that that "sacred document" was written in the interests of certain economic classes and that the Founding Fathers themselves stood to profit personally from ratification of the Constitution. In 1917, Beard resigned from the Columbia faculty in protest of the dismissal of three colleagues who had criticized the United States' intervention in World War I. He never held another teaching appointment but continued to write (he had inherited a substantial amount of money from his father).

Mary Ritter Beard (1876–1958) in many ways was typical of many well-

CHAPTER 11

THE
REINVENTION
OF AMERICA:
WHO "OWNS"
OUR HISTORY?

educated women from affluent families who in the late nineteenth and early twentieth centuries had to balance their own professional aspirations with the expectations of society that they become model wives and mothers. Mary Ritter met Charles Beard when they were students at DePauw, and they were married in 1900, three years after her graduation from DePauw. When Charles and Mary were in England, she became as involved as her husband in working-class movements and also worked in the woman suffrage movement. When the couple returned to America in 1902, they enrolled in graduate school at Columbia, but Mary withdrew from graduate school when the couple's first child was born. When her husband resigned from the Columbia faculty in 1917, the two of them collaborated on many works, including the classic textbook *The Rise of American Civilization*. (Mary Beard also wrote six books by herself.) She remained committed to social causes and was one of the founders of the Women's party.[6]

As one can deduce from their biographical material, the Beards came of age in the climate of the reform-minded Progressive era. The widespread belief in the goodness of humankind was linked to the calls for political, economic, and social reforms to improve the lives and environments of these essentially good people. Like those living in Bancroft's climate of opinion, Progressives thought in

6. See Susan D. Becker, *The Origins of the Equal Rights Amendment: American Feminism Between the Wars* (Westport, Conn.: Greenwood Press, 1981).

terms of conflict, but they saw this conflict in economic terms, between the wealthy and the dispossessed.

The third selection is from one of the most popular textbooks of the 1960s through the 1980s, *The American Nation* by John A. Garraty (1920–). Born in Brooklyn, New York, Garraty was educated at Brooklyn College (B.A. 1941) and at Columbia University (M.A. 1942, Ph.D. 1948), where he ultimately returned (in 1959) to teach for the remainder of his career. *The American Nation* (first edition published in 1966) profited from a great deal of work by postwar historians who sought to redirect the study of American history away from an emphasis on economics and class conflict (too Marxist for historians writing during the cold war) and toward an emphasis on continuity and the commonalities of all Americans.

The climate of opinion in which Garraty wrote (1950s to early 1960s) was one characterized by the cold war and a simultaneous striving by Americans for homogenization. As suggested above, conflicts were de-emphasized, and *consensus* was the dominant spirit of the age. Thus, to people living in that climate, all Americans were pretty much the same, whether Democrat or Republican, liberal or conservative, black or white (the goal of integration in the civil rights movement was but one case in point). This striving for homogeneity could best be seen in the new postwar suburbs, where Americans sought to fit in and not stand out (too dangerous in the era of McCarthyism, when being *too* different could lead to charges of being a Communist).

The fourth selection is from *A People's History of the United States* (1980) by Howard Zinn. Born in New York City in 1922, Zinn received his B.A. from New York University (1951) and his Ph.D. from Columbia (1958). He has been active in several liberal and left-of-center activities, and his research and writing often reflect those interests, especially his excellent work on the history of the civil rights movement. He has taught at Upsala College, Spelman College, and Boston University.

Although close together in time, Zinn's climate of opinion was markedly different from Garraty's. The heightening struggle for civil rights, unrest on America's college campuses, and the conflict over the Vietnam War made the climate of opinion in which Zinn wrote (1960s through 1970s) less a striving for homogenization and more an openly self-critical climate. In that climate, the emphasis was not on how far America had come but (in the view of many in that era) on how little it had achieved—whether in civil rights for minorities, the equality of women, help for the dispossessed, or putting a stop to American "imperialism" overseas. Little wonder that people called some historians who wrote during this period Neo-Progressives, thus linking them with the Beards and other historians of the Progressive era. In some ways, they are similar.

The author(s) of your own textbook probably are well-known people in their respective fields of American history. Ask your instructor for assistance in collecting information about them (your instructor might well have met the author[s] at a professional meeting). *The Directory of American Scholars* (volume on history) contains a listing of most of the people who are authors of contemporary American history texts. See if you can deduce what that person's (or persons') climate of opinion was. How would you go about doing this? (See the previous chapter for some suggestions.)

To repeat, your task in this chapter is to examine and analyze separate textbook accounts dealing with the nature (character) of the American Revolution published during five separate time periods (1858, 1927, 1966, 1980, and your own text). How does each selection portray the nature of the American Revolution? How does the climate of opinion in which each author wrote help to explain these different perspectives?

As you read each selection, make a chart similar to the one that follows, filling in the appropriate places after reading each selection. As you read each selection and complete the chart, you soon will see how America has been constantly reinvented by historians and why such reinventions take place.

CHAPTER 11

THE
REINVENTION
OF AMERICA:
WHO "OWNS"
OUR HISTORY?

Author(s)	Climate of Opinion	Nature of American Revolution	Example to Support Nature
Bancroft			
Beards			
Garraty			
Zinn			
Your text			

⚬⚬ THE EVIDENCE ⚬⚬

Source 1 from George Bancroft, *History of the United States, from the Discovery of the American Continent,* 11th ed., Vol. VII (Boston: Little, Brown and Co., 1872; originally published 1858), pp. 291–296.

1. George Bancroft.

At two in the morning, under the eye of the minister, and of Hancock and Adams, Lexington common was alive with the minute men; and not with them only, but with the old men also, who were exempts, except in case of immediate danger to the town. The roll was called, and of militia and alarm men, about one hundred and thirty answered to their names. The captain, John Parker, ordered every one to load with powder and ball, but to take care not to be the first to fire. Messengers, sent to look for the British regulars, reported that there were no signs of their approach. A watch was therefore set, and the company dismissed with orders to come together at beat of drum. Some went to their own homes; some to the tavern, near the southeast corner of the common. . . .

The last stars were vanishing from night, when the foremost party, led by Pitcairn, a major of marines, was discovered, advancing quickly and in silence. Alarm guns were fired, and the drums beat, not a call to village husbandmen only, but the reveille to humanity. Less than seventy, perhaps less than sixty, obeyed the summons, and in sight of half as many boys and unarmed men, were paraded in two ranks, a few rods north of the meeting-house.

How often in that building had they, with renewed professions of their faith, looked up to God as the stay of their fathers, and the protector of their privileges! How often on that village green, hard by the burial place of their forefathers, had they pledged themselves to each other to combat manfully for their birthright inheritance of liberty! There they now stood side by side, under the provincial banner, with arms in their hands, silent and fearless, willing to fight for their privileges, scrupulous not to begin civil war, and as yet unsuspicious of immediate danger. The ground on which they trod was the altar of freedom, and they were to furnish its victims.

The British van, hearing the drum and the alarm guns, halted to load; the remaining companies came up; and at half an hour before sunrise, the advance party hurried forward at double quick time, almost upon a run, closely followed by the grenadiers. Pitcairn rode in front, and when within five or six rods of the minute men, cried out: "Disperse, ye villains, ye rebels, disperse; lay down your arms; why don't you lay down your arms and disperse?" The main part of the countrymen stood motionless in the ranks, witnesses against aggression; too few to resist, too brave to fly. At this Pitcairn discharged a pistol, and with a loud voice cried, "Fire." The order was instantly followed, first by a few guns, which did no execution, and then by a heavy, close, and deadly discharge of musketry.

In the disparity of numbers, the common was a field of murder, not of battle; Parker, therefore, ordered his men to disperse. Then, and not till then, did a few of them, on their own impulse, return the British fire. These random shots of fugitives or dying men did no harm, except that Pitcairn's horse was perhaps grazed, and a private of the tenth light infantry was touched slightly in the leg.

Jonas Parker, the strongest and best wrestler in Lexington, had promised never to run from British troops; and he kept his vow. A wound brought him on his knees. Having discharged his gun, he was preparing to load it again, when as sound a heart as ever throbbed for freedom was stilled by a bayonet, and he lay on the post which he took at the morning's drum beat. So fell Isaac Muzzey, and so died the aged Robert Munroe, the same who in 1758 had been an ensign at Louisburg. Jonathan Harrington, junior, was struck in front of his own house on the north of the common. His wife was at the window as he fell. With the blood gushing from his breast, he rose in her sight, tottered, fell again, then crawled on hands and knees towards his dwelling; she ran to meet him, but only reached him as he expired on their threshold. Caleb Harrington, who had gone into the meeting-house for powder, was shot as he came out. Samuel Hadley and John Brown were pursued, and killed after they had left the green. Asahel Porter,

CHAPTER 11

THE
REINVENTION
OF AMERICA:
WHO "OWNS"
OUR HISTORY?

of Woburn, who had been taken prisoner by the British on the march, endeavoring to escape, was shot within a few rods of the common.

Day came in all the beauty of an early spring. The trees were budding; the grass growing rankly a full month before its time; the blue bird and the robin gladdening the genial season, and calling forth the beams of the sun which on that morning shone with the warmth of summer; but distress and horror gathered over the inhabitants of the peaceful town. There on the green, lay in death the gray-haired and the young; the grassy field was red "with the innocent blood of their brethren slain," crying unto God for vengeance from the ground.

Seven of the men of Lexington were killed; nine wounded; a quarter part of all who stood in arms on the green. These are the village heroes, who were more than of noble blood, proving by their spirit that they were of a race divine. They gave their lives in testimony to the rights of mankind, bequeathing to their country an assurance of success in the mighty struggle which they began. Their names are had in grateful remembrance, and the expanding millions of their countrymen renew and multiply their praise from generation to generation. They fulfilled their duty not from the accidental impulse of the moment; their action was the slowly ripened fruit of Providence and of time. The light that led them on, was combined of rays from the whole history of the race; from the traditions of the Hebrews in the gray of the world's morning; from the heroes and sages of republican Greece and Rome; from the example of Him who laid down his life on the cross for the life of humanity; from the religious creed which proclaimed the divine presence in man, and on this truth as in a life-boat, floated the liberties of nations over the dark flood of the middle ages; from the customs of the Germans transmitted out of their forests to the councils of Saxon England; from the burning faith and courage of Martin Luther; from trust in the inevitable universality of God's sovereignty as taught by Paul of Tarsus, and Augustine, through Calvin and the divines of New England; from the avenging fierceness of the Puritans, who dashed down the mitre on the ruins of the throne; from the bold dissent and creative self assertion of the earliest emigrants to Massachusetts; from the statesmen who made, and the philosophers who expounded, the revolution of England; from the liberal spirit and analyzing inquisitiveness of the eighteenth century; from the cloud of witnesses of all the ages to the reality and the rightfulness of human freedom. All the centuries bowed themselves from the recesses of a past eternity to cheer in their sacrifice the lowly men who proved themselves worthy of their forerunners, and whose children rise up and call them blessed.

Heedless of his own danger, Samuel Adams, with the voice of a prophet, exclaimed, "Oh! what a glorious morning is this!" for he saw that his country's independence was rapidly hastening on, and, like Columbus in the tempest, knew that the storm did but bear him the more swiftly towards the undiscovered world. . . .

Source 2 from Charles A. Beard and Mary R. Beard, *The Rise of American Civilization* (New York: Macmillan, 1927), pp. 193–203.

2. Charles A. Beard and Mary R. Beard.

Out of the interests of English landlords and merchants, illuminated no doubt by high visions of empire not foreign to their advantage, flowed acts of Parliament controlling the economic undertakings of American colonists and measures of administration directed to the same end. These laws and decisions were not suddenly sprung upon the world at the accession of George III in 1760. On the contrary, they were spread over more than a century, beginning with the rise of the mercantile party under Cromwell; they crowded the pages of the statute books and the records of the British colonial offices from the coronation of Charles II in 1660 to the outbreak of the American Revolution. Far from being accidents of politics, conceived in the heat of controversy, they were the matured fruits of a mercantile theory of state which regarded colonial trade as the property of the metropolis, to be monopolized by its citizens and made subservient in all things to their interests—a theory which, with modifications here and there, still thrives under the guise of milder phrases and loftier sentiments. . . .

The origins of this legislation, or at least the most salient pieces of it, are more or less clearly revealed in the records. Certainly, the restriction on American woolen manufactures flowed from the protests of a competing industry—English landlords and wool-growers, as well as merchants and manufacturers, uniting in the protection of a business which furnished about one-third of England's total export trade when the restrictive act was passed in 1699. Parliamentary legislation against colonial hat and iron industries was likewise the result of specific protests made by interested parties.

Such also was the origin of the prohibition on colonial paper money. According to Franklin's testimony, that irksome ban was devised at the request of a handful of creditors. "On the slight complaint of a few Virginia merchants," he lamented, "nine colonies had been restrained from making

CHAPTER 11

THE
REINVENTION
OF AMERICA:
WHO "OWNS"
OUR HISTORY?

paper money, become absolutely necessary to their internal commerce, from the constant remittance of their gold and silver to Britain." Applying the same argument to other statutes, he added: "The hatters of England have prevailed to obtain an act in their own favor restraining that manufacture in America. . . . In the same manner have a few nail makers and a still smaller body of steelmakers (perhaps there are not half a dozen of these in England) prevailed totally to forbid by an act of Parliament the erecting of slitting mills or steel furnaces in America; that Americans may be obliged to take all their nails for their buildings and steel for their tools from these artificers." The measures laying duties on foreign sugar and molasses were passed on the insistence of British planters in the West Indies, of whom, it was alleged at the time, seventy-four were actually sitting in Parliament when the bills were enacted.

There was accordingly some foundation for the complaint published in the Boston Gazette of April 29, 1765: "A colonist cannot make a button, a horseshoe, nor a hobnail, but some sooty ironmonger or respectable button-maker of Britain shall bawl and squall that his honor's worship is most egregiously maltreated, injured, cheated, and robbed by the rascally American republicans. . . ."

[*At this point, the Beards admit that the British mercantile system held "distinct advantages" for the American colonies, such as a monopoly on timber and naval stores, preferential treatment in tobacco sales, and bounties paid for hemp and masts. Yet the Beards maintain that the British imperial policy "restricted American economic enterprise in many respects." The Beards then describe the British Board of Trade, which they claim favored English merchants and manufacturers in its "grasping activities." In all, the Beards claim, the Board of Trade was designed to profit the mother country at the expense of its colonies.*]

Considered in the light of the English and provincial statutes spread over more than a hundred years, in the light of the authentic records which tell of the interminable clashes between province and metropolis, the concept of the American Revolution as a quarrel caused by a stubborn king and obsequious ministers shrinks into a trifling joke. Long before George III came to his throne, long before Grenville took direction of affairs, thousands of Americans had come into collision with British economic imperialism, and by the middle of the eighteenth century, far-seeing men, like Franklin, had discovered the essence of the conflict.

In a letter written in 1754, six years before the accession of George III, the philosopher of Poor Richard set forth the case in terms that admitted of no misinterpretation. With reference to matters of politics, he declared that royal governors often came to the New World merely to make their fortunes; that royal officers in the provinces were frequently men of small estate subservient to the governors who fed them; and that the Americans in reality bore a large share of English taxes in the form of enhanced prices for English goods thrust upon them by monopolistic laws. Turning to questions of commercial economy, Franklin insisted that the acts of Parliament forbidding Americans to make certain commodities forced them to purchase such goods in England, thus pouring more tribute into the English chest; that statutes restraining their trade with foreign countries compelled them to buy dearer commodities in England, adding that golden stream to the same treasury; that since the Americans were not allowed to stop the importation and consumption of English "superfluities," their "whole wealth centers finally among the Merchants and Inhabitants of Britain." In short, in enumerating grievances that had flourished for many a decade, Franklin gave a clue to the friction which was soon to burst into an agrarian war.

In a larger sense the American Revolution was merely one battle in the long political campaign that has been waged for more than two centuries on this continent. The institutions of metropolis and colony and the issues of their dispute were analogous to the institutions and issues that have figured in every great national crisis from that day to this. On the side of the mother country, a Crown and Parliament sought to govern all America somewhat after the fashion of the President and Congress under the federal Constitution of 1787. The central British government regulated the inter-state and foreign commerce of the thirteen colonies in the interest of the manufacturing and commercial classes of England; it directed the disposal of western lands; it struck down paper money and controlled the currency; it provided for a common defense and conducted the diplomacy of the continent. With a view to protecting practical interests, the British Crown and judiciary nullified acts of local legislatures similar in character to those declared void long afterward by Chief Justice Marshall.

On the American side of the colonial conflict, the agent of local power was the popular assembly which aspired to sovereignty and independence, placing all rights of person and property at the disposal of passing majorities. It authorized the issue of paper money; passed bankruptcy acts in the interest of debtors; stayed the collection of overdue obligations; sought to control the sale of western lands, and assumed the power of regulating local trade and industry. The British government brought heavy pressure upon it; an explosion resulted. For a decade the state legislature was sovereign, and it worked its will in matters of finance, currency, debts, trade, and property. Then followed the inevitable reaction in which were restored, under the ægis of the Constitution and under American leadership, agencies

CHAPTER 11

THE
REINVENTION
OF AMERICA:
WHO "OWNS"
OUR HISTORY?

of control and economic policies akin to those formerly employed by Great Britain. In a word, the American Revolution was merely one phase of a social process that began long before the founding of Jamestown and is not yet finished.

Source 3 from John A. Garraty, *The American Nation: A History of the United States* (New York: Harper and Row, 1966), pp. 114–115, 123–124, 133–137.

3. John A. Garraty.

The decision to use troops against Massachusetts was made in January 1775, but the order did not reach General Gage until April. In the interim both sides were active. Parliament voted new troop levies, declared Massachusetts to be in a state of rebellion, and closed the Newfoundland fisheries and all seaports except those in Great Britain and the British West Indies, first to the New England colonies and then to most of the others. The Massachusetts "Patriots," as they were now calling themselves, formed an extralegal provincial assembly, organized a militia, and began training "Minute Men" and other fighters. Soon companies of men were drilling on town commons all over Massachusetts, and other colonies too.

When Gage received his orders on April 14, he acted swiftly. The Patriots had been accumulating arms at Concord, some 20 miles west of Boston. On the night of April 18 Gage dispatched 700 crack troops to seize these supplies. The Patriots were forewarned. Paul Revere set out on his famous ride to alert the countryside and warn John Hancock and Sam Adams, leaders of the provincial assembly, whose arrest had been ordered. When the Redcoats reached Lexington early the next morning, they found the common occupied by about 70 Minute Men. After an argument, the Americans began to withdraw. Then someone fired a shot. There was a flurry of gunfire and the Minute Men fled, leaving eight dead. . . .

One great difficulty in the way of establishing a central government was the lack of precedent: there had never been an *American* government. Another was suspicion of authority imposed from above, resulting from British behavior after the French and Indian War. British oppression had forced the colonies to combine, but it had also strengthened their conviction that local control of political power was vital. Remembering Parliament's treatment of them, they refused to give any central authority the right to tax.

Fortunately, neither of these problems blocked the creation of effective state governments. Using their colonial charters as a basis, the states soon

[332]

framed new constitutions. The new governments were all quite similar and not drastically different from those they replaced. Each provided for an elected legislature, a governor, and a system of courts. In general the powers of the governor and of judges were closely limited—a natural result of past experience, if somewhat illogical now that these officials were no longer appointed by an outside authority. The locus of power was in the legislature, which the people had come to count upon to defend their interests. Nevertheless, the constitutions also contained bills of rights protecting the peoples' civil liberties against all branches of the government. In general the state governments combined the best of the British system, including its respect for fairness and due process, with the uniquely American stress on individualism and a healthy dislike of too much authority. The idea of drafting written frames of government—contracts between the people and their representatives, carefully spelling out the powers and duties of the latter—grew out of the experience of the colonists during the years after the French and Indian War, when the vagueness of the unwritten British Constitution had caused so much controversy. It also evolved logically from the compact implicit in the Declaration of Independence. It represented one of the most important political results of the Revolution, for it provided a peaceful method for altering the political system. In the midst of violence the states changed their frames of government in an orderly, legal manner, a truly remarkable achievement that became a beacon of hope to future reformers all over the world.

Many states seized the occasion of constitution-making to introduce important reforms. For example, in Pennsylvania, Virginia, North Carolina, and certain other states the seats in the legislature were reapportioned in order to give the western districts their fair share. Primogeniture, entail (the right of an owner of property to prevent his heirs from ever disposing of it), and quitrents were abolished wherever they had existed. Steps toward greater freedom of religion were also taken, especially in those states where the Anglican Church had enjoyed a privileged position. While most states continued to support religion after the Revolution, funds were usually distributed roughly in accordance with the numerical strength of the various Protestant sects.

The spirit of the Declaration of Independence led many states to strike blows against slavery. In 1783 the Massachusetts Supreme Court decided that the state's Bill of Rights made the ownership of human beings illegal. Other northern states soon followed this precedent, and even in the south, where prominent men like Jefferson and Washington had criticized slavery and where the decline of tobacco and rice cultivation made it less attractive economically, many talked of doing away with the institution. Between

CHAPTER 11

THE
REINVENTION
OF AMERICA:
WHO "OWNS"
OUR HISTORY?

1782 and 1790 in Virginia alone, 10,000 slaves were given their freedom by their owners voluntarily. Nearly all the states outlawed the importation of new slaves from Africa. Prison reform, the abolition of harsh punishments, and the improvement of education were also undertaken in many states. A few tried, without much success, to stamp out the barbaric but aristocratic practice of dueling.

However, there was little of the social or economic upheaval generally associated with revolutions. The property of Tories was frequently seized by the state governments, but almost never with the idea of redistributing wealth or providing the poor with land. While some large Tory estates were broken up and sold to small farmers, others passed intact to rich men or groups of speculators. After all, in most cases the men who framed the new constitutions had possessed power even before the Revolution.

That the new governments were liberal but moderate reflected the spirit of the times, best typified by a man like Jefferson, who had great faith in the democratic process but who owned a great estate and many slaves and had never suggested a drastic social revolution. The framers wanted to create a new and better world but had no desire to overturn a privileged class. A certain amount of conflict developed at this time between rich and poor, between established merchant and frontier farmer, but these were merely local squabbles. No single class or interest triumphed in all the states or in the national government. In Pennsylvania where the western radical element was strong, the constitution was extremely democratic; in South Carolina the conservative tidewater planters maintained control handily. Many great landowners were ardent Patriots: others became Tories—yet so did many small farmers. . . .

American independence and control of a wide and rich domain were the most obvious results of the Revolution. Changes in the structure of society, as we have seen, were relatively minor. Economic developments, such as the growth of new trade connections and the expansion of manufacturing in an effort to replace British goods, were also of only moderate significance. By far the most important social and economic changes involved the Tories, and thus were by-products of the political revolution rather than a determined reorganization of a people's way of life. Yet there was another extremely important result of the Revolution: the growth of American nationalism. Most modern revolutions have been *caused* by nationalism and have *resulted* in independence. In the case of the American Revolution the desire to be free antedated any very intense national feeling. The colonies entered into a political union not because they felt an overwhelming desire to bring all Americans under one rule, but because unity seemed to offer the only hope of winning a war against Great Britain.

[Here Garraty cites some examples of American nationalism, including a common enemy in the war, the interaction of people from different states, the American flag, the stimulating of interstate trade, and the unspoken agreement that the former colonies eventually would form one nation.]

Finally, the Revolution fostered nationalism by giving the people their first commonly revered heroes. Every colony had had its leaders, many of them wise, colorful, and popular men, but none widely known in other regions. However, out of the drama and hardships of the Revolutionary era came a few truly national figures. Benjamin Franklin was widely known before the break with Great Britain through his experiments with electricity, his immensely successful annual, *Poor Richard's Almanack,* and because of his invention of the Franklin stove. However, his staunch support of the Patriot cause, his work in the Continental Congress, and his diplomatic successes in France, where he was extravagantly admired, added greatly to his fame. Franklin demonstrated, not only to Europeans but to Americans themselves, that all Americans need not be ignorant rustics. Thomas Jefferson was also a national figure by the 1780's. His writing of the Declaration of Independence (to which, it will be recalled, Franklin also contributed) was enough to make him a hero to all Americans. Especially in retrospect, when the boldness of the document and its felicity of expression could be fully appreciated and when the success of the revolt made it even more significant, the Declaration and its author were revered in every state.

And then, most notable of all, there was Washington, "the chief human symbol of a common Americanism." Stern, cold, inarticulate, the great Virginian did not seem a likely candidate for hero worship. But he had qualities that made him truly "the Father of his Country": his personal sacrifices in the cause of independence, his unyielding integrity, his devotion to duty, his commanding presence, and above all, perhaps, his obvious desire to retire to his Mount Vernon estate (for many Americans feared *any* powerful leader and worried lest Washington seek to become a dictator). As a general, Washington was not a brilliant strategist like Napoleon, although his design for the complicated Yorktown campaign was superb. Neither was he a tactician of the quality of Caesar or Robert E. Lee. His lack of genius made his achievements all the more impressive. He held his forces together in adversity, avoiding both useless slaughter and cata-

CHAPTER 11

THE
REINVENTION
OF AMERICA:
WHO "OWNS"
OUR HISTORY?

strophic defeat. He learned from experience and won the respect—if not the love—of his men and the cooperation of Congress and his French allies. Men of all sections, from every walk of life, looked upon Washington as the embodiment of American virtues: a man of deeds rather than words; a man of substance accustomed to luxury, yet capable of enduring great hardships stoically and as much at home in the wilderness as a wild Indian; a bold Patriot, quick to take arms against British tyranny, yet eminently respectable. The Revolution might have been won without Washington, but it is unlikely that the free United States would have become so easily a true nation had he not existed. . . .

Source 4 from Howard Zinn, *A People's History of the United States* (New York: Harper and Row, 1980), pp. 76–89.

4. Howard Zinn.

The American victory over the British army was made possible by the existence of an already-armed people. Just about every white male had a gun, and could shoot. The Revolutionary leadership distrusted the mobs of poor. But they knew the Revolution had no appeal to slaves and Indians. They would have to woo the armed white population.

This was not easy. Yes, mechanics and sailors, some others, were incensed against the British. But general enthusiasm for the war was not strong. While much of the white male population went into military service at one time or another during the war, only a small fraction stayed. John Shy, in his study of the Revolutionary army (*A People Numerous and Armed*), says they "grew weary of being bullied by local committees of safety, by corrupt deputy assistant commissaries of supply, and by bands of ragged strangers with guns in their hands calling themselves soldiers of the Revolution." Shy estimates that perhaps a fifth of the population was actively treasonous. John Adams had estimated a third opposed, a third in support, a third neutral.

Alexander Hamilton, an aide of George Washington and an up-and-coming member of the new elite, wrote from his headquarters: ". . . our countrymen have all the folly of the ass and all the passiveness of the sheep. . . . They are determined not to be free. . . . If we are saved, France and Spain must save us."

Slavery got in the way in the South. South Carolina, insecure since the slave uprising in Stono in 1739, could hardly fight against the British; her militia had to be used to keep slaves under control.

The men who first joined the colonial militia were generally "hallmarks of respectability or at least of full citizenship" in their communities, Shy says. Excluded from the militia were friendly Indians, free Negroes, white servants, and free white men who had no stable home. But desperation led to the recruiting of the less respectable whites. Massachusetts and Virginia provided for drafting "strollers" (vagrants) into the militia. In fact, the military became a place of promise for the poor, who might rise in rank, acquire some money, change their social status.

Here was the traditional device by which those in charge of any social order mobilize and discipline a recalcitrant population—offering the adventure and rewards of military service to get poor people to fight for a cause they may not see clearly as their own. . . .

The military conflict itself, by dominating everything in its time, diminished other issues, made people choose sides in the one contest that was publicly important, forced people onto the side of the Revolution whose interest in Independence was not at all obvious. Ruling elites seem to have learned through the generations—consciously or not—that war makes them more secure against internal trouble.

The force of military preparation had a way of pushing neutral people into line. In Connecticut, for instance, a law was passed requiring military service of all males between sixteen and sixty, omitting certain government officials, ministers, Yale students and faculty, Negroes, Indians, and mulattos. Someone called to duty could provide a substitute or get out of it by paying 5 pounds. When eighteen men failed to show up for military duty they were jailed and, in order to be released, had to pledge to fight in the war. Shy says: "The mechanism of their political conversion was the militia." What looks like the democratization of the military forces in modern times shows up as something different: a way of forcing large numbers of reluctant people to associate themselves with the national cause, and by the end of the process believe in it.

Here, in the war for liberty, was conscription, as usual, cognizant of wealth. With the impressment riots against the British still remembered, impressment of seamen by the American navy was taking place by 1779. A Pennsylvania official said: "We cannot help observing how similar this Conduct is to that of the British Officers during our Subjection to Great Britain and are persuaded it will have the same unhappy effects viz. an estrangement of the Affections of the People from . . . Authority . . . which by an easy Progression will proceed to open Opposition . . . and bloodshed."

Watching the new, tight discipline of Washington's army, a chaplain in Concord, Massachusetts, wrote: "New lords, new laws. The strictest gov-

CHAPTER 11

THE
REINVENTION
OF AMERICA:
WHO "OWNS"
OUR HISTORY?

ernment is taking place and great distinction is made between officers &
men. Everyone is made to know his place & keep it, or be immediately tied
up, and receive not one but 30 or 40 lashes."

The Americans lost the first battles of the war: Bunker Hill, Brooklyn
Heights, Harlem Heights, the Deep South; they won small battles at Tren-
ton and Princeton, and then in a turning point, a big battle at Saratoga,
New York, in 1777. Washington's frozen army hung on at Valley Forge,
Pennsylvania, while Benjamin Franklin negotiated an alliance with the
French monarchy, which was anxious for revenge on England. The war
turned to the South, where the British won victory after victory, until the
Americans, aided by a large French army, with the French navy blocking
off the British from supplies and reinforcements, won the final victory of
the war at Yorktown, Virginia, in 1781.

Through all this, the suppressed conflicts between rich and poor among
the Americans kept reappearing. In the midst of the war, in Philadelphia,
which Eric Foner describes as "a time of immense profits for some colonists
and terrible hardships for others," the inflation (prices rose in one month
that year by 45 percent) led to agitation and calls for action. One Philadelphia newspaper carried a reminder that in Europe "the People have
always done themselves justice when the scarcity of bread has arisen from
the avarice of forestallers. They have broken open magazines—appropriated
stores to their own use without paying for them—and in some instances
have hung up the culprits who created their distress."

In May of 1779, the First Company of Philadelphia Artillery petitioned
the Assembly about the troubles of "the midling and poor" and threatened
violence against "those who are avariciously intent upon amassing wealth
by the destruction of the more virtuous part of the community." That same
month, there was a mass meeting, an extralegal gathering, which called
for price reductions and initiated an investigation of Robert Morris, a rich
Philadelphian who was accused of holding food from the market. In October
came the "Fort Wilson riot," in which a militia group marched into the city
and to the house of James Wilson, a wealthy lawyer and Revolutionary
official who had opposed price controls and the democratic constitution
adopted in Pennsylvania in 1776. The militia were driven away by a "silk
stocking brigade" of well-off Philadelphia citizens.

It seemed that the majority of white colonists, who had a bit of land, or
no property at all, were still better off than slaves or indentured servants
or Indians, and could be wooed into the coalition of the Revolution. But
when the sacrifices of war became more bitter, the privileges and safety of
the rich became harder to accept. About 10 percent of the white population
(an estimate of Jackson Main in *The Social Structure of Revolutionary*

America), large landholders and merchants, held 1,000 pounds or more in personal property and 1,000 pounds in land, at the least, and these men owned nearly half the wealth of the country and held as slaves one-seventh of the country's people.

The Continental Congress, which governed the colonies through the war, was dominated by rich men, linked together in factions and compacts by business and family connections. These links connected North and South, East and West. For instance, Richard Henry Lee of Virginia was connected with the Adamses of Massachusetts and the Shippens of Pennsylvania. Delegates from middle and southern colonies were connected with Robert Morris of Pennsylvania through commerce and land speculation. Morris was superintendent of finance, and his assistant was Gouverneur Morris.

Morris's plan was to give more assurance to those who had loaned money to the Continental Congress, and gain the support of officers by voting half-pay for life for those who stuck to the end. This ignored the common soldier, who was not getting paid, who was suffering in the cold, dying of sickness, watching the civilian profiteers get rich. On New Year's Day, 1781, the Pennsylvania troops near Morristown, New Jersey, perhaps emboldened by rum, dispersed their officers, killed one captain, wounded others, and were marching, fully armed, with cannon, toward the Continental Congress at Philadelphia. . . .

[*Zinn describes the insurgence at Morristown and two others, another in New Jersey and one in Pennsylvania.*]

What soldiers in the Revolution could do only rarely, rebel against their authorities, civilians could do much more easily. Ronald Hoffman says: "The Revolution plunged the states of Delaware, Maryland, North Carolina, South Carolina, Georgia, and, to a much lesser degree, Virginia into divisive civil conflicts that persisted during the entire period of struggle." The southern lower classes resisted being mobilized for the revolution. They saw themselves under the rule of a political elite, win or lose against the British.

In Maryland, for instance, by the new constitution of 1776, to run for governor one had to own 5,000 pounds of property; to run for state senator, 1,000 pounds. Thus, 90 percent of the population were excluded from holding office. And so, as Hoffman says, "small slave holders, non-slaveholding planters, tenants, renters and casual day laborers posed a serious problem of social control for the Whig elite."

With black slaves 25 percent of the population (and in some counties 50 percent), fear of slave revolts grew. George Washington had turned down

CHAPTER 11

THE
REINVENTION
OF AMERICA:
WHO "OWNS"
OUR HISTORY?

the requests of blacks, seeking freedom, to fight in the Revolutionary army. So when the British military commander in Virginia, Lord Dunmore, promised freedom to Virginia slaves who joined his forces, this created consternation. . . .

Even more unsettling was white rioting in Maryland against leading families, supporting the Revolution, who were suspected of hoarding needed commodities. The class hatred of some of these disloyal people was expressed by one man who said "it was better for the people to lay down their arms and pay the duties and taxes laid upon them by King and Parliament than to be brought into slavery and to be commanded and ordered about as they were." A wealthy Maryland landowner, Charles Carroll, took note of the surly mood all around him:

> There is a mean low dirty envy which creeps thro all ranks and cannot suffer a man a superiority of fortune, of merit, or of understanding in fellow citizens— either of these are sure to entail a general ill will and dislike upon the owners.

Despite this, Maryland authorities retained control. They made concessions, taxing land and slaves more heavily, letting debtors pay in paper money. It was a sacrifice by the upper class to maintain power, and it worked.

In the lower South, however, in the Carolinas and Georgia, according to Hoffman, "vast regions were left without the slightest apparition of authority." The general mood was to take no part in a war that seemed to have nothing for them. "Authoritative personages on both sides demanded that common people supply material, reduce consumption, leave their families, and even risk their lives. Forced to make hard decisions, many flailed out in frustration or evaded and defied first one side, then the other. . . ."

Washington's military commander in the lower South, Nathanael Greene, dealt with disloyalty by a policy of concessions to some, brutality to others. In a letter to Thomas Jefferson he described a raid by his troops on Loyalists. "They made a dreadful carnage of them, upwards of one hundred were killed and most of the rest cut to pieces. It has had a very happy effect on those disaffected persons of which there were too many in this country." Greene told one of his generals "to strike terror into our enemies and give spirit to our friends." On the other hand, he advised the governor of Georgia "to open a door for the disaffected of your state to come in. . . ."

In general, throughout the states, concessions were kept to a minimum. The new constitutions that were drawn up in all states from 1776 to 1780 were not much different from the old ones. Although property qualifications for voting and holding office were lowered in some instances, in Massachusetts they were increased. Only Pennsylvania abolished them totally. The new bills of rights had modifying provisions. North Carolina, providing for religious freedom, added "that nothing herein contained shall be construed to exempt preachers of treasonable or seditious discourses, from legal trial and punishment." Maryland, New York, Georgia, and Massachusetts took similar cautions. . . .

One would look, in examining the Revolution's effect on class relations, at what happened to land confiscated from fleeing Loyalists. It was distributed in such a way as to give a double opportunity to the Revolutionary leaders: to enrich themselves and their friends, and to parcel out some land to small farmers to create a broad base of support for the new government. Indeed, this became characteristic of the new nation: finding itself possessed of enormous wealth, it could create the richest ruling class in history, and still have enough for the middle classes to act as a buffer between the rich and the dispossessed.

The huge landholdings of the Loyalists had been one of the great incentives to Revolution. Lord Fairfax in Virginia had more than 5 million acres encompassing twenty-one counties. Lord Baltimore's income from his Maryland holdings exceeded 30,000 pounds a year. After the Revolution, Lord Fairfax was protected; he was a friend of George Washington. But other Loyalist holders of great estates, especially those who were absentees, had their land confiscated. In New York, the number of freeholding small farmers increased after the Revolution, and there were fewer tenant farmers, who had created so much trouble in the pre-Revolution years.

Although the numbers of independent farmers grew, according to Rowland Berthoff and John Murrin, "the class structure did not change radically." The ruling group went through personnel changes as "the rising merchant families of Boston, New York or Philadelphia . . . slipped quite credibly into the social status—and sometimes the very houses of those who failed in business or suffered confiscation and exile for loyalty to the crown."

Edmund Morgan sums up the class nature of the Revolution this way: "The fact that the lower ranks were involved in the contest should not obscure the fact that the contest itself was generally a struggle for office and power between members of an upper class: the new against the established." Looking at the situation after the Revolution, Richard Morris comments: "Everywhere one finds inequality." He finds "the people" of "We the people of the United States" (a phrase coined by the very rich Gouverneur Morris) did not mean Indians or blacks or women or white servants. In fact, there were more indentured servants than ever, and the Revolution "did nothing to end and little to ameliorate white bondage."

Carl Degler says (*Out of Our Past*): "No new social class came to power through the door of the American revolution. The men who engineered the

CHAPTER 11

THE
REINVENTION
OF AMERICA:
WHO "OWNS"
OUR HISTORY?

revolt were largely members of the colonial ruling class." George Washington was the richest man in America. John Hancock was a prosperous Boston merchant. Benjamin Franklin was a wealthy printer. And so on.

On the other hand, town mechanics, laborers, and seamen, as well as small farmers, were swept into "the people" by the rhetoric of the Revolution, by the camaraderie of military service, by the distribution of some land. Thus was created a substantial body of support, a national consensus, something that, even with the exclusion of ignored and oppressed people, could be called "America." . . .

It seems that the rebellion against British rule allowed a certain group of the colonial elite to replace those loyal to England, give some benefits to small landholders, and leave poor white working people and tenant farmers in very much their old situation.

What did the Revolution mean to the Native Americans, the Indians? They had been ignored by the fine words of the Declaration, had not been considered equal, certainly not in choosing those who would govern the American territories in which they lived, nor in being able to pursue happiness as they had pursued it for centuries before the white Europeans arrived. Now, with the British out of the way, the Americans could begin the inexorable process of pushing the Indians off their lands, killing them if they resisted. In short, as Francis Jennings puts it, the white Americans were fighting against British imperial control in the East, and for their own imperialism in the West. . . .

The situation of black slaves as a result of the American Revolution was more complex. Thousands of blacks fought with the British. Five thousand were with the Revolutionaries, most of them from the North, but there were also free blacks from Virginia and Maryland. The lower south was reluctant to arm blacks. Amid the urgency and chaos of war, thousands took their freedom—leaving on British ships at the end of the war to settle in England, Nova Scotia, the West Indies, or Africa. Many others stayed in America as free blacks, evading their masters.

In the northern states, the combination of blacks in the military, the lack of powerful economic need for slaves, and the rhetoric of Revolution led to the end of slavery—but very slowly. As late as 1810, thirty thousand blacks, one-fourth of the black population of the North, remained slaves. In 1840 there were still a thousand slaves in the North. In the upper South, there were more free Negroes than before, leading to more control legislation. In the lower South, slavery expanded with the growth of rice and cotton plantations.

What the Revolution did was to create space and opportunity for blacks to begin making demands of white society. Sometimes these demands came from the new, small black elites in Baltimore, Philadelphia, Richmond, Savannah, sometimes from articulate and bold slaves. Pointing to the Declaration of Independence, blacks petitioned Congress and the state legislatures to abolish slavery, to give blacks equal rights. . . .

The inferior position of blacks, the exclusion of Indians from the new society, the establishment of supremacy for the rich and powerful in the new nation—all this was already settled in the colonies by the time of the Revolution. With the English out of the way, it could now be put on paper, solidified, regularized, made legitimate, by the Constitution of the United States, drafted at a convention of Revolutionary leaders in Philadelphia. . . .

⚭ QUESTIONS TO CONSIDER ⚭

All the authors of the five selections you read (the four selections in the Evidence section of this chapter and the account in your own textbook) offer what they consider to have been the *true nature* (that is, the intrinsic *character*) of the American Revolution. And yet, as you have learned, each author's account was influenced by the climate of opinion in which the author lived and wrote. How does each selection portray the nature of the American Revolution? How was each portrayal influenced by the author's climate of opinion?

Only George Bancroft (born in 1800) could have known anyone who lived during the Revolutionary era. In fact, as a child and young man, he knew many. And yet Bancroft's account goes far beyond a straightforward reconstruction of the events that took place on Lexington Green based on the memories of people he knew. What did Bancroft add to his "simple retelling" of the events? How are the colonists

treated? How are the British treated? Where did Bancroft place the colonists in history? Why do you think he did that? Finally, in what ways do you think Bancroft's climate of opinion (Jacksonian democracy, a northern Democrat in a period of increasing sectional tension) influenced his reinvention of America?

Charles and Mary Beard's discussion of the American Revolution is dramatically different from that of George Bancroft. Indeed, one sometimes wonders whether they are writing about the same event. How do the Beards treat the American Revolution? In their view, why did that conflict take place? What roles did the following play: British merchants and manufacturers, the Board of Trade, George III? Both Bancroft and the Beards portray the American Revolution as part of a continuing struggle. In the Beards' view, what was the nature of that struggle? Finally, in what ways did the Beards' climate

CHAPTER 11

THE
REINVENTION
OF AMERICA:
WHO "OWNS"
OUR HISTORY?

of opinion (Progressive era) influence their treatment of the American Revolution?

The American Nation (1966) by John A. Garraty set a new standard for United States history textbooks that in many ways is still with us. For one thing, it was the first college-level textbook by a major publisher to use color illustrations to make the text more attractive. The writing style was purposely more conversational, written more for students than for their professors. For our purposes, however, it is Garraty's treatment of the American Revolution that is most interesting. How does Garraty's telling of the story of Lexington differ from that of Bancroft (see especially their respective accounts of how firing first broke out)? How would you explain these differences? Did the two climates of opinion (Garraty wrote during the cold war period when Great Britain was a strong ally) help to explain these differences? In the view of Garraty, how "revolutionary" was the American Revolution? What influence do you think Garraty's climate of opinion had on his treatment? In what ways, specifically?

Howard Zinn's 1980 interpretation not only benefited from a great deal of research done by him and other historians in the 1960s and 1970s, but was also written in a markedly different climate of opinion from that of John A. Garraty. What was Zinn's climate of opinion (1960s through 1970s)? How did that climate help Zinn to see the American Revolution in different terms? What were the chief differences between Zinn's treatment and those of his predecessors? Pay special attention to groups that Zinn included in his discussion that were not included by his predecessors. How does the inclusion of those groups alter our "reinvention" of America?

Now look at your own textbook's discussion of the American Revolution. Based on the book's copyright date, in what climate of opinion was the book written? In your view, how does your book's treatment of the American Revolution differ from (or how is it similar to) the selections you read in this chapter? How would the climate of opinion help to explain those differences? How does your textbook's treatment help you to identify some of the principal issues of our own times? Put another way, how can our reading of history help us to understand our own climate of opinion?

Finally, look back over the five accounts. How does each selection portray the nature of the American Revolution? How does the climate of opinion in which each selection was written help us to understand why each portrayal was written in the way it was?

ᏮᏮ EPILOGUE ᏮᏮ

By now you have come to an understanding that this chapter is not really about the American Revolution. Rather, it is about how people use history to understand the major issues, concerns, anxieties, and fears of their own times. Whether it be Bancroft, the Beards, Garraty, Zinn, or you yourself, no one can escape from the present into the past. Instead, we all use history to understand the present and our own respective climate of opinion.

This chapter marks the end of this book, but it is by no means the end of American history. There will be different climates of opinion in the future and, inevitably, new reinventions of America's past. How, then, can we tell when our history (or histories written in the future) comes closest to the past?

One scholar, Benjamin R. Barber, sees a difference between history and mere storytelling (the invention of events to teach some lesson). But he admits that "history is the story we choose to believe in."[7] Does one treatment of history (Bancroft's, the Beards', Garraty's, Zinn's, or any other's) come close to the past simply because we "choose to believe" that it does?

Though partially true, that answer is not nearly enough. By using the skills you have learned or sharpened while reading this book, you can make certain judgments about how others use (or misuse) evidence. That is one reason you need to know how to analyze evidence for yourself and not merely rely on others to do it for you.

How can present and future Americans analyze the momentous choices before them? They can do so only by using the knowledge and skills at their disposal to examine and analyze the evidence presented to them, by questioning that evidence, and by reaching mature and responsible conclusions. Whether that evidence is presented in the form of speeches, debates, cartoons, advertisements, posters, interviews, newspapers and magazines, or television programs (the new "textbooks"), Americans must be able to see that evidence in its historical and contemporary contexts. To that end, we sincerely hope that this book has made a contribution.

In one of his more philosophical moods, Thomas Jefferson once wrote that the earth belongs to the living. As you have seen in this chapter, so also may the past.

---

7. Barber, *An Aristocracy of Everyone,* p. 62.

Acknowledgments continued from p. iv.

CHAPTER THREE

Sources 1–4, 8–9: Catalogue ads Courtesy of Sears, Roebuck & Co.

CHAPTER FOUR

Source 1: Sunken Gardens. Smithsonian.

Source 3: Negrito tribesman. Library of Congress.

Source 5: Igorot tribesmen. Library of Congress.

Source 9: Igorot dance and spectators. Library of Congress.

Source 12: American school. National Archives.

CHAPTER FIVE

Source 6: Uncle Sam Poster. Library of Congress.

Sources 18–21: From *War as Advertised: The Four Minute Men and America's Crusade, 1917–1918*, pp. 70, 72–73, 122, 60, and 27. Copyright 1984. Reprinted by permission of American Philosophical Society.

CHAPTER SIX

Source 2: From *The Plastic Age* by Percy Marks. Copyright 1924 by the Century Company, renewed. Used by permission of the publisher, Dutton, an imprint of New American Library, a division of Penguin Books USA Inc.

Source 3: Margaret Sanger, *Woman and the New Race*, 1920, pp. 93–95. Copyright © 1920 by The Putnam Publishing Group. Reprinted with permission.

Source 5: Copyright © 1927 by *Harper's Magazine*. All rights reserved. Reprinted from the October issue by special permission.

CHAPTER SEVEN

Sources 1, 10: John Vachon/Library of Congress.

Sources 2, 5, 7–9, 11: Dorothea Lange/Library of Congress.

Sources 3–4, 15: Arthur Rothstein/Library of Congress.

Sources 6, 14: Carl Mydans/Library of Congress.

Source 12: Ben Shahn/Library of Congress.

Source 13: Marion Post Wolcott/Library of Congress.

Source 16: Walker Evans/Library of Congress.

Source 17: Russell Lee/Library of Congress.

CHAPTER EIGHT

Source 1: From Harry S Truman, *Memoirs: Years of Decisions*, pp. 10–11, 416–423. Copyright 1955. Reprinted by permission.

Source 2: Excerpts from *On Active Service in Peace and War* by Henry L. Stimson. Copyright 1948 by Henry L. Stimson. Copyright renewed 1976 by McGeorge Bundy. Reprinted by permission of HarperCollins Publishers.

Source 5: Excerpts from *Turbulent Era: A Diplomatic Record of Forty Years, 1904–1945* by Joseph C. Grew, edited by Walter Johnson. Copyright 1952 by Joseph C. Grew. Copyright